D1617580

Praise for

GEORGE MASON

"*George Mason: The Founding Father Who Gave Us the Bill of Rights*, is a welcome contribution to the literature about one of the most important—yet least known—founders of the American Republic. Drawing heavily upon original documents and research, author Hyland has produced a valuable work which should put all of us in his debt. Highly recommended for scholars, students, and the general public alike."

> —**ROBERT F. TURNER,** professor of law at the University of Virginia and co-founder, distinguished fellow, and associate director of the Center for National Security Law

"William Hyland's eloquent work is a welcome addition to the growing library of books about George Mason, author of the Virginia Declaration of Rights. In this new book, Mason's often underappreciated contributions to the Revolutionary period and to the U.S. Constitution, as well as his relationships with family and contemporaries, are explored and examined in a personal and engaging fashion. Anyone interested in Mason and the founding of the United States would enjoy reading this intimate portrait of one of America's greatest statesmen."

> —**SCOTT STROH,** executive director of George Mason's Gunston Hall

"George Mason has always been considered one of the Founding Fathers, but one who stood just outside the main spotlight. Now, fortunately, William Hyland has moved Mason into that spotlight by his illuminating and carefully researched biography of this intriguing figure. Hyland provides a scholarly portrait of Mason with new emphasis on the complete Mason—his wives, children, friends, business affairs, physical ailments, and his treasured Gunston Hall—with this splendid and balanced new chronicle. Hyland's clear-eyed review will enlighten anyone seeking to understand the special role that Mason played in breaking from England and creating a new nation with a governing structure that rests on safeguarding human rights."

—**ARTHUR DOWNEY,** author of *The Creole Affair: The Slave Rebellion that Led the U.S. and Great Britain to the Brink of War* and *Civil War Lawyers: Constitutional Questions, Courtroom Dramas, and the Men Behind Them*

"Thomas Jefferson called George Mason 'the Cato of his country,' and the renowned biographer of Jefferson, Dumas Malone, claimed that 'more than any other single American...George Mason may be regarded as the herald of this new era." Such praise and acclaim were also voiced by James Madison, George Washington, and a host of American Founding Fathers. But Mason's name is hardly known today, and the studies of his life and thought are few. But William Hyland in this seminal biography has set the record straight. In close, scholarly examinations of Mason's writings, Hyland demonstrates the profound influence he had on Revolutionary America's history and thought; and he does so in a way which presents to us the man we have forgotten. Textual study and biography are hand in glove. The former sheds great light on Mason the fiery opponent of slavery, the man of unbending principle who voted against the Constitution though it cost him his friendship with his life-long friend and neighbor, George Washington, and who shunned public life out of an intense devotion to his family, home, and fields. William Hyland set the scholarly bar very high in this great and much needed book, and we are in his debt for seeing his task through successfully."

—**WILLIAM WILSON,** professor emeritus of religious studies at the University of Virginia and former director of graduate studies at the Jefferson Scholars Foundation

GEORGE MASON

GEORGE MASON

THE FOUNDING FATHER WHO GAVE US THE BILL OF RIGHTS

William G. Hyland Jr.

REGNERY
HISTORY

Regnery History™ is a trademark of Salem Communications Holding Corporation; Regnery® is a registered trademark of Salem Communications Holding Corporation

Cataloging-in-Publication data on file with the Library of Congress

ISBN 978-1-62157-926-7
ebook ISBN 978-1-62157-947-2

Published in the United States by
Regnery History, an imprint of
Regnery Publishing
A Division of Salem Media Group
300 New Jersey Ave NW
Washington, DC 20001
www.RegneryHistory.com

Manufactured in the United States of America

10 9 8 7 6 5 4 3 2 1

Books are available in quantity for promotional or premium use. For information on discounts and terms, please visit our website: www.Regnery.com.

To Lourdes, my love, my life, and the woman who mended a broken heart. When we met, my life began again. You are my true soul mate, a blessing, and my love for you shall live forever.

Contents

Preface

*George Mason was the most respected founder in his
own time, [but] ... virtually invisible in our time.*

—JOSEPH J. ELLIS, *Founding Brothers: The Revolutionary
Generation* (2002)

*Reputation, what they sometimes called character,
had been paramount in the minds of the founders
from the earliest phases of the Revolution. A man's
actions would now determine his reputation. Character was performative, for outward consumption.*

—LORRI GLOVER, *Founders as Fathers* (2014)

America was woven together by three pieces of political
paper: the Declaration of Independence, the Constitution,
and the Bill of Rights.[1] George Mason had a decisive role
in shaping all three documents. Mason, one of the ablest constitu-
tionalists of all time, left an indelible footprint on the founding of
our nation. Mason was the dean of the intellectual rebels in Virginia, as historian Robert Rutland has observed: "The directness,
the scholarly validity of his arguments belied the fact that he was
not a lawyer. Logic born of a love affair with the classics gripped
his mind when confusion seized others. Demagoguery was his chief
irritant, integrity his palliative."[2]

The creation of the American experiment is Mason's true enduring legacy. But his contribution has been obscured by the accidents of
history and his self-effacing character. Mason's creative capacity lies
buried in the inner folds of the man's personality, beyond the reach
of traditional biographical methods of discernment.

Mason's role in the Revolution and the Founding has been buried
in almost two and a half centuries of public oblivion. It is time Mason
was rescued from this historical abyss as one of the least known of
America's founding patriots. The sum of Mason's writings is an astonishing accomplishment, yet in each instance, Mason's individual work
was absorbed by a political coalition—and his name lost to public fame.
Anonymity, however, was more than a historical byproduct of the
character of his work. It was also a matter of preference for Mason. His
advice to his sons, "to prefer the happiness and independence and a
private station to the troubles and vexations of a public business," was
advice he himself followed. His contemporaries' efforts to elect him to
office were met with persistent refusals. "George Mason," it has been
said, "was a thinker and advisor rather than a publicist."[3]

The chronological terrain over which Mason's story moves is
highly contested ground. My task is to attempt a meticulous personal
and professional recovery of George Mason, a man whose enormous
political and intellectual capacities were crucial to the founding of the
American Republic. This book is not a free fall into Mason idolatry.
It is a broad portrait of Mason and of the world in which he lived.
While not scanting his vibrant intellectual life, I have also collected
anecdotes that bring this brilliant man to life. The resulting account
of Mason's life and work will, I hope, offer an interpretation fresh
and surprising even to those best versed in the literature of the Revolutionary period. The political and personal sides of Mason's story,
blended together, lead to an inevitable conclusion: George Mason
deserves careful and renewed focus.

Every fact bearing upon the character and service of Mason, whose visionary mental gifts helped create a form of government that is a model for the world, should receive warm appreciation from anyone who cares about individual freedoms. Mason's understanding of liberty is at the heart of America. His philosophy of the citizens' authority and control over their government is the basis for our self-rule.

Quite simply, given the influence of Mason's political writings, his name should be more known. Mason should be on the same level with Thomas Jefferson, James Madison, and Alexander Hamilton.[4] Mason's pragmatic mind minted constitutional principles and infused them with expansive life, turning abstract theory into living realities. And Mason never wavered on his core cherished convictions—while both Jefferson and Madison changed their views with the political climate of the times, falling prey to what one prominent historian has termed a "disarming ideological promiscuity."[5] Unfortunately, that same scholar concluded that only "four men made the transition from confederation to nation happen. They are George Washington, Alexander Hamilton, John Jay, and James Madison. If they are the stars of the story, the supporting cast consists of Robert Morris, Gouverneur Morris (no relation), and Thomas Jefferson."[6]

No mention of George Mason.

History has consigned Mason to the second tier of Founders. The public renown of patriotic icons Jefferson and Washington as votaries of liberty is so monumental that nothing can profoundly affect their reputations. The goal of this book is not to take recognition away from them, but to assign more public credit to Mason. Jefferson himself admitted that the Declaration of Independence he wrote was "neither aiming at originality of principle or sentiment ... it was intended to be an expression of the American mind, and to give to that expression the proper tone and spirit called for by the occasion."[7]

And while Jefferson said, accurately, that the Declaration was not literally "copied from any particular and previous writing," nevertheless the blueprint for it—the original text Jefferson worked from—was the Virginia Declaration of Rights written by Mason.[8] Jefferson never made a secret of the fact that he revered Mason. The sage of Monticello called George Mason the wisest man of his generation. Jefferson's famed biographer Dumas Malone agreed, summing up Mason's marquee contributions to the Revolution: "He was the author of the Virginia Declaration of Rights, which was adopted three weeks before the national Declaration of Independence; and in this he charted the rights of human beings much more fully than Jefferson did in the immortal but necessarily compressed paragraph in the more famous document. Of the contemporary impact of Mason's Declaration there can be no possible question. More than any other single American ... George Mason may be regarded as the herald of this new era."[9] Mason's Virginia Declaration of Rights has been said by another historian to have "more wisdom and concentration of thought in one sentence of it, than all former writings on the subject."[10]

And Mason was directly responsible for famous language in the Constitution, as well. He supplied the phrase "aid and comfort" in the definition of treason. And it is due to Mason that the president can be impeached for "high crimes and misdemeanors." He also wrote major portions of the presidential oath of office.[11]

Yet Mason's writings and activities generally did not strike even his contemporaries as epoch-making. He was not a bold commander like Washington, nor a fiery orator like Patrick Henry,[12] but gained his chief fame as the draftsman of documents. He rarely had a national audience outside of "his country" (Virginia), and only the slow passage of time has revealed the full significance of his work.[13] His elegant articulations of the American creed laid out a vision that set the course for history. But Mason did not rest once his words were written or his ideas entered circulation. Historian Joseph Ellis has called him "a political strategist" with a great gift for "intellectual agility."[14]

Although some have dismissed George Mason as simply a man who refused to sign the Constitution, this is not a historically accurate portrayal. Mason was both a dissenter and a builder, the chief architect of the Bill of Rights, in what one scholar has called "arguably the most creative and consequential act of political leadership in American history."[15] Indeed, Mason's political influence cannot be overstated. The historian R. Carter Pittman described Mason as "The father of the Bill of Rights and the wisest statesman America has ever known. The contributions of George Mason to every Bill of Rights and Constitution that has been adopted in this world since 1776, including the Federal Constitution and Bill of Rights and those of our various States, are such as to leave his mark and impress indelibly on the world."[16]

At the time of the Constitution's bicentennial, historian Josephine F. Pacheco wrote that James Madison "gets credit for the bill of rights, whereas he opposed the concept and agreed to support such a document only as a last resort."[17] George Mason, by contrast, "is brushed aside as an opponent of the Constitution, whereas the truth is that he was a major intellectual contributor to its creation. Except for Madison," Pacheco declares, "probably no one contributed more to the actual document than did Mason. He rightly deserves to be considered one of the fathers of our national government."[18] Indeed, our greatest political documents, the Declaration of Independence and the Bill of Rights to the Constitution, all form a series of concentric circles leading back to Mason.

Although professional historians are familiar with Mason's legacy, it seems that his name has drowned in public obscurity. He is one of the most unknown figures in American history, a remote, enigmatic man more respected by scholars of the Revolutionary era than known by the general public. Mason lacks the folksy appeal of Benjamin Franklin, the robust dominance of George Washington, and the charms of Thomas Jefferson. In fact, Mason has receded so much in our collective memory that he has become nothing more than a modest bronze statue in Washington, D.C. But in his own time and place, his contemporaries grasped at superlatives to describe the Virginian. James Madison judged that "Mason possessed the greatest talents for debate of any man I have ever seen or heard speak."[19] Patrick Henry pronounced him "the greatest statesmen I ever knew." Jefferson complimented his mind as "great and powerful." Philip Mazzei, the Florentine physician and world traveler, met Mason in Williamsburg within days of arriving in America. "In my opinion," Mazzei wrote, "he is not well enough known. He is one of those brave, rare—talented men who cause nature a great effort to produce." The Italian ranked Mason as one of the intellectual giants, writing that, "[Mason] is one of those strong, very rare intellects, which are created only by a special effort of nature, like that of a ... Machiavelli, a Galileo, a Newton."[20]

While the private worlds of Hamilton and Jefferson have recently attracted a great deal of attention and ink, Americans know little of Mason's private and family life. This book reexamines George Mason by telling his personal as well as his political journey.

Mason loved his wife, his children, his books, his estate, good wine, architecture, horseback riding, hunting, fishing, history, Virginia, and the very latest in farming ideas. He was a devoted husband and father with twelve children and twenty-five grandchildren, a farmer, philosopher, botanist, amateur musician, and architect. At Gunston Hall, the home he built on Dogue's Neck, Mason indulged in the quiet pleasures of scholarly pursuits in alternation with the family bustle that was his tonic. A devoted family man, unlike some other Founders, George Mason had a personal life with no hint of scandal or suspicion of smarm. Indeed, it is not possible to fully understand Mason's intense commitment to liberty, sacrifice, and virtue—words that had very explicit meanings in the eighteenth century—apart from his commitment to his family. Surviving letters and documents reveal a caring husband and doting father. His son John's written *Recollections* give us an additional window into the private life of George Mason at Gunston Hall. It seemed almost impossible for Mason to be intimate with anyone outside of his immediate family. He concentrated his attention on them, not on posterity.

His generosity to his family was unmatched. He was solicitous to his beloved mother while she lived, and caring toward his younger brother and sister. And even when he lost his dear wife at age thirty-nine, and his life-long friendship with Washington over his opposition to ratifying the Constitution, Mason believed in the fundamental goodness of life. His contributions to the political life of America grew out of his local commitments—as a vestryman in his community parish, an officer of the militia, a trustee for the town of Alexandria.

Mason remained a somewhat reclusive figure until the Revolutionary War, which precipitated his constitutional brilliance. The War for Independence did not progress swiftly. It was a tedious struggle, demanding patient faith from a small cadre of patriots. As England's national policy toward the colonies became ever more oppressive, Mason met it with a resolution no less fixed—and expressed in forceful language. "Though we are [Britain's] subjects," he wrote, "we will use every means, which Heaven hath given us, to prevent our becoming its slaves." Mason's commanding strength of intellect was aroused by the emotional appeal and vigor of words. "Our all is at stake," he wrote to Washington, "and the little conveniences and comforts of life, when set in competition with our liberty, ought to be rejected, not with reluctance, but with pleasure."[21]

Although born to privilege, Mason opposed all the trappings of an aristocratic society. He believed in America, and in Americans. Liberty was his chief concern, the freedom of the spirit and the mind. Mason was a forward-looking man, consumed by a relentless yearning for knowledge. A cultivated gentleman, although he did not attend college, the Virginian was a life-long advocate of education for all in proportion to their merit. To call him a votive of the Enlightenment is the best way to sum up the character of his mind.[22]

Mason's political strength lay in his many friendships among the leaders of all shades of politics. Mason never ceased to prefer the companionship of a superior mind and prized good manners. He assumed responsibilities by virtue of his towering intellect, just as Jefferson and Madison did. At times he may have seemed remote, and his sensitivity to criticism was recognized by some as a character flaw. But his colleagues also recognized Mason as a devoted family man and loyal friend, assets in any private circle. Mason's industry could not be questioned. Though his age and poor health prevented him from becoming a soldier during the war, he was recognized by his peers as a man of capacity and courage.

His personal papers are not voluminous, compared with the official papers of Jefferson, Madison, and Washington. The definitive edition of Mason's papers runs a comparatively scant three volumes, not the thousands of pages produced by the more famous Founders. This divergence arises from both politics and family considerations. George Mason and Patrick Henry curtailed their political careers after the constitutional debates of 1787–1788, so they amassed far fewer papers than the first three presidents. In 1820, when Mason's grandson George Mason (VI) began to correspond with prominent men who knew his grandfather, including James Madison, Madison sympathized with the young man's struggle to recover Mason's rightful place in history. "It is to be regretted," Madison wrote of Mason's achievements, "that highly distinguished as he was," accounts "are more scanty than of many of his contemporaries far inferior to him in intellectual powers and in public services."[23]

It is unfortunate that Mason is remembered best as the dissenting delegate to the "Federal Convention" (as it was called in its day) in Philadelphia in 1787, one of three men who refused to sign the Constitution. Losers receive little credit from history. Historical accounts of Mason depict him as a grumpy old patriot who lost the political argument, then refused to sign the Constitution for his own vain reasons. But the first six words of his famous "Objections" to signing the Constitution were heard in every town and village: "There is no Declaration of Rights." He was one of the strongest proponents of religious liberty—of all our liberties—in American history. George Mason carried his struggle to the people and lived barely long enough to see his efforts crowned with his greatest victory, our Bill of Rights.

Mason also had other grounds for refusing to sign the Constitution. His warnings about the dangers of the powers given to the president were prophetic.

But finally, Mason could not sign the Constitution because of the bargain by which it allowed the slave trade to continue for twenty years. Mason, at great personal cost, confronted the tangled issue of slavery in an era of political revolution. This book seeks to sort out Mason's actions and beliefs regarding slavery, the slave trade, and states' rights.

George Mason was one of the preeminent architects of the Revolutionary War and of the American nation to which that conflict gave birth. His Virginia Declaration of Rights should be part of the common stock of political and journalistic discourse. Mason had the sharp mind of Jefferson, the determination of Washington, the literary skills of Madison, and the irascible temperament of John Adams.[24] Why is Mason not among the sacred gallery of famed patriots? It is lamentable that most Americans do not know Mason as well as they should, especially when we reflect on who he was and what he achieved.

At the inception of the American Revolution, Mason labored to hammer out a pragmatic theory that would divide government powers so effectively that the hand of a king could never eliminate the freedoms of the people.[25] His constitutional and political knowledge and compelling oratory helped propel the colonies toward independence. Then, a dozen years later, his dissenting voice was raised against what he deemed a fatally flawed Constitution of 1787, and nearly defeated the same. Mason drafted some of the most creative and consequential political texts in revolutionary history, yet history has anointed others with fame while Mason has languished in relative obscurity.

It is said that biography ends with death. But like most great statesman, Mason thought of the next generation. Had he lived longer, perhaps he could have found a viable solution for the next generation to end slavery (an institution he condemned in the most stringent of terms, though he never freed his own slaves). I hope this book presents Mason so the reader can feel the patriot, the father, the husband, the farmer, the scholar. No doubt he was a hard man to know intimately and still is, but it must have seemed a privilege to know him then as it does now. I also hope this biography will invite the reader to define "patriotism" as Mason did in its broadest sense, while appreciating the necessity of political debate in a free society. As one historian eloquently concluded, "In historic evaluations, as in religion, panegyric is vain and empty. Actions speak louder than words. Emulation rather than rhetorical evaluation by men of wisdom and virtue is the better test. By that rule let Mason be judged."[26]

For in the end, his sober judgment, deep knowledge, personal maturity, and principled convictions are woven into the fabric of the Constitution and the country's DNA. George Mason remains one of the wisest statesman America has ever known.

Prologue

As 1776 dawned, George Mason was a sober fifty years of age, his raven hair not yet sprinkled with gray. Mason's bearing was dignified, his complexion swarthy, his face grave, with radiant dark eyes that retained the fire of youth. Nearly six feet tall with a husky frame, his presence was commanding. On the eve of the American Revolution, Mason ranked among the most prominent and established patriarchs in Virginia society. But he saw family obligations, not politics, as his main responsibility, and he filled his personal writings with planting concerns, not political theory. Mason experimented with new crops, worried about the capabilities of his overseers, and pressed for government protection of his expanding western lands. He managed his estate meticulously, even corresponding with his workmen refinishing a cellar at Gunston Hall about the best mortar to keep out the summer cockroaches.

Over the past ten years, Mason had become one of the wealthiest Virginia planters, indifferent to the temptations of political office. He devoted his leisure time to study and books. His love of the outdoors had preserved his relatively good health, and he was fond of hunting and fishing on the Potomac River. Exposure to the open air and water revived him. As befitted a studious scholar from the Tidewater, Mason was "plain dressing" for a wealthy member of Virginia gentry. His oft-stated pleasures were his family, his farm, his books and writing table, an occasional pipe, a cup of tea or preferably a glass of good Madeira. In the warm seasons in Virginia he relished long, contemplative walks in his manicured gardens and time alone on horseback. He loved the open fields of his estate, and the soft breezes from the river. Mason was a man who cared deeply for his friends, and they were to be his friends for life, despite severe political strains. And to no one was George Mason more devoted than to his cherished wife, Ann. A hint of a smile always grooved his cheeks when Ann entered a room.

Mason was also, as many could attest, a persevering man of uncommon ability with a brilliant mind. He was beyond scrupulous and everyone recognized it. Extremely independent by nature, hard-working, frugal—all traits instilled by his parents—he was anything but cold or angry, as some historians have portrayed him. By temperament and disposition, he possessed the internal agility to be high-spirited and affectionate, but he was sometimes cranky, self-absorbed, and fiercely stubborn. Yet he also could be generous, entertaining, and all-forgiving to family and friends. With a core of deep, moralistic simplicity, Mason was subject to periods of despair, especially when separated from his devoted family. He had an honest aversion to political power, and much preferred domestic life to public service.

But when the Crown and Parliament began to assert obsessive control over his daily life, it bred a smoldering distrust. George Mason's "Revolution" was effected long before the war commenced.

The Revolution was in his mind and heart, as his loyalty to the Crown turned into rage and rebellion, producing a patriot firebrand. Mason became the full-throated voice of liberty with ideas, courage, and perseverance that would fuel an impossible victory. He rallied his colleagues around an amorphous idea greater than themselves. Mason and his Virginia patriots literally created a country where none had existed.[1]

Jump forward eleven years, to the spring of 1787. We can imagine a crucial day in March 1787, as Mason faced what would be one of the most momentous decisions in his illustrious life. There is no historical record of a visit from George Washington to Gunston Hall at that time, but it is probable that Washington paid a visit to his old friend as they both reluctantly considered whether to attend the Philadelphia Convention in May of that year, which had been called to amend the failed Articles of Confederation, and which would end by proposing a wholly new Constitution for the United States.

On this day in the early spring of 1787, George Mason is facing a painful choice. Mason—author, statesman, scientist, and farmer—had spent most of his life nurturing his five-thousand-acre estate nestled in the rolling Northern Virginia countryside. Gunston Hall, Mason's elegant home near the Potomac River, was a few miles south from Mount Vernon, George Washington's plantation.

Imagine an absorbed Mason, now portly in a blue frock coat with a few well-earned gray hairs, standing at the river entrance that morning, supervising his busy carpenters, the aroma of rich maple wood in the air. The view is stunning. The vista from the porch of Gunston Hall prompted amazed silence from guests, which was Mason's intended reaction. On this occasion, Mason's own eyes register the spring frost blanketing the cherry tree orchard, pale rows of peas bursting out in Gunston Hall's garden. He relished such simple moments as he refined his ideas about republican government. Wide

gravel paths separated four symmetrical gardens, bordered by manicured boxwoods that overlooked his scenic grounds. There were
glorious views of the Potomac River just steps from the house.[2] One
guest described the splendor of the scenery as "certainly the most
noble, excellent and beautiful river I ever saw, indeed it can be excelled
by no other river in the universe. The situations and gentlemen's seats
on this river are beyond comparison or description."[3] Mason took
periodic breaks down by the river to "walk for a considerable time
wrapped in meditation, and return again to his Desk."[4] The pristine
landscape was also a welcome reprieve from the bustle of his growing
household of nine children.

It was no coincidence that George Mason sprang out of the Virginia soil with a group of men who, for ability, character, and political genius, have few equals in any period of history. At almost the
same point of time and location, within a radius of one hundred miles,
George Mason, James Madison, Patrick Henry, Thomas Jefferson,
John Marshall, James Monroe, and George Washington were born.
The life stories of these Founders largely make up the early history of
our country, and it was their words that gave form to modern democracy. Mason and Washington, in particular, had much in common.
Before they presided over vast plantations and land holdings, each
had lost his father at an early age: Mason's father drowned in a ferry
accident crossing the Potomac when Mason was only ten; Washington's father died shortly after George turned eleven. "These personal
experiences," one scholar has said, "made these men daring and careful—qualities that served them well in the challenges they faced as
leaders of the Revolution and American nation."[5]

As dusk on this momentous day settles, picture Mason walking
gingerly, with a slight limp, through a row of boxwoods with his
lifelong friend and neighbor, General George Washington, a man
seldom seen in public, but whispered about in private.[6] Mason, seven

years older than his guest, has earned an honest fatigue during the day, most of which he has spent on horseback, supervising work around his tobacco crop. Tobacco and land ownership were paramount to Mason, which is why he speculated often in land and bought as much property as he could. Tobacco had long been Gunston Hall's signature crop. It was so important in Virginia that the Old Dominion was often called "the tobacco colony." Some planters even paid their taxes in tobacco. Mason had honed his proficiency at tobacco cultivation, bringing in a lucrative tobacco crop from seed to hogshead year after year.[7] Mason's horseback riding around the plantation played fits with his gout, a type of debilitating rheumatoid arthritis that affected him throughout his later years. In the Virginia twilight, the Occoquan River was streaming on the south of what was called Dogue's Neck, pouring into the great Potomac River. As the cool breeze wrinkled the water, one can visualize Mason's fond memories drifting back through the years: as a boy on his father's shoulders, arms raised in triumph, holding two caught fish; spring leaves floating off a thick magnolia tree that Mason's great grandfather had planted decades ago; cool, crystalline honeysuckle scenting the Virginia air; lavender irises painting Mason's elaborate gardens, the bees murmuring among the flowers.

As the last sliver of sun sets, the two patriots inspect Mason's crop of tobacco being planted for the coming summer season. Their friendship is of long standing. The two men have bought neighboring pews at the Pohick Church and occasionally speculated together on land. When George Mason hired tutors to come to Gunston Hall, including a dance instructor, Washington's stepdaughter Patsy Custis attended classes there. Washington has sought Mason's advice about a teacher for his stepson, Jacky Custis, and often relied on Mason for help with delicate matters.[8] When legal issues developed with respect to his stepdaughter's estate or his stepson's assets, Washington turned to Mason for sage advice. Only four months before, he asked Mason to loan his brother John Washington, "four, five, or six hundred pounds," a substantial sum. If any man could speak with Washington as his peer and friend, it was George Mason. They have hunted deer, talked politics, and shared farming strategies. Both are local leaders, serving as vestrymen for Truro Parish and trustees of the City of Alexandria. Dedicated farmers, the men talk easily of the freezing weather that has delayed their spring planting, and of the grafts Mason recently sent for Mount Vernon's budding cherry trees.[9]

As they retire into Gunston Hall for the evening, Mason and Washington discuss the simmering political problems plaguing the fledgling nation. A crackling fire in the west parlor pushes back the evening chill. The woodwork is dark walnut, the furniture elegant, and the air smells of wine and candle smoke. Both men favor sweet Madeira in the evening, and Gunston Hall's house servants have made sure the revered General, stroking a jaw that tapers to a diamond-shaped chin, has everything he wants.

The firelight exaggerates the contrasts between the two Virginians. Dressed in a mahogany brown suit with a set of silver buttons featuring eagles, Washington has features of granite. Tall and charismatic, with large hands and a face marked by smallpox scars, Washington is the palpable projection of authority. He has confided to Mason that he sometimes rides atop a pillow to protect his ailing backside from the pain of hemorrhoids.[10] Yet his posture is gracefully erect, his shoulders tight and muscular—"dignity with ease and complacency, the gentleman and soldier look agreeably blended in him," in the description of Abigail Adams.[11] Known to crack walnuts with a single hand, the strapping General has thrived on outdoor living and battlefield dangers. A doctor in the Continental Army saw Washington "as the perfect gentleman and accomplished warrior. He is remarkably tall, full six feet, erect and well proportioned."[12] At fifty-three, Washington retains the power of a superb horseman, but it is an inner power that commands every room he enters.

Mason has "clear gray eyes" and "few white hairs."[13] Squinting age lines around his eyes create a starburst effect. Mason radiates dignity and calm, with the look of a man who has seen much, yet retained at least some of the joy of youth. His hands, corded with blue veins have the long, tapered quality of a surgeon's. Like Washington, Mason has the superior equestrian skills required of all true gentlemen and is known for his prowess on horseback. He is fond of leaping fences and dashing across fields during fox and stag hunts. Rotating the daily use of his horses in order not to exhaust them, Mason refuses to whip his animals. He makes it a habit to visit their stables every morning to check on their well-being.[14]

George Washington's military service has made him a hero; his retirement, a legend. He could have been a king, but he spurned a crown and absolute power. It was no accident that Napoleon would say on his deathbed, "They wanted me to be another Washington."[15]

Mason, in contrast, is a private man by inclination—in his own description, "a man who spends most of his time in retirement and has seldom meddled in public affairs, who enjoys a moderate but independent fortune, and is content with the blessings of a private station."[16] A man of deep political thought and firm political convictions, he participates in politics only when he has to. He has already written one of the most influential documents of the Revolution, the 1776 Virginia's Declaration of Rights, the blueprint for Jefferson's eloquent Declaration of Independence.

Washington is literate, but not as well-read as Mason. James Madison went to Princeton, Thomas Jefferson to William and Mary, but George Washington went to war.[17] During the Revolution, Washington—not so well-versed in political theory as his neighbor and friend, or so knowledgeable about the rights of Englishmen, which were being trampled by Parliament's dictatorial claims over the colonies—deferred to the erudite Mason on such constitutional issues. Mason is respected and admired for his extraordinary abilities, the wide range of his knowledge, and the strong and eager intellect he has acquired by persistent self-education.

Mason can be direct, sardonic, and blunt with critics, while Washington is much more guarded and reserved.

As the two men talk over glasses of Madeira, behind them stand tall wooden book cases swelled with biographies and legal treatises of seventeenth-century philosophers. And now the conversation between the two Virginians turns more serious. They are discussing the deepening crisis in their nascent country. Mason's tone betrays his passion on the subject. The General listens intently to his old friend, whose insights he trusts.

When Mason finishes speaking, Washington admits, "This is a subject to which I confess I have paid very little attention. My time has been so much occupied in the busy and active scenes of life … that but a small portion of it could have been devoted to researches of this nature."[18] Mason has the better grasp of the current political crisis. While in 1776 the political issue was freedom and independence, now, in 1787, it is nationhood. The political apparatus of the young government is operating on a level of dismal incompetence. The War had knitted the states into a tenuous whole. A nascent political entity, the "Confederation Congress," had given a veneer of legitimacy to the Union between the thirteen United States. But the so-called "Articles of Confederation" had been inadequate from the start, and the tenuous Union they had created is now endangered by economic bickering among the new states. The diversity of climates, competing regional interests, and long-standing political disagreements are making it impossible to imagine that Americans can ever, in the words of British pamphleteer Josiah Tucker, "be united into one compact Empire, under any species of Government whatsoever."[19]

The two friends and neighbors agree about the current deplorable—and dangerous—state of affairs. As Mason lays out the perilous situation of the tenuously "United" States, George Washington seconds his conclusions, point by point.

Mason understands that the Articles of Confederation were never intended to be a political framework for a national government. They had created only a "Confederation" of states, all thirteen of which were "nations" themselves.[20] It was one thing to win a Revolution. It was quite another to create an entirely new system of government that would preserve the freedoms for which people had died. This is the problem now facing the thirteen states. To fight the war, they had joined together into a loose federation. But the Confederation Congress is now in a state of paralysis. Under the Articles, Congress cannot engage in war, enter into treaties, coin money, appropriate funds, or essentially do anything of significance without the consent of nine state delegations. All real power rests not with the Continental Congress, but with the states. There is no president of the country, no national court system, no Washington, D.C. In fact, the French government had intended to send thirteen separate ambassadors, one to each of the states. The War of Independence is over, but the fate of the American Revolution has yet to be decided.

The General has recently received a series of letters from Alexander Hamilton,[21] who had been his aide-de-camp during the war, in despair that without an army or a navy America is powerless to deal with international problems: "Spain blocks our ships from the Mississippi. How do we defend our rights as a country? Do we have troops, a national treasury, or even a national government? We have a shadow of a federal government, where 13 petty republics must agree on every point of every measure the Union wants to execute. The result? Nothing happens. The states have brought the wheels of national government to a standstill ... I hate Congress. I hate the world, a mass of fools and knaves. I hate myself."[22]

Washington, who would never express himself in these histrionic terms, is nonetheless deeply concerned. He nods and agrees with Mason that a great turning point seems to be at hand. "Your sentiments, that our affairs are drawing rapidly to a crisis, accord with my own," he tells his neighbor.[23] Mason savors his Madeira, and speaks firmly but quietly. (One of the keys to his success as a businessman is to speak softly and make others listen. It forces them to be quiet.) The Articles are almost useless, he urges—a fact demonstrated by "Shays' Rebellion," the recent bloodshed in New England. Daniel Shays was a former captain in Washington's army. Shays had led one of three rebel columns of debt-ridden Massachusetts farmers on a snowy day in late January 1787, when, armed with guns and pitchforks, they shut down courts to prevent bankruptcy proceedings. Like his men, Shays wore remnants of his old Continental Army uniform with a sprig of hemlock in his hat to distinguish himself from the official militia. Mason, who has read explicit descriptions of the lethal rebellion, detects a whiff of anarchy in the air.

For Washington, too, Shays' Rebellion has crystallized the need to overhaul the Articles of Confederation. "What stronger evidence can be given of the want of energy in our governments than these disorders?" he asks Mason. "If there exists not a power to check them, what security has a man of life, liberty, or property?"[24] What most troubles both men is the fact that their own countrymen are on the cusp of flouting the political order for which they had risked their lives. As Washington points out, "It is but the other day we were shedding our blood to obtain the constitutions under which we now live—constitutions of our own choice and framing—and now we are unsheathing the sword."[25]

Washington shows Mason a copy of a letter he received a few days before Christmas—a letter that he had dreaded: a plea from Virginia's governor, Edmund Randolph, that included a copy of an act passed by the Virginia General Assembly, appointing delegates to a "federal" Convention in Philadelphia. As Governor Randolph explained, the Assembly was alarmed by the "storms" that threatened to cripple the fledgling American nation. "To you I need not press our present dangers," Randolph had written. His letter explained that the Convention was being called "for the purpose of revising the federal constitution"—that is, the Articles of Confederation. Topping the list of the seven delegates who had been selected to represent Virginia at the Convention were George Washington and George Mason. Only those "who began, carried on & consummated the revolution," urged Randolph, could "rescue America from the impending ruin."[26]

Washington wished to remain in seclusion. But duty called once again, and the General has agreed to attend the Convention. The object of his visit to Gunston Hall is to convince Mason to accompany him. Washington appeals to his friend, telling him that this Federal Convention will represent a dramatic change in the direction of the country, transforming a confederation of states to a federal republic. He urges his dear mentor to join him in Philadelphia. He needs him, and the country needs his constitutional expertise. But Mason is reluctant as ever to leave home to play a role in public affairs. He has never ventured outside his native Virginia and does not relish the thought of leaving his cloistered family and farm. He draws strength and security from his wife and children, who have remained a constant source of comfort throughout his life.

Forming a new Constitution will be arduous, complicated work. And Mason foresees that the Convention will have to address inflammatory issues. In fact, the delegates will be forced into a tumultuous political confrontation on the proper balance between a strong national government and individual liberties. Mason's lifelong passion for liberty gives him instinctive reservations about sanctioning too much authority in a federal government.[27] Perhaps Mason intuits that his skepticism about government power may put him on a collision course with Washington and threaten their political alliance and personal friendship—which on this night seems as solid as at any point in their long lives. But Mason agrees to consider Washington's gracious request and escorts the General to the upstairs guest bedchamber. Mason gives Washington's hand a forceful squeeze and retires to his study, where he watches a sizzling log crumbling upon itself.

Mason could not know that he had just written *finis* to his thirty-year friendship with George Washington, By the end of the famous Philadelphia Convention in September, just six months from this evening of intimate agreement and mutual respect, Mason would find himself immersed in the most profound political and personal maelstrom of his life. And his relationship with Washington would be utterly ruptured.

George Mason's place in history would be sealed forever.

CHAPTER ONE

Origins

—

My father was a man of much note and influence
in Virginia ... and a stern and active patriot during
the Revolutionary war. And he was, as I can confirm
with truth, greatly beloved and admired.

—JOHN MASON, *Recollections* (1830)

The first half of the eighteenth century was a time when it was thrilling to be young, male, wealthy, and a Virginian. There was money was to be made, land to be claimed, tobacco to be planted and sold. There were plenty of ambitious men about—men with the boldness and the drive to develop farms, build estates, and accumulate fortunes in land and slaves in the wilderness of the mid-Atlantic. This was the time and place into which George Mason was born.

"We begin in Virginia," as one historian has written, "for the story of the creation of the American Republic is ... the story of Virginia. The plantation masters who presided over the largest, oldest, and most influential of England's North American colonies were used to their word holding sway."[1] George Mason had longstanding roots in the Virginia colony. His father, also named George Mason and known in the family as George III (not to be confused with the British monarch of that title) thrived as a surveyor and planter. Our George Mason (George IV) was a fourth-generation

1

Virginian, born on December 11, 1725, into a comfortable gentry life at Dogue's Head plantation in Stafford County. His parents were wealthy by eighteenth-century standards. Like George's father, his mother, Ann, came from a well-off gentry family with deep family ties in Virginia.[2]

Hugging the Eastern seaboard, the loyal British colony of Virginia was connected to the trading world of London by commerce and culture. As one scholar explains, "The all-powerful planters in this provincial sphere strove to ape their English cousins, who remained the unquestioned model of everything superior and cosmopolitan." And yet, in contrast to life in the mother country, "As the economic basis of this undemocratic world, slavery was commonplace and unquestioned, fostering an idle, dissolute existence for rich young Virginians."[3]

But despite the slave economy of Virginia, classical liberalism—or what was known at the time as the Whig view—was in the Mason blood. George's paternal ancestors were firm advocates of the largest measure of freedom consistent with the law. Mason's great-grandfather (George Mason I), the first in the family to immigrate to the New World, sat in Sir Francis Bacon's Assembly. His grandfather (George II), was a vigorous supporter of the Whig principles to which William of Orange was pledged when he came to the throne, and his father (George III) was a disciple of Alexander Spotswood, the most progressive of the colonial governors, who brought the writ of habeas corpus to Virginia. According to family tradition, Mason's great-grandfather, the first to reach the Old Dominion, was a Royalist who fled England after the defeat of pro-Stuart forces at the battle of Worcester in 1651. "Colonel Mason" (George I) commanded a troop of horses on the battleground, and barely escaped from this fatal field. He disguised himself and was concealed by some peasants until an opportunity offered him to escape to America. A younger brother is said to have accompanied him to Virginia. They landed at Norfolk, Virginia, and the brother, William Mason, married and died at or near Norfolk. The first George Mason in Virginia sailed up the Potomac River and settled at "Accokeek," lying in the peninsula called Potomac between Aquia and Potomac Creeks. George I initially located in Northumberland County but later moved to Westmoreland, Prince William, and finally to Stafford County. Some years after his death, Accokeek was sold by his son and the family moved further north on the Potomac River to extensive lands called Dogue's Neck (afterwards known as Mason's Neck). The Mason's vast land holdings stretched far into the entire peninsula.[4]

In his *Recollections*, great-great-grandson John Mason wrote of Colonel Mason (George I) as "a man of considerable talent and great influence in Virginia." He described an incident in which a "tribe of Indians lived on the Maryland shore who were continuingly murdering and plundering the inhabitants. Mason raised a party of men in the neighborhood where he lived, came up the river in boats and canoes in the night, surrounded the Indian town just as the dawn of the day and put them all, men, women and children to the sword."[5] Colonel Mason and his son were "great Indian fighters." Under their direction companies of men called "rangers" were formed for the protection of the colonists. As late as the year 1700, there was a brutal Indian uprising in which whole households of settlers were killed only twenty miles from Mason's home. This danger was close enough to require Mason's official military action.[6]

George Mason I "patented," or claimed, nine hundred acres in Northern Virginia based on eighteen "headright" claims in 1655, quickly entering the ranks of the local gentry.[7] His first wife, Mary French Mason, gave birth to George Mason II in 1660, apparently an only child. The eighteenth-century tradition of recycling names—to honor and reinforce connections to relatives—can be confusing.

Our George Mason (George Mason IV) was not only the fourth in his family line to share that name, but he also gave it to his firstborn son, who in turn gave the same name to his first son. In fact, six of George Mason's children named sons George, and five named daughters Ann, after their mother, Ann Eilbeck Mason. Patrick Henry had no fewer than ten grandchildren named Patrick.[8]

George Mason II bought hundreds of additional acres in Northern Virginia. He patented seventy-nine acres of land in 1704, including the site of the present village of Occoquan. He held diverse tracts of land totaling thousands of acres, and his home seat was at Dogue's Neck, the peninsula that juts out between Pohick and Occoquan creeks into the Potomac River, where George IV would build Gunston Hall. When George II and his third wife died during an epidemic in 1716, he owned more than nine thousand acres.

The life of the second Mason followed closely the pattern of his father's. He also inherited his father's political liberalism and was one of the most outspoken critics against the doctrines of King James II.[9] George II served as county lieutenant. This was the highest office in his county, carrying the rank of colonel. It was something more than a ceremonial title, certainly in earlier days.

The second George Mason had married three times. By Mary Fowke Mason he had five children, the eldest of whom was George Mason III, our George Mason's father. The three groups of children grew up in what later was to be called the Old Plantation, near the river's edge at Dogue's Neck.

George III, born in 1690, also became a successful planter. He kept family traditions alive and followed in the footsteps of his father as county lieutenant. A Virginia blueblood belonging to a family secure in privileges and vast, inherited estates who added vast sums of land in Virginia and Maryland, he was a prominent man engaged in the affairs of the colony, rising to justice of the peace and the sheriff of Stafford County, and then, in 1715, was elected to the prestigious House of Burgesses.[10] But our George Mason's father seems to have been somewhat lackadaisical about his political obligations. During his eleven-year tenure in the House of Burgesses, Mason received a formal reprimand for being absent. He was anything but relaxed, however, in his ambitious quest for land and his diversifying business interests—planting, land speculation, and shipping goods on the Potomac. While others still placed their honor in the trappings of a fortunate birth, Mason's father demonstrated talent, ambition, and a virtuous devotion to his family. He was too busy acquiring land to be lashed to lineage.[11]

As a large landholder and tobacco planter, George Mason III had extensive commercial transactions with the Scottish tobacco merchants, who were also brought into close relations with him in his position as county lieutenant, which gave him the power to extend financial courtesies. To show their appreciation, they gave Mason the "freedom" of the city of Glasgow, equivalent to a modern-day "key to the city," in 1720.

George Mason III, seemingly the most charming of the early Masons, had a profound early influence on his young son George. Our George Mason's father was the picture of Southern affability. George III, with a shining personality, seemed to be the picture of the wealthy and charming young planter. Our first vivid glimpse of him is as a "Knight of the Golden Horse Shoe." In 1716 he accompanied Governor Spotswood on a party of "gay and gallant gentlemen who formed the governor's escort" to Virginia's Western hills to encourage English exploration of the West. Each cavalier was given a small gold horseshoe pin stud, with jewels to represent nails. Horses went unshod on the soil in those times, but horseshoes were necessary in the rocky hills. These little golden horseshoes were symbols of an elegant chivalric order and became valued Mason family heirlooms.[12]

In 1718, George Mason III made his first appearance in the Virginia House of Burgesses, he and his brother-in-law George Fitzhugh representing Stafford County. A seat in the Virginia legislature was a high goal for the colonial gentry, a position held in esteem before and after the Revolution. Celebrated for his courage, the third George Mason had shown "loyalty, courage and conduct" in defense of the frontier people, who still required protection from the native Indians.[13] He excelled at riding, hunting, and fishing, passing those passions to his young son, our George Mason. Family tradition held that George Mason III single-handedly uprighted two huge "hogsheads" of tobacco that weighed a thousand pounds each—a remarkable feat, if not apocryphal. His father's standing mattered greatly to young George, who remembered him in superlative and fond terms in letters to his own children. As we trace the life of our George Mason, the story of these first generations seems to flow smoothly from generation to generation. Each successive Mason seems to have acquired more land, more wealth, and a more assured status as an established member of Virginia.

As Mason's father rose in stature, he made a fortuitous marriage in 1721 to Ann Thomson, the heiress of an influential royal appointee. Inheriting her father's estate made Ann a much sought-after bride, attractive to men like Mason. According to the recollections of his grandson John, George Mason III may have been married previously, to a "Miss Thompson of Chapawoscic who died without child. He then married another 'Miss Thompson,' ... an English lady by whom he had three [surviving] children George, Thompson and Mary. They also had three other daughters (who died ... of an 'eruptive disorder'—smallpox) and were buried in the same coffin." No other documentation, however, exists to support or disapprove the first marriage to a Miss Thompson. There was a "Thomson" family living in Stafford County, though, so the first marriage may have taken place. Our own George Mason was one of the three surviving children from the marriage to Ann Thomson.

In 1735, family tragedy struck. Mason's father died at the age of forty-nine. George Mason III drowned when his sailboat capsized as he was crossing the Potomac River. It was said he was buried at "Newtown," the seat of his brother-in-law, a Mr. Bronaugh. But it is probable that his remains were afterwards removed to Gunston Hall to be placed next to those of his wife. George Mason was only ten years old when his father died.[14]

Ann Thomson Mason, Mason's mother, would be remembered by the family rector, Reverend John Moncure, as "a good woman, a great woman and a lovely woman."[15] With almost perfect skin and shoulders powdered with freckles, Ann was the daughter of prominent attorney Stevens Thomson and much sought after as a wife. During the reign of Queen Anne, Stevens Thomson's distinguished career impressed the queen, who authorized Governor Nicholson to appoint him as Her Majesty's attorney general. Descended from a distinguished Yorkshire family, Thomson had earned his degree at Cambridge and been admitted to the Middle Temple for the study of law. Little is known of his public life, as the records of the general court were destroyed by the burning of the Richmond courthouse on April 3, 1865, during the Civil War. But one contemporary wrote that the Virginian was "an astute Atty. General." Ann was the only Thomson child who survived to adulthood, the sole heir to a substantial estate, and by all accounts a beautiful and intelligent girl.

By eighteenth-century standards, George Mason's parents were wealthy. In fact, fourth-fifths of present-day Fairfax County, Virginia, was once owned by the Mason family. George's father substantially expanded the family's holdings in Northern Virginia and into Charles County, Maryland, generally preferring to lease land to tenants rather than to work it with his own slaves.

But he was also a busy tobacco farmer. Although London merchants considered Mason's local "Orinoco" tobacco inferior to the
sweet-scented tobacco grown further south, a substantial market
existed for Orinoco tobacco on the European continent.[16]

By the time our George, George Mason IV, was born in 1725, his
family had become quite prominent in Virginia.[17] A first son born into
a family of the Virginia aristocracy, he was bred to be a Virginia
planter-patriarch. Baptized in early 1726, Mason matured amid the
prosperous farmland of Tidewater Virginia, the Eastern territory
washed by four broad rivers: the James, York, Rappahannock, and
Potomac. Young George grew up with every advantage. One indication
of his parents' vast land holdings: Mason and his two siblings, Mary
and Thomson, were all born on different plantations. The Masons were
a prosperous, cultured, and sophisticated family. They dined with silver,
danced with grace, and entertained. Their Virginia and Maryland
estates demonstrate that the Mason family wished to participate in
upper social culture, even if they lived on a relative frontier. The Masons
set their table with knives, forks, spoons, and napkins in an era when
many people still ate with only a spoon or their hands. Mason and his
siblings did not have to seek refinement outside of their own home.
Virtually everything he needed was right there. Although Fairfax
County was still a wilderness in many ways, the Masons acquired fine
goods and taught their children the impeccable manners required to
enter Virginia gentry society. As one German visitor sniffed, about the
typical young Virginian: "At fifteen, his father gives him a horse and a
negro, with which he rides about the country, attends every fox hunt,
horse race and cockfight."[18] Nathaniel Hawthorne wrote mockingly
that a child of the Virginia gentry was "born with ... hair powdered
and made a stately bow on his first appearance in the world."[19]

But there was nothing pampered about Mason's provincial boy-
hood. His mother would wake young George at dawn for chores

about the plantation, a farmer's habit that Mason retained for the rest of his life. The early lessons from his mother were internalized by her son. A dark walnut grandfather clock clicked seven deep gongs before the silence returned. One can imagine it took an incredible amount of effort for George to drag himself out of bed. His firm but loving mother did not tolerate the indulgence of sleeping in. Ann did not bend easily to others but stayed true to her own industrious standards. Rising early with the sun, she instilled habits of thrift and arduous work into her children.

Mason's childhood seems happy, but it was ultimately unsettled by his father's unexpected death. That demise, like the early death of George Washington's father, stole any chance of a lighthearted youth. George grew accustomed to assuming family burdens from his mother. George developed a toughness not uncommon in children forced to assume adulthood at a tender age. He discovered his ability to perform many adult tasks, and he never forgot the sudden, painful loss of his father. One can imagine Mason's overwhelming sense of loss and loneliness, but early on he learned the importance of endurance and improvisation. He learned it the way his father wanted him to: through action, not theory. And quite naturally, George turned to older men as sponsors and mentors, seeking out influential figures such as his uncle, John Mercer.

Mason often referred to family heirlooms he knew from his childhood. There was his father's big seal, which he had pressed decisively into blobs of hot red wax on the letters he wrote to the governor. It left an imprint of a heart pierced with two arrows, surmounted by a crown. The young George became so fond of it that in later years he used this same design for a ring of rubies and diamonds to give to one of his daughters. His father's "Burgesses" ticket to the Virginia assembly in Williamsburg with its gray, red, and blue coat of arms and scrolling motto was another beloved heirloom. And most delightful of all, because it carried with it so many breathtaking stories, was the "Golden Horseshoe," his father's diamond-studded, inscribed brooch given to George's father by Governor Spotswood.

With his father's tragic death, George was propelled into the role, if not the reality, of "the man of the house." The family would now be dominated by George's mother, Ann, who almost certainly exerted as great an influence on her eldest son as the memory of his father did. In her late thirties at the time her husband's death, she inherited the mantle of mother and father to her three surviving children and became both mistress and master of the family estate, managing a plantation with sixty-six slaves and almost three thousand acres. Family members would remember Ann as a woman of a clear and strong purpose, managing a demanding plantation, tending three children, and overseeing dozens of slaves. By all family accounts, Ann was an agreeable, intelligent woman, as well educated as other Virginia ladies of the day. When she died in 1773, the *Maryland Gazette* eulogized her: "She discharged her duty, in her several characters of a Wife, Parent, a Mistress, a Friend, a Neighbor and a Christian with that distinguished Lustre, which everyone would wish to imitate, but few have ever equaled."[20]

She returned from Maryland to Virginia, settling her young family on Thomson family property on Chopawamsic Creek, just a short distance north of where the first George Mason had built his plantation. A bit of a martinet, Ann ran things as she saw fit. Literate, social, fond of cultivated things—from fancy plates and crockery to well-made furniture to fine clothing—she endured the death of a husband, coped with the deaths of children, and remained in control to the end, immersed in the world around her and in the lives of those she loved. That her eldest son grew to become such a resourceful and resilient man is no surprise.[21]

Mason inherited one quality from both of his parents that became his most important character trait: perseverance. Mason was also taught by his father and mother, and later by his tutors and mentors, that a Virginia gentleman owed service to his family, to his county, and to his colony—in that order. Mason came of age with the confidence instilled by his wise mother and his learned paternal uncle by marriage, John Mercer, who undertook George's formal education.

Ann's influence on George cannot be overstated. It was from her that he inherited his delicate facial features, and also the culture and intellectual legacy of a prominent British family. Her father and brother were distinguished lawyers in England, and she was born and bred in London, a descendant of the British aristocracy who boasted of a family crest. Tradition holds that George Mason's mother was a great favorite with her maternal great-uncle, the prominent Sir William Temple. Ann cherished a family relic from Temple, later passed down to her son George—the Lord's Prayer written elegantly upon a circle parchment the size of a quarter. Interestingly, Ann's younger son gave one of his children the name William Temple, and his place in Loudoun County was called Temple Hall.[22] Ann had the mental endowments that were to be expected from her distinguished lineage and inheritance. She was also impressive in her own right, a woman of force and character. George Mason's mother was the most important early influence him. She was his tender succor and champion in his youth.

Ann, a young and beautiful woman when widowed, never married again, though tradition reports that her hand was sought by numerous suitors. Ann was an attractive, wealthy, and intelligent woman. But she had little practical need for a husband. She devoted herself to her children, and they owed much to their wise and affectionate mother. Ann was said to have possessed all the brilliant intellectual qualities of her father, and to be a woman with a most amiable and domestic disposition.[23]

Also a careful and fastidious business woman, Ann kept meticulous records and made shrewd land investments. Because Mason's father died without a will, all the family's land would be inherited by young George when he turned twenty-one. Worried about leaving the younger children without an inheritance, Ann wisely bought ten thousand acres in Loudoun County for Mary and Thomson. She proved herself an incredibly careful and prudent guardian. Ann saved all the money she could to purchase the acres of what was then called "wildlands" in Loudoun County, for which she paid only shillings per acre. No sooner had she completed the purchase than she divided the land between her younger children, Mary and Thomson. She did not delay this until her death, because she did not wish her younger children to grow up with a sense of envy or inequality regarding George's inheritance. Her investment turned out a most lucrative one. In the end, she made her two younger children wealthier than their older brother.[24]

Ann also made sure her children dressed their status: ruffled linen shirts for the brothers and fashionable petticoats for Mary. We know that she bought George a beaver hat, a wig, a razor, and some school books when he turned seventeen. She carefully managed her household without accruing debts. Ann's accounts as guardian of her children give great detail on their "expenses." Each child was "charged" one thousand pounds of tobacco yearly for board and other items. On one occasion Thomson was charged for linen and making three ruffled shirts. Mary was charged with wooden heeled shoes, petticoats, one whole petticoat, and linen.

A warm, quiet bond endured between Mason and his mother. Ann Thomson Mason raised a son who was bookish, infused with a lifelong need for knowledge, and exhibited the reserved personality that would later define him. The similarities between Ann and her eldest son were striking. She was a fine horsewoman, enjoyed dancing, was frugal in money matters, superintended her farm, and displayed independence. Both mother and son exhibited supreme willpower and earnestness.[25]

The relationship might have been different had Mason attended college. His lack of the formal education that some distinguished gentlemen had set him apart from more famous peers such as Jefferson and Madison. But the lack of a university education did not thwart Mason's intellectual curiosity or mean he was uneducated. We can glean details of his education from several sources. Although Mason did not have a formal college education, he was tutored and read widely in his uncle's vast library. Mason was tutored in Latin, Greek, and French. Ann's account book reflects George's tutoring by a "Mr. Williams" during the years 1736 to 1739, and that in addition a "Mr. Wiley" received 845 pounds of tobacco for schooling and books for George in 1738. There were no public schools then, so children received an education in many ways. When he turned twelve, Mason went to a private school, called an academy, in Maryland. The family minister also assisted his education by ordering books for him from Great Britain. Although there is no certain documentation, the evidence of Mason's later adult speeches and writings demonstrate not only the power of his mental processes but a broad education that made him a "universal" man.[26]

Perhaps the degree to which Mason dwelt upon the importance of education in his advice to his children reveals his regret at having missed college. He shared the view of Washington, who also did not attend a formal college and who lectured a young nephew about to enter college that "every hour misspent is lost forever," and that "future years cannot compensate for lost days at this period of your life."[27] Both Washington and Mason were subject to a modicum of condescension on this account, particularly from the snobbish John Adams, who disparaged Washington as "too illiterate, unlearned, and unread for his station and reputation."[28]

But Mason's lack of a university education never gave him a sense of intellectual inadequacy like Washington's. On the contrary, Mason was secure in his intellectual achievements all his life. And by any ordinary standard Mason was a highly educated man with a keen ability to grasp complex ideas ranging from constitutional structure to the planting and harvesting of a successful wheat crop. Mason seized every hour of leisure to improve himself and retain useful knowledge. George's father's extensive library included Shakespeare and Jonathan Swift. As an adolescent, Mason read numerous works of fiction, history, philosophy, and geography. An avid reader of periodicals, he sampled *The Spectator* by the age of sixteen and read Henry Fielding's *Tom Jones* and Tobias Smollett's *The Adventures of Peregrine Pickle*. He relished English law and military history. It is often said that Mason's neighbor and friend George Washington absorbed his lessons from action, not books. Mason was just the opposite. He formed his thoughts, his writing, and his political ideas from English history books.[29]

Mason enjoyed many other pursuits besides his books. In the summer he loved to swim in the cool, deep waters of the Potomac and Rappahannock rivers. He excelled at riding, liked to hunt, learned fencing, attended a dancing school, played billiards, and frequented horse races. Despite his love for nature and the outdoors, he also had the social graces necessary for a member of the Virginia gentry. At the same time, he was a sober young man. In countless letters in later years, he advised his children that adolescence could be a precarious time.

His gentle personality earned him many friends. While Washington held himself aloof from political disputes, and Jefferson abhorred debating—once advising a grandson "When I hear another express an opinion which is not mine, I say to myself, 'he has a right to his opinion, as I to mine' ... be a listener only, keep within yourself, and endeavor to establish with yourself the habit of silence, especially in politics"—Mason regarded a robust argument as the ideal form of a conversation, though in later years his seniority and his wit allowed him to float above political infighting. Mason could be direct and blunt. As he grew older, he became somewhat sardonic, similar in nature to John Adams.

The foundations for Mason's political career were laid in his adolescent years under the tutelage of John Mercer. Soon after his father died, Mason came under the guidance of his temperamental maternal uncle by marriage, a prominent lawyer who shared guardianship of him after his father's death. There is no doubt that Mercer was the greatest intellectual and scholarly influence on young George. The cultivated and sophisticated Mercer presented an appealing model of urbanity for young George. Mercer would have a tremendous intellectual influence on young George, forming his early academic interests and thoughts.

And fortuitously, Mercer found himself unexpectedly unemployed just when his nephew's education required his attention. He had begun a law practice upon his arrival in the colony in 1726 but his Celtic temper got the best of him in court, and he was disbarred because of insulting language. But the disbarment proved to be of short duration. Ten years later Mercer was allowed to practice again and given a legal commission for his county.

John Mercer of Marlboro was a man of substance who owned one of the best private libraries in the Virginia colony. It contained fifteen hundred volumes, including books on law as well as works by Milton, Pope, Swift, Grotius, and Voltaire. Half of Mercer's collection consisted of legal treatises, including an extensive collection of the writings of the great English jurist Sir Edward Coke. But Mercer's tastes were eclectic, running from classical works such as the *Iliad*, the *Odyssey*, and Plato to more pedestrian books on farming, gardening, and medicine.

During the years he taught George Mason, Mercer was also working on his *Abridgement* of the laws of Virginia. There is no doubt that Mason owed to Mercer his classical scholarship, his familiarity with the law and many of his philosophical ideas. No casual antiquary, Mercer directed Mason's reading toward useful objects. George became a diligent student of British and Virginia history, studying historical sources, years before his involvement in the Declaration of Independence and the Bill of Rights. The notes Mason would compile in the 1770s on land charters, as well as his surviving correspondence about the debates in the Constitutional and Ratification Conventions of 1787 and 1788, disclose that Mason had a wealth of knowledge about the law, although he was never admitted to the bar. He had studiously learned the details of British and Virginia land law from Mercer. Mason knew about the laws and legal forms for protecting and transmitting estates, and how to sue to collect a debt. He also studied in detail the laws and customs of domestic and international commerce. His knowledge of law and public policy were impressive for a man who did not attend college.

A passion for individual liberty and freedom ran deep in Mason's psyche from a very early age. Its roots can be traced back to his voracious instruction and reading in his uncle's library. It was there that he learned the history—dating back to Cromwell's time, and beyond—of the rights of a free people and the restraint of government. British law and philosophy influenced Mason's thoughts and helped form the ideas that would shape his contributions to the Constitution and the Declaration of Independence.

At the age of twenty-one, George Mason took possession of his inheritance and returned to the home of his early childhood at Dogue's Neck. There he would build Gunston Hall and live as its master for the next forty years.

CHAPTER TWO

Ann Eilbeck
Mason

The household establishment at Gunston Hall
was conducted with great regularity much under
the particular inspection of my revered parents
while my mother lived.

—JOHN MASON, *Recollections* (1830)

F ew events in George Mason's life story are more striking than the arrival of his true love Ann Eilbeck into his cloistered life. Young, beautiful, and charming, Ann caught the eye of many suitors, including a fourteen-year-old George Washington, who found early disappointment in his pursuit of her. Ann's youthful charms made havoc in more than one susceptible heart, but no one else had a chance once she met George Mason. Nearly eight years her senior, darkly handsome, Mason was grave and studious. Perhaps it was these qualities she was looking for, because Mason won her over and she became mother and mistress of his estate for the next twenty-three years.

In 1749, as the winter days grew longer, young Mason's interest in the tobacco warehouse being built upon his Maryland plantation increased steadily. His overseer must have wondered at the frequency of the young owner's visits. Mason's trips across the

Potomac River always included a stop at the house on Mattawoman Creek, the home of sixteen-year-old Ann Eilbeck. On one such occasion, Mason found Mr. and Mrs. Lawrence Washington from Mount Vernon dining with the Eilbecks, for he, as well as Mason, owned land on the Maryland side of the Potomac. Lawrence Washington was a frail young man, and appeared even more so when compared with his strapping half-brother George who accompanied him.

In the presence of the beautiful Ann, Mason initially may have been awkward and reserved. Ann's mother, presiding with ease at the head of her dinner table, would have drawn young George into the conversation. Ann must have encouraged his attentions, since he soon returned. It was a busy time for Mason even before he began to woo Ann. Mason's plans for his permanent home on the river were forming. Now he had a reason to build a family estate: a potential wife.

Ann was well educated for her day, and a constant reader. Shared tastes in literature may have brought her closer to George; they would read *The Poems of Ossian* together after they were married. She had her father's method and industry. Her daughter would describe Ann as "lavish with her charms," a woman of great personal attractions, with a mind of no ordinary caliber. Mason became determined to have Ann, and to give her the best of everything.[1]

He had finally found a woman who set his studious nature ablaze with a yearning for romantic love. She possessed an abundance of a virtue that Mason valued above all other attributes, sweetness of temper. This was a virtue that his mother had, and that Mason needed to find in a wife. Two other qualities were attractive to Mason: Ann's sprightliness and sensibility.[2]

Ann captured what "Virginians prized in female character and conduct. Ann Mason was ... 'blessed with a clear and sound judgment, a gentle and benevolent heart, a sincere and a humble mind, with an even, calm and cheerful temper.'"[3] It was what Ann Mason did with those traits that made her a model woman. Content with the blessings of a private station, Ann would place all her happiness here, where only it is to be found, in her own family. Mason would praise his wife for fulfilling every desirable role of a woman: "An easy and agreeable companion, a kind neighbor, a steadfast friend, a humane mistress, a prudent and tender mother, a faithful, affectionate, and most obliging wife."[4]

At some point Mason emerged as the leading contender among Ann's numerous suitors. Some seven years her senior, six feet tall, brilliant and studious, he was lean, with blackish hair, dark eyes, and a fair complexion. His nose was patrician, the mouth firmly set. Mason, who was slightly shorter than George Washington but long-limbed and loose-jointed, was a man with a reserved charm, but his mild manner belied his fierce convictions and intellect. His first biographer described the young Mason as a man with an engaging appearance, a face that beamed with intelligence. He was also a fine dancer and a dashing horseman.[5]

What, apart from their looks and literary tastes, drew Ann and George together? Both were products of plantation life. Their similar upbringings may account for their strong attraction to each other. The correspondence between their social circumstances and the influence of their fathers is uncanny. Both Mason and Ann were very much a product of their class. Ann was bred to be a plantation mistress, and during her years of married life with George, she would work hard at being a successful one.

Ann was the only child of Sarah Edgar and Colonel William Eilbeck, a wealthy planter and merchant whose Mattawoman plantation lay near the Masons' Maryland estate. Ann's father was not only a longtime Mason family friend and business ally, but also one of the richest men in Charles County. And Ann was his sole heir. One historian has commented that his father's example showed George

Mason the advantage of courting a woman whose wealthy father had no sons.[6] Well-off and accomplished, Ann—who already owned some property and stood to inherit massive land holdings from her father— would have been an incredibly attractive candidate for marriage to any Virginia gentleman.

No doubt Mason was also physically attracted to Ann from the start. Delicate, with dark eyes, Ann was a "Beauty of ... Person, & the Sweetness of her Disposition, she was equaled by few, & excelled by none."[7] Family tradition and Mason's own description of Ann show her as strikingly beautiful—and Mason adored her. Ann's complexion was brilliant, her luxuriant hair of the finest tint of black. Mason himself gave a detailed description of Ann in the family Bible: "She was something taller than the middle size, and elegantly shaped. Her eyes were black, tender and lively; her features regular and delicate; her complexion remarkably fair and fresh. Lilies and roses (almost without a metaphor) were blended there, and a certain inexpressible air of cheerfulness and health. Innocence and sensibility diffused over her countenance [which] formed a face the very reverse of what is generally called masculine."[8] Ann's impeccable manners had been imposed on her by her parent's stern admonitions but gentle discipline. Her magnolia-white skin was guarded with bonnets, veils, and mittens against both the sun and the chafing Virginia cold. Her wedding dress would set off to perfection her seventeen-inch waist.

Little recorded evidence is left of the early courtship of Ann by George. If the couple did not originally meet at Mattawoman plantation, as some historians have surmised, perhaps their first meeting was at Governor Botetourt's royal ball, or at a dinner party at the governor's mansion in Williamsburg, the colonial capital. If they met at the governor's mansion, in the eighteenth-century tradition, the dinner table, on trestles upon the ballroom floor, would have been set for sixty people. The tablecloth would have been homespun linen and laden with the fruits of three days of work: quails and sausages, squash-corn salad, kidney-mutton savories, and sweet potato biscuits. Ann would have been dressed in the "gay and splendid" style for which Virginia was famous, her hair "craped" high with rolls on each side, topped by a cap of gauze and lace. Mason would have looked almost as splendid in clockwork silk stockings, lace ruffles, breeches, and a waistcoat of blue, green, scarlet, or peach. Mason would have worn a wig set with curlers using a pomade made from animal fat and dusted with a powder made from wheat flour. He also would have worn some sort of tie or scarf, hand sewn of locally made linen or cotton fabric, but taken it off and put it in his haversack if he became heated dancing the minuet with Ann.

In the spring of 1750, the marriage bans for George and Ann were read in the church near Port Tobacco on three successive Sundays, in accordance with Church law. The happy wedding day came on April 4, 1750, and the service was performed by the Reverend John Moncure, Mason's close friend. (Mason was godfather to three of Moncure's children.) Mason married Ann at her father's estate, Mattawoman Plantation, in Charles County, Maryland. The *Maryland Gazette* reported the marriage on May 2, 1750, describing the bride as "a young lady of distinguished merits and beauty and a handsome fortune": "George Mason, of Stafford County, Virginia, aged about twenty-five years, and Ann Eilbeck, the daughter of William Eilbeck, of Charles County, Maryland, merchant, aged about sixteen years, were married on Wednesday, the 4th day of April, in the year 1750, by the Rev. Mr. John Moncure, Rector of Overwharton parish, Stafford County, Virginia."[9]

It was customary in those days in Virginia and Maryland for young women of affluent families to be married at home. As one historian describes these eighteenth-century weddings, "Cards and dancing immediately succeed," followed by "an elegant supper, a cheerful glass and the convivial song." The wedding celebrations often lasted several days and sometimes would move from one house to another. The wedding party, in one such case, occupied six well-filled carriages, with "the Bride and Bridegroom leading the van in a new Phaeton."[10]

We may be sure that George and Ann had a traditional and beautiful wedding. Wedding veils were not worn then, nor were brides dressed in white. We can only guess at Ann's wedding dress, but we know that a fashionable young lady of that period might wear a fawn-colored gown with fabric of purple, red, yellow, and white scattered over it, with pleats at the back ending in a graceful train. Lace may have adorned the front of Ann's dress, held in with a row of dainty silk bows. Her hair would have been powdered and adorned with pearls. Mason, like any bridegroom, was probably speechless when he saw Ann in her wedding gown. As custom dictated, he would give her his deepest bow when Ann gave her curtsey. In honor of the occasion, Mason would have powdered and tightly curled his hair, something he seldom troubled to do. Was Mason nervous? Did his firm voice shake when he said his vows?

The marriage ceremony probably began with the three "causes for which matrimony is ordained," the first being for "the procreation of children, to be brought up in the fear and nurture of the Lord, and to the praise of His holy name," the second, "as a remedy against sin, and to avoid fornication," and the third, the "help and comfort, that the one ought to have of the other, both in prosperity and adversity."[11] They made their vows, according to the rites of the Church of England, as embodied in "The Form of Solemnization of Matrimony" in the Book of Common Prayer. Invocations followed: that the couple be blessed with children and live long enough to give those children a Christian upbringing; that in the marriage, representing "the spiritual marriage and unity between Christ and his church," Mason would love his wife and Ann would "be loving and amiable, faithful and obedient to her husband, and in all quietness, sobriety and peace, be a follower of holy and godly matrons."[12] It was customary for the minister to remind the couple of Saint Paul's advice on the duties of husbands and wives, directing Mason to love his wife even as himself, weaker vessel that she was, and reminding Ann to "submit to your husband as unto the Lord, for the husband is the head of the wife, even as Christ is the head of the church."[13] Mason promised to love Ann, "honor her, comfort her and keep her in sickness and in health." Ann swore to "obey him, serve him, love, and honor and keep him in sickness and in health."[14]

Then music and feasting would have been the order of the day. Perhaps as the couple danced in the Eilbeck ballroom, Frances Alberti, a little Italian music instructor with bowed legs and a most ill-fitting wig, played the violin. In fact, Alberti may have taught music to both Ann and George separately, as he did to Thomas Jefferson and his children. Mason was probably generous in his tips to the musicians and trusted servants. When the celebration was well along, Mason would have taken Ann's hand and the couple would have climbed together upstairs to their wedding chamber. There it was that the newlywed couple slept together for the first week of their married life. Ann doubtless treasured the memory of closing the door, pegging it, and climbing into their bed, alone together as they had never been before.

The twenty-three years of marriage that followed were the happiest period in George Mason's life. Those years were in stark contrast with the period of almost equal length that followed, when Mason's talents carried him into the stream of momentous events leading to the American Revolution.

Ann possessed advantages that set her apart from the vast majority of colonial women.[15] She had money and education. But even though the cities on the Eastern seaboard were growing, with their shops and conveniences, most women, even wealthy women like Ann, still lived on farms and produced everything they used. "As towns sprouted up," observed author and historian Cokie Roberts, "women started specializing—one doing the soap making, another the cheese and butter churning, another the weaving. They bartered with each other for goods and services, creating an off-the-books economy entirely run by women."[16]

In fact, despite their lack of legal rights, many women ruled their households. There was an elaborate view of separate "spheres." The men were "in the world," whereas a woman's place was in the house, the "domestic sphere." "The men handled relations with England—deciding whether to declare independence and what kind of government should be formed; the women handled pretty much everything else," wrote one scholar: "That's not to say that these women were unaware of the sphere outside of their homes, quite the contrary. Their letters and diaries are filled with political observations and, in the case of Abigail Adams, instructions. Newspapers and magazines of the day kept women as well as men up to date on the news, as well as the fashions, both at home and in England."[17]

In addition to her domestic and childrearing duties, Ann also played a vital role in Mason's gentry life, as hostess and social companion. As his family grew, Mason began schooling the younger children. But in the evenings, he and Ann played games or read to each other from their favorite books.

Ann's formal education probably included music, since the ability to sing and play at the keyboard was considered a valuable social skill. A young woman of her status would have invariably studied dance with a dancing master, and Ann would have been encouraged to draw and paint. Ann also read poetry and novels suitable for ladies. Indeed, reading was often one of her main amusements. Robert Carter, a neighbor at Nomini Hall, boasted of his own wife that he "would bet a Guinea that Mrs. Carter reads more than the Parson of the parish!"[18]

How Ann dressed herself reflected her prosperity; her clothing was expected to be suitably stylish and tasteful. Although there were professional milliners, dressmakers, and tailors in the larger towns such as Richmond and Williamsburg and clothing was purchased regularly from England, no plantation mistress could afford not to be able to sew. "At a fancy ball in Williamsburg, Virginia ... held for the governor and ladies and gentlemen of the town," author Cokie Roberts observed, "women arrived at the gala affair in simple home-spun gowns, leaving their imported silks and brocades at home."[19]

"Almost all of the women who mothered and married the Founders," according to Roberts, "were of the wealthier classes, and even if they had no formal education, they did know how to read and write, and many of them, like Abigail Adams, read exten-sively, though they never went to school. Abigail never got over the injustice of excluding girls from proper schools, and she advocated vociferously for women's education."[20] Although many of the mar-riages of the Founders, like that of Ann and George Mason, were true partnerships, in the context of the marriage itself, the women literally owned nothing, not even their own jewelry. "Some colonies allowed for divorce," observed one historian, "but since it was not legal in England, the subject became another bone of contention between the Mother Country and her colonies. In fact, Catharine Littlefield Greene, the widow of Revolutionary War hero Nathanael Greene, caused a scandal by living with a man not her husband. Her old friend President Washington advised her to marry when she and her gentleman came to visit. Kitty was to petition Congress for repayment of her husband's payouts to clothe his soldiers, but Wash-ington thought her sinful state of cohabitation caused resistance to her cause. But Kitty Greene, rambunctious, flirtatious, and highly competent, had legal reasons to resist marriage: she wanted to control her own property."[21]

In addition to family duties, Ann would eventually take a deep interest in the Mason land and farms. An Italian neighbor and acquaintance, Philip Mazzei, had brought Ann several kinds of European seeds when he arrived to stay with the Masons while his own estate was being completed in Charlottesville. Ann was pleased, especially at the "fifty-day Indian corn," and the winter wheat. Mazzei explained to Ann that these crops would grow very well in the fields, and that they thrived in the mountainous sections of Italy, near Casentino and Valdarno.

"The wheat pleased the men; the corn, the women," Mazzei wrote in his *Memoirs*. "In Virginia, and I think it is also true of other States, the wife is in full charge inside the house; the husband, outside; he does, however, see to the purchase of whatever provisions his wife tells him are needed."[22] Mazzei's recollections of Ann and George Mason give significant insight into their everyday lives on a plantation. He noted that, "If the wife needs indoors someone working outdoors, she asks her husband for him; and the husband, his wife if he needs outside someone working indoors. Hostesses just love to have their dinner guests find uncommon fare, especially early fruits or vegetables. Of their nine or ten varieties of Indian corn preferable to our own none mature as early as our fifty-day corn, and over there they make a very appetizing dish with corn that is not fully ripe. That is why the ladies were grateful to me for the fifty-day corn."[23]

Mazzei shared with the Masons and Jeffersons a great deal about farming and crops. For example, Mazzei related that "it is a well-known fact that plants produced by pear or apple seeds always degenerate and generally produce fruit so bad that even hogs will not eat some of it. Sometimes, however, an excellent new species is generated by them. This generally happens where the vastness of the land seeded makes it impossible for its owner to graft more than a small portion of the trees." One of Mazzei's ungrafted trees produced a cider apple "superior to the best of Brittany and England ... it is called Becker's apple because it originated on his land. In New York State the same was true of a winter eating apple, better than any I know, and there it must be known by the name of the man on whose land it originated, but in Virginia and the other States it is called New York apple."[24] Because New York apples kept well, the Masons, as well as other Virginians, probably bought and sold many of them, shipping them to other states in barrels.

Ann would have also overseen, at least in part, some of the stables and construction work at Gunston Hall while Mason was away in Williamsburg or Alexandria. Because Ann was herself an accomplished rider, she would have overseen the stable of beautiful saddle mares and draft horses to make long trips in comfort.[25]

Life for the newlyweds was a warm portrait of harmony. It was the life Mason had long hoped for—the kind of life his father had built and his mother had maintained, and which he now gave his own family. Possessing an estate and being blessed with an accomplished husband, Ann seemed prepared for a prosperous and happy life voyage. From Mason's account books, his income was a handsome one for that day. This was later to be increased substantially by the receipt of Ann's fortune when her father died.[26]

No doubt, like any young bride, Ann's thoughts were less focused on money, in which she was adept and frugal, and more on her fledgling new family. She surely dreamed of a garden of her own making. She had knowledge from her father working on a plantation, but she also depended on Mason's gardening expertise. She would have known her husband owned numerous books on gardening and planting, for example, *James on Gardening*, translated from Leblond's manual of the French formal style of gardening, as well as other books that gave examples of English landscape gardens.

As the plantation village expanded, Ann supervised the production of all that the family ate and everything that the numerous servants used for food and clothing. There was, of course, a smokehouse for meat, a dairy, and a garden for vegetables, herbs, and flowers. She improved the gardens with the planting of a variety of fruits and vegetables, including fig and cheery trees. By the first summer, the Masons were enjoying cucumbers, peas, snap beans, and Irish potatoes. And there were chickens, hams, and beef in abundance.

Ann oversaw the slaughtering of ducks, geese, and hogs, weaving, and sewing. Her accounts record the production of fabrics in a spectrum of quality: "fine linen shirts," "fine mixt cloth for the children," "mixt cloth for the house servants," and, for the "out negroes," "hemp linen" and "coarse linen." She traded bacon to the slaves for their chickens, and she supervised the preparation of meat for her own family. In fact, Ann delighted in taking personal direction of the work of the kitchen on more sophisticated foods. As some of her servants recalled, she came to the kitchen on occasion to give cooking instructions, carrying a cookery book in her hand and read out to her servants how to make cakes, tarts, and breads.[27]

On grand dining social occasions with neighbors and dignitaries, Ann had small wheeled carts that could be drawn up beside each guest so each could serve himself subsequent courses without interruption. She clearly wished the dishes at dinner to be an accompaniment to conversation, not to take center stage. A typical Gunston meal would probably have consisted of fish, fried apples, and bacon. A favorite dish was squab pie, and of course, "spoon bread," a Southern favorite. (The story goes that on one special occasion at Ash Lawn–Highland, James Monroe's estate, in the cook's effort to make good cornmeal mush, she put it into the oven where it baked into a soft "pudding" with a crisp crust—and thus "spoon bread" was invented.)

When not entertaining, Ann oversaw life at Gunston Hall, which included the normal household duties of preserving meat, dairy, and fresh foods and supervising their preparation; knitting or sewing bedding materials, linen, and slave clothing; and manufacturing soap, candles, and dyes. Ann, as well as her scientific husband, would have been the plantation physician, too. She most probably tended to the illnesses of her own family and of the families of the household slaves. We know that the Masons, in all likelihood, like the Jeffersons, inoculated their slaves against smallpox. Ann also managed the feeding and clothing of the house servants and was the arbiter of their disputes.

Ann may have also supervised the messy task of making soap. In those days, soap was produced by adding assorted fats to lye that had been made by leaching water through ashes gathered from the plantation fireplaces. The lye was strong enough and ready for use if an egg floated in it. The lye and fat were boiled, usually in a large kettle over an open fire outdoors. Making soap was normally a cold weather chore, when ashes were plentiful and pork was butchered. Hard soap, made by adding salt to the lye, was used for general-purpose cleaning as it is today. Gunston Hall's soft soap had the color and consistency of butterscotch pudding and was used for the plantation laundry.[28]

But a Virginia plantation wife's principal duty was to provide her husband with an heir, and Ann fulfilled that expectation. Not quite three years after their wedding, Ann gave birth to their first child, a boy they named George. In fact, throughout much of her marriage to Mason, Ann was either pregnant, nursing, grieving the death of an infant, or sick from the complications of childbirth. She bore these pregnancies during the difficult years leading up to the American Revolution and in a constantly changing household, while simultaneously undergoing the physical and emotional stress of multiple pregnancies. By all accounts, Ann was a very loving and nurturing mother to all her nine children. Her youngest son, John, remembered Ann as an "affectionate parent and excellent woman," who "was beloved and admired by everybody for her virtues and charities." He would write that it was "his mother's constant habit to make him and the other younger children, one or two at a time, kneel down before her sitting, putting our hands on her lap and say our prayers every night before we went to bed."[29]

But the first few years of marriage for the Masons were not all happy times. Mason recorded the death in a margin of his family Bible of their fifteen-month-old son William. In all probability little William was suffering from a severe ear infection and high fever, and even laudanum could not ease his pain. We can only envision the emotional scene that Ann must have endured at the death of her child. The surprise of William's death no doubt cut through Ann with grief and shock.

Mason noted that William "was buried at the Family Burying Place at Newtown." Newtown was the plantation established by Mason's grandfather, George Mason II. The site of the Newtown house is about fifteen hundred feet north of the Gunston Hall mansion, in what is presently a much-overgrown wooded area. In the early 1890s, Mason's distant relative and his first biographer, Kate Mason Rowland, visited Gunston Hall for the purpose of gathering material for a two-volume biography of Mason. She wrote, "'New Town' ... has passed away utterly; the very name of it is unknown in the neighborhood today. And recent owners of the land have ruthlessly ploughed up the old graveyard, one of the old tombstones having been left leaning against a tree in one of the fields."[30] It is not clear whether Rowland actually knew where the Newtown burying ground was located. However, it appears Newtown has been lost to history—first under a plowed field and then under a forest that replaced the field.

Ann gave birth to twelve children, three of whom died in infancy. At the end of her last pregnancy, she gave birth to twin sons two months prematurely. Both sons died the next day, and Ann never recovered her health. She died three months later. Her oldest son was twenty, her youngest, three. Mason and other family members all recounted Ann's agonizing death-bed scene. In a glimpse into his deep love for Ann, Mason recorded her death in their 1759 family Bible: "About three o'clock in the morning ... Mrs. Ann Mason, in the thirty-ninth year of her age [died at Gunston Hall]; after a painful and tedious illness of more than nine months, which she bore with truly Christian Patience and resignation, in faithful hope of eternal Happiness in the world to come."[31]

Ann's death brought an overwhelming sorrow to Mason. His son John years later would remember his father's visceral emotional reaction. Suddenly the gravity of Mason's loss hit him for the first time as he staggered from the room in a state of stricken grief to his study. Ann's death had cut out his heart. For the next week Mason was sequestered in his bedroom and study. Grief was not an irrational response, but for a man like Mason, who attempted to order his life according to rationality, it was a foreign emotion.

Ann's death shredded Mason's future plans and dreams. And, perhaps, his thoughts had to confront an ironic but dreadful fact: Ann's death had been caused not by her weakness of will or lack of determination to survive but by her multiple pregnancies. Perhaps Mason held himself partially responsible for Ann's death. Ann's young son John put pen to paper, remembering the agonizing death of his beloved mother and its devastating impact on the family: "I remember well her funeral, that the whole family went into deep mourning suddenly prepared, that I was led clothed in black to her grave, that I saw her coffin lowered down into it by cords covered with black cloth, and that there was a large assemblage of friends and neighbors of every class and of the slaves of the estate present; that the house was in a state of desolation for a good while, that the children and servants passed each other in tears and silence or spoke in whispers, and that my father for some days paced the rooms, or from the house to the grave (it was not far) alone."[32]

Mason's deep loss was palpable to the entire family. He recorded his abiding love after Ann's death, commemorating her memory: "In the Beauty of her Person, & the Sweetness of her Disposition, she was equalled by few, & excelled by none of her Sex.... [Ann] was bless'd with a clear & sound Judgement, a gentle & benevolent Heart, a s[incere] & an humble Mind; with an even calm & chearful Temper to a very unusual degree Affable to All, but intimate with Few."[33]

Mason ordered the following inscription on the tombstone that marks Ann's grave in the Gunston Hall burial ground:

Ann Mason, Daughter of William Eilbeck of Charles County in Maryland Merchant, departed this Life on the 9th Day of March 1773 in the 39th Year of her Age, after a long & painful illness, which She bore with uncommon Fortitude & Resignation.

Once, she was all the cheers and sweetens Life,
The tender mother, daughter, friend, and Wife,
Once, she was all that makes mankind Adore,
Now, view this marble and be vain no more.[34]

The phrase "unchequered happiness," which Jefferson used to describe his union to Martha Jefferson, could also describe George and Ann's marriage and their relationship. Regardless of external turmoil, nothing had been allowed to intrude upon their deep love affair. "But we now see how strongly the founders ... stressed the importance of a happy marriage in a man's life," declared historian Thomas Fleming. By the scant evidence we can accumulate, it becomes apparent that Ann's spirit must have soared with Mason, her days and nights filled with books, music, gardens, the man she loved, her unique house, and her abundant children. To Mason, Ann was the fairest bride who ever gave her hand in marriage. She had charm, sophistication, grace, education, and a profound sense of family. Ann would have been an exceptional woman in any era, but for her to do what she did in eighteenth-century America was truly remarkable.

George Mason continued firm in his deep love for Ann many years after her death, wearing black mourning clothes for the rest of his life.

CHAPTER THREE

Gunston Hall

Had Mason never dealt with statecraft, Gunston Hall
would still rank as an American treasure.

—CALDER LOTH, architectural historian,
Virginia Department of Historic Resources[1]

T he prominent colonial artist John Hesselius painted George
Mason's portrait shortly after his marriage to Ann. The
Hesselius portrait has since been lost, but a copy depicts
a somber and pudgy Mason. His dark eyes are large and sensitive,
evoking a poet or a scholar. It is Mason's best-known likeness,
but nothing in the picture suggests the strong will, the fierce independence, or the blistering tongue for which Mason would
become known in later years. In the elegant painting, Mason wore
a wig, the hair hung straight but curled up in back and tied with
a black ribbon, called a "club." Mason owned several wigs. His
trusted mulatto house servant, James, always kept one dressed
and powdered.

For Mason, as for most eighteenth-century Americans, home
and family provided a focus for life. Important family milestones—
births, deaths, christenings, and marriages—commonly took place
at home. At twenty-one, Mason inherited his father's large estate.
It consisted of thousands of acres of farmland in Virginia and

37

Maryland, as well as thousands of acres of uncleared land in the Western country. Mason returned to the peninsula of land on which he had lived for the first nine years of his life. Known as Dogue's Neck, the peninsula was defined by a high ridge running east to west and bordered by the Potomac River. Mason's grandfather had purchased "the Neck" in the late seventeenth century, and his father was born there. Mason also inherited his father's slaves—about three hundred—and began taking care of the tobacco plantations he had inherited as well. This was a huge and complex task, since there were thousands of acres of land.

As a planter, Mason would conduct most of his business operations from the elegant but simple mansion he was about to build and live in for the next thirty years: Gunston Hall. His five sons and four daughters, like the children of most plantation owners, would all be taught at Gunston Hall by private tutors. Mason's home would be the scene of many social activities, including dinners, teas, balls, fish fries, and games. Hospitality was one of the great virtues of the age. Business associates and travelers of distinction were also welcome guests at the Mason estate. Hence, entertaining became a way of life for gentlemen like George Mason.

From a young age, Mason had a decidedly private and reserved temperament. Gunston Hall would become the symbol of his need to seclude himself from the rest of the world, and create a haven for domestic harmony. Mason could have built a much grander house, but he planned Gunston Hall exactly as he approached most endeavors—with moderation and thoroughness. From the outside, the story-and-a-half brick house looked deceptively small, but in fact it was quite roomy.[2] For Mason, life at Gunston Hall was defined by family.

By the time Mason inherited his father's property, he had become an accomplished surveyor, carrying out an extensive survey of Dogue's Neck in preparation for the building of his new home. Mason might have chosen a number of fine home sites upon his vast plantations, but he selected a site he had known since childhood, a few hundred yards from the house, called Newtown that had been built by his grandfather in 1694. His early drawings and notes of Gunston Hall reveal much about Mason's personality: self-discipline, his insistence on personal privacy, his need to save and account to the smallest of detail—money, books, and records. Mason's sketches and designs he gave to his English architect were executed precisely, with rule and compass. His mansion would overlook a panoramic view of the Potomac River and open fields.

As Mason matured into adulthood, he had often talked with his influential mother about his craving for a tranquil refuge from what he considered the flurry of the world. He would have been in perfect agreement with the sentiments of Jefferson, who said that he much preferred "to withdraw myself totally from the public stage and pass the rest of my days in domestic ease and tranquility, banishing every desire of afterwards even hearing what passes in the world."[3] Gunston Hall was always the preferred destination in Mason's imagination. But the American Revolution would intervene, then the Constitutional Convention, and finally the Virginia Ratifying Convention, all taking him away from his beloved sanctuary.

Before Mason settled in at Gunston Hall with Ann, he felt compelled to carry on the Mason legacy and briefly ventured into politics. Like his father, he was elected into the Virginia House of Burgesses; he would represent Fairfax County until 1761. As he matured into adulthood, his sense of duty thrust him into the local governmental affairs of his Northern Virginia community. As a trustee, Mason fostered the development of the burgeoning city of Alexandria. As a justice of the peace, he helped to administer his county. As vestryman in his church, he brought his influence to bear upon his parish. Out of this constant experience in local government grew the political ideas and themes which Mason subsequently expressed in detail years later. The roots of his later political work, defending the power of state government over concentrated national power, can be fully understood only when Mason's political philosophy is seen against the background of his local activities in the town, his county court and his Alexandria church.

Finishing second among twelve successful candidates, Mason was elected to the vestry of Truro Parish along with George Washington. Service to Truro Parish became one of the constants of Mason's life, helping to form his views of religious tolerance and freedom early in life. Mason remained on the vestry for twenty-two years, serving four separate terms as a church warden.[4] The twelve-man vestry oversaw the temporal affairs of the church at Pohick, which formed part of the Anglican or "established" Church. During the next decade Mason performed standard church duties, such as helping to pay the minister, balancing the church budget, choosing a site for a new church, and scrutinizing its construction. In addition to his responsibility for the construction and maintenance of church buildings, Mason also supervised the relief of the poor. An entry in the vestry minutes is typical: "400 pounds of tobacco were allotted to Elizabeth Palmer 'towards the support of her child, a Lame Idiot.' Indeed, in part because of its responsibility for the aid of the destitute and disabled, Truro Parish had a larger budget than Fairfax County."[5] At the newly built Christ Church in Alexandria, Mason also joined the vestry, bought a pew, and contributed funds to buy gold leaf for religious inscriptions on the altar.

Mason was a deeply religious and faithful man. He began most days with a Bible reading and ended with "grace" every night at dinner, then supervising the children's bedtime prayers. Mason's five sons and four daughters who lived to maturity were all baptized in the large silver bowl which Mason mentions in his will, as that "in which all my children have been christened, and which I desire may remain in the family unaltered for that purpose."[6] Mason's personal papers and his son John's recollections reveal glimpses of his deep faith. Mason seems, by all accounts, to have been a virtuous young man. He shared with his friends and family his belief that the handiwork of God was all about him, confirmed by the order and beauty of nature. When the present-day Pohick Church was completed, Mason bought two pews—numbers three and four on the south aisle. Mason's will, which he wrote in middle age and never revised, began with an expression of religious sentiment; he resigned his soul to an "Almighty Creator ... who hateth nothing that he hath made," and "willingly and cheerfully" trusted the "unbounded mercy and benevolence ... of my blessed Savior, (for) a remission of my sins."[7]

And as historian Josephine F. Pacheco observed, "Mason, more than any other revolutionary leader, insisted on the necessity for morality in public life." He confided to Patrick Henry, for example, that "Justice & Virtue are the vital Principles of republican Government."[8] In the early days of the Revolution when Congress set a day of prayer and fasting, Mason wholly supported the measure, commenting that "solemnities, if properly observed, & not too often repeated, have a good Effect upon the Minds of the People." He passionately believed that "if ever there was a national Cause in which the supreme Being cou'd be safely & confidently appealed to, ours is one."[9] While his future colleague Thomas Jefferson would endure fierce attacks from his political enemies for his alleged atheism and deism, Mason had no such critics or doubts in God. And he was not the type to be shy about his opinions on religion, or any other subject for that matter.

According to historian Elwyn A. Smith, this time period "was perhaps the most significant in the history of the United States for the evolution of religious liberty."[10] An early historian of Truro Parish called Mason "the Father of Religious Liberty" for both defending the separation of church and state and for opposing punitive treatment of the Episcopal Church after it was disestablished.[11] Historian Robert Rutland went so far as to suggest that, of all the Framers, Mason may have been the most consistent opponent of an established Church.[12] For, although Mason was a member of the Church of England, to him the privileged position of the established Church seemed inconsistent with the promise of religious liberty.

From the earliest days of adulthood, Mason exhibited an awareness of, and sensitivity to, the interests of religious citizens such as his neighbor George Brent, whose right to vote was challenged because he was a Catholic.[13] Eventually, drawing on his strong faith and principles, Mason would include a specific article on religion in his seminal Virginia Declaration of Rights. His original draft boldly declared "That as Religion, or the Duty which we owe to our divine and the Manner of discharging it, can be governed only not by Force or Violence; and therefore that all Toleration in the Exercise of Religion, according unpunished and unrestrained by the Magistrate, unless, any Man disturb the Peace, the Happiness, or Safety And that it is the mutual Duty of all, to practice Christian Charity towards Each other." Mason believed that freedom of religious exercise was inexorably linked to freedom of conscience, and to liberty as a natural right.

Few among the founding generation would play such a noteworthy role in establishing religious liberty as Mason.[14] And yet for Mason the call to public service was always an unwelcome distraction from the domestic tranquility and Gunston Hall.

Until he built Gunston Hall there, Dogue's Neck was farmed and maintained, but no member of the Mason family lived there. It is clear that Dogue's Neck held special meaning for Mason. "Over the next 46 years," observed one historian, "Mason applied vision, energy, passion, creativity, and expertise to the transformation of this distinctive natural place. He initiated sizeable agricultural enterprises, built a wharf providing deep-water access to the river, constructed numerous buildings to support the operation of the plantation, planted gardens and enhanced the natural beauty of the place with one-of-a-kind landscape features, terraced the ridge leading down to the river plain, and perhaps most significantly, built a home for his growing family."[15]

This effort created a working plantation house that was completed by design, through careful planning, over three years of construction.[16] Mason wanted the house to reflect his family legacy and his gentry status in Virginia, but in his deepest recesses he wanted a house that he could truly call a "home." His chief concerns would be comfort, privacy, and serenity for himself and his family. It would be a mansion where he wished to spend the rest of his life and leave for his descendants. And he ultimately did, leaving for us a portrait of himself in brick, plaster, and paint. It was a home that started as a portrait in Mason's young mind, reflecting his need for the civilizing comforts of home and hearth.[17]

Gunston Hall was to be Mason's asylum, a home where he could retire to his study and enjoy the intellectual companionship of his colleagues. He would name the house "Gunston Hall," for an ancestral home in Staffordshire, England. The name had come down through several generations of Mason ancestry: his grandmother was Mary Fowke of Gunston Hall in Charles County, Maryland, and her grandfather was Gerard Fowke of Gunston Hall in Staffordshire. The habit of naming new homes in America after ancestral homes in England was popular among the planters of Virginia Tidewater.

Set among the rosy color of the Virginia clay, Gunston Hall seemed to glow under the warmth of the Virginia sunlight. The mansion Mason ultimately built had symmetry, style, and solid foundations—it was an architectural wonder, designed with ornate wood carving, of brick laid in stylish Flemish bond, a "Chinese Chippe Room," the only one of its kind in Virginia. Guests were charmed and amazed by the hall's double arch and the fluted balusters of the staircase, as well as a formal drawing room in the Palladian style. Chippendale- and Palladian-styled rooms reflected Mason's wealth and taste, while the rest of the house demonstrated his more practical side and the demands of a large family. To the left of the landward entrance stood a modest master bedroom that was distinguished mainly by two closets on either side of a fireplace. Mason's wife, Ann, would keep her clothes and "the Green Doctor"—a riding crop used sparingly to spank the children—in the closet.

The design Mason ultimately settled on was derivative of the architectural pattern books he had been reading, particularly Robert Morris's *Select Architecture*. The house would consist of a central two-story block of rooms with wings on each side, a design typical of small country estates for aristocratic gentlemen. "It was an architectural style," observed author Jack McLaughlin, "well suited for the Virginia climate: it had high ceilings and two walls of windows in every room for ventilation in the summer, and its brick construction and massive fireplaces made it a tight, warm house in winter."[18] But the crucial decision for Mason was to build his house of brick, instead of the more traditional wood structures in eighteenth-century Virginia. Gunston Hall was one of the first brick structures in Northern Virginia. Mason designed his home so that no misplaced window or missing support beam might bring down the roof. And he was a stickler for detail. Ten years after building Gunston Hall, he remembered Washington's formula given to him for combinations of lime and sand to make mortar at Gunston Hall, "good pit sand, out of your cellars or well."[19] In the end, Mason designed institutions of government in similar fashion—a rock solid foundation for freedom, to safeguard liberty.[20]

When Kate Mason Rowland, a Mason descendant and early biographer, inspected Gunston Hall in the late 1880s, she found that it "has been well preserved, and the ravages of time, with the more fatal devastations of war, have so slightly affected it that it may be taken today as one of the best types of the Virginia colonial mansion."[21] Rowland went on to describe the interior of Gunston Hall: "The hall is wainscoted and paneled in North Carolina pine, and the woodwork is elaborately carved—every door, window, and cornice. The wide staircase leading up to the second floor has a baluster of mahogany, also ornamented in the same manner. And the doors, it should be said, are likewise of mahogany. In the center of the hall is a carved arch with a huge acorn as a pendant in the middle, and this is also elaborately carved. The hall opens out on a pentagonal porch at the river-front of the house, and on the left of this entrance is the drawing-room. Here the woodwork is exquisitely carved doors, windows, and mantel—the cornices almost reaching to the high ceiling. All this hand carving is reported to have been the work of convicts sent from England."[22]

After its completion in 1759, few changes were made to Gunston Hall. From the outside it is graceful, but neither large nor imposing. The interior, however, is one of the most impressive of any home of the colonial era. The view of the Potomac from the east door, framed by the twelve-foot-high Boxwood Allee planted by Mason, is one of the most famous sights in Virginia. The gardens fall on either side and below the 250-foot avenue of boxwood bushes. It was Mason's escape, washed upon Virginia's shores.

Mason adored nature and greenery and loved his second career as an amateur gardener. His son recalled the double rows of Black Heart cherry trees his father had proudly planted: "On the north front ... was an extensive lawn kept closely pastured, thro' the midst of which led a spacious avenue girded by long, double ranges, symmetrical rows of that hardy and stately cherry tree, the common black-heart … commencing at about 200 feet from the house and extending for about 1,200 feet, the carriage way being in the center and the foot ways on either side between the two rows forming each double range of trees."[23]

Mason was greatly influenced by both English and French designs for his plantation that created avenues of trees making the house the focal point. He even installed a "magic" trick of the eye, where unsuspecting guests standing at the center of the doorway and looking back would only see four trees until moving off center, an unusual feature in colonial American gardens. The optical illusion Mason achieved is not one suggested in contemporary literature. John Mason recorded his father's immense pleasure in displaying the "magic" concealed within the Avenue and reveals the subtle nature of George Mason's humor.[24]

Beyond the allée on the east side were Mason's extensive orchards, Newtown Pippin apple trees. Mason gave cuttings from Newtown Pippins growing at Gunston as a gift to neighbors and friends such as George Washington. On the west side of the enclosed lawn, as described by Mason's son, were woods "just far enough within which, to be out of sight, was a little village called Logtown, so called because most of the houses were built of hewn pine logs. Here lived several families of the slaves serving about the mansion house. Among them were Mason's body servant, James, a mulatto man and his family, and those of several negro carpenters."[25]

No doubt the decisive event for Mason in his construction of Gunston was his fortuitous acquisition of the services of the soon-to-be-famous English architect, William Buckland. Mason was determined that Gunston Hall would have stylish interiors and asked his brother, Thomson, who was living in England at the time, to find an artisan who could create decorative woodwork for the first-floor spaces. Mason seemed especially close to his younger brother, Thomson, who would become a Burgess in the Virginia Assembly and one of the first trustees of the town of Leesburg.[26] Luckily, Thomson secured the young English carpenter William Buckland, just twenty-one at the time, but highly trained in the latest architectural fashions. Buckland, a "Citizen and Joiner" of London, was hired, or "indentured" for four years as "Carpenter and Joiner," and brought to Virginia in 1755 by Thomson Mason. On the back of the indenture are a few words written by Mason, noting that Buckland "had the entire Direction of the Carpenters and Joiners work of a large House," namely Gunston.[27]

Buckland would later move to Annapolis and become one of the outstanding architects of the colonial period in an extensive line of English architects brought to America. Mason was pleased with Buckland's work on Gunston Hall and later remembered him as a man of "a very good Character" and "an honest sober diligent Man, & I think a complete Master of the Carpenter's & Joiner's [trades]."[28] Buckland devised designs for the interior woodwork and supervised the craftsmen and carvers in their execution. In his work at Gunston Hall, Buckland produced some of the finest, most elaborate interiors surviving in the Chesapeake Bay colonies.[29]

The actual physical construction of Gunston Hall involved long, arduous, and back-breaking work for skilled and unskilled laborers, including slaves. These men, and particularly Buckland, were paid a relatively modest sum for their work, approximately four shillings a day. Wages in the North were much higher. Workmen at Clivedon, a stone Palladian mansion in Germantown, Pennsylvania, outside Philadelphia, received nearly twice as much as Mason's workers. An unskilled worker was paid three shillings and nine pence a day, a master mason made six shillings and six pence. These wages, however, did not include food or lodging, according to one historian.[30] Mason became so personally involved in overseeing the construction of his home, he even managed the making of mortar and plaster. Mason's following letter indicates that oyster shells were used for lime in "outside-work" as well as "inside-work": "When I built my house I was at pains to measure all the Lime & Sand as my Mortar was made up, & always had two Beds, one for outside—Work 2/3 ds. Lime & 1/3 d. Sand, the other equal parts of Lime & Sand for Inside-work—it is easily measured in any old Tub or Barrel, & there is no other way to be sure of having your mortar good without Waste, & the different parts of yr. Building equally strong."[31]

Mason seemed an exacting but not harsh employer and supervisor. When present, he supervised each detail of the construction process personally. As his architectural knowledge and skills increased, he became more demanding of his workers. Gunston Hall had become a passion for him. By the time it was fully completed, he had not merely built a fashionable home for his wife and growing family, he had created a domestic haven and family legacy.

In 1759, Mason completed construction of his beloved estate and moved in with his new wife and kindred spirit. When Mason brought Ann to Gunston Hall, their future together on this hill overlooking the Potomac River was full of promise. They had, no doubt, spent many hours going over the drawings of the mansion he intended to build for her. It is likely that Ann took part in its design, and certainly the decisions dealing with the utilization of space. Like any housewife of that time and place, Ann undoubtedly spent her time conferring with their cook and other servants, ordering furniture and rugs to decorate the mansion emerging before her delighted eyes. And, amid the chaos of construction and rebuilding, in the summer of 1760, Ann became pregnant. Theoretically, she must have considered it good news, but there was an undercurrent of worry in Ann's joy. In those days of high infant mortality, a woman accepted the need to have many children as a fact of life.

When completed, Gunston Hall was an elegant home to a family that entertained the most famous of Americans, including George Washington, Thomas Jefferson, James Madison, James Monroe, and Patrick Henry. When visitors approached Gunston they would see seven or eight separate buildings, giving them the impression that they had rolled into a small rural village. The splendid view of the river set the stage for many social and political gatherings. When the weather was temperate, guests could enjoy alfresco dining, cooled by river breezes and serenaded by chirping birds. Mason's dining room was executed in a grander and more refined style than anything else in the house, its height emphasized by tall Palladian windows. At the time, yellow was a rare and the most expensive imported pigment, prompting a status-conscious Mason to opt for bright yellow wallpaper, which gave the room a cheerful mood by day with a soft sheen at candlelit dinners.

When not entertaining guests or family, George Mason would read and write for hours in strict solitude in his library. His study was adorned with modest furniture, a small walnut writing table and a vertical folding ladder, identical to the one at Monticello and said to have been a gift from Thomas Jefferson. As was typical for a Virginia planter, Mason's library included the Book of Common Prayer, a handbook for justices of the peace, and a form book for real estate conveyances. The classics and ancient history were his favorite books. He also owned a copy of John Locke's *Two Treatises of Government*, copies of legal treatises by Coke and Pufendorf, Algernon Sidney's *Discourses concerning Government*, and Edward Wortley Montagu's *Reflections on the Rise and Fall of the Ancient Republics*.[32]

In Mason's bedroom were two huge closets, one for all the children's clothing, which was accessible to the house servants as well, and the other closet for Mason and Ann's clothes, as well as a pantry for sweets and other delicacies. Across a narrow hall running perpendicular to the foyer was a small room that doubled as Mason's office and a family dining room. Mason cluttered the windowsill and bookcase with papers and probably composed his famous Declaration of Rights in this study. Upstairs, a central hallway divided the front and rear of the house, with five separate rooms on each side, enough for the children, a few guests, and perhaps a house servant.

Mason's estate occupied more than five thousand acres on Dogue's Neck, yet he also farmed four other tracts of four to five hundred acres apiece, each with its own overseer. Mason's principal crops were tobacco and corn, but wheat became more important as time went by. He also raised cattle and hogs. The big house itself stood among smaller buildings—a smoke-house, a school, a spinning and weaving house, a laundry, a blacksmith's shop, a stable, barns, and, at some distance, the slave quarters. Gunston Hall also had its own orchard, its own distillery to make, among other things, persimmon brandy, and its own barrel-making operation to provide storage for its produce.

On the slope between the house and the river, Mason laid out a deer park in the English style, with a mixed herd. Deer abounded on the two-thirds of the estate that was forest, and the fence across the landward side restrained the deer from encroaching. In the surrounding pastures and fields, Mason planted a variety of trees. In the spring and summer, the plantation was radiant with the bloom of peach, cherry, apple, apricot, lilac, and dogwood blossoms. All of this impressed visitors with the magnitude of the owner's wealth. Unlike many large planters, Mason tended his own financial books and personally managed several sprawling plantations that may have ultimately included seventy-five thousand acres in Northern Virginia and Maryland. Indeed, Mason affected a yeoman's tone about farming because it was his livelihood.

His love of agricultural expertise was spurred by a practical need: what to do with his vast soil that had been depleted by tobacco cultivation. What Virginia Governor Edmund Randolph called "that baleful weed tobacco" was "the only commodity which could command money for the planter on short notice."[33] No doubt Mason agreed with Randolph, who listed tobacco's defects in his history of colonial Virginia: tobacco sustained the "pollutions and cruelties of slavery"; it exhausted the soil; and by swallowing up "in its large plantations vast territories," it discouraged the immigration of white settlers.[34]

Unlike Patrick Henry and Thomas Jefferson, who inserted themselves into the public arena, Mason seemed content with his loving family, his farm, and his library. Indeed, he was not a typical Virginia planter-politician. Mason was a cloistered and contemplative family man. The single element of Mason's life, one essential for understanding the man, is often forgotten: his family. "Before they even thought about being founders," according to one author, "these men were Virginia planter-patriarchs, fathers in their small corner of the British Empire. In the plantation culture of colonial Virginia, a respectable father not only raised dutiful children and secured his household's finances, but also provided for extended kin, ran a thriving estate, mastered slaves, and even served in political office."[35]

These were gay family times at Gunston Hall: card games in the drawing room, sumptuous dinners served with great ceremony in the family dining room, and dancing in the hall. The fiddlers played in the little musicians' gallery at the head of the stairs while the planters and their ladies danced to measured minuets. There were children's dancing classes when the dancing master was in residence. Sometimes children from neighboring families, in powdered hair and miniature gowns, came by water in barges which delivered their precious cargo at the landing below the garden.

The Masons were a very tight-knit family, according to John's recollections. Family oil portraits lined the walls of Gunston Hall. "All the children lived together in great harmony at the mansion ... that the most sincere constant affection and interchange of kindly offices subsisted afterwards among us all ... and that there was never ... a single quarrel or even a transient coolness that ever took place between any of us."[36] And Mason was a busy man, with a new wife, new home, and a growing family of eventually nine children.

In everyday life at Gunston Hall, Mason's personal staff consisted of one or two slaves, especially his reliable servant James. Mason did not employ a formal overseer for his estate. He and Ann personally managed Gunston Hall. Mason drank coffee and tea at breakfast, sometimes cider with dinner. While he avoided most hard liquor, he enjoyed two or three glasses of wine each day. John remembered his father " ... was abstemious ... but he drank his toddy ... every day ... and two or three glasses of wine."[37] Formal afternoon tea for the Masons was also an important eighteenth-century social custom, one that provided the opportunity for them to show off their finest teawares. The Masons had some of the finest imported china in the colonies. Artifacts excavated in the kitchen yard at Gunston Hall have revealed the presence in the household of table and teawares of expensive Chinese export, including porcelains and ceramics.[38]

Rising with the sun regardless of the season, Mason usually got five to eight hours of sleep. His sleep routine was contingent upon the retirement hour or his current reading material, which could be voluminous. Like many thrifty farmers, he rose early and accomplished much work while others slept. The Virginian began most mornings with a contemplative walk around his brick walkway overlooking shaped boxwoods, azaleas, and grass that grew like a deep green carpet overlooking the Potomac River. One can envision Mason savoring the cool breeze and smell of freshly turned soil in the dawn.

Mason bathed his head in icy water, both in winter and summer, in an open porch.[39] He told his son this was a practice he had followed all his life. One of John's first memories of his father was wearing a wig, "as I believe he had long before. It was a club wig with curls at the sides, that is the straight hair was turned up behind and collected in what was called a 'club.'" In the summer, Mason wore a white linen cap. In cooler weather, Mason wore a green velvet cap under his hat.[40]

Before breakfast, Mason worked an hour in his library, reading, writing, and responding to correspondence. He devoted time to prayers before James laid out his clothes for the day. He also liked to check his horses before breakfast, inspect his stables, and talk with the grooms about their feed and condition. Then Mason ate a hearty breakfast of corn cakes, tea, and honey. After breakfast, James would help him pull on tall black boots and mount his horse, and then Mason surveyed his farms. Each day he rode about twenty miles, supervising field work, tree planting, and dozens of other plantation tasks. An active presence in his early years, before his gout restricted his physical activities, Mason showed his slaves how specific tasks should be done.

He loved foxhunting, horseback riding, and horse racing—the sport of Virginia patriarchs. Dogue's Neck was long famous for its game, the native deer, turkeys, and wild fowl. And Mason was considered one of the best shots and keenest sportsmen of his day. Washington, Governor Sharpe of Maryland, Colonel William Fairfax, Colonel Blackburn, and other distinguished men, both before and after the Revolution, were often guests and associates in the hunt on Mason's grounds.[41]

Mason actively grew and sold crops at Gunston Hall. When he realized that tobacco, his original cash crop, was not sustainable, he switched to grains, especially wheat. Reading the latest books on farming, Mason implemented the newest methods of husbandry, using innovative fertilization and crop rotation plans. Although wheat was not a principal export crop in the eighteenth century, Mason and others were shipping quantities abroad for profit. In one year Mason shipped 1,289 bushels of wheat, and thirteen "hogs heads" (barrels holding a thousand pounds or more) of tobacco to Bordeaux, France, on the ship *Becky* to his son's company, Fenwick and Mason.[42] Always fastidious with money, Mason requested that "my remittances are to remain to the credit of my own proper account."[43] Mason also devoted his life to the improvement of American agriculture. While his initial interest in farming was driven by his own need to earn a living at Gunston Hall, in later years Mason realized his experimentations could assist his fellow farmers.

Despite Virginia plantation society's reputation for lavish entertaining, Mason was a serious businessman. Keeping his own books, he had turned his and Ann's inheritances into a vast estate and personally managed a sprawling enterprise that ultimately included seventy-five thousand acres spread across Northern Virginia and Maryland, and on the Western frontier. By his mid-thirties, Mason had made the most of his family legacy and claimed his status of Virginia gentleman. Mason's grandson, also a George Mason, would laud his grandfather's accomplishments as statesman and intellectual, but also celebrate "his still more admirable talents for acquisition and economy." Commenting on the vast lands and wealth Mason amassed, his grandson concluded, "his enterprise and economy in private fully equaled his genius and ability in public life."[44]

During his own lifetime Mason was known by his neighbors not just for his farming prowess but for his fierce independence. He made up his own mind and had such confidence in his own judgment that the differing opinions of other men did not always meet with patience from the master of Gunston Hall. Mason was not afraid to lose the support of his neighbors to earn the respect of the world. During one winter and spring Mason apparently waged a one-man crusade in Fairfax County against the ruthless slaughtering of deer during the deep snows. He filed legal complaints against eighteen citizens for the unlawful killing of fifty-two deer with dogs in his neighborhood and promised further complaints. Mason's letter told a poignant story: "There has been such shameful havock made of the deer during this snow, when the poor creatures could not get out of any dog's way, that I hope the magistrate and gentlemen of the county will think it their duty to make an example of the offenders." Mason felt for "poor creatures" that "could not get out of the ... way," whether those "creatures" were man or beast.[45]

Mason was well-read, intelligent, discerning, and a good conversationalist, but he was seldom at ease at public functions. His son's memoir provides an intimate view of Mason reading and pondering alone in his study at Gunston Hall, or taking long walks in his formal gardens. During these times of work and reflection, Mason would become even more secluded, "absented as it were from his Family sometimes for weeks together." John described his father's study as "a small dining room which was devoted to his service. He used to write ... often until very late at night during the Revolutionary war, when he was much absorbed in public affairs and frequently from home at Williamsburg or Richmond attending the public councils several months at a time. This room looked ... on to the garden. My father was fond of his garden and took most of the exercise ... during the times of close occupation in it."[46]

John later recalled his father often strolled out of doors "wrapped in meditation," oblivious to anyone around him.[47] The children knew not to interrupt the patriarch when he wrote in his study or strolled in the garden. Mason would eat with the family, but between his preoccupation with business and politics and the challenge of keeping up with nine children, one of them could be gone for days before Mason noticed. All the household understood that Mason was not to be interrupted in these times of deep introspection. Even at mealtimes when he joined the family, Mason often remained preoccupied and soon retired to the comfort of his books and study. John recalled that his father "was always sent for when these [meals] were served and nobody sat down until he came in. He always had Grace said; most generally he performed that office himself but sometimes he desired one of his elder sons to do so. That 'grace' was uniformly delivered in the following words, 'God bless us and what we are going to receive.' At such times he was not morose but often taciturn and would leave the table early. And I have frequently known his mind though always kind and affectionate to his children so diverted from the objects around him.... "[48]

Before dinner was served, Mason's habit was to send for one of his sons "to make the bowl of toddy which was compounded always of West Indian spirits, low sugar and water. Everybody drank out of the same bowl," John wrote, "and uniformly it was the practice with my father when the bowl was presented to him ... to [say to] the son so presenting it, 'I pledge you sir', which was to say drink for yourself sir."[49] Mason would drink a weak toddy just before dinner every day. John described his father as "remarkably cheerful" when not deeply engaged with politics or business. Mason became fond of being "ample in his conversation" with his family. With young children, he was "jocular."[50]

The family always dined "in those days at 2 o'clock" on a variety of vegetables, fish, and oysters. Mason made sure that he returned for dinner precisely at two, when the first bell sounded for the large mid-day meal. According to oral family tradition, the clatter of Mason's approaching horse often coincided with the bell's loud ring. Mason then washed, dressed, powdered his hair, and supervised the family supper by the stroke of three, leading the meal with prayer. Mason preferred a dinner of fish from the Potomac, sometimes meat and poultry, but he always had a hearty appetite. The meal for guests or dignitaries was quite elaborate when the Masons entertained. A bill of fare found at Gunston Hall suggested a two-course dinner for numerous guests, with dishes arranged symmetrically on the table according to the prevailing mode. He would habitually then retire to his library before a light supper, sometimes enjoying a long-stemmed clay pipe strolling his garden. After a period in which he smoked his own tobacco, Mason seems to have quit the habit altogether. Before going to bed, usually at nine o'clock, he would often read to the family from the newspaper or lead a game of cards or backgammon.[51]

George and Ann Eilbeck Mason would eventually have twelve children during their twenty-three years together at Gunston Hall, with nine surviving to adulthood. This was a miraculous ratio for the eighteenth century when death rates were high among newborns without modern medicine. We know much about the Mason children and family life through John Mason's memoirs in honor of his parents. Although Mason's sons may have studied briefly at local academies, he employed a series of Scottish tutors for the boys:

> there being but a few public schools in the county in those days, my father, as was the case with most of the gentlemen of landed estates in Virginia, kept private tutors for his children in the family. The private tutors in my father's family as far back as I can remember were: first a Mr. McPherson of Maryland and next a Mr. Davidson and then a Mr. Constable of Scotland both. The last two were especially engaged in that country to come to America (as was the practice in those times with families who had means), by my father to live in his house and educate the

children. I remember I was so small when the first of these three gentlemen had charge of the school that I was permitted to be an occasional visitor of it rather than made a regular attendant. The tutoreses for my sisters was a Mrs. Newman. She remained in the family for some time. Mrs. Newman also taught the girls needlework, cooking, etiquette, dance, and music.[52]

From time to time, Gunston Hall also served as a home for members of Mason's extended family, and when it did, Mason assumed responsibility for their affairs. Mason tried, without success, to obtain a military commission for his young cousin French Mason as, he explained to George Washington, "the only means of getting him clear of a very Foolish Affair he is likely to fall into with a Girl in this neighborhood."[53]

George and Ann were powerful influences and role models to all their children. A letter by Mason gives insight into his philosophy of parenting: "I have endeavour'd to impress upon the Minds of my Boys, from their earliest Years" a reverence for "the Cause of Liberty" and an unwavering dedication to "Republican & independent Principles." To Mason, instilling virtue, character and industry in his children was paramount. "Everything," Mason advised his son John as he commenced a business partnership, "depends upon Diligence, Frugality, and Prudence; for without these, the fairest Prospects will quickly dwindle into Nothing." George Mason cherished his family and did not allow anyone or anything to interfere with his time with them.

As Mason grew older, he complained often about his health. By the time he turned thirty, he was already suffering from health problems that would plague him for the rest of his life. In August of 1755 he wrote his neighbor George Washington, "I fully intended to have waited on you this evening at Belvoir"—the Fairfax plantation halfway between Dogue's Neck and Mount Vernon—"but find myself so very unwell after my Ride from Court, that I am not able to stir abroad."[54] Mason's letter to Washington, the oldest surviving document in a series of chronic complaints of ill health, identified no specific ailment. But "gout," a catch-all phrase that covered numerous ailments, would persistently trouble Mason for the rest of his life. Here Mason was suffering in good company. His fellow sufferers included Benjamin Franklin, Horace Walpole, Samuel Johnson, and Edward Gibbon.[55] Indeed, the eighteenth century experienced something of a "gout wave." Mason's gout was so debilitating in later years that he had to use crutches to walk. He was only thirty-nine years old when he wrote this, in a March 12, 1764, letter: "but I am so weak at present that I can't walk without crutches and very little with them, and have never been out of the house but once or twice, and then, though I stayed but two or three minutes at a time, it gave me such a cold as greatly to increase my disorder."[56]

Mason's gout affected his stomach, hands, and feet. The pain would usually dissipate within twenty-four hours, but soreness in the joints could last for weeks. No evidence exists that Mason sought professional help and, given the crude state of medicine, it was probably just as well. Some doctors even believed gout served a useful purpose. It was, they speculated, the body's way of forcing dangerous elements away from vital organs and into the extremities.[57] Doctors tended to agree that stress of almost any kind could weaken a patient's resistance to the disease. Richard Blackmore, a London doctor, blamed gout on what he called "fright," or the stresses of life in the hectic eighteenth century. According to one authority, gout attacked those "who follow their studies too closely, especially in the night, with an intense application of mind."[58] That description fit Mason. He also liked to enjoy two or three glasses of wine at dinner almost every night.

Apparently, Mason evolved into something of an amateur doctor and scientist himself, reading quite extensively in the journals and treatises of medicine for homemade, natural cures. For example, Mason sent this recipe to his friend and neighbor Martin Cockburn at Springfield Plantation as a cure "for the bloody flux:" "2 handfuls white oak bark (only the clean inner bark) 1 handful flowering ash root (2 handfuls of sweet gum bark may be substituted) 1 handful pear tree root ½ handful bark of dogwood root 1 handful root of crosswort (if unavailable, increase indigo root to 1 handful) ½ handful wild indigo root; 1 gallon of water 2 cups new milk 1 small slice of rancid bacon."[59]

George Mason's gout often made it difficult for him to travel, and sometimes made it hard for him even to leave his study. His poor health kept him at his books and papers, mulling over political philosophy and historical precedents. One could say that Constitutional liberty in America today is a child of Mason's suffering, and his solitude.

The home George Mason built was an essay in architectural design and decoration. Alexander Pope once wrote of "Nature to advantage dressed, What oft was thought but ne'er so well expressed." Mason's plan for Gunston Hall on his hilltop fit those words. For its day and its place, it had elegance and style, but more important, it reflected Mason's sense of family, solitude, and culture. He loved Gunston Hall as much as Jefferson loved his cherished obsession, Monticello. It became a safe retreat where he could retire to solitude. Mason relished his domestic affairs, the tranquility of his family, and the agricultural challenges of the farm. Mason was at the very core of his being "domestic," and he always looked forward to returning to his books, his farm, and his family.

It would take a bloody war to destroy this sheltered scene.

CHAPTER FOUR

The Two Georges

I could think of no person in whose friendship,
care, and abilities I could so much confide ...

— **GEORGE WASHINGTON** to George Mason (1786)

Gunston Hall and Mount Vernon, two strikingly different eighteenth-century plantations, still stand overlooking the Potomac River as it flows through Fairfax County, Virginia. Separated by only a few miles, the homes of George Mason and George Washington have been preserved as memorials to two of America's most distinguished Founders. The efforts of these two men to create the American nation became one of the greatest cooperative triumphs in history, but it ended in one of the most unfortunate personal estrangements among the Founders.

The two men were friends and colleagues for, essentially, all their lives. They worked together in local church affairs and politics for decades. For example, Washington's diary for December 1–2, 1768, reads: "Went to Election of Burgesses for this County and was there, with Colo West, chosen. Stayd all Night to a Ball Well I had given" (and which cost, according to the entry in his account book, for cakes, ale, and the fiddler). The next day, he "returnd home after dinner accompanied by Colo Mason, Mr. Cockburn,

61

and Messrs. Henderson, Ross and Lawson." Indeed, throughout the 1760s and early 1770s, when court days took them both to Alexandria, Mason almost invariably stopped at Mount Vernon on his way to or from the sessions. Washington returned the visit when vestry meetings called them both to Pohick Church. During the six years following 1769, Mason's relationship with Washington was even closer than before. And their collaboration throughout the Revolutionary period gives great public importance to their relationship.

Through the early decades of the friendship between Washington and Mason, the latter was the older, wealthier, more established, and dominant member of the partnership. Mason advised the young Washington on both politics and farming. He also prepared public papers for Washington, and sponsored his leadership role during the Revolution.

After the war, however, Washington was the dominant man in America, not just Fairfax County or Virginia. During the war the two kept up a scattered correspondence, and Mason was among the first to greet the returned General upon his Christmas Eve homecoming to Mount Vernon in 1784. From then on, however, both men had a hard time accepting the role reversal. "Washington poses," as one historian observed, "what we might call the Patriarchal Problem in its most virulent form: on Mount Rushmore, the Mall, the dollar bill and the quarter, but always an icon—distant, cold, intimidating ... he is in our wallets but not in our hearts." Leading up to the Revolution, Mason and Washington had built their friendship and political partnership on shared principles. But the value which Mason put on political freedom came into conflict with the value Washington placed on political unity. When clashing principles sent them in different directions after the Constitutional Convention, Washington's pride prevented reconciliation.

History has portrayed the two men as close and longtime friends, with Mason acting as Washington's mentor. According to this traditional view, their friendship suffered a severe breach following Mason's decision to oppose the Constitution. This was George Mason's own belief about their relationship. He wrote his favorite son, John, "You know the friendship which has long existed (indeed from our early youth) between General Washington and myself ... but it is possible my opposition to the new government, both as a member of the national and of the Virginia Convention, may have altered the case."[1]

A careful examination of the historical record, however, demonstrates that their friendship was an unequal one from the beginning, Mason having more genuine affection for Washington than was returned. Indeed, as one historian has remarked, "it never was what could be called a close friendship, at least on Washington's part. Mason's warmth and unfeigned admiration for the general was never fully reciprocated."[2] As one Washington scholar has concluded, " ... their friendship was an uneven one and was in fact ended by Washington, not Mason, as a result of differences over the Constitution. Washington never forgave Mason for not signing the constitution in Philadelphia."[3]

All along, Washington's feelings toward Mason may have been more neighborly respect and political camaraderie than genuine personal affection. The two men had much in common. Both were in frequent contact, as close neighbors and farmers. Though they would help make a Revolution together, there was no hint when they were born into the Virginia gentry that either Mason or Washington would work to overthrow the system that had made their families powerful and wealthy. As leading citizens of Fairfax County, both were members of the land venture business, the Ohio Company, both were justices of the peace, vestrymen for Truro Parish, trustees for the city of Alexandria, and delegates to the Constitutional Convention in Philadelphia. Although they never sat together in the House of Burgesses, they served at the same time. The two prominent

Virginia patriots often collaborated to defend colonial rights. That collaboration resulted in the Non-Importation Agreement of 1769, the Fairfax Resolves of 1774, and the organization of the Fairfax militia before the start of the Revolutionary War.[4] The two men shared an enjoyment of horse racing and hunting. Mason adored the sport so much that he decorated Gunston Hall with hunting prints. Taught to ride by his father, Mason sat straight and relaxed on horseback. He broke his own horses, though as he grew older he delegated that task to his field slaves. Mason's love of horses lasted throughout his life, and he often rode with Washington, whom he recognized as "the best horseman of his age and the most graceful figure that could be seen on horseback."[5]

Both Georges exemplified the self-motivated American, constantly bettering himself to rise above his origins. Neither received an extensive formal education in youth. Training from parents, an occasional itinerant tutor or local academy, and home schooling by a relative provided the basics for both men. Washington's school copybooks attest to some formal study, although the work may have been done under the watchful eye of his mother or older brother. The books are filled with geometric, gauging, and surveying problems, with some notes on astronomy, literature, and world geography.[6] There is speculation that a Henry Williams may have taught Washington at a school near Church Point in Westmoreland County after teaching Mason in Stafford County. Washington's brother Lawrence was an instrumental instructor, whereas Mason mastered the law, classics, and political philosophy that made him one of the most learned and educated people in Virginia in his uncle John Mercer's library. But Mason would continue to actively pursue a scholarly life through self-teaching, while Washington would not.

"Unlike many of the nation's founders," wrote one historian, "both men remained largely self-educated. Experience, reading and conversation were their greatest instructors. Unlike John Adams, James Madison, or Thomas Jefferson they never attended college. Washington had probably dreamed of studying in London as his two older siblings had done, but his father's death ended that possibility and he dutifully used his father's instruments as a surveyor."[7] Later Washington wrote that Americans should not go to Europe to study because they would imbibe principles "unfriendly to republican government" and "the rights of man." Years later, John Adams would bluntly remark, "That Washington was not a scholar was certain. That he was too illiterate, unread, unlearned for his station and reputation is equally past dispute." Washington acknowledged his insecurity in a letter he wrote to David Humphreys, in which he expressed "a consciousness of a defective education."[8]

Research points to a library of fewer than one hundred books for Mason at his death. Many were purchased from his uncle John Mercer. This was a substantial practical library, but far fewer than the more than six thousand books amassed by Thomas Jefferson. Mason's books were mostly practical, political, or instructional. Among the titles Mason is known to have owned are Edmund Wingate's *Abridgement of All Statutes*; Richard Brownlow, *Declarations, Courts and Pleadings*; Edward Button, *Rudiments of Ancient History*; Herman Moll, *Geographia Classica*, and books by Plutarch, Cicero, and Sallustius. On the lighter side, Mason had *Terence's Comedies Made English*, *The Tattler* and Joseph Addison's *The Spectator*. Washington's library included a plethora of how-to books on husbandry and farming, and treatises on history, religion, and geography. Washington also sought out additional information on the military and had forty volumes on military arms, including Thomas Webb's *A Military Treatise on the Appointments of the Army*. By the time of his death, Washington's library totaled almost twelve hundred books. Many were gifts from authors hoping for an endorsement from America's most famous citizen. Despite this impressive library, however, Washington seems to have been much more sensitive to his lack of education than Mason, who was the better-read man, respected for his knowledge of English and constitutional law.

George Mason cultivated few friendships throughout his life and he did not have many intimates outside his immediate family. Mason's reserve—some would say shyness—was instilled in him at an early age. Washington's advice to his nephew Bushrod—"Be courteous to all, but intimate with few, and let those few be well tried before you give them your confidence. True friendship is a plant of slow growth"[9]—could have been written to describe Mason's own practice. Outside of his immediate family and uncle John Mercer, Mason rarely invited people into his confidence. He tended to be much more revealing among his own close family members and reserved with everyone else.

One of the rare exceptions to that rule was his neighbor and colleague George Washington, one of Mason's few close friends.

On hunting days with Washington, Mason's routine was to rise before sunrise, then breakfast by candlelight before riding off with his hounds while the sun rose. On most occasions, he was accompanied by his servant, James, who assisted Mason in exhaustive hunts of black and gray foxes. For a man of Mason's work ethic, it is interesting to note how much he loved the outdoors and the time he spent hunting, even in the winter. Though he enjoyed fishing the Potomac River, it never matched his interest in hunting, learned at an early age by the side of his father. In January 1769, for example, he went foxhunting eight times with Washington in a twelve-day period even though the ground was hard with frost.

Mason and Washington enjoyed culture and the arts and attended plays in Williamsburg and Alexandria. Two touring companies, the American Company and the Virginia Company, performed at the Williamsburg theater and usually timed their visits to coincide with meetings of the House of Burgesses. They offered rich and varied programs, running the spectrum from Shakespeare to contemporary plays. During one busy week in June 1770, Mason and Washington may have attended the theater five nights out of seven. Joseph Addison's *Cato* was one of Mason's favorite plays. He also quoted Shakespeare and his letters refer to both *Hamlet* and *The Merchant of Venice*. Washington also quoted Shakespeare—not surprisingly, in wartime, the Bard's Roman plays, including *Julius Caesar* and *Antony and Cleopatra*.[10]

But perhaps their greatest shared passion was their farms. At Gunston Hall, Mason experimented with different seeds, grafted fruit trees, tested grapes for a homegrown wine, and collected cuttings from and for neighbors. Washington, for his part, ingeniously devised a new plow that could till and seed the fields at the same time. Through Washington, Mason learned of his neighbor's correspondence with renowned English agronomist, Arthur Young, who sent Washington his four-volume tome, *Annals of Agriculture*. No doubt Washington shared his newly acquired agricultural knowledge with Mason. According to Washington biographer Ron Chernow, "[Washington] saw the agricultural system of the whole country as bogged down in outdated methods and was especially critical of Virginia planters who exhausted their soil with endless rounds of tobacco, Indian corn, and wheat. Deciding to conserve his soil through crop rotation, Washington ordered a variety of new seeds from Young— including cabbage, turnips, rye, and hop clover—and under Young's tutelage eventually planted sixty different crops at Mount Vernon."[11]

As Washington wrote to George William Fairfax, "It may not in this place be amiss to observe to you that I still decline the growth of tobacco ... and to add that it is my intention to raise as little Indian corn as may be. In a word, that I am desirous of entering upon a compleat course of husbandry as practiced in the best farming counties of England."[12] Mason, too, believed that American farming practices had to change, and both men looked to England as their role model.

Both men were fastidious and frugal. Mason kept a tightfisted grip on his estate and his finances, as, together with Washington, he tried to modernize postwar farming techniques. Mason found farming congenial to his temperament and corresponded enthusiastically with Washington about his plantation. Washington shared Mason's enthusiasm for the land, writing that "the life of a husbandman, of all others, is the most delectable.... To see plants rise from the earth and flourish by the superior skill and bounty of the laborer fills a contemplative mind with ideas which are more easy to be conceived than expressed."[13]

Dinner guests noted that Mason's attention seemed to perk up whenever planting was discussed, providing a pleasant distraction from political controversy. But while Mason's plantations throve, with agricultural prices depressed during the 1780s, Washington found it hard to make any profit. He wrote Fairfax that he never viewed his plantations "without seeing something which makes me regret having [continued] so long in the ruinous mode of farming which we are in."[14]

At one time, the two neighbors were so friendly that Washington frequently received additions to his stock of fruits and flowers from his friend at Gunston Hall. In 1763 Washington wrote in his journal about grafting cherries, apples, pears, and plums, the cherries and plums coming from Colonel Mason.[15] Mason and Washington enjoyed talking gardens and plants with each other. While in Philadelphia as delegates to the Constitutional Convention both men visited the famed garden of the Bartram brothers John and William, known for their collection of American trees, shrubs, and flowers.[16]

And the two patriots had much in common with their upbringing as well. While the loss of loved ones was a reality of everyday life in the eighteenth century, newborns, children, and mothers were the most common casualties. The drowning of Mason's father in an accident while crossing the Potomac when Mason was not yet ten and Washington's similar loss of his father when he was eleven gave them another point of commonality. And both were eldest children. Mason had a younger sister Mary, age four, and brother Thomson, age two at the time of their father's death. Washington had four younger siblings (and two older half-brothers). The death of their fathers coupled with the fact that neither of their mothers would marry again saddled both Georges with additional responsibilities at an early age—responsibilities that helped mold both men into the leaders they would become. As one historian has concluded, it was "[p]erhaps due to the loss of their fathers and familial responsibilities" that "neither of these men would have the opportunity to receive a formal education."[17]

While Washington spent many of his formative years at Ferry Farm in Stafford County and Mason spent time at Chopawamsic Plantation, these men would end up settling near one another along the Potomac River. Mount Vernon is only a few short miles north of Gunston Hall.

Both men lived in a house in the center of a small plantation village populated mainly by their dependents and people they owned. "You can imagine either George," wrote one historian, "going out to their back porch—relieving himself, brushing his teeth, grabbing a bucket of water, rinsing out his mouth, and pouring the remainder over his head. Morning ablutions now complete, the plantation master could survey his surroundings in detail."[18] One can imagine that the smells, sights, and sounds of both these plantation villages would overwhelm the senses of a person from the twenty-first century. As one writer describes,

The smells of dozens of farm animals, decaying plants, and excrement of all kinds wafted through the air. Dozens of

unwashed humans and animals tromped through unsani-
tary soil and puddles of liquids. Rodents competed with
domestic animals and people for food and water. Dogs
barked, while cats and other critters ran under foot. Rats,
mice and birds scurried for scraps. People cried out in joy
and pain. Horses, cows, pigs, and fowls neighed, mooed,
grunted, and cackled. Dust, hair, feathers, leaves, seeds,
and dried dung floated through the air to be inhaled,
tasted, and spat out. The sounds of people getting up and
going about their normal routines joined the cacophony.
Manual fans stirred the hot and fetid air in the summer.
Fireplaces and occasional stoves battled the cold in winter.
No central water or sewerage systems existed at Mount
Vernon or Gunston Hall. A present day visitor would be
incapacitated within days or certainly weeks by intermittent fevers, intestinal fluxes, or infectious diseases that they
had never been exposed to and not seasoned against. This
was normal life for neighbors Washington and Mason in
a more advanced part of rural America.[19]

Like Mason, Washington had inherited the property on which he
lived in a beloved home. Civil obligations meant that, as we have seen,
they sat on committees together and were both elected to the House
of Burgesses in Williamsburg.[20]

Throughout their lives they corresponded on many subjects. On
one occasion Mason offered to help Jacky Custis, Washington's stepson. The General responded with surprising warmth, writing, "I could
think of no person in whose friendship, care and abilities I could so
much confide, to do Mr. Custis and me this favour as yourself; and
therefore, take liberty of soliciting your aid."[21] In April of 1769, Washington turned to Mason to resolve the disputed estate of Patsy Custis,

Washington's stepdaughter. When Patsy's brother died in 1781, Washington again asked Mason's assistance. The letters between the men reveal their personal familiarity. In one Mason asked Washington if he would "be kind enough to get me two [pairs of] gold snaps made at Wms. burg for my little girls."[22]

The two men were in frequent personal and social contact as well. As leading citizens of Fairfax County, both were trustees for Alexandria, members of the Committee of Safety, and participants at the Mount Vernon Conference. Frequently they were appointed to arbitrate disputes among their neighbors.[23] In the face of growing British aggression leading up the Revolution, Mason and Washington often collaborated to defend colonial rights. In fact, it was with Mason's counsel that Washington first played a leadership role in the House of Burgesses. On May 18, 1769, Washington presented a proposal calling for a colony-wide boycott of specific English goods, to include a cessation of the slave trade. Mason had actually drafted the proposal, but he could not present it himself due to his long-standing reluctance to leave the confines of Gunston Hall. "This was an important moment in Washington's public career," according to historian Joseph Ellis, "for he now became an acknowledged leader in the resistance movement within Virginia's planter class."[24] Washington's political vocabulary grew more radical because of increased interaction with Mason in the summer of 1774. At that time, Mason was generally regarded as Virginia's most well-versed student of political theory. "He and Washington conferred several times," observed Ellis, "in July as Mason was drafting the Fairfax Resolves, which also warned of a concerted British plan to make all colonists into slaves and imposed the dramatic dichotomy of English corruption and American virtue over all its recommendations."[25] Washington's deep and abiding respect for Mason's remarkable intellectual abilities grew each year. Washington must have had Mason in mind when he wrote,

"Much abler heads than my own hath fully convinced me, that [British action] is not only repugnant to natural right, but subversive of the laws and constitution of Great Britain itself."[26]

Hearing that Mason would lead the fight against inflation in the Virginia General Assembly in 1781, Washington informed his stepson, "I know of no person better qualified ... than Colonel Mason, and shall be very happy to hear he has taken it in hand."[27] Washington clearly respected Mason's abilities and valued his advice. Amid his myriad duties as commander-in-chief, he wrote his old neighbor in 1779: "Though it is not in my power to devote much time to private correspondences, owing to the multiplicity of public letters (and other business) I have to read, write, and transact; yet I can with great truth assure you, that it would afford me very singular pleasure to be favored at all times with your sentiments in a leisure hour, upon public matters of general concernment as well as those which more immediately respect your own State."[28]

In the early years of their acquaintance, Washington no doubt viewed Mason as a highly capable man but also as a friend and fellow patriot. In writing letters of introduction to Benjamin Franklin and Marquis de Lafayette on behalf of Mason's son, Washington characterized Mason as "a Gentln. of fortune and influence ... a zealous and able supporter of the liberties of this country and a particular friend of mine."[29] And Washington told Mason that he was glad to write the introductions "as I wish for instances in which I can testify the sincerity of my regard for you." In the same letter, Washington hinted at the troubles facing the young nation and then continued to Mason, "Were I to indulge my present feelings and give a loose to that freedom of expression which my unreserved friendship for you would prompt me to, I should say a great deal on this subject."[30] Mason returned the warm sentiments, writing, "For I can truly say there is not a Man in the World, who more cordially wishes you every

Blessing, has a higher Sense of the important Services you have rendered our common Country, or who feels more Satisfaction in being inform'd of your Prosperity and Welfare; and if any thing shou'd occur in your Affairs here in which I can be of any Manner of Service, you can't confer a greater Obligation on me than in giving me the Occasion."[31]

But a closer examination of the historical record provides us with a keener sense of the intellectual and emotional ingredients that defined their relationship. Despite outward appearances, the relationship between Mason and Washington was always somewhat complex. The two Georges, upon closer scrutiny, were worlds apart.

Washington was active and athletic, travelling the wilderness as a surveyor and soldier, leading the Continental Army during the Revolutionary War. At least on the physical side, appearances were not wholly deceptive. Washington had a tall, muscular, strong constitution and excellent health. He was a charismatic man of action—a natural leader. Although Washington occasionally suffered from dysentery or "the bloody flux," (nearly dying from it in the winter of 1757) and later had an anthrax tumor removed from his thigh, he was of remarkably strong constitution. His years of military campaigns without chronic illness attest to that fact. Throughout his retirement Washington experienced no debilitating injury or deterioration of his mental or physical powers. A day in the life of Washington in retirement began before the sun rose: "If my hirelings are not in their places at that time, I send them messages of my sorrow for their indisposition."[32] Less than a month after his retirement. Washington wrote that "we are all on litter and dirt, occasioned by Joiners, Masons & Painters working in the house, all part of which, as well as the out buildings, I find, upon examination, to be exceedingly out of Repair."[33] By seven o'clock in the morning Washington was on horseback, riding around his farms for six hours, ordering drainage ditches to be widened, or inspecting the operation of a new distillery. When he arrived back at the mansion, no one needed to take the reins of his horse. Washington simply slapped him on the backside and commanded him to trot over to the barn.[34]

Mason, on the other hand, was continually plagued by chronic gout and intestinal problems. From his portrait, Mason appears to have been a plump, stocky man, with chronic stomach colic and gout, reticent and given to intellectual pursuits. Mostly sedentary, he preferred his cloistered home, leisurely walks in the gardens, and books. Mason, like Cato, believed that "The Post of honour is a private station." The "vine and fig tree" motif that he preferred, wrote one scholar, "suggested bucolic splendor, afternoon naps in the shade, relaxed routines aligned with the undulating contours of rolling hills. Nothing could have been more alien to Washington's temperament."

Indeed, the fundamental personalities of the two men were quite different. Afflicted by gout and "convulsive cholic," forced to lead an inactive life, Mason was often irritable and annoyed by the pettiness of politicians surrounding him. Writing to his son from Philadelphia he lamented, "I begin to grow heartily tired of the etiquette and nonsense so fashionable in this city." Yet as historian Douglas Southall Freeman noted, "Washington enjoyed, in his dignified manner, the social affairs that Mason detested."[35] As a living legend, Washington recognized that he was public property, though even he found it somewhat disconcerting to realize that he and Martha had not sat down for a meal by themselves in over twenty years. As one historian wrote, "Even the sheer gawkers, he acknowledged, 'came out of respect to me,' then added, would not the word curiosity answer as well?" After dinner Washington liked to show guests his collection of medals, the key to the Bastille sent by Lafayette, and prints done by John Trumbull depicting famous battles in the War of Independence, all this done with becoming modesty about his own contribution to the cause."[36]

Mason had nine children and forty-eight grandchildren who survived to adulthood. Washington had none.

Mason wore a wig, Washington did not.

Despite both coming from Virginia planter stock, there were differences between the family heritages of the two men, as well. George Mason III (Mason's father) and Augustine Washington (Washington's father) were vastly different men and their sons reflected those differences. To be the eldest son of a very wealthy planter, like George Mason, guaranteed you wealth, position, and social position. To be the middle son of a less well-off member of the Virginia gentry, like Washington, gave you advantages but meant that you would have to earn wealth and social prestige. While both men were raised by single mothers and relatives after the early deaths of their fathers, there is no evidence that young Mason struggled with his maternal relationship. Washington, on the other hand, battled his stern mother throughout his life. She often complained Washington ignored her needs, and one of his last letters was a successful attempt to convince his mother she would not want to live with him at Mount Vernon.[37]

The two men's houses reflected the different personalities of their owners. Both houses were built on high ground with a panoramic view of the Potomac River, though Mount Vernon was merely yards from the river, while Gunston Hall was nearly a mile. Both estates had formal gardens in a patterned English style. Both mansions had long, tree-lined approaches. But as one historian concluded, "Mt. Vernon was built to prove that its owner had arrived in the upper ranks of Virginia gentry—an eighteenth century version of mine is bigger than yours. Gunston Hall was built to demonstrate the solid life of an established gentleman."[38]

Gunston Hall, built in the classic Georgian style under George's direction, was located "about four miles from the great public road from North to South [now basically Route One] on a high bluff

overlooking the Potomac River and sitting between the Occoquan
River and Pohick Creek." Like Mason, Gunston Hall was solid and
efficient, constructed of brick and finely finished. Mason's house was
built for family life with no large reception rooms but with a multitude
of bedrooms. Mount Vernon, in contrast, was much larger and out-
ward-looking, like its owner. Washington's father, Augustine, had
begun Mount Vernon as a simple four-room planter's house. George's
brother Lawrence enlarged it into a first floor with almost thirteen
hundred square feet of four rooms divided by a central hall and a
half-story attic with more bedrooms and storage before his death.
After George purchased the widow's rights to Mount Vernon from
Lawrence's widow, Anne Fairfax, he began the first of two major
renovations. Wrote one Washington biographer, "Mount Vernon was
rebuilt entirely of wood in the neoclassical Georgian style. The wood
was shaped and painted to resemble stone. Most of the first floor was
designed for the entertainment of guests and the rooms on the main
floors were large. Although Mt. Vernon would pale in comparison to
contemporary English country estate houses, it was certainly more
pretentious than most plantation houses, including Gunston Hall."[39]

So in many ways the two men were very different. And there were
other factors that kept Washington from feeling a particular sense of
affection to Mason. Mason was seven years older, possessed a large
family fortune, and was Washington's superior in both intellectual
ability and knowledge. Historian John E. Ferling has argued that
Washington's internal makeup was such that it did not enable him to
get close to a man like Mason. Washington "was at ease with—and
closest to—only those who accommodated his needs, principally
aspiring young men who basked in his presence and women who, in
the customs of the times, treated him with deference."[40]

Reviewing their correspondence and the accounts of contemporaries, it must be said that the Mason-Washington relationship was

never an intimate friendship, at least on Washington's part. Mason's warmth and unfeigned admiration for the General was never fully returned. The basis for Washington's long connection with Mason appears to have been more respect than affection. Although George Mason was not a lawyer, Washington called on him to draw practically every important state paper that ever bulged from Washington's pockets. Mason's Fairfax Resolves of July 1774, by way of Washington's pockets, became the Virginia Resolves. By way of other pockets, it became the Resolves of the Continental Congress on October 14, 1774.

The historical record demonstrates that the two men were more colleagues than true friends. One leading scholar has commented on their complicated relationship: "Mason's affection for Washington and pleasure in his company were not fully reciprocated. *The Diaries of George Washington* offer a detailed if brief summary of how and where the master of Mount Vernon spent his time. The diaries reveal that Washington spent the night at Gunston Hall on only two occasions. The first was in 1771 and the second nearly fourteen years later. Only one other visit to Gunston Hall is recorded."[41] Considering that Gunston Hall is only a short trip by water from Mount Vernon, it is significant that Washington made only three known visits there in twenty years. Mason, by contrast, was often a visitor at Mount Vernon, frequently staying more than one night.

Other facts support the notion that Mason valued their friendship more than Washington. Mason wrote Washington approximately three letters for every one he received, and constantly sent a variety of seeds, plants, and other gifts to Mount Vernon. "Again, part of the explanation lies in the fact that Mason's plantation was much better established," concludes one historian, "and had a wider variety of plants, shrubs, and trees. Yet the volume of this largely one-way traffic testifies to Mason's desire to please his neighbor by continually supplying specimens that would be of interest."[42]

Mason's letters evince his deep respect and personal affection for Washington. "When I am corresponding with you," Mason wrote, "the many agreeable Hours we have spent together recur upon my Mind; I fancy myself under your hospitable Roof...."[43] Mason thought himself one of Washington's closest friends. "I believe there are few men in whom he placed greater confidence," Mason declared. There is no reliable evidence that Mason ever changed his high opinion of or affection for Washington. Even during his intense struggle against ratification of the Constitution, Mason's correspondence does not contain a single derogatory remark about Washington personally. For example, in warning about the power of the president, Mason pointed out that "so disinterested and amiable a character as George Washington might never command again."[44] Although Mason was "condemning the pomp and parade" and "the useless ceremonies" of the new government, he also swore, "By God if the President was not an uncommon man we should soon have the devil to pay." Mason "did not fear so long as it pleased God to keep [Washington] at the head." Only months before his death, Mason reaffirmed his belief that the president was "strongly attach'd to the Rights & Liberty of our country."[45]

Mason was truly a private man. He did not need or seek popular acceptance. As he stated, "I would not forfeit the approbation of my own mind for the approbation of any man, or all the men upon earth."[46] Possessing an independent fortune, Mason declared himself to be, "content with the Blessings of a private Station" from which he could equally disregard "the Smiles & Frowns of the Great." Months before his death, he wrote his son John, "For at my time of Life, my only Satisfaction and Pleasure is in my Children; and all my Views are centered in their Welfare and Happiness."[47]

Washington was childless—and in any case he would never have written that kind of emotional letter. For the Father of Our Country, the "greatest of earthly rewards was the approbation and affections of a free people."[48] A powerful need for approval and personal loyalty lies at the center of Washington's character. As Douglas Southall Freeman concluded, "Other men might want ships or mistresses or race horses and luck at cards; his ambition was that of deserving, winning and retaining the goodwill of right-minded Americans. The most compelling argument that could be offered to Washington was duty and defense of his reputation. When confidants wished him to serve a second term of office as president, this was the successful line of argument they followed."[49]

Several specific episodes demonstrate strains on Washington's relationship with Mason. Although Washington and Mason may have engaged in a good-natured disagreement over the new location of Pohick Church, their most serious differences, before the Constitutional Convention fatally strained their friendship, appear to have involved finances. Historian Julian P. Boyd has commented, "It was no secret among the political leaders of Virginia that along with his undeniably great abilities as legislator, Mason possessed a shrewd and unabashed talent for improving his own interests through public office."[50] George Washington shared those qualities. Yet there appears to have been something in Mason's attitude toward money that concerned Washington. A hint of this may be gleaned from a little-known letter from Lund Washington, Washington's confidant as well as his plantation manager.[51] The letter describes the 1783 elections in Fairfax County for the House of Delegates. In one historian's summary, "Charles Broadwater, a man Washington did not like, won by a mere three votes over David Stuart, who was to marry the widow of Washington's stepson. Lund Washington blamed Mason, in part, for Stuart's loss. 'Mason was not present, but he had said he should vote for Broadwater although he was a very ignorant man and the other a very clever man.' Lund explained why: 'Mason whose whole mind

is taken up with saving and accumulating wealth' recognized that
Stuart was no friend of those who wished to monopolize land.'"[52]

An entry in Washington's financial ledger may indicate Washington's distrust of this aspect of Mason's personality. When Washington paid Mason £100 for a parcel of land, he took the unusual
step of listing the names of three witnesses to the transaction. By
way of contrast, when Washington paid Sampson Darrell the con-
siderably larger cash sum of £260 for his land, the General did not
list any witnesses.[53]

Although for all practical purposes Mason's relationship with
Washington was permanently over after the Constitutional Convention, it appears Washington never lost his appreciation for Mason's
sage advice. He wrote one of his final letters to Mason on March
23, 1789, requesting a recommendation for a coachman who was
employed by Mason. At the time, Washington was president-elect,
due to be sworn in as president at the end of April. A trusted coach
driver would be needed for his long carriage ride to New York.
Washington asked if Mason could vouch for the man's "sobriety,
skill, honesty, and industry." Washington wrote "I shall make no
overtures to him, nor will I employ him (Altho' I want a Coachman)
unless it is with your knowledge and consent he leaves you." Mason's
reply to Washington was written quickly, dated March 23. Mason
identified the coachman as a "redemptioner" from Germany; Mason
had bought the remaining two years of his indenture.[54] In answer
to Washington's concerns about the coachman's "sobriety, skill,
honesty, and industry," Mason told the General in no uncertain
terms: "[I shouldn't] have employed him the second Year, if I cou'd
have got another Coachman or had any Servant of my own capable
of driving. I think him an excellent driver, & careful of Horses, if
he has anybody to do the Drudgery of the Business for him. I believe
him honest. He is also, if he pleases, a handy Servant in waiting at

Table. He is exceedingy lazy, incorrigibly addicted to Liquor, very turbulent & quarrelsom among the Servants, insufferably so when in Liquor tho' he has never presumed to be insolent to me. If therefore you chuse to employ him, I have no Objection to parting with him, as I am sure will be the Case soon, if you do not."[55] Unfortunately, the exchange of letters ends here, so it is not known if Washington was driven to his inauguration by a lazy, alcoholic, and quarrelsome German coachman.[56]

In the end, it seems unfortunate that the two patriots' political differences, as well as their differences in personality, temperament, and philosophy, kept the friendship from being repaired. The end of Mason's thirty-year relationship with his neighbor and friend was an unfortunate consequence of the polarizing and heated debate over the Constitution. But Mason's lost relationship with Washington seemed to be a pattern with the General: perceived disloyalties ended many of Washington's relationships. A political imbroglio with James Monroe signaled the demise of yet another one of Washington's friendships with a prominent Virginian, a list that would eventually include George Mason, James Madison, Thomas Jefferson, and Edmund Randolph. And during his presidency Washington would draw the ire of another Revolutionary War icon: Thomas Paine. "Paine believed that Washington had made no effort to free him after he was imprisoned in France," wrote one author, "as a British-born resident and a Girondin supporter who had opposed the execution of the king. Having advanced a dubious claim to American citizenship, he accused Washington of "connivance at my imprisonment."[57] Paine was finally released with help from Monroe, who then invited him to lodge in his residence. Paine published an open letter to Washington in the *Aurora* newspaper, accusing him of "a cold deliberate crime of the heart" in letting him rot in prison—but also criticizing Washington's command of the Continental Army. "You slept away your time in the field till the finances of the country were completely exhausted," Paine fumed.[58]

When James Mercer wrote Washington of Mason's October 7, 1792, death, Washington replied laconically, "I will also unite my regret to yours for the death of our old friend, and acquaintance Colo. Mason." Washington was in Philadelphia and could not attend the funeral.

By the time Washington himself died in 1799, he had lost his personal friendship with or become estranged from each of the leading Virginians—Mason, Jefferson, Henry, and Madison. For Washington, unlike for Mason, preserving friendships seemed less important than preserving his place in history. And history can never take away from Washington's monumental achievements. As historian John Rhodehamel writes, "A tawdry mythological excrescence oozing Victorian pieties and wooden teeth has gained a greater hold on the national imagination than the epic of Washington's indispensable leadership in the making of the great nation that probably would not have come to be without him. It hardly matters … the true Washington monument is the United States of America."[59]

Historian Joseph Ellis seems to agree, noting, "It seemed to me that Benjamin Franklin was wiser than Washington; Alexander Hamilton was more brilliant; John Adams was better read; Thomas Jefferson was more intellectually sophisticated; James Madison was more politically astute. Yet each and all of these prominent figures acknowledged that Washington was their unquestioned superior. Within the gallery of greats so often mythologized and capitalized as Founding Fathers, Washington was recognized as *primus inter pares*, the Foundingest Father of them all."[60]

But Mason, who valued private relationships over public reputation, was also respected by his fellow Founders, those who knew him best. In 1821, Jefferson wrote in his autobiography, "I had many

occasional and strenuous coadjutors in debate, and one most steadfast, able and zealous; who was himself a host. this was George
Mason, a man of the first order of wisdom among those who acted
on the theatre of the revolution, of expansive mind, profound judgment, cogent in argument, learned in the lore of our former constitution, and earnest for the republican change on democratic principles.
his elocution was neither flowing nor smooth; but his language was
strong, his manner most impressive, and strengthened by a dash of
biting cynicism, when provocation made it seasonable."

As one historian has succinctly summed up the two patriots,
"One is a provincial and international celebrity by age twenty. Only
his neighbors and a small political elite know the other at the time of
his death. Washington became recognized as the one indispensable
man of the nation's founding. But Mason's writings form the back-
bone of individual rights in the United States. Both were indispensable
to the creation of the United States."[61]

CHAPTER FIVE

The Ohio
Company

Descendants not of the Conquered,
but of the Conquerors....
—**GEORGE MASON**, Extracts from the Virginia Charters (1773)

A
lthough he loved his native state of Virginia, George
Mason was by nature a Westerner, greatly interested in
acquiring land on the frontier. Besides his love of Gunston
Hall, and his impatience with politics, the other constant in
Mason's life was his preoccupation with the land company he
helped form, the Ohio Company. It was Mason's greatest business
venture, an association of wealthy citizens who tried to obtain a
huge tract of land in the Ohio Valley on the basis of a grant to them
by the English Crown.[1] Mason's original intention was to open up
the Western lands which had lain unexplored for a hundred years,
to compete with the Pennsylvanians for trade with the Indians, and
to place permanent settlers as the frontier moved west.

All the time that Mason was making money in various local
businesses and land investments, he was also involved in land speculation. Although Mason's local land speculations were generally
shrewd and made money for him, with the Ohio Company his luck
finally ran out. Lured by the promise of fine land, Mason was one

of the most determined investors. Others might have been discouraged and cut their losses, but Mason held on through two wars and many changes of fortune—much to his eventual disappointment, financially and personally.

The Ohio country had caught the imagination of Mason as a young man. And his interest in the Ohio tract was reinforced by his family's values. Generations of Masons had built their fortune by increasing their land holdings. His father, who had traveled in 1716 to the peaks of the Blue Ridge with Governor Spotswood, told Mason enchanting stories about the "lands on the western waters," lands that could make them wealthy. As a boy Mason had seen his mother turn successful land speculation into solid estates for his younger siblings. Since he, too, wanted to leave children—all nine of them—substantial estates, the lands in the Ohio Valley must have seemed a tempting investment.

Mason's great interest in Westward expansion and the development of Virginia's frontier was shared by George Washington. In this vein of Western land expansion, both men were visionaries. Mason's first appearance in published records outside of his own county was in connection with the Ohio Company. In 1749 the British Crown had approved a land grant to the Ohio Company to be administered by the Colony of Virginia. The grant covered the Ohio territory, a collective term for what is now modern-day West Virginia, much of Ohio, Western Pennsylvania, and parts of Maryland. Lieutenant Governor Robert Dinwiddie, a portly, bewigged Scot, was a prime investor in the Ohio Company. Born in Glasgow, he had a beefy face with a drooping chin, which one person described as the "face of a longtime tax collector."[2] Dinwiddie wanted to secure the Ohio Company's interests as well as the lucrative fur trade with the Indians. Upon Mason's urging, he lobbied London for permission to erect forts and settle one hundred families to secure the grant. The company also employed frontiersman Christopher Gist to survey the area of the grant in 1750. Gist became the representative of the Ohio Company, and Colonel Joshua Fry represented the Colony of Virginia at the land negotiations. But the Ohio territory was also claimed by the French, who began erecting forts in the Ohio Valley.

George's involvement with the Ohio Company began when he was in his early thirties, but through the busy years which followed, his interest never faltered. To Virginians like Mason, Ohio was the new land, the symbol of the future, the child of the Old Dominion. Mason's interest in Ohio was stoked by his continuous correspondence with the young frontiersman, George Rogers Clark. This young adventurer wrote often to Mason, whose paternal advice he appreciated. Persuaded by Clark, Mason had been one of the first members of the Company to advocate for the promotion of trade with the Indians.

The Ohio Company consisted, in essence, of twenty shareholders. The company had as its object the colonization of Virginia's Western territory and the promotion of trade with the Indians on the Ohio River. Initially, the Ohio Company seemed successful. In 1749, the members were initially granted two hundred thousand acres by the king with the promise of an additional three hundred thousand acres if they built a fort and brought people in to settle the territory. Mason planned to develop a large fur trade with the Indians so he could make money while he waited for the Company's land to become valuable. But eventual problems with the Ohio frontier—tensions between Great Britain and the American colonies arising out of war with the French and Indians over the Western lands, and the Crown's continual interference in the Ohio Company members' rights—would help give rise to the Revolution. One could argue that it was this ill-fated business venture of his that distilled the ingredients of Mason's revolutionary ideology.

Mason's entry into the company reflected its need for initial capital, although Mason never invested more than he could afford to lose.
Eventually, Mason became the Ohio Company's valued treasurer, a
position he held to the end of his life. The company represented the
trading and land prospecting interests of a handful of wealthy Virginia planters, including Mason. Thomas Lee was appointed president, Nathaniel Chapman initially served as treasurer, and Mason's
uncle John Mercer served as both secretary and general counsel.
Mercer's son George Mercer was appointed the company's representative in England. Other members of the company included brothers
Lawrence and Augustine Washington, as well as George Washington,
Governor Robert Dinwiddie, and British merchant John Hanbury.
Unlike a modern corporation, the Ohio Company did not pay for
professional management. Much of the routine transactional business
of the company was performed by Mason himself. Mercer was paid
to draft a legal agreement that made him a shareholder and the cor-
porate secretary. He and Mason acted, for all intents and purposes,
as the company's chief executives.[3]

With the assistance of the company's agent, a prominent merchant
in London, Mason and his shareholders ultimately obtained a total
grant of six hundred thousand acres of land, lying mostly west of the
mountains and south of the Ohio. They sent Gist as their agent to
oversee the construction of roads and survey the ground for a perme-
ant settlement to be situated near the present site of Pittsburgh. Gist
became the first white settler west of the Alleghany Mountains. The
Ohio Company literally made the first road in this locality, permitting
eleven families to settle there, mostly German immigrants and settlers.
Mason's goal was the colonization of the backcountry with German
Protestants, mainly because German and Swiss Protestants enjoyed
a good reputation for faith, morality, and industry. Consistent with
his interest in Westward expansion, Mason undoubtedly saw religious

freedom as an incentive for immigration. He agreed with Patrick Henry, who observed that "a general toleration of Religion appears to me the best means of peopling our country."[4] When the Ohio Company received an inquiry from John Pagan, a merchant who was considering assisting a group of Germans to immigrate, Mason enthusiastically responded with an invitation, puffing the many freedoms that would be accorded the new settlers. "German Protestants, Pagan was told, would enjoy religious freedom, could become citizens, and would be allowed to vote. They would enjoy the protection of 'the English Laws of Liberty and Property,' which were 'universally allowed to be, the best in the World for securing the people's lives and fortunes against Arbitrary power.' Virginia's 'moderate' taxes 'don't amount to above the value of eight shillings per poll,' and food and clothing went untaxed."[5]

The Ohio Company had initially been established by Mason and his colleagues in large part to secure a share of the rich Indian trade west of the Alleghenies. Yet an examination of the history of the Ohio Company shows that it was far more than a money-making scheme. That history involves Indian problems and policy, colonial jealousy and conflict, trade problems, the land struggle between France and England for North America, and British colonial policy.[6]

Several unforeseen events would arise to disappoint Mason's hopes for land riches. An initial problem was that the boundaries of the Ohio Company's original land grant were not clear. The colonial charters of Virginia and Pennsylvania actually overlapped, and some Pennsylvanians also thought they had rights to this land. And the French were also claiming this area. The Ohio Valley sat between French New Orleans and French Canada, and uniting her colonial empire was important to France. In addition, the native Indians who lived there believed the land belonged to them. In 1753, French claims to this territory erupted into the bloody French and Indian War. The fighting between Great Britain and France (and France's Indian allies) on American soil was, in Mason's view, disastrous for the Ohio Company's land claims. The war was precipitated by competing French and British claims to the Ohio country. The French began to build more forts throughout the country and declared that any English who traded there would be captured. The British quickly mobilized. Much of the Ohio Company's claimed land became used for military purposes. Roads established by the company became military transport lines, and an Ohio Company trading post at the forks of the Ohio River became Fort Duquesne, later Fort Pitt. Once the British military gained control of that outpost, various Virginia groups sought further Western land grants. There were soon overlapping claims between military and private interests, as well as between competing land companies. Adding to the confusion, Virginia Governor Dinwiddie promised the Ohio Company land to Virginians who fought in the campaigns.

The Ohio Company had actually played a key role in the outbreak of the war in the first place. Governor Dinwiddie, a member of the Ohio Company, saw the French as a threat not only to the English Colony of Virginia, but to the private interests of the Ohio Company. He had sent a small force led by George Washington to protect the fort the company had built at the fork of the Ohio River. Although Mason did not fight, he helped by finding flour, pork, and beef for the troops. During this period of service, he became known as "Colonel Mason." George Washington's 1754 expedition to the fort precipitated hostilities between the French and the British and so, according to one scholar, it can be argued that the Ohio Company was one of the catalysts for the inevitable French and Indian War:

> The company's aggressive construction program alienated the Indians and prodded the French to assert their claims in the Ohio Valley. Emboldened by the Logstown treaty, the

Ohio Company made plans to build a fort on Shurtees, or Chartier, Creek about two miles below the fork of the Allegheny and Monongahela rivers. Mason, in July 1753, ordered twenty swivel guns for the fort from John Hansbury in London. Captain William Trent was sent to take charge of construction. Trent and a small party met Gist and Cresap at the site in the early spring of 1754, but apparently informed that a large French force was on the move, Trent left to seek reinforcements. A young ensign Edward Ward was left in command. The French arrived on 17 April, before Trent could return and before the fort was completed. Ward had little choice but to surrender the post, which the French quickly finished and renamed Fort Duquesne.[7]

The Battle of Jumonville Glen, which took place in the month after the surrender of the fort to the British between the party led by Washington and a group of French Canadian scouts, was the engagement that started the war.

Late in November 1758, a British-American force led by General John Forbes recaptured Fort Duquesne. The victory, however, did not save the Ohio Company's declining prospects. With the French removed, Pennsylvanians once again claimed the land. Also, as a result of the French and Indian War, there were now the bounty claims from soldiers for land in the Ohio Valley. In essence, the outbreak of hostilities ended the Ohio Company's efforts at colonization and brought ruin on its trading posts. According to one historian's assessment, " ... the military commanders seized the company's property and, in Mason's view, never fully compensated the company. In reality, the distinction between the company's interests and those of the empire, which had never been sharp, virtually disappeared in the fog of war. The catastrophic defeat of

General Edward Braddock at the Battle of the Wilderness, outside Fort Duquesne ... ended all hope of further English settlement in the West within the foreseeable future."[8]

And the war brought about a change in British policy, one with ominous consequences for Mason and his Ohio Company. The treaty signed after the war prohibited white settlement in Pennsylvania territory west of the Allegheny Mountains without the consent of the Indians. After the bloodshed of the French and Indian War, royal authorities wanted to avoid further provoking the tribes. Francis Fauquier replaced Dinwiddie as Virginia governor the same year the treaty was signed. The new governor originally wanted to pursue Virginia's Western land claim. But Fauquier was quickly pressured by British officials to adhere to the policy that no white settlement west of the mountains would be approved without the formal consent of the Indians.

When the political tides turned against the Ohio Company, Mason took the offensive. In September 1761 the Company, through an executive committee on which Mason served, submitted a petition to George III asking the king to confirm earlier royal instructions to the governor to issue the company another land grant.[9] The deadline to complete the first phase of settlement had passed, but the French and Indian War constituted an extenuating circumstance, Mason claimed. Until fighting had begun, the company had done everything asked of it. The war had reduced its frontier trade to shambles; its "debtors in those parts, were for the most part either killed, dispersed, or ruined." Above all, "your petitioners ... have been from time to time put off, by divers pretences, particularly, that the Indians would not suffer the said lands to be settled." The company retained Charlton Palmer, a London solicitor, to press its case before the king, and Mason tried to use Robert Dinwiddie as a lobbyist. "As we may expect a peace next winter," Mason wrote the ex-governor in September 1761, "his Majesty's subjects" will soon be at liberty "to settle the lands on the Ohio."[10]

In the end, the king denied the Company's petition. In April 1762 the British Board of Trade ruled that "a few Indians" could not convey land on behalf of all the tribes.[11] In a decision that was upheld by the Privy Council, the Board ordered that no further land grants be made in Indian territory. King George's famous Proclamation of 1763 formalized a strict territorial policy: there would be no English settlement west of the Appalachian Mountains in the immediate future, and no more Western land could be purchased from the Indians. The Proclamation forbade settlement on Indian lands west of the Allegheny Mountains, and inflicted a death blow to the Ohio Company and its fortunes. The British wanted no more trouble on the American frontier, and hoped that the mountains would be a good buffer zone between their settlements on the East, and the Indians in the West. Mason concluded "that the proclamation was an express destruction of our grant." He now believed that the company should change its strategy and seek compensation "for the great trouble and expense we had been at."[12] Although Mason never entirely abandoned his dream of a real estate empire in the Ohio River Valley, he soon began to hedge his bets by collecting headrights in his own name. He would not rest all his dreams on the Ohio Company grant.

The Ohio Company had been an ill-fated venture from the beginning. Some of the obstacles it faced—competition from rival land companies, opposition from the French, the Pennsylvania-Virginia border dispute—were beyond its control.[13] And the Company had lost much of its valued leadership before it could establish permanent settlements. Thomas Lee died of tuberculosis in 1750. Lawrence Washington, George Washington's respected half-brother, replaced Lee as president, but died two years later, and Hugh Parker died in 1751. Two prominent members, William Fairfax and Thomas

Nelson, resigned from the Ohio Company and joined the rival Loyal and Greenbrier Companies. This left the Ohio Company with, essentially, no paid professional management, and much of the day-to-day business of the company fell to Mason.[14]

In the end, Mason's attempts to complete the Ohio Company's land acquisitions and surveys were doomed to failure. It seems probable that had no other vested interest intervened, his persistent efforts might have been successful. But such was not the case. The result was that the Ohio Company claims failed to receive official recognition, and all of Mason's years of work went for nothing. With the failure of these plans, Mason's interest in Western lands came to an end. A major goal of the venture had been profit, but an equally important goal for Mason was the expansion of his nascent country. And in the final analysis, he did not lose a significant amount of money on the venture. When nothing appeared likely to revive the Ohio Company's grant, Mason had "judiciously located" his headright claims so as not to be affected financially.[15]

But the struggles over property rights between the Ohio Company and the Crown ignited a fire in Mason and sparked his revolutionary ideas. His experience with the Ohio Company undermined Mason's allegiance to Britain, and fueled his reasons to embrace a revolution.

The making of a revolutionary can be seen in Mason's failure to persuade imperial authorities to make good on the terms of the Ohio Company's land grant. Mason, one could argue, may have been radicalized by the king's reneging on the Company's grant. George Mason had not given up without a fight. He became an expert in land law and defended the interests of the Ohio Company in the courts, before the governor, and in the House of Burgesses. That he was also a highly skilled surveyor helped him in land disputes. But none of this worked with the governor or the Crown. Rival political interests and shifting laws kept the Ohio Company's grant just out of reach. The whole frustrating chain of events changed Mason's attitude toward the king, making him more keenly aware of the tension between the colonists' rights and the Crown's prerogatives.

But the French and Indian War was a contributory cause of the American Revolution for another reason as well. When the fighting ended, Britain maintained troops in the colonies to prevent expansion beyond the frontier. The War had proved costly for Great Britain and the remaining troops further increased the financial burden. Consequently, government officials in Britain began looking for new sources of revenue and decided the colonists should contribute to their own defense. The end of the war had left Britain with a vast new domain to administer, a large standing army, and a large and growing national debt. Britain's national debt had increased from about £70 million in 1755 to more than £122 million by 1763. Despite the mounting indebtedness, British taxpayers believed their taxes were already high. Worse yet, the British economy was mired in a postwar recession.

In the spring of 1764, the new Chancellor of the Exchequer, George Grenville, pushed through the House of Commons a legislative package of invasive taxes on the colonies intended to put the empire back on firm financial footing. On the question of the authority for taxing the colonies, Grenville relied on the great British jurist William Blackstone, who, in his *Commentaries on the Laws of England*, insisted that there must in every state reside "a supreme, irresistible, absolute, uncontrolled authority, in which the *jura summi imperii*; or the rights of sovereignty reside." In the British Empire, that supreme authority was Parliament. "The colonists had resisted that constitutional interpretation," noted one historian, "resting their case on the semi-sacred Whig principle that no British citizen could be taxed or required to obey any law that was passed without his consent. And since the American colonists were not represented in

Parliament, the statutes passed by that body were not binding on them, who needed to obey only the laws passed by their own colonial legislatures."[16]

The notes Mason compiled in the early 1770s on the charters and land laws of Virginia were initially made in aid of the Ohio Company's land rights. But one can see in them the seeds of colonial protest against Britain's attempt to levy a series of invasive taxes on the colonies. Mason's notes served not only as business documents in defense of his entrepreneurial interests, but also as legal theory on the best avenues for protest against the king—in essence, they formed, in embryo, Mason's fierce objection to "taxation without representation."

When the Crown finally revoked the Ohio Company's land rights grant, Mason wrote his first major political protest paper, *Extracts from the Virginia Charters, with Some Remarks upon Them*. It was a detailed statement of the Ohio Company's case against the Crown. This document was prepared to clarify the circumstances of the Ohio Company's particular case, but contained principles applicable to far wider issues. Its initial purpose was to refute the contention that the Crown was justified in disposing of lands ceded by the Indians because the title was vested in the Crown rather than in the colonies. The document was entered on the Company's books and "for their justification to posterity sent a copy thereof to the Governor and Council, to be entered if they thought fit, on their journals." Mason also presented it to the Virginia Assembly, where it contributed to the simmering sense of grievance against the king and Parliament.

This document, in which Mason defended Virginia's claim to the Western territory, would eventually be used as justification for the Lewis & Clark expedition and boundary settlement with the British. Mason had made elaborate extracts from Virginia's colonial charters, with his own commentaries appended. For Mason, every clause relating to the people and inhabitants in general ... under the Faith of which our Ancestors left their native land, and adventured to settle an unknown country, operated and inures to the benefit of their posterity forever, notwithstanding the dissolution of the Virginia Company, had such dissolution been ever so legal.... When America was discovered, the sending abroad colonies had been unknown in Europe from the times of the ancient Greeks and Romans ... the people removing from thence, to settle Colonies in America, under the auspices and protection and for the benefit of Great Britain, would by the laws of Nature and Nations, have carried with them the Constitution of the Country they came from, and consequently been entitled to all its advantages.[17]

Mason's Ohio Company had relied upon the colonial charters of Virginia. As trusted treasurer of the Ohio Company, it inured to Mason's financial benefit to understand the complicated legal issues involving them, competing claims arising from the charters of other colonies, and relevant British and American court decisions. In annotating his abstracts of the charters, he also paid close attention to loopholes that might allow some unethical persons to advance his private interests. His research helped educate Mason about historical and legal precedents, which he put to effective use in his dissents during the Revolution.[18] As one historian commented: "the date of the 'Extracts from the Virginia Charters' is the last possible date at which [Mason] can be thought of solely as the private gentleman of Gunston Hall. After that he is clearly to be numbered among the statesmen of the Virginia colony."[19]

As Mason negotiated the business waters with the Ohio Company, British policy was changing toward the colonies. Radicalized by his grievances with the Crown over the Ohio company, and now by additional taxes imposed by Parliament, Mason slowly gravitated from the periphery to the center of the colonial resistance. He played a noteworthy role in the controversy over the 1765 Stamp Act and by 1769 had become a leader in Virginia's efforts to organize a boycott of British goods and thereby force Parliament to repeal the "Townshend Duties." If Mason took his time in assuming a position of leadership, he recognized immediately the explosive character of the imperial crisis, and understood that, if mishandled, it could lead to war. Apart from an occasional levy on personal property, Virginians paid three direct taxes, each essentially a poll tax. A public levy, imposed by the House of Burgesses, financed the colonial government. The county courts levied a county tax to support local government, and the parish vestries collected a separate assessment.

The 1764 Sugar Act had imposed a series of new and increased export duties.[20] Although the Sugar Act was intended to raise revenue, it could be rationalized by Great Britain as a trade regulation and, hence, as a legitimate exercise of Parliament's legislative power. A more egregious threat to colonial rights soon overshadowed the Sugar Act. Debt-ridden from war, Britain passed the Stamp Act in 1765, imposing a tax on legal documents, newspapers, even playing cards. To Mason this plainly violated the tradition that only their own legislatures could tax the colonies, and it set off a storm of protest. The Stamp Act imposed a direct internal tax by requiring Americans to buy stamps for almost all printed material. The Stamp Act crisis added salt to Mason's wounds over the Ohio company's treatment by the Crown, which had left him with permanent political scars. He may have considered himself an Englishman, but he knew the English government considered him to be a rude provincial. Edmund Randolph later wrote that "until the era of the Stamp Act almost every political sentiment, every fashion in Virginia appeared to be imperfect unless it bore a resemblance to some precedent in England."

The Virginia House of Burgesses, urged on by Mason and Patrick Henry, passed a set of resolves opposing taxation without representation, and a Stamp Act Congress, meeting in New York and representing nine other colonies, condemned the Stamp Act and called for its repeal.[21] George Washington and George William Fairfax, then Fairfax County's delegates to the House of Burgesses, asked Mason for legal help in protesting the Crown's new taxes. He provided them with a scheme for addressing one of the principal issues raised by the Stamp Act: the problem of collecting delinquent rent during the Crown's suspension of litigation. Under the common law, a landlord could restrain, or seize, a debtor's property for nonpayment of rent. The debtor, in turn, could "replevin" the seized property by posting a bond. But under the Stamp Act, the tenant could not post a legal bond without purchasing a stamp. Mason's proposal was to allow the tenant to submit a "confession of judgment" for back rent to a single justice of the peace, who could enforce the judgment without convening the other justices if the tenant failed to satisfy the debt within a reasonable period. Mason's "Scheme for Replevying Goods & Distresses for Rent" demonstrated an impressive knowledge of English land law, and it showed Mason's willingness to help sabotage the Stamp Act. Mason told Washington and Fairfax that the replevin proposal was "much longer than it might have been," but asked them to excuse it "as a natural Effect of the very idle Life I am forced to lead," an apparent reference to his poor health.[22]

The Stamp Act proved to be unenforceable. The American boycott hurt the British economy, and in January 1766 a group of London merchants petitioned the House of Commons to repeal the Act. Lord Rockingham replaced Grenville as Chancellor, and in March it was repealed. Mason's replevin scheme never took effect. Parliament had yielded to political reality and economic necessity. Yet it still refused to take the American constitutional arguments seriously.[23]

Now Mason, sensing the impending crisis with Great Britain, made a prescient prediction. "Such another Experiment as the Stamp-Act wou'd produce a general Revolt in America," he warned, a revolt that would invite foreign intervention in support of the Americans. "There is a Passion natural to the Mind of Man, especially a free Man, which renders him impatient of Restraint." At the same time, Mason professed his loyalty to "his Majesty's sacred Person & Government," and rested his case squarely on "the Liberty & Privileges of Englishmen." Americans, Mason believed, were legally equal to the English, and morally superior. "Let our fellow-subjects in Great Britain reflect that we are descended from the same Stock as themselves, nurtured in the same Principles of Freedom ... that in crossing the Atlantic Ocean, we have only changed our Climate, not our Minds, our Natures & Dispositions remain unaltered; that we are still the same People with them, in every Respect; only not yet debauched by Wealth, Luxury, Venality, & Corruption." Their greater virtue made Americans more apt to defend their rights, and by force if necessary. Mason's letter was apparently never published in England, but it placed Mason firmly in the camp of the more zealous advocates of American rights.[24]

CHAPTER SIX

Revolutionary

---

*If I can only live to see the American union firmly
fixed and free governments well-established in our
Western world, and can leave my children but a Crust
of Bread and Liberty, I shall die satisfied....*
—**GEORGE MASON** (1778)

At the private level, George Mason had already built his
personal enclave of domestic tranquility at Gunston Hall.
At the public level, Mason prepared to launch his formidable
pen against a royal king who was threatening to destroy his country.
Oppressive British actions and taxes had prompted Mason's reentry
into the public arena, this time in the form of protest writing. In 1769
he edited the Nonimportation Association Agreement for Virginia,
an attempt to force British recognition of political rights through
application of economic pressure by boycotting English goods.[1]
Mason's aim was to have British merchants suffer curtailed trade
with the colonies and exert pressure on Parliament.

Then Mason drafted the now famous twenty-four articles of
protest against the British government, the so-called Fairfax Resolves,
a sweeping denial of excessive Parliamentary authority over the Virginia
colony. Mason historian Robert Rutland believes Mason also
wrote a similar, if less well known, set of resolves for neighboring
Prince William County. The Resolves and the Nonimportation

Agreement were two of Mason's more prominent political writings; they thrust him to the forefront of Revolutionary leaders.[2]

Mason was better prepared intellectually than most to advocate separation and independence. The impending war now called Mason out of his cloistered world at Gunston Hall. His political career effectively began when he was elected to the House of Burgesses as a representative from Fairfax County. Very soon he would pen the famous Virginia Declaration of Rights, which would serve as the blueprint for the Declaration of Independence. "When any government shall be found inadequate or contrary to these purposes," Mason declared, "a majority of the community has an indubitable, inalienable, and indefeasible right to reform, alter, or abolish it, in such manner as shall be judged most conducive to the public will."[3]

The Virginia Convention assembled in Williamsburg on Monday, May 6, 1776, with a plethora of familiar faces: Edmund Pendleton from Caroline County, Archibald Cary from Chesterfield, Patrick Henry from Hanover, Robert Carter Nicholas from James City, Richard Bland from Prince George, Thomas Ludwell Lee from Stafford, Dudley Digges and Thomas Nelson Jr. from York, and George Wythe from Williamsburg. Two of the younger delegates, James Madison of Orange County and Williamsburg's ubiquitous Edmund Randolph, would soon rise to national prominence.[4] Mason dined with George Washington and widowed hostess Christiana Campbell, "a little old woman about four feet high and equally thick, [with] a little turn[ed] up pug nose, [and] a mouth screw[e]d up to one side," as one Scottish traveler described her.[5]

Mason joined his colleagues and took his seat in the Virginia Convention of 1776. The most splendid stage on which he paraded in these years was the colonial capital at Williamsburg, now overseen by Royal Governor Francis Fauquier. Fauquier, described by Jefferson as the "ablest man who had ever filled that office,"[6] was well liked by the colonists. Unlike his despised successor, Lord Dunmore, Fauquier was a charming man of eclectic interests, a fellow of the Royal Society who had published papers on science and economics. The town of Williamsburg was characterized by "the manners and etiquette of a court in miniature," and stood forth as a glittering symbol of British royalty, a showplace of surface brilliance whose major social priorities were "precedence, dress, imitation."[7] To jaded European eyes, Williamsburg might have appeared provincial, but its elaborate government buildings, including the governor's palace, formal gardens, and spacious streets with brick sidewalks, surpassed anything seen in rural Virginia. On one occasion, Ann Mason asked her husband if she could join him for the upcoming session at the House of Burgesses, and they traveled there in the full regalia of rich tobacco planters—a coach with uniformed slaves riding as coachmen. Once at the capital, the Masons lodged at the most fashionable Inn, the Raleigh Tavern on the Duke of Gloucester Street.

But Mason had no stomach for the puffery and trappings of regal living that he saw in Williamsburg. He preferred the simple things in life: routine, family, and the intellectual work of defining true liberty. And the cost of renting lodgings and purchasing meals while in Williamsburg meant that the ever-frugal Mason was losing money while serving the public interest. Mason seemed to perennially tire of his constant trips to the colonial capital. In those days, it was no inconsiderable trip as it took Mason a good five days to travel from Gunston Hall to Williamsburg, and four days from Stafford County. Mason wrote his neighbor and friend, Martin Cockburn, two weeks into his stay in Williamsburg, "I begin to grow heartily tired of this town and hope to be able to leave it sometime next week ... I beg to be tenderly remembered to my children."[8]

And yet it was in Williamsburg that Mason would make what may have been his greatest contribution to the American Revolution and Founding: his draft of the Virginia Declaration of Rights, which served in turn as a model for the Declaration of Independence that Jefferson wrote for the United States.

Before fame was thrust upon him, Mason had thoroughly familiarized himself with a long tradition of writing on political and religious freedom—what he regarded as fundamental rights. Most assuredly, we can trace Mason's first influences to his uncle John Mercer's diverse library as a young man. Three high walls of Mercer's library were lined with books, leather-bound biographies, and legal treatises. From the writings of English Enlightenment philosopher John Locke, Mason had come to a radical insight: that a republic had to begin with the formal, legally binding commitment to the principle that individuals had inalienable rights that were superior to any government, including Great Britain's.[9]

Mason did not think and write in a vacuum. Like Jefferson, who was beginning to distill his own ideas on individual liberty at the same time, Mason drew upon a long tradition of English political literature to express what he regarded as inherent, natural laws and rights. No one will assert that, in preparing the Virginia Bill of Rights, Mason discovered a wholly unexplored field. On the other hand, no one will deny that he exhibited astonishing originality in what can only be regarded as an important creative achievement. Thoroughly acquainted with the history of the Old World, Mason had familiarized himself with the major attempts to define the limits and qualities of individual freedom. He was of course familiar with the Magna Carta. The dominant feature of that instrument was the submission of the king to the demands of the feudal lords—in addition to which it guaranteed certain rights to those who were called "freemen." The Magna Carta also forbade excessive bail and cruel and unusual punishments and required trial by jury. Mason recognized the Magna Carta as a landmark in the progress from political darkness toward the light. Mason had also studied the English Bill of Rights of 1689, enacted upon the accession to the throne of William of Orange. Nearly all of its thirteen articles denounced the tyranny of the Stuart Kings in violation of the authority of Parliament. The English Bill of Rights, adopted less than one hundred years before Mason's Virginia Bill of Rights, sprung from the pen of the English Whig jurist John Somers. But that Bill of Rights does not approach the complex instrument written in the quiet of Gunston Hall and the Raleigh Tavern. Somers gave little detail on how to structure a popular government, and he left the power of the Parliament unrestrained. Yet Mason drew on the spirit of Somers.[10]

Mason's notes and his surviving correspondence demonstrate that he was extremely knowledgeable about the law, although he never practiced law. He had analyzed the details of British and Virginia land law with his uncle, an attorney, and he knew about the laws and legal forms for protecting and transmitting estates. He also knew how to sue to collect a debt, as well as the laws and customs of domestic and of international commerce. Mason's knowledge of law and public policy was impressive for someone who served only a few terms in the General Assembly and avoided service as a justice of the peace. In fact, Mason was only one of two non-lawyers appointed in 1776 to Thomas Jefferson's committee to revise the laws of Virginia, a tribute to his colleagues' estimation of his political talents.

In writing the Virginia Declaration of Rights, Mason drew on a long tradition of statements of rights and liberty, but none had more influence on him than John Locke's *Second Treatise on Civil Government* (1690). Mason closely studied Locke's writings, including his *Fundamental Constitution for the Carolinas* of 1669–1670. Locke had argued that government's sole purpose was to protect the natural rights, liberty, and property of the people. Government had a contract with the people, and if it broke that contract, the people had a right to rebel. Locke's ideas became the cornerstone of Mason's rationale for independence and for a new government.[11] Locke had insisted that the "social contract" was also binding on the sovereign. Author Christopher Hitchens condensed Locke's theory of government, as it influenced both Mason and Thomas Paine, the author of the famous pamphlet *Common Sense*:[12]

> First, they are to govern by promulgated established laws, not to be varied in particular cases, to have one rule for rich and poor, for the favourite at Court, and the country-man at plough. Secondly: These laws also ought to be designed for no other end ultimately but the good of the people. Thirdly: They must not raise taxes on the property of the people without the consent of the people given by themselves or their deputies ... Paine added that lawmakers should never surrender their power to make law, "or place it anywhere but [with] the people. But when a long train of abuses and usurpations, pursuing invariably the same course, evinces a design to reduce them under absolute despotism, it is their right, it is their duty to throw off such government, and to provide new guards for their future safety.

But Mason argued for a more radical version of Locke's critique. He broke with Locke and some of the other English philosophers in explicitly requiring a greater degree of separation of functions than in the English government. In fact, Mason argued that no person might exercise more than one public office. This insistence on the separation of powers—which, as we shall see, Mason found in the writings of the eighteenth-century French political philosopher Montesquieu—is one of the strongest themes that permeates all of Mason's major political contributions, from his notes on nonimportation of British goods to his criticisms of the Constitution more than twenty years later. He included the principles of separation of powers and rotation in office in the Virginia Declaration of Rights, indicating that they were prerequisites of a trustworthy, competent government.[13]

Mason's other political and intellectual influences were manifold; he quoted Machiavelli on representative government and cited the experiences of the Greeks in defeating the Persians, the Dutch in holding off the Spanish, and the Swiss in maintaining independence "in the midst of the most powerful Nations." The philosophers of the Scottish Enlightenment were also among Mason's direct influences, as was James Wilson's pamphlet *Considerations on the Nature and Extent of the Authority of the British Parliament.* Mason had read the works of Rapin, Bolingbroke, and others. He understood history as a war for political power between the few and the many. The government George Mason wanted for his new country was that of a balanced Constitution that protected individuals from the power of the government—and he and his fellow Virginia patriots would go to war for it.

Mason's colleagues, especially Washington, came to recognize and admire Mason's literary and constitutional expertise. Jefferson said that Mason was "learned in the lore of our former Constitution"—that is, of the British government. Indeed, he was. Mason was "learned in the lore" of every Constitution that had ever existed in the world. For example, the English philosopher Algernon Sidney, executed for treason in 1683, had taught Mason much in his *Discourses concerning Government.* In fact, every martyr to human liberty had spoken his philosophy to Mason, and he could trace the development of constitutional law along lines that began in ancient Greece and Rome. Mason was intimately familiar with the classical and contemporary scholars from Aristotle onward.

He knew the arguments on both sides, having studied writers who opposed popular sovereignty as well as those in support thereof. One such book, in the former category, was found in Mason's personal library (his copy is now in the Library of Congress): *Patriarchal,* by Protestant theologian Robert Filmer, the court theologian to King James I. Filmer's treatise was a defense of the Divine Right of Kings.

Mason was also influenced by the works of Cardinal Robert Bellarmine on the notion of individual freedom. Mason analyzed Bellarmine's voluminous writings, which revealed a man committed to God and to the notion of popular government two hundred years before the founding of our nation. Mason embraced Bellarmine's principles of self-government, restrained authority, and liberty over license.[14] Imagine what Mason must have thought as he read the opening paragraphs of Bellarmine: "... there hath been a common opinion maintained ... which affirms: 'Mankind is naturally endowed and born with freedom from all subjection, and at liberty to choose what form of government it please, and that the power which any one man hath over others was at the first by human right bestowed according to the discretion of the multitude ... the common people everywhere tenderly embrace it as being most plausible to flesh and blood, for that it prodigally distributes a portion of liberty to the meanest of the multitude, who magnify liberty as if the height of human felicity were only to be found in it."[15]

Mason adapted the fundamental premise of Bellarmine's writing on government to his own thinking: that people are autonomous, and that they have popular sovereignty. Mason agreed with Bellarmine that all power came from God but saw each nation as a political unit composed of a naturally free people. Being free and equal, none had any more or less right to rule than another. Yet a civilized society depended on a modicum of orderly government. Civil authority was necessary for stability, Mason concluded, but the individual members of society should determine who governs them. Political authority may come from God, but the question of who will exercise that political authority is determined by the free will of the people.

Mason, a sober and mature fifty-one years old in 1776, was well prepared in law and constitutional theory. Among other things, he had thoroughly acquainted himself with the early Virginia charters and their guarantees to settlers in Virginia of the "liberties, franchises, and immunities" of Englishmen. Mason had had occasion to study and make extracts from those charters. His Fairfax County Resolves had decried the destruction of "our ancient laws and liberty, and the loss of all that is dear to British subjects and free-men."[16]

Mason's colleague George Washington introduced the Fairfax Resolves into the House of Burgesses. The Resolves were intended, Washington explained, to "defend our Constitutional Rights" and to set forth our fundamental principles. A nineteenth-century historian described Mason's Fairfax Resolves as the "first great movement on the theatre of the Revolution."[17] Similar resolves from some thirty-one Virginia counties survive, but Mason's Fairfax Resolves were the most detailed and influential.

The Resolves declared that the colonists' most precious rights belonged to them "by the laws of nature." This is of major historical importance: when a meeting attended by the citizens of Fairfax County adopted Mason's Fairfax Resolves on July 18, 1774, it was the first declaration by a representative body in America that the colonists had the exclusive right to enact laws governing their own affairs. Mason's Resolves proclaimed "that the claim, lately assumed and exercised by the British Parliament, of making all such laws as they think fit, to govern the people of these colonies, and to extort from us our money without our consent, is not only diametrically contrary to the first principles of the Constitution, and the original compacts by which we are dependent upon the British Crown and government; but it is totally incompatible with the privileges of a free people and the natural rights of mankind, will render our own legislatures merely nominal and nugatory, and is calculated to reduce us from a state of freedom and happiness to slavery and misery."[18]

As a Virginian, Mason had an acute sense of the tightening of royal authority. Before 1729, no royal governor in Virginia had suspended an act of the colonial legislature. Then, in the nine years between 1764 and 1773, there were seventy-five such suspensions—a steady, and infuriating, rate of increase that the most powerful Virginians felt directly.[19]

To Mason, consent of the people was the nonnegotiable essence of any republic worthy of its name.[20] One historian has pointed out that although the will of the people, the *vox populi*, was an old idea in Western culture: "it took on enhanced significance [for Mason and others] in the latter half of the eighteenth century in response to the steady democratization of Western society. During the revolutionary era many American leaders, echoing David Hume and other enlightened thinkers, had become convinced that public opinion ought to be the 'real sovereign' in any free government like theirs."[21]

For Mason, the Revolution was effected before the war commenced. The Revolution was in his mind and heart. It came long before the bloody battles with the Redcoats, even before taxation without representation. Those events only sharpened Mason's resolve, mental faculties, and moral responsibility to his "country" (Virginia) and its laws, not Parliament's. By the time they took place, the Revolution had already happened for Mason, with his adoption of the principles of self-government and individual rights. And Mason was not a man to put on and then shed his principles "like some shabby old coat at the door."[22] The man who rode into Williamsburg in May 1776, was the same man who would ride into Philadelphia in May 1787, eleven years later. The principles that inspired him to defy

Parliament were the very same principles that would not allow him to accede to a Constitution with no Bill of Rights.

Although other issues played a role in bringing the leading Virginians around to proposing independence in the summer of 1776, the part played by Mason's desire to preserve personal liberties was strong, and there is no doubt that he genuinely believed that his personal, political, and economic liberties were seriously threatened by the British parliament. Mason and his beloved state of Virginia were now at the center of opposition to British colonial rule. Mason had learned that Parliament, angered by the "Boston Tea Party,"[23] had adopted the Boston Port Bill, which closed the port of Boston until restitution was made for the tea. The legislation infuriated Mason and his circle. Jefferson wrote that "we must boldly take an unequivocal stand in the line with Massachusetts."[24] Patrick Henry, Richard Henry Lee, and other members of the House of Burgesses joined Mason in the capital's Council Chamber, home to a library of parliamentary precedents edited by John Rushworth, a historian who had fought in the English Civil War. "We were under [the] conviction of the necessity of arousing our people from the lethargy into which they had fallen as to passing events," Jefferson recalled, "and thought that the appointment of a day of general fasting and prayer would be most likely to call up and alarm their attention."[25]

Now the full light of publicity began to fall on the sage from Gunston Hall. Mason soon became identified with the proposals that a "Congress" of the colonies should be organized, and that Virginia should hold a Convention. Mason was impatient with London's attitude that the colonists should be grateful for Britain's slight accommodations to the colonies. When England repealed the oppressive Stamp Act, Mason wrote, "All we hear from that side of the water is pray be a good boy for the future; do what your Papa and Mama bid you, & hasten to return to them your most grateful

Acknowledgements for condescending to let you keep what is your own; and then all your Acquaintance will love you, & praise you, & give you pretty things."[26]

England had undermined basic American freedoms, and no one understood this more clearly than George Mason. But he knew independence could not to be gained easily. Mason and his revolutionary compatriots imagined themselves as seizing a rare moment. Their language was incredibly inflammatory by eighteenth-century standards. Mason insisted that "North America is the only great nursery of free-men, now left upon the face of the earth. Let us cherish the sacred deposit.... In all our associations; in all our agreements let us never lose sight of this fundamental maxim—that all power was originally lodged in, and consequently is derived from, the people. We should wear it as a breastplate, and buckle it on as our armour."[27]

Since the battles of Lexington and Concord, a deep trench of blood divided British and Americans. From this point forward, "the dispute between England and the colonists ceased to be fraternal and became fratricidal," remarked one historian.[28] The haughty royal governor of Virginia, Lord Dunmore, flush with a victory over the patriots at Kemp's Landing, proclaimed martial law and freed those slaves and indentured servants willing to fight for Great Britain. The next day Robert Carter Nicholas, the president pro tempore of the third Virginia Convention, summoned Mason and his colleagues to reconvene in Williamsburg. Three days later, Mason and his colleagues declared that Dunmore's action amounted to "tearing up the foundations of civil authority and government," and urged Virginia "to resist to the utmost the arbitrary government intended to be established therein." Mason recommended that if the Convention found it necessary to establish a new form of government, it should "call a full and free representation of the people, and that the said representatives, if they think it necessary, establish such form of government as in their judgment will best produce the happiness of the people, and most effectually secure peace and good order in the colony, during the continuance of the present dispute between Great Britain and these colonies."[29]

Both Mason and Jefferson understood the importance of the work at hand; they anticipated the sweeping historical significance of the events of the summer of 1776.[30] Mason's wealth, political experience, and intellectual talents combined to make him a natural choice to serve in the Continental Congress in Philadelphia. But Mason declined. Traveling to Philadelphia would be another matter entirely from trips to Williamsburg. It would make politics a full-time job, with precedence over his family. Mason worked closely with the Virginia delegation going to the Continental Congress, and he spent the night at Mount Vernon with Patrick Henry and Edmund Pendleton before they left for Philadelphia.[31] As Mason anticipated in his will, it was not always possible to avoid political "troubles and Vexations." The year before, he had tried to decline a seat in the Virginia Convention by reminding his Fairfax neighbors about his motherless family: "I entreat you, Sir, to reflect on the duty I owe to a poor little helpless family of orphans to whom I now must act the part of father and mother both, and how incompatible such an office would be with the daily attention they require."[32] When his neighbors persisted, Mason's sense of patriotic duty had prompted him to fill the vacant seat left by George Washington. Mason was "personally applied to by more than two thirds of the Members" of the Virginia legislature to serve in the Second Continental Congress. He asked them not to name him, but twenty proceeded to do so. When he declined, Patrick Henry and Thomas Jefferson reminded Mason that the cause needed him. By repeated appeals to family duty Mason did avoid going to Philadelphia, but he complained to Martin Cockburn, "my getting clear of this Appointment has avail'd me little." He was soon called to join the Committee of Safety, "which," he groused, "is even more inconvenient & disagreeable to me than going to the Congress. I endeavour'd to excuse myself.... "[33]

As war seemed inevitable in the summer of 1776, Mason assumed a leadership role in the Virginia Convention as Fairfax County's delegate to Williamsburg. In May 1776, the Virginia Convention passed a resolution creating a committee to draft a Bill of Rights and a new Constitution. The Bill of Rights, Edmund Randolph later wrote, was intended to serve two purposes. One was to bind the legislature, "the other, that in all the revolutions of time, of human opinion, and of government, a perpetual standard should be created, around which the people might rally and by a notorious record be forever admonished to be watchful, firm and virtuous."[34] Madison was added on May 16, and Mason was appointed on May 18, his first day in the Convention, when he was also named to the Committee of Privileges and Elections and the Committee of Propositions and Grievances.

It was in this Committee that Mason drafted his most famous contribution to American history: the Virginia Declaration of Rights, the antecedent to the Declaration of Independence and the Bill of Rights. Edmund Pendleton wrote that "Colo. Mason seems to have the Ascendancy in the great work, I have Sanguine hopes it will be framed so as to Answer it's end, Prosperity to the Community and Security to Individuals." Edmund Randolph's later recollection that Mason's proposals "swallowed up all the rest" confirmed Pendleton's assessment of his "Ascendancy."[35] In fact, Mason's prolific words flowed first—before Jefferson, Madison, Hamilton, or Washington's. They famously read, "That all men are created equally free and independent and have certain inherent natural rights among which are the enjoyment of life and liberty with the means of acquiring and possessing property and pursuing and obtaining happiness and safety."

While writing his draft of the Virginia Declaration of Rights in Williamsburg that summer, Mason would rise at dawn most mornings, bathe, dress, and then eat a simple breakfast of coffee, cold ham, and bread.[36] He would then pen a letter to his son almost every day. For Mason, caught up in the most turbulent of political and military times, his family remained implanted foremost in his mind. Mason could plausibly write, "[A]t my time of life, my only satisfaction and pleasure is in my children, and all my views are centered in their welfare and happiness." One scholar describes Mason's familial commitment: "Mason willingly served Virginia in ways that did not compromise his duty to his motherless children, but he was exceedingly loath to do more. Though he drafted Virginia's Declaration of Rights ... family remained George Mason's first priority after 1775, just as it had been before. He simply would not leave home for long periods because his 'numerous family of children' required 'constant attention.' ... Successfully pleading his paternal duties reflected the degree to which men of his station understood prioritizing family life."[37]

In the evening, Mason would enjoy a meal and perhaps some wine or grog (a mix of rum and water) with his colleagues at the Raleigh Tavern or the Kings Arms Inn.[38] Mason did not dare linger in the evening air, however. The Tidewater region of Virginia, where Williamsburg is located, was known for being malarial in the heated months. One unfortunate death from malaria was that of John Parke Custis, George Washington's twenty-six-year-old stepson.[39]

On May 15, 1776, the Convention instructed the Virginia delegates to the Continental Congress to make a motion for independence from Britain. The Convention then immediately called for the writing of a Constitution and Bill of Rights. Mason arrived too late for the vote on independence because of "a smart fit of the gout."[40]

When he did arrive, he was glad to see familiar faces. He admired Patrick Henry, whom he had met two years earlier in the House of

Burgesses.[41] Mason thought Henry "the first man upon this continent, as well in abilities as public virtues." The two would later become fierce political allies in the Virginia Ratifying Convention of 1788, criticizing the final version of the Federal Constitution.[42] Jefferson held a different view of Henry "as a gifted orator who was otherwise shallow and selfish. Henry's storied legal career, in Jefferson's version of history, derived not from his mastery of the legal details but from bamboozling juries. Most significantly, Jefferson said Henry's contributions to the patriot cause were superficial and fleeting—'he had a talent for soaring rhetoric but made no substantive intellectual, political, or legislative contributions.'"[43]

Edmund Pendleton, president of the Convention, appointed twenty-eight men to a "committee" to draft a Declaration of Rights and Constitution for Virginia. The committee eventually expanded to thirty-six. Most prominent among the members was Mason. His expertise and reputation made him a natural choice for drafting both documents. Also on the committee were Meriwether Smith, Patrick Henry, Edmund Randolph, William Cabell Jr., Joseph Jones, James Blair, Cuthbert Bullitt, John Banister Sr., Mann Page Jr., and James Madison. Except for Madison and Henry, Mason seemed unimpressed by these men, complaining to Richard Henry Lee that "the committee appointed to draft a plan of government was overcharged with useless Members. We shall, in all probability have a thousand ridiculous and impracticable proposals."[44] Mason immediately took the lead in outlining a fundamental human rights statement and prepared his first draft of the Virginia Declaration of Rights. The group met for several hours in the cool of the morning and again in the evening, after lengthy Convention sessions that consumed most of the day. These sessions exasperated Mason and left him feeling faint and disgusted. "Party's & Factions," Mason grumbled, "ran so high that we frequently had no other Way of preventing improper Measures but by Procrastination, urging the previous Question, and giving men time to reflect."⁴⁵ Other delegates drew Mason's wrath as "Babblers." Another "greatly disgusted" delegate said, "We are of as many different opinions as we are men.... [And] are undoing one day what we did the day before." For weeks, the Convention drifted.⁴⁶

Service in Williamsburg that summer was "hard duty," according to Mason. But his formidable intellect allowed him to take the lead. Mason methodically prepared a Declaration of Rights in a matter of days. A little more than a week later, on May 27, the chairman of the group read the last version of Mason's Declaration of Rights to the Convention. This final draft was largely the work of Mason, as can be verified by a comparison between the adopted draft and Mason's copy of his original sent to George Mercer in 1778 and now preserved in the Virginia State Library. Very few alterations were made to Mason's original work.

Mason intended his Declaration of Rights to serve as a preamble to the Convention's new Virginia Constitution, and indeed, the Declaration of Rights was a conscience in search of a constitutional mind.⁴⁷ Mason's Virginia Declaration of Rights has been called one of "the most influential constitutional documents in American history."⁴⁸ Among the influential principles Mason laid out were "That all power is derived from the people and that government officials are their trustees and servants. That no government official is entitled to a hereditary office. That the legislative, executive and judicial branches of government should be separate from one another. That freedom of the press is a 'bulwark of liberty.' That free exercise of religion is a right to which all are entitled. That standing armies in time of peace should be avoided as dangerous to liberty. At all times the military should be under civilian control."

Mason's draft was approved by the Convention on June 12, 1776, and quickly printed in the *Virginia Gazette*, reprinted in the

Pennsylvania Gazette, and in Williamsburg newspapers, nearly a full month before Jefferson's draft of the Declaration of Independence.[49]

George Mason produced a document that revolutionized a world. His Virginia Declaration of Rights, with its simple delineation of the inherent rights of men was arguably one of the most influential documents ever penned. In Mason's mind, man stood forth in freedom as the natural master of his own government. His Declaration also separated the powers of government, striking the hand of executive and legislative powers from the courts of justice. In addition, for the first time, the press found its freedom elevated to historic, constitutional status. "Scores of other fox holes," wrote one scholar, "of liberty were reconstructed by Mason's fabulous mind from the bitter struggles of man to achieve liberty and dignity in all ages, and were framed into a governmental structure by his pen for the first time, thence to re-echo forever down the corridors of time."[50]

Mason's Virginia Declaration of Rights directly influenced Jefferson's Declaration of Independence. Both documents boldly proclaimed that all men were born free and that the duty of government was to protect their safety, liberty, and happiness. Jefferson would later write in his autobiography that Mason's "elocution was neither flowing nor smooth, but his language was strong, his manner most impressive, and strengthened by a dash of biting cynicism when provocation made it seasonable."[51] Much of Mason's original Declaration of Rights is a statement of governmental principles, with emphasis on frequent elections, separation of powers, and a ban on hereditary office holding. The parts of the Declaration of Rights that are most remembered now, though, are the paragraphs that proclaim personal liberties. Mason's draft contained a condemnation of taxation without representation, a statement affirming the principle of religious toleration, and one paragraph of such importance that it requires full quotation: "That in all capital or criminal Prosecutions, a Man hath a right to demand the Cause and Nature of his Accusation, to be confronted with the Accusers or Witnesses, to call for Evidence in his favor, and to a speedy Trial by a Jury of his Vicinage; without whose unanimous Consent, he cannot be found guilty; nor can he be compelled to give Evidence against himself. And that no Man, except in times of actual Invasion or Insurrection, can be imprisoned upon Suspicion of Crimes against the State, unsupported by Legal Evidence. That in all controversies respecting Property, and in Suits between Man and Man, the ancient Trial by jury is preferable to any other, and ought to be held sacred."[52]

Mason's Declaration of Rights combined a succinct statement of the republican principles that underlay the Revolution with constitutional doctrine designed to protect individual civil liberties. The opening paragraphs throb with a richer emotion than any other public document Mason ever wrote. Mason's second article confirmed that magistrates derived their powers from the people, and in a third article Mason asserted the people's "indubitable, inalienable and indefeasible Right to reform, alter or abolish" any government that failed to provide "for the common Benefit and Security of the People, Nation, or Community." Mason's fourth article repudiated the notion of a hereditary aristocracy. "The Idea," he wrote, "of a Man born a Magistrate, a Legislator, or a Judge is unnatural and absurd."[53]

Mason recognized the pursuit of happiness as a fundamental, natural right, writing of man's "natural right to promote happiness." Mason was equally clear in asserting that the obligation of man to his Maker was the source of these natural rights, writing. "Now all … legislature apparently contrary to natural right and justice, are, in our laws, and must be in the nature of things, considered as void. The laws of nature are the laws of God: A legislature must not obstruct our obedience to him from whose punishments they cannot protect us. All human constitutions which contradict His laws, we are in conscience bound to disobey. Such have been the adjudications of our courts of justice."[54]

Mason's Declaration of Rights was disseminated and reprinted all over America and beyond the seas. Philadelphia newspapers carried it on June 6, 8, and 12, 1776. Jefferson was in Philadelphia, but he was preoccupied with the ongoing events at the Virginia Convention. According to one prominent Jefferson biographer, "Jefferson, like a good many other delegates in Philadelphia, presumed that the most crucial political business was now occurring at the state rather than national level. The act of drafting new state constitutions, [Jefferson] noted, 'is the whole object of the present controversy.' He meant that the establishment of state governments was the most discernible way to declare American independence, indicating as it did the assumption of political responsibility for the management of American domestic affairs."[55]

Throughout late May and early June 1776, couriers moved back and forth between Williamsburg and Philadelphia, carrying drafts of the Bill of Rights. The couriers also reported on the Virginia debate to the Continental Congress. Thus the case can be made that George Mason should be credited with an original draft of what ultimately became the famed Declaration of Independence. One could reasonably argue that Jefferson essentially smoothed, edited, and pruned Mason's language from the Virginia Declarations of Rights—written three weeks before Jefferson's final product.

For example, Mason's Declaration of Rights begins with the following famous language: "All men are by nature equally free and independent, and have certain inherent rights ... namely, the enjoyment of life and liberty, with the means of acquiring and possessing property, and pursuing and obtaining happiness and safety." Jefferson's draft of the Declaration of Independence read, "We hold these truths to be self-evident: that all men are created equal; that they are endowed by their Creator with certain [inherent &] inalienable rights ..."[56]

Did Jefferson plagiarize Mason's work? Absolutely not. Did he borrow heavily in constructing his own document, to famous effect? Yes. Jefferson eloquently condensed Mason's language, ultimately making the document his own while retaining its essential content. As historian Pauline Maier observed, "I dissent from any suggestion that Jefferson was alone responsible for the Declaration of Independence, or that the document most worth studying and admiring is his draft."[57] Prize-winning author Joseph Ellis went even further— too far, in my view—suggesting that Jefferson was merely "editor in chief" of Mason's work. "Since Jefferson's version of the same thought was drafted sometime that following week," according to Ellis, "and since we know that he regarded the unfolding events in Virginia as more significant than what was occurring in Philadelphia and that he was being kept abreast by courier, it also strains credulity to deny the influence of Mason's language on his own."[58] In the end, however, Ellis gives due and fair credit to Jefferson's eloquent prose, concluding, "the draft Declaration of Independence submitted to Congress by the Committee of Five was so much the work of Thomas Jefferson that it can justly be called 'Jefferson's draft.'"[59]

Historian David O. Stewart opines that "the resemblances between the two documents are too close not to conclude that Jefferson began with Mason's Declaration before him and revised it for his purposes."[60] Prominent historian David McCullough agrees that Jefferson "borrowed readily from his own previous writing, particularly from a recent draft for a new Virginia constitution, but also from a Declaration of Rights for Virginia, which appeared in the *Pennsylvania Evening Post* on June 12. It had been drawn up by George Mason, who wrote that "all men are born equally free and independent, and have certain inherent natural rights ... among which are the enjoyment of life and liberty."[61]

Pauline Maier declares, of Jefferson's draft, "By modern lights, Jefferson's use of texts by other authors might be considered to detract from his achievement. In the eighteenth century, however, educated people regarded with disdain the striving for novelty. Achievement lay instead in the creative adaptation of preexisting models to different circumstances, and the highest praise of all went to imitations whose excellence exceeded that of the examples that inspired them.... Jefferson had not only a good memory but, as his biographer Dumas Malone observed, 'a rare gift of adaptation.'"[62] Mason's Declaration of Rights, no doubt, caught the approving eyes of Jefferson and his committee members in Philadelphia, "who asked their draftsman to incorporate language like Mason's into the Declaration of Independence," Maier writes, "or perhaps Jefferson decided to do that on his own. In any case, his use of those texts suggests that the Declaration of Independence should be understood first and foremost not as a philosophical but, in the language of the day, as a constitutional document, that is, one that concerned the fundamental authority of government."[63]

Maier notes that Jefferson—perhaps with some help from Franklin, "made the same kind of careful editorial adjustments in the opening lines ... which, as an examination of successive drafts of the document reveals, were based upon the first three provisions of the Mason/committee draft of Virginia's Declaration of Rights."[64]

According to Maier,[65] both Jefferson's preamble to the Virginia Constitution and Mason's Declaration of Rights were direct descendants of the English Declaration of Rights: "The lineage is obvious in Mason's case since the child bore its ancestor's name, and a few other features as well. But Jefferson's preamble corresponded to the first part of the English Declaration, which formally ended the reign of James II, while Mason's Declaration fulfilled the second function of the English document in stating 'which rights do pertain to us and our posterity, as the basis and foundation of government.' Mason's Declaration was far more radical than its parent, which set out simply to reaffirm 'antient rights and Liberties.'"[66]

Mason's draft Virginia Declaration of Rights included eighteen provisions, which the Virginia Convention later cut to sixteen, a few more than the thirteen in the English document. Jefferson, however, began with Mason's statement "that all men are born equally free and independant," which he rewrote to say they were "created equal & independent," then (on his "original rough draft") cut out the "& independent." Mason said that all men had "certain inherent natural rights, of which they cannot, by any compact, deprive or divest their posterity," which Jefferson compressed marvelously into a statement that men derived from their equal creation "rights inherent & inalienable," then moved the noun to the end of the phrase so it read "inherent & inalienable rights." Among those rights, Mason said, were "the enjoyment of life and liberty, with the means of acquiring and possessing property, and pursuing and obtaining happiness and safety," which Jefferson again edited first to "the preservation of life, & liberty, & the pursuit of happiness," and then simply to "life, liberty, & the pursuit of happiness."

Mason's idea of the 'pursuit of happiness' was ancient, yet until Williamsburg it had never been granted such a prominent place in a new scheme of government—"a pride of place that put the governed, not the governors, at the center of the enterprise," argues historian Jon Meacham: "As with so many things then to understand the Declaration we have to start with Aristotle. 'Happiness then,' he wrote, 'is the end of action'—the whole point of life. Scholars have long noted that for Aristotle and the Greeks ... happiness was ... an ultimate good, worth seeking for its own sake. [Happiness] evokes virtue, good conduct and generous citizenship."[67]

Mason had already completed his Declaration of Rights when
John Adams, Benjamin Franklin, Thomas Jefferson, and Richard
Henry Lee were all in Philadelphia struggling to compose the "original" Declaration of Independence.[68] Their combined wisdom had the
task of framing a powerful preamble justifying revolution that would
appeal to the hearts, the reason, and the sense of justice of all men.
Nothing like that had ever been penned by man. No doubt, they read
Mason's completed manuscript and later saw it reprinted in the newspapers. Mason's Declaration of Rights was personally handed to
Jefferson in manuscript form by Richard Henry Lee, who had received
it from his brother, T. L. Lee, in late May 1776. Lee knew George
Mason better than any other man in Philadelphia, as Jefferson
affirmed in a letter to Madison near a half century later, where he
also said that "Richard Henry Lee charged [Mason's Virginia Declaration of Rights] as copied from Locke's treatise on government." Lee
had guessed wrong. George Mason was a constitutional polymath.
In his ample library at Gunston Hall, he had filtered three thousand
years of history and political philosophy with a mind that worked
with dazzling speed. The principles he expressed in the Virginia Declaration of Rights were the distilled essence not simply of Locke, or
of the 1689 English Declaration of Rights, but of three millennia of
human wisdom.

Jefferson's first draft of the Declaration seems to have been
extremely similar to Mason's Declaration of Rights. We know this
because, though Jefferson's first draft has never been found, when
John Adams borrowed from it, he copied Mason's language, specifically the word "born." Both Franklin and Adams, who were on the
committee with Jefferson in Philadelphia, later prepared Bills of
Rights for their respective states.[69] Yet neither of them adopted Jefferson's version of the Declaration. The Pennsylvania Bill of Rights of
September 28, 1776, used Mason's language: "All men are born

equally free and independent, and have certain natural, inherent and inalienable rights, amongst which are, the enjoying and defending life and liberty, acquiring and possessing and protecting property, and pursuing and obtaining happiness and safety."

And John Adams's Massachusetts Bill of Rights of 1780, similarly read: "All men are born free and equal, and have certain natural, essential, and inalienable rights; among which may be reckoned the right of enjoying and defending their lives and liberties; that of acquiring, possessing and protecting property; in fine, that of seeking and obtaining their safety and happiness."

It will be recalled that Mason had originally begun his Declaration this way: "That all Men are born equally free and independent, and have certain inherent natural Rights, of which they cannot by any Compact, deprive or divest their Posterity; among which are the Enjoyment of Life and Liberty, with the Means of acquiring and possessing Property, and pursuing and obtaining Happiness and Safety."

And all the while, Mason never left Virginia. But the delegates at the Continental Congress in Philadelphia knew where Jefferson's words had come from. Mason's Declaration of Rights had been copied and sent to the other colonies. Up and down the Atlantic seaboard, it emerged in public places, printed in newspapers, considered, debated, and admired. There was not a man in Philadelphia who had not seen Mason's Declaration or knew who its author was. And one after another, first Pennsylvania, then Maryland, then Delaware, then North Carolina and others, took most or all of Mason's Declaration of Rights and either made them amendments to their own constitutions or incorporated them directly into their constitutions.[70]

Scholar and author R. Carter Pittman analyzed the sequence of events as to the various drafts as follows: "Jefferson told Henry Lee that he didn't know whether or not any of the ideas embodied in the preamble to the Declaration had come from 'Aristotle, Cicero, Locke,

Sidney, etc.' Of course he didn't know. He never asked George Mason. He asked Richard Henry Lee and ... Lee charged it as copied from Locke's treatise on government, so Jefferson told Madison. Lee ... knew Jefferson didn't copy from Locke because he knew that Jefferson copied from Mason's Virginia Bill of Rights he himself [had] handed to Jefferson in Philadelphia."[71]

Perhaps Jefferson revealed a tinge of jealousy in connection with the framing of the Declaration and the Virginia Declaration of Rights. Julian Bond, the editor of Jefferson's voluminous official papers, points out in footnotes that there are several conflicts between what Jefferson said in his 1821 autobiography and what the historical record actually shows. In his autobiography Jefferson perhaps hedged his claim of sole authorship of the Declaration by giving Mason credit of a sort: "In giving this account of the laws of which I was myself the mover and draughtsman, I, by no means, mean to claim to myself the merit of obtaining their passage. I had many occasional and strenuous coadjutors in debate, and one, most steadfast, able and zealous; who was himself a host. This was George Mason, a man of the first order of wisdom among those who acted on the theatre of the revolution, of expansive mind, profound judgment, cogent in argument, learned in the lore of our former constitution, and earnest for the republican change on democratic principles."

John Adams gave Mason due recognition for writing the first draft of what would later become the Declaration of Independence: "He (Franklin) is a great philosopher, but as a legislator of America he has done very little. It is universally believed in France, England, and all Europe, that his electric wand has accomplished all this revolution. But nothing is more groundless. He has done very little. It is believed that he made all the American constitutions and their confederation; but he made neither. He did not even make the constitution of Pennsylvania, bad as it is. The bill of rights is taken almost verbatim from that of Virginia which was made and published two or three months before that of Philadelphia was begun; it was made by Mr. Mason."[72]

Adams could not remember the first name, "George," so he let it go as "Mr. Mason." Seventy-five years later Charles Francis Adams, son of John Quincy and grandson of John, could remember neither the first nor the last name. Nevertheless, he recorded in *The Works of John Adams* "that his grandfather had no sooner disembarked from the Sensible to embrace his wife, grandmother of Charles Francis, than he was called away to write the Massachusetts Declaration of Rights."[73] The grandson disclosed that in August 1779 his grandfather did exactly what Benjamin Franklin did in August 1776: John Adams too copied "almost verbatim" from the Virginia Declaration of Rights.[74]

Popular and scholarly accounts of the pursuit of liberty in Virginia properly credit the major contributions of Jefferson and Madison. Curiously overlooked in many accounts are the consequential contributions of George Mason. "The Declaration of Rights and the Virginia Constitution in their final forms were collaborative efforts," concluded one scholar, "although Mason was the principal architect of both documents."[75] Perhaps the best evidence of Mason's profound influence is the tribute that Jefferson paid to him, praising Mason as the "Cato of his Country, without the avarice of the Romans."[76]

CHAPTER SEVEN

The Virginia Constitution

*The fact is unquestionable, that the Bill of Rights and
the Constitution of Virginia were drawn originally by
George Mason, one of our really great men, and of
the first order of greatness.*

— **THOMAS JEFFERSON** to Judge Woodward (1825)

The vote for independence that humid summer in Williamsburg had changed everything. It was treason, pure and
simple. It was a vote for war, a war Mason had already
begun with his pen. Mason waged a battle for lasting change; he
wanted few remnants of the English traditions. Now his mind
worked frantically, as did his writing hand, on forming a new
model of government. Mason believed that most of Virginia's existing laws must be rewritten or abandoned. Virginia had, after all,
been a royal colony; now it would be an independent state.[1] Mason
put his prodigious thoughts on paper each day, organizing the
various issues facing America into a wide-ranging collection of
constitutional notes. His desire to advance individual rights and
promote social order became his central struggle in American
political life. Even before independence, notes one historian, politically astute colonists like Mason "understood the adversarial

relationship between liberty and power. Power, they knew, was aggressive and would, if not vigilantly monitored, destroy liberty. Power was not by its nature evil but could be easily corrupted and, in turn, corrupted men who wielded it. Individual liberty rested on checking governmental power...."[2]

The Virginia Convention meeting in Williamsburg had unanimously adopted Mason's Declaration of Rights on June 12. Now Mason was asked to draft a new Constitution, which he titled, "Constitution and Form of Government" for Virginia. Historian Joseph Ellis sets the scene for Mason's historic work: "Knowing the outcome of the American Revolution has also blinded us to the problematic character of this intense moment, when everything was in the balance, history was happening at an accelerating pace, and both sides—especially the Americans—were improvising on the edge of catastrophe. The delegates...were forced to make highly consequential decisions without knowing what the consequences would be. In this compressed moment, they were living, as Adams put it, 'in the midst of a Revolution,' which almost by definition meant that they were making it up as they went along."[3]

Mason's Declaration of Rights and his republican Constitution for the state of Virginia are among the most important documents emanating from the Revolution itself. They are classic examples of Mason's political thought, which was seminal in the creation of the first major republic in the modern world. Mason's Virginia Constitution was a model for the governments of other states, and most important, for the national government of the United States. It was also influential abroad during the French Revolution.

Mason worked rapidly and, to judge by surviving drafts, with a sure command of his material—for these two documents, the Virginia Declaration of Rights and the Virginia Constitution, are two sides of a single story, incomprehensible unless sewn together. Thus, to analyze the evolution of our constitutional form of government, we must recover the psychological context of Mason, and capture his political mentality as he negotiated the unknown.[4]

After the adoption of the Virginia Declaration of Rights, Mason devoted considerable energy to writing the first draft of a Virginia Constitution during two weeks in June of 1776, staying up long past sunset most evenings, editing, reading and pruning a document full of soon-to-be-famous words such as "Senators" and "House of Representatives." Before the Virginia Convention reconvened to take up the form of government, Mason skimmed *The History of Florence*, a historical account first published by Niccolò Machiavelli in 1532. "Nobody should start a revolution," Machiavelli insisted, "in the belief that he can stop it at will or regulate it as he likes."[5] An unwavering advocate for independence, Mason understood that a formal Constitution must be fashioned to govern the new country he and his fellow patriots had built. The success of the Revolution would depend on a profound commitment to constitutionalism, which guided Mason's thoughts and actions. He, and his fellow Virginians, had made two radical decisions that summer: first, to declare independence and constitute themselves a separate country; second, to create a republican form of government for that new country. Mason brought ideas drawn from different traditions of political thought and experience to his task of laying the foundations for that new government.

Mason's authorship of the Virginia Declaration of Rights is widely recognized, but his draft of what could be considered America's "first" Constitution does not get as much credit. One historian has remarked that Mason was "widely acknowledged as having the most profound understanding of republican government of any man in Virginia. Madison and Jefferson always deferred to him as their mentor on matters of political theory."[6] The passage of Mason's

Declaration of Rights in the Virginia Convention established the general basis for a new state, and ultimately a new country. Remember that the Declaration was not merely a statement of individual rights; it also separated judiciary power from the legislature and the executive, forbade any person from holding two offices at once, and laid out the principle of separation of powers. The task at hand now was to establish a formal government with offices through which the general principles of self-government and fundamental natural rights could be put into effect.

Though the final version of the Virginia Constitution was not the product of any one hand, there is no doubt that its chief architect was George Mason. As in his Virginia Declaration of Rights, Mason set out to write a document that embodied the fundamental principles he had gleaned from a lifetime of study of history and political philosophy. His blueprint for the Virginia Constitution was intended to lay out the fundamentals of a society, to frame its government, to set limits on that government's power, and to guard the people's individual liberties. Mason's Constitution (a mere fifteen hundred words) would serve as a draft not only for the new Constitution of Virginia, but for the Federal Constitution drafted in Philadelphia some twelve years later.

Mason attempted to make his Constitution serve a dual purpose: stating the principles of the social contract that created a new government, and establishing institutions that would secure the purposes for which the new government was designed. Mason's cardinal principle throughout his draft was absolutely clear: good government requires a written Constitution to secure the liberty and welfare of the people and to guard against a "strong Byass of human Nature to Tyranny and Despotism."[7]

Mason's draft Constitution did not suggest significant changes in governmental structure, and he paid little attention to local government.

Mason's form of government so closely resembled that of the colonial government of Virginia that it did not alarm many of his colleagues. It is ironic that every political paper that Mason had written up to this point had been a protest statement against some aspect of British policy. So it is interesting to note that his initial effort at a practical vision of government recommended a constitutional structure that adopted the general form of the old colonial governments. The exception, however, was Mason's diminution of executive authority, clearly in response to the lessons he had learned in the colonial resistance to gubernatorial claims of royal prerogative.[8]

Mason's draft proposed our modern-day form of government with three branches: executive, legislative, and judiciary. Mason thought and wrote along republican lines, organizing a government that rested on the civic virtue of its citizens. His brief Constitution established a bicameral legislature and separate judicial and executive branches. Power was to be separated, Mason reasoned, but it was not to be shared equally. Mason intended the legislature, as the people's representatives, to be paramount among the three branches of government. Mason's two-house legislature and his executive with an advisory council were similar to what Virginia had in existence. Mason insisted upon lodging the largest measure of power with the people, in a popularly elected lower house of the assembly.[9] Mason saw legislative power as the purest expression of the popular will.

By June 10, Mason had submitted his proposal to Archibald Cary's committee on the Constitution, and it became the committee's working draft.[10] The legislature, consisting of two houses elected at short intervals, would meet at least once a year. Delegates were to be chosen annually by the people for a lower house, senators elected to an upper house for four-year terms, according to Mason's plan. Mason's draft, like some rival plans, established that all legislation was to be originated in the popularly elected lower house.

Except for "money bills," the upper house could accept, reject, or amend any bill sent to it, but it could only vote tax and appropriations bills up or down.

The governor would be elected by joint ballot of the two houses and would exercise his executive powers jointly with a "privy council." The two houses would jointly elect all the other principal officers of government: the attorney general, the treasurer, state court judges, and the eight-member privy council, or council of state. The governor could serve three consecutive one-year terms and then was ineligible to hold office for three years. Two of the privy councilors would be replaced every three years and be ineligible to serve on the council for the next three years.

Judicial duties, formerly a prerogative of the Governor's Council, were transferred to a new system of courts. Judges would be appointed by the legislature, and county courts would be given a significant role in the selection of county officers.

According to Mason's draft, all "officers of government" could be impeached "for maladministration, or corruption" by the lower house and tried before a supreme court. Commissions, writs, and indictments would be made in the name of the new "commonwealth" of Virginia—wording taken from John Locke and intended to signify the supremacy of the legislature in Mason's Constitution.[11] To Richard Henry Lee, Mason's Virginia Constitution was more "democratic than anything in his previous experience."[12]

Mason had not begun his work on the Constitution with a *tabula rasa*. Its forebears were the "Agreement of the People" and the "Instrument of Government" prepared for the Cromwellian Commonwealth, the "Fundamental Orders" of Connecticut, and Locke's "Fundamental Constitutions of Carolina." Mason's Virginia Constitution, however, was the first revolutionary Constitution to be written after passage of the Resolution for Independence. It was designed as the permanent "future form of government of Virginia." In fact, Mason's Constitution endured without change well into the nineteenth century.

While the Virginia Constitution was substantially Mason's work, the absence of a first draft in his handwriting makes it impossible to compare his plan and the version finally adopted in Williamsburg. Unfortunately, no record exists of the debates of the Virginia Convention to shed light on these issues. When the revolutionaries met to discuss their new state Constitution, they felt no need to document what was said for posterity. Mason was probably influenced by several able alternatives that had been circulating. John Adams's *Thoughts on Government*, for example, had been widely disseminated, as had a draft from the pen of Carter Braxton called *Address to the Convention of the Colony and Ancient Dominion of Virginia; on the Subject of Government in General and Recommending a Particular Form to their Consideration: by a Native of the Colony.*

Adams's *Thoughts on Government* had actually developed from a request by Richard Henry Lee that John Adams put down on paper his suggestions for a Virginia government. The Massachusetts leader sent his initial thoughts in a November 15, 1775, letter to Lee: "The course of events naturally turns the thoughts of gentlemen to the subjects of legislation and jurisprudence; and it is a curious problem what form of government is most readily and easily adopted by a colony upon a sudden emergency....A legislative, an executive, and a judicial power comprehend the whole of what is meant & understood by Government. It is by balancing each of these powers against the other two, that the effort in human nature towards tyranny can alone be check'd & restrained, and any degree of freedom preserved in the constitution."[13] The letter was followed in January 1776 by Adams's *Thoughts on Government*, written at the request of George Wythe and published by Lee with Adams's consent. Thomas Jefferson, who was attending Congress in Philadelphia at the time of the Virginia

Convention, also sent his own version of a Constitution, titled *Bill for New Modelling the Form of Government and for Establishing the Fundamental Principles of Our Future Constitution*. It contained many proposals that would later became law under the Commonwealth.[14] Unfortunately, the document did not arrive until the day Mason's committee reported to the House, when, as Wythe wrote him, "they were worried with the contentions it [the proposed Constitution] had produced, and could not, from mere lassitude, have been induced to open the instrument again."

Mason's authorship of the main body of the Virginia Constitution is not in doubt, as corroborated by Jefferson's own testament, written in April 1825, to Judge Woodward: "The fact is unquestionable, that the Bill of Rights and the Constitution of Virginia were drawn originally by George Mason." A September 1824 letter from Madison to the same correspondent, substantiates Jefferson's statement: "You have fallen into a mistake in ascribing the Constitution of Virginia to Mr. Jefferson as will be inferred from the…versions on it in his 'Notes on Virginia.' Its origin was with George Mason, who laid before the Committee appointed to prepare a plan a very broad outline…& after being varied on some points & filled up, was reported to the Convention where a few further alterations gave it the form in which it now stands. The Declaration of rights was subsequently from the same hand."[15]

In fact, Mason's original plan for the Constitution had been laid ten years before, in 1766, when the colonies were protesting the Stamp Act and other British taxes. He had previously written that the American colonists claimed "nothing but the liberty and privileges of Englishmen, in the same degree, as if we had still continued among our brethren in Great Britain." In all the documents he drafted out of his knowledge of history and political philosophy, Mason returned to his constant theme: the natural rights of mankind. Life and liberty were the natural rights that would form the basis of his draft Constitution.

Mason's philosophy of natural rights was championed by other Founders such as his Virginia colleague, Richard Henry Lee. Lee would rise to his feet at the Philadelphia Convention and echo Mason's bold sentiments, his left hand wrapped in a black silk handkerchief to conceal the absence of four fingers lost in a hunting accident.[16] The thirty-year-old planter and legislator descended from one of Virginia's most esteemed families. Using words similar to those Mason had penned, Lee began: "Life and liberty, which is necessary for the security of life, cannot be given up when we enter society."

Mason drew heavily on his previous writings in preparing his draft Constitution. His proposed Constitution for Virginia was compact and succinct, with an emphasis upon his core political philosophy: a balance of governmental power which was served by a separation of authority and powers. He pronounced that "the legislative, executive, and judicial branches should be separate and distinct, so that neither exercise the powers properly belonging to the other."[17] This arrangement was the essence of Mason's design for a republican government. The legislature, he argued, was the necessary counterweight to potential executive misconduct

"If the theory was mangled in execution, the Virginia charter was the first constitutional document in America to endorse expressly the separation of powers and the first to recognize the courts as a distinct branch of government," according to historian Jeff Broadwater.[18] Mason sought to draft a Constitution that would preserve individual rights, protecting them from the corrupting touches of power. Mason's general distrust of executive power, with its locus in the king and royal governor, was reflected in his draft for the Constitution, which concentrated power in the legislature and reduced the executive to an "administrative" figure deprived of the power to veto legislation. Had Mason's structure prevailed, American government might have morphed into a more parliamentary form, akin to the modern British political system. Mason explicitly required a greater degree of "separation of powers" than in the Virginia colonial government and decreed that no person might exercise more than one public office: "And be it further enacted by the authority aforesaid that the following fundamental laws and principles of government shall henceforth be established. The Legislative, Executive and Judiciary offices shall be kept forever separate; no person exercising the one shall be capable of appointment to the others, or to either of them. Legislation shall be exercised by two separate houses, to wit a house of Representatives, and a house of Senators, which shall be called the General Assembly of Virginia." This separation of powers principle is one of the strongest and brightest threads that permeates all of Mason's political writings, from his notes on colonial charters to his criticisms of the federal Constitution of the United States.

In fact, all of the various draft constitutions circulating in that time period, including Mason's, Adams's, and Jefferson's, reveal an interesting consensus: agreement on the principle of separation of powers. Conceived by French philosopher Montesquieu, the tenet of "separation of powers" was an article of faith to Mason. Few political theorists were more highly regarded or more often cited by Mason than Montesquieu. And none of the French philosopher's ideas had greater influence in America than the theory of the separation of powers—by way of George Mason's seminal political writings. Indeed, every draft and plan of government that Mason penned included the fundamental postulate that there must be a separation of the powers of government among its principal branches. The Constitution finally agreed upon by the Virginia Convention on June 29, 1776, incorporated this influential doctrine.

Ironically, separation of powers was more a theory than a fact under Mason's version of the Constitution. All constitutional proposals of the day embodied this doctrine, yet not all of them created such a weak governor as did Mason's version—an executive elected by the legislature with little power. While the theory of separation of powers was something people could agree on, the Virginia Constitution carried the seeds of divisive controversy on this issue. Of the changes effected in Mason's governmental structure put in place on the transition from Colony to Commonwealth, none was more notable than the relegation of the executive to a position of total dependence. Edmund Randolph wrote that the Convention "gave way to their horror of a powerful chief magistrate without waiting to reflect, how much stronger a governor might be made."[19] To Mason, executives meant kings such as George III, whom he had indicted in the Virginia Declaration of Rights, and governors such as Lord Dunmore, whose ships had laid waste to Norfolk in January 1776. Indeed, as Mason met with his fellow delegates in Williamsburg, a constant military threat loomed over the Virginia leaders.

In Mason's plan of constitutional government, the governor was to be elected by the Legislature and was to be dependent on it for his salary. Not all delegates agreed with Mason's emasculation of executive power. Randolph complained that the executive office was, "clogged with a council of state, who were to be elected by that assembly, and to court them for their favor." James Madison put it more bluntly. He believed that "our executive is the worst part of a bad Constitution." And St. George Tucker, an esteemed lawyer and professor of law at the College of William and Mary, thought that no feature of the Virginia Constitution of 1776 cried out more sharply for reform than the executive: "Though the Constitution professed to make the departments of government independent of each other, yet the executive is chosen, paid, directed, and removed, by the legislative. It possesses not a single feature of independence.... If the union of these powers [executive and legislative] in the same men or body of men be dangerous to the state, is that union less dangerous when the legislature has the executive at its devotion, than when the executive dictates to an obedient legislature?"[20]

Certain sections of Mason's Virginia Constitution evoked criticism and protests almost immediately. Some of them were sufficiently well-founded to lead to its amendment during the nineteenth century. One frequently repeated criticism was that the Constitution was invalid without submission to and ratification by the people. It was objected that the Constitution contained no provision for its future interpretation or amendment. Critics argued that the division of power between governor and legislature was faulty. According to Madison, it paralyzed the governor while leaving the legislature unrestrained—"a grave of useful talents." Critics also charged that Mason's Constitution institutionalized the aristocratic status quo. Five years after its adoption, Jefferson, in his *Notes on Virginia*, pointed out that the roll of freeholders entitled to vote under the Virginia Constitution included less than one half the names on the roll of the militia or the list of tax collectors, and the geographic disproportion was even greater.[21] Similar doubts were expressed about the new Constitution by those who were there when it was made. George Wythe, for one, was dubious. He wrote to Jefferson, "The system agreed to in my opinion requires reformation."[22]

So Mason's draft of the Virginia Constitution had its share of critics. Some were simply unwilling to view any change as a good thing. John Randolph made it clear that nothing anyone had said at the Convention had made him ready for changes in the system under which he had been born and under which "I had hoped to be carried to my grave." Crying out against the "lust of innovation," Randolph wrote, "for my share, this is the first Convention in which I ever had a seat; and I trust in God, it will be the last. I never had any taste for Conventions; or for new Constitutions, made per order, or kept ready made, to suit casual customers." [23] Indeed, Randolph went so far as to oppose any provision for amending the new Constitution, just as he had preferred not changing the old one. To allow amendments, argued Randolph, was to introduce a state of "perpetual uncertainty," rather like "introducing into a marriage contract a provision for divorce."[24]

But those personally closer to Mason expressed optimism for his blueprint of government. Richard Henry Lee wrote to Charles Lee from Williamsburg, "The desire of being here at the formation of our new Government brought me from Philadelphia the 13th of this month. I have been in this City a week where I have had the pleasure to see our new plan of Government go on well. This day will put a finishing hand to it. 'Tis very much of the democratic kind".[25]

Lee sketched the primary features of Mason's plan of government and concluded, "These are the outlines of our political machine, which hope is sufficiently guarded against the Monster Tyranny." Years later, Jefferson and Madison exchanged considerable correspondence canvassing the possibility of a revisory Convention to address amendments to the Constitution. Jefferson wrote to his friend and political protégé on December 11, 1783, "You have seen G. M. I hope and had much conversation with him. What are his sentiments as to the amendment of our Constitution? What amendments would he oppose? Is he determined to sleep on, or will he rouse and be active? I wish to hear from you on this subject." The letter crossed one from Madison declaring, "On the article of the Convention for revising our form of state government he was sound and ripe and I think would not decline a participation in the work."[26]

Mason's attitude toward revision is difficult to determine, as he expressed ambivalence. A letter from Mason to William Cabell questions whether it would not "be better to defer it [the revisory Convention] for a year or two until the present ferment (occasioned by the late sudden change) has subsided, and men's minds have had time to cool." Jefferson departed for France shortly after this correspondence, and calls for a Convention to revise the Virginia Constitution ceased. There is, however, no doubt that Mason considered some parts of the final version of the Constitution problematic. Perhaps, he would have agreed with Edmund Randolph's final analysis: "By a further analysis of the Constitution a lesson will be taught, that the most expanded mind as that of George Mason's, who sketched the Constitution, cannot secure itself from oversights and negligences in the tumult of heterogeneous and indistinct ideas of government, circulating in a body, unaccustomed to much abstraction."[27]

Indeed, there remained a fundamental flaw to the last version of the Virginia Constitution: no institutional means for enforcing the provisions of the Declaration of Rights or any other part of the Constitution. Yet this blemish would be cured within a few years when the courts of Virginia would implement the practice of "judicial review." Though imminent, judicial review of "unconstitutional" laws was still in the future at the time of the Virginia Convention of 1776. For Mason, the principal means for preserving the rights of the individual and of the people were elections, public opinion, a properly constructed Constitution, and the ultimate preservative—revolution—in that order. Section Fifteen of Mason's draft Constitution was a repository of these fundamental rights, including the right to take up arms against tyranny. The Virginia Constitution was not intended to be a document for lawyers and judges only. It was intended to express the will of the people and to inform that will.

The Virginia Convention moved quickly once the committee completed its work. Archibald Cary presented the committee's report on Monday, June 24, 1776. On Friday, the Constitution received a third reading, which reflected a few amendments made by the Convention. The Constitution was passed on Saturday, June 29, a mere formality. In its final draft, the upper and lower houses of the assembly became, respectively, the "House of Delegates" and the "House of Senators."[28] Writing years later, Mason himself expressed satisfaction with the work of the Virginia Convention and with the public's reception of his handiwork: "We have laid our new Government on a broad Foundation, & have endeavoured to provide the most effectual Securities for the essential Rights of human nature, both in Civil and Religious liberty; the People become every Day more & more attach'd to it; and I trust that neither the Power of Great Britain, nor the Power of Hell will be able to prevail against it."[29] But as one historian has commented, "The essential structure of the government George Mason laid out early in June survived committee review and convention debate largely intact, yet the constitution, important as it was, contributed less to Mason's reputation than did [his] Declaration of Rights."[30]

With independence and a new, republican government thus established, the Virginia Convention adjourned on July 5, 1776. The men who had entered the Capitol as British subjects took their leave of Williamsburg as citizens of a new Commonwealth. At the end of this historic summer, the task before Mason and his colleagues was not to discover the weaknesses of their Constitution, but to implement the strengths of the document they had just completed. To put the Constitution into motion, the Convention proceeded to the election of a governor and council. The conservatives nominated Thomas Nelson Sr. for the executive office, the Movement Party nominated Patrick Henry, and the Convention supported Henry. Mason was chairman of the committee that notified the fiery orator of his election and installed him in the Governor's Palace. Ironically, just over a year earlier, Lord Dunmore had issued a proclamation urging that "the said Patrick Henry" receive no aid from anyone "but be opposed by every means."

As a perfecting touch, Mason (with George Wythe's assistance), served as chairman of the committee that designed the new Seal of the Commonwealth of Virginia. On one side of the great seal was a female figure personifying the Roman virtue of *Virtus* selected by Mason to represent the genius of the new Commonwealth. *Virtus* is a figure of peace, standing in a pose which indicates a battle already won. She rests on her long spear, its point turned downward to the ground. Her other weapon, a parazonium—a long triangular dagger—is sheathed; it is the sword of authority rather than that of combat. On the other side of the seal is the motto *Sic semper tyrannis*, "Thus always to tyrants." The Seal of Virginia was officially described in the Code of Virginia as follows:

> On the obverse, *Virtus,* the genius of the Commonwealth, dressed as an Amazon, resting on a spear in her right hand... and holding in her left hand, a sheathed sword...pointing upward; her head erect and face upturned; her left foot on the form of Tyranny represented by the prostrate body of a man, with his head to her left, his fallen crown nearby, a broken chain in his left hand, and a scourge in his right. Above the group and within the border conforming therewith, shall be the word "Virginia," and, in the space below, on a curved line, shall be the motto, "Sic Semper Tyrannis." On the reverse, shall be placed a group consisting of *Libertas*, holding a wand and pileus in her right hand; on her right, *Aeternitas*, with a globe and phoenix in her right hand; on the left of Libertas, Ceres, with a cornucopia in her left hand, and an ear of wheat in her right; over this device, in a curved line, the word "Perseverando."[31]

A final round of Madeira, some nervous congratulations, and it was all over for the delegates in Williamsburg. The work had gone well, considering the magnitude of the legal and political issues at hand. Mason, the legislator, had completed his assignment, but Mason, the father, had one further duty: to find a "supply of ribbons, buckles, buttons, and other elemental fineries" for his journey home to his beloved family, his gardens, his fields, and his library. Mason's journey back to Gunston Hall would not be easy. The roads were unpaved and rutted; there were many rivers and streams to ford, and few places for proper lodging. Indeed, after the first fifty miles of travel, Mason entered the wilderness and thick forests.

And he was about to enter a brutal military wilderness he and his family would endure for the next five years.

CHAPTER EIGHT

War and Death

*He who is the author of a war, lets loose the whole
contagion of hell, and opens a vein that bleeds a
nation to death.*
—THOMAS PAINE (1776)

In March of 1773, George Mason's beloved wife lay dying. Ann
Eilbeck Mason had given birth prematurely to twin boys. Neither child lived. Ann had fallen ill during her difficult pregnancy and never recovered. This was the twelfth pregnancy she had
endured in twenty-three years of marriage. Nine children would
reach adulthood, but her favorite may have been one of her youngest, John. Surviving correspondence suggests that George Mason
was also closest to John.

John had been born in 1766, the last surviving child of George
and Ann. John would write his forty-nine-page memoir, titled
Recollections, in the 1830s as a tribute to his father. John's recollections provide a detailed portrait of family life at Gunston Hall:
"I had during my youth, constant intercourse with all these people,
I remember them all and there are several employments as if it was
yesterday. As it will convey a better idea of the state of the family
and the habits of the times, I will describe them all."[1]

According to his *Recollections*, John was born at Mattawoman, the home of his Eilbeck grandparents. He was first tutored at Gunston Hall by a Scottish tutor, a "Mr. Davidson," who arrived at Gunston Hall around 1770. Another tutor, David Constable, stayed with the Masons for almost seven years. After the Revolution, John, his brother Thomas, and a cousin studied under the Reverend Buchnan, rector of Aquia and Pohick Churches. To finish his formal education, John was apprenticed to a Quaker merchant in Alexandria, William Hartshorne of the firm of Harper & Hartshorne. Perhaps the most interesting incident of young John's life was accompanying his father to the famous Constitutional Convention in Philadelphia in the summer of 1787. But John soon returned to continue his apprenticeship with Hartshorne before the Convention ended.[2]

From his childhood, John remembered his father's conversations with some of his colleagues about King George III, "and all conversations and so universal was the idea that with it was treason and death [to] speak ill of the King." John remembered a scene on a Sunday when the family was spending the day in the garden: "Several of the children having collected in the garden after hearing the talk among the elders of many complaints and distressing for forebodings as to the oppressive course toward our country were talking ... and I cursed the king. But I immediately begged and obtained the promise of the others not to tell on me."[3] The boy was mimicking his father's views. Given Mason's blunt temperament, it is easy to imagine his children overhearing his incendiary language against George III. And yet resentment to royal authority was one thing, revolution quite another.

As late as 1770, George Mason was flatly dismissing the idea of American independence, writing, "The wildest Chimera that ever disturbed a Madman's Brain has not less Foundation in Truth than this Opinion. The Americans have the warmest Affection for the present Royal Family; the strongest Attachment to the British Government & Constitution … there are not five Men of Sense in America who wou'd accept of Independence if it was offered."[4]

"The idea of breaking away from the British Empire," wrote one historian, "came remarkably quickly, though not easily."[5] In a few short years Mason, as we have seen, would reverse that opinion and craft the foundational argument justifying that "wildest Chimera" and ending the North Americans' long-standing allegiance to the "Royal Family."

John, who had been so embarrassed by his own defiant words against King George as a boy, would later have a successful business career and become a Georgetown merchant and civic leader in the District of Columbia, living to old age, eighty-three, almost twenty years longer than his father. But, as one source has written, "his hometown newspaper obituary gave the barest of details about [John] Mason's life: it reported only where he died, the time and location of his funeral, and that he was 'the last surviving son of Colonel George Mason.' The eulogist filled the remainder of his essay admiring John's father."[6]

John's brother, George Mason V, was also educated by private tutors at Gunston Hall. When George came of age in 1774, his father gave him part of the fifty-five-hundred-acre Gunston Hall tract. On this tract, called "Lexington," George V built his mansion house and estate. The plantation was so named in 1775 to commemorate the famous revolutionary battles of Lexington and Concord in Massachusetts. Lexington would eventually become the property of Mason's third son, William Eilbeck Mason, who served in the Fairfax Militia, fighting under "Light Horse" Harry Lee during the Revolutionary War. He fought with Lee in South Carolina and was commissioned a captain.

Sarah Eilbeck Mason (Sally) was George's second daughter and the first to marry, at age eighteen. Sally married Daniel McCarty Jr., the son of a prominent neighbor who lived at Cedar Grove (on Mason's Neck). McCarty also served in the Revolutionary War, fighting in the battles of Brandywine Creek and Germantown.

The Mason family did not escape the dangers and deprivations visited on America by the Revolutionary War. While Mason was not young and fit enough for military service, his sons and sons-in-law saw action. The War of Independence also, as we shall see, threatened Mason's sanctuary at Gunston Hall, disrupting the life of his family there. In a time before modern medicine, the vicissitudes and griefs of ordinary life and death also took their toll on the family, and on its patriarch.

The strong ties of affection Mason felt for Sally are revealed in a letter he wrote to her after she suffered the death of her infant daughter: "I most sincerely condole with you for the loss of your dear little girl, but it is our duty to submit with all the resignation human nature is capable of to the dispensation of Divine Providence which bestows upon us our blessings, and consequently has a right to take them away. A few years' experience will convince us that those things which at the time they happened we regarded as our greatest misfortunes have proved our greatest blessings. Of this awful truth no person has lived to my age without seeing abundant proof. Your dear baby has died innocent and blameless, and has been called away by all wise and merciful Creator, most probably from a life of misery and misfortune, and most certainly to one of happiness and bliss."[7]

Mothers had to expect to lose a large proportion of their offspring. George Mason and his wife were lucky to have nine surviving children. But twelve difficult pregnancies had devastated Ann Eilbeck Mason's petite body. She had recovered slowly from each ordeal, with Mason fussing over her, doing his utmost to restore her health and happiness. She may have been in failing health for some time before her death, since Mason made several payments to doctors on her behalf.

Still, the end came more suddenly than anyone expected.

Dr. James Craik, George Washington's close friend and personal physician, attended her.[8] Mason wrote that Ann suffered from "a slow fever ... after a painful tedious Illness." Ann's eventual death would devastate Mason. Death afflicted all at Gunston Hall, and Mason's devastating loss was pivotal to the political roles he played—and declined—after her death. Ann's greatest heartbreak, as she accepted her mortality, lay in being torn from her doting husband and adoring children. It was a lesson in priorities that Mason took to heart, and her death would leave him the single father of nine children, at the very time when his country most needed his public service.[9]

Ann would leave behind weeping children—her oldest not yet twenty—and a grief-stricken widower. Ann was only thirty-nine, but her body was exhausted. The tensions and exertions of the political situation in the prelude to the Revolutionary War no doubt exacerbated the state of her distressed health. By the early spring, Ann had been confined to her bedroom. Her young son John recalled that "my revered mother was afflicted for a considerable time and confined to her room or bed for some months by the disease which terminated in her death. Long as that has been ago and young as I then was yet I'm confident in the recollection of her and some of the scenes of her latter days."[10] Among the prescriptions Dr. Craik used for Ann was "weak milk punch" to be taken in bed in the morning. John would come into his mother's bedroom at times to comfort Ann and "drink a little of this beverage, which I loved very much from the bottom of the cup."[11]

Mason all but refused to leave Ann's side. Day after day, week after week, Mason was never out of calling, his son recalled years afterward. Mason spared himself few details of his wife's care, helping her take medicines and guiding cups to her lips. Either at her bed or in the small parlor nearby that opened onto hers, he kept vigil.

Ann, too, craved Mason's company. "Her eyes ever rested on him, ever followed him," according to family tradition. "The last I remember of that affectionate parent," her son John recalled, "an excellent woman, is that she took me one day in her arms on her sickbed told me she was going to leave us all, kissed me and gave me her blessing, and charged me to be a good boy to love and obey my father, to love and never quarrel with my brothers and sisters, to be kind to the servants, and if God spared me, when I grew up to be an honest and useful man."[12]

At a quarter to noon on a cool March day, Ann Mason, daughter, wife, and mother died.[13] When Ann passed, John later wrote, his "father for some days paced the rooms, or from house to the grave (it was not far) alone." Mason penned a loving eulogy to Ann in the family Bible, idealizing both her character and her death. Mason lovingly described Ann as kind, honest, cheerful, and steadfastly dedicated to her family. The tribute ended with these words: "Her ... irreparable Loss I do, & ever shall deplore; and tho' Time I hope will soften my sad impressions, & restore me greater Serenity of mind than I have lately enjoyed, I shall ever retain the most tender and melancholy Remembrance of One so justly dear."

Mason received the news of Ann's death with "a swollen heart," and the children "fell immediately into a hardy and long cry."[14] According to family oral history, Mason kept to his room for days. When Mason emerged, he walked almost incessantly night and day, only lying down occasionally, when he was completely exhausted. Mason's only source of consolation was long rides on horseback with one of his children, rambling about the Gunston Hall property. The whole family went into deep morning, and the children were led, clothed in black, to her grave.

Mason wrote George Brent that after Ann's death he was overcome by a "settled melancholy ... from which I never expect, or desire to recover." He told Brent that he had "determined to spend the Remainder of [my] Days in privacy & Retirement with my children."[15] Mason did not quickly take a new wife, nor did he send the children to live with female relatives, common options of widowed fathers in eighteenth-century century Virginia. He kept the children at home and rarely left them.

As Mason returned to Gunston Hall from his drafting of the Virginia Bill of Rights and the Virginia Constitution in Williamsburg in the summer of 1776, he must have felt excitement and perhaps a sense of dread, knowing that declaring independence from Britain had made war inevitable. The public reading of the formal Declaration of Independence after the Fourth of July had led to such wild enthusiasm that Washington's soldiers had sprinted down New York streets. They toppled the equestrian statue of George III at Bowling Green, decapitating it, then parading the head around town to the beat of fifes and drums. The patriots melted down the lead statue and made forty-two thousand musket bullets. Hearing of this treason, British Lord Sandwich, in a speech in the House of Lords, arrogantly responded: "Suppose the colonies do abound in men, what does that signify? They are raw, undisciplined, cowardly men."[16]

Perhaps more than his younger colleagues, Mason fully realized that his Declaration of Rights screamed treason. He knew the grisly punishments the British meted out to traitors to the Crown. Only recently a British judge had handed down this gruesome sentence to Irish revolutionaries: "You are to be drawn on hurdles to the place of execution, where you are to be hanged by the neck, but not until you are dead, for while you are still living your bodies are to be taken down, your bowels torn out and burned before your faces, your heads then cut off, and your bodies divided each into four quarters."[17]

Treason was a capital crime, and he had passed the point of no return. Mason was well aware of how the British had treated the colonist traitors in Boston. British methods of discipline ranged from whippings to hanging, carried out on the Boston Common, for all to see. The punishments applied not only to rebellious colonists, but to British soldiers who neglected their duties. If the punishment was flogging, the traitor or soldier was stripped to the waist, tied to a tree or post, then lashed across the back with a whip known as a "cat-o'-nine-tails."[18] It was not uncommon for a man convicted of treason to receive several hundred lashes. It was considered a sign of weakness to cry out during this punishment, so soldiers crushed a lead bullet between their teeth while being whipped. In some extreme cases, the excruciating lashings lasted several days, so that the wounds were not allowed to heal. The "cat" became covered in blood during the torture, and when not in use it was kept in a bag made of coarse crimson cloth. The color was deliberate, meant to hide the blood seeping through the fabric.[19]

George Washington wrote that he and his colleagues had fought "with halters about their necks." In the event of defeat, Mason and Washington both knew they would be hanged as chief culprits. Washington had decided that he would "neither ask for nor expect any favor from his most gracious Majesty."[20]

By the spring of 1776, when Mason was drafting the Virginia Declaration of Rights and Constitution in Williamsburg, British and American troops had already been killing each other for more than a year. While the engagements at Lexington and Concord had been small skirmishes, the battle at Bunker Hill turned into a bloodbath. The British lost more than a thousand men, half their force. The American dead numbered in the hundreds, a figure inflated by the fact that the wounded left on the field were killed with bayonets by British execution squads. In London, one retired British officer commented sarcastically that with a few more victories like this, the British Army would be thrashed.[21]

Although the War for Independence was in its early stages, it already had a hero: George Washington, the commander of the collection of militia units now being referred to as the Continental Army. "Over six feet tall and just over two hundred pounds," wrote one historian, "Washington was a physical specimen produced by some eighteenth-century version of central casting."[22] Washington not only fit the hero image physically, "he was also almost perfect psychologically, so comfortable with his superiority that he felt no need to explain himself. While less confident men blathered on, he remained silent."[23] Washington called the American Revolution "the last great experiment, for promoting human happiness."[24] But the happiness would not be easily won.

The bloody war continued to ebb and flow. Mason wrote to Washington to congratulate him on a "glorious & important Event"— the retaking of Boston. When General Howe's British army finally abandoned Boston, Mason sent an effusive letter to Washington. The British withdrawal would render the General's "memory to the latest Posterity, and entitle him to those Thanks which Heaven appointed the Reward of public Virtue. I think we have some reason to hope," he declared to Washington, "the Ministry will bungle away another summer, relying partly upon Force, & partly Fraud & Negotiation."[25] Mason understood that his friend's military exploits would "render General Washington's Name immortal in the Annals of America."

Mason was active in the war effort from the beginning, even if he did not actually fight. On July 19, 1776, the Virginia Convention passed a resolution declaring "that a sufficient armed Force [should] be immediately raised and embodied, under proper Officers for the Defence and protection of this Colony." Mason was appointed to a committee to draft an ordinance to implement the resolution.

Throughout the war years in Fairfax County, Mason organized men into a voluntary militia—the first in the colony—who elected

Washington their commander. Borrowing the colors of the English Whig party, the Fairfax Independent Company wore blue uniforms with buff facings and white stockings. They armed themselves with bayonets and cartridge boxes for muskets, along with sharpened tomahawks. Washington knew of the unit's formation while he was still in Philadelphia, for they had asked him to order drums and fifes. To that he added his own personal order for a silk sash, gorgets, epaulettes, and a copy of Thomas Webb's *A Military Treatise on the Appointments of the Army*. Across Virginia, Washington recorded, men were "forming themselves into independent companies, choosing their officers, arming, equipping, and training for the worst event."[26] General Washington accepted the field command of four independent companies: in Prince William, Fauquier, Richmond, and Spotsylvania counties.

Mason also helped organize American defenses along the Potomac. The Fairfax County Committee of Correspondence sent instructions to its Convention delegates, Mason and Charles Broadwater. Although the early skirmishing had centered on Norfolk, the committee complained that Lord Dunmore "still continues to pester us." Complaining of the inadequacy of "the Minute System," the committee asked for more regular troops and for the "fitting out a few vessells of war, to protect the Bays & Rivers, from Lord Dunmore's Pirates." Trying to rally support for the British, Dunmore had horrified Virginians by promising to free the slaves and indentured servants who joined the British army. As the Fairfax committee put it, "The Sword is drawn, the Bayonet is allready at our Brests."[27] The Committee of Safety authorized Mason and John Dalton, another member of the Fairfax Committee of Correspondence, to raise two row galleys and three cutters for the defense of the Potomac. Mason and Dalton, who apparently advanced some of the costs, had the galleys under construction, and they had purchased "three Sloops for

Cruisers." The largest of the sloops, the *American Congress*, mounted fourteen guns and carried a crew of ninety. Guns, powder, and musket balls were in short supply, so Mason had to beg and borrow for supplies. He also supported the establishment of a munitions factory at Fredericksburg and stockpiled tobacco to be traded in Europe for military supplies.

As war invaded their homes, patriots sent their sons into the battle. Patrick Henry's sons and Washington's nephews served. And all of Mason's sons fought in the war—after they finished their educations. To their father's gratification, all served valiantly. But there were clear limits to what the Mason sons would contribute, at least in their father's eyes.

Ever the concerned father, he urged his son George Mason V not to volunteer for the Continental Army, but he had no objection to young George's service as a minuteman. "I look upon it to be the true natural, and safest Defence of this, or any other free country." Young George accordingly served in one of the first minuteman regiments. He was first of the Mason family to wear the new uniform of the fledgling country. George V served as an ensign in the first militia company raised by Virginia and soon rose to the rank of captain. As a young captain he was in attendance, in his uniform of Whig-inspired buff and blue, when the second Continental Congress met in Philadelphia. With emotion and pride he saw the tall, quiet George Washington, a man he had known all his life, appointed general and commander-in-chief of all the Continental forces. George V's health, however, proved even more fragile than his father's. When he was struck by the same painful gout and "violent Rheumatic Disorder" which had followed his father from his youth, young George was forced to resign his commission.[28] But he continued to act as supply agent for troops commanded by Washington. What dreams of glory, never to be fulfilled, must have thrilled the boy's heart.

In a December 1780 letter, Mason, ever the concerned father, would refuse an offer by Harry Lee to extend the military service of another son. William Eilbeck Mason, who as we have seen was serving under Lee with the Fairfax Militia: "I have received your favor of the 30th November, and have the warmest sense of your very friendly offer to my son William, whose inclination I well know would strongly incline him to accept it, in which I would most cheerfully indulge him if I had any thought of continuing him in the military line.... But I have ever intended him for civil and private life; his lot must be that of a farmer and gentleman...."[29] Later, his proud father would speak of William's "coolness and intrepidity" under fire in the defense of Williamsburg.

George Mason himself carried a loaded pistol with him at all times during the war. He was recognized as one of the best shots in Fairfax County. In the April 1830 issue of *American Turf Register and Sporting Magazine*, there is mention of George Mason of Gunston Hall being "one of the best shots and keenest sportsmen of his day." This opinion was echoed by Mason's son John who referred to his father as a "great sportsman" in his *Recollections*.[30] Mason taught all his boys how to shoot expertly.[31]

For Mason's younger sons John and Thomas, there were no more pleasant hours of them hunting along the shores of the Potomac River. Mason considered these places unsafe for his boys. Instead, they often rode with their father to Colchester to see the troops passing through on their way south. There they met the dashing young Marquis de Lafayette, while one of their father's friends, Mr. Richard Chichester, gave out the quantity of wheat allocated to the Marquis's command. The boys thrilled with pleasure when they heard their father invite the Frenchman to spend the night at Gunston Hall. In fact, John Mason would recall that during "the Revolutionary war particularly, the officers of the different core of Army passing from north to south, knowing how welcome they would always be, very often took up their quarters at these houses for a night at least and sometimes for some days. From my earliest days, I saw all these things at my father's house. His neighborhood was an excellent one in those times."[32]

Throughout the war, Mason played an organizational and intellectual role in defending Virginia, but did not see the battlefield due to his age, infirmity, and obligations to his motherless children. Like Jefferson, he would wield the pen rather than the sword. He helped raise taxes for war needs and worked continuously to procure clothing, food, weapons, ammunition, and equipment for the soldiers throughout the war years.[33] He inspired his fellow Virginians to service, calling on men to remain "firmly determined, at the hazard of our Lives, to transmit to our Children & Posterity those sacred Rights to which ourselves were born." Mason repeated this call to duty in an April 1776 letter to Washington, expressing the hope that if the soldiers serving in the Continental Army could not return to their domestic lives, they would "bear our present & future Sufferings, becoming Men determined to transmit to our Posterity, unimpair'd, the Blessings we have received from our Ancestors!" For Mason, the death of every soldier was an irrefutable argument for persevering in the fight for Independence: "Can they restore the Husband to the widow, the Child to the Parent, or the Father to the Orphan? The die is cast—the Rubicon is passed—and a Reconciliation with Great Britain ... is impossible."[34]

Through the stages of the war, Washington complained to Mason about the dire circumstances of his army. At one point in 1780, the "present distresses" were "so great and complicated, that it is scarcely within the powers of description to give an adequate idea of them. We are without money, & have been so for a great length of time, without provision & forage except what is taken by Impress—without Cloathing—and shortly shall be (in a manner) without Men.... The history of this War is a history of false hopes, & temporary devices."[35] Washington's description of the Continental Army—"half starved, always in Rags, without pay"—was a tribute to the suffering troops who had stayed with him out of patriotic duty. But it was also a caustic criticism on a political pattern that only deepened over the ensuing war years: namely, the Continental Army was kept on life support but was never fully provided the necessary money and men Washington had requested.[36] The General came to believe that winning the war required nothing short of "an entire new plan." The starting point: a permanent and reliably funded military, followed by a redesign of government. Washington concluded that without real and immediate change, "our efforts will be in vain."[37]

Mason echoed Washington's declining confidence in the militia. As the war tediously wore on, Mason now put little faith in Virginia's "badly armed and appointed" militia. He had a terrible experience with Virginia's recurring inability to equip the troops it raised. Mason wrote Governor Jefferson to ask that William's company be provided with muskets and bayonets: "It is a most discouraging Circumstance to a young-fellow to lead Men into Action, without proper Arms." Supplying and equipping an American army proved to be more difficult than raising one because money was harder to command than men. Mason had reported to Washington that Virginia's initial levy of troops had been made "with surprising Rapidity," but added ominously, "as to Arms," the new regiments were "very deficient." Dismissing the militia as "ineffectual," he pleaded for a "speedy and powerful reinforcement of Continental troops."[38] Mason also grew hopeful about the "draft" for a standing army, writing to Jefferson that the "late Draught, for regular Service, was not only quietly, but chearfully executed in this, and the neighboring Countys." Little resistance would develop, he assured Jefferson, "where the leading men are true Whigs, & possessed of common Discretion."[39]

In 1778, there was finally some good news about the war. France had signed a treaty of alliance, and the British army had abandoned its grip on the American capital, Philadelphia. Washington pursued the retreating redcoats and claimed a victory in a brutal clash at Monmouth, New Jersey. Mason and Jefferson hoped peace was imminent. In May 1779, Jefferson informed his friend Edmund Pendleton—prematurely, it would turn out—that he was planning to retire from both state and national politics with the war quickly settled.

But it dragged on—through 1779 and 1780, and into 1781. And as it dragged on, no one was safe. Grisly reports of British atrocities terrified Virginians. One account told of two soldiers in the Queen's Rangers who were robbing a local home when they came upon a nine-year-old girl. According to contemporaneous journals and letters, the soldiers "ravished" her. The commander of the Queen's Rangers, John Graves Simcoe, investigated the incident and informed General Cornwallis that "I have not the least doubt but that Jonathan Webster & Lewis Terrpan ... of the Queen's Rangers, were guilty of a rape on Jane Dickinson yesterday." After a brief trial, the two men were given an hour "to prepare for their death." By order of Cornwallis, the men were then hanged "in the presence of the whole army." Word of the crime spread quickly, terrifying Mason's family and their fellow Virginians.[40]

And as the war raged on, British raiding ships came up the Potomac River with increasing frequency and threatened the river plantations, including Mason's Gunston Hall. In a letter he wrote to his son George on June 3, 1781—coincidentally, the same day Jane Dickinson's rapists were hanged—Mason discussed the progress of the war, writing that the Americans under Nathanael Greene were fighting bravely, but were overmatched by the British, who seemed intent on taking Virginia. Mason mentioned that Cornwallis and his men had just arrived in Virginia to support Benedict Arnold's troops. He discussed the forces of Lafayette and General Wayne in Pennsylvania and hoped that a French fleet would soon arrive. Mason wrote that most Virginians supported the Revolution and the alliance with the French. But many Virginians, he wrote "grow uneasy, & restless, & begin to think that our Allies are spinning out the War, in order to weaken America, as well as Great Britain, and thereby leave us, at the End of it, as dependent as possible upon themselves."[41] Mason did not doubt France's commitment to the war but wished they would quickly send more troops. He ended the letter saying that he believed "France surely intends the Separation of these States for ever from Great Britain; but by drawing out the thread too fine, & long, it may unexpectedly break in her Hands."[42] Only the arrival of a fleet, he thought, could check the British, but Mason feared the French might be extending the war to weaken America.[43]

In the letter, Mason also gave his son news about how the war was affecting the Mason family:

> Your Brother William writes you by this opportunity. He returned some time ago from South Carolina, where he commanded a company of volunteers, 70 fine young hellions from this country. He had a rough campaign of it and has acquired the reputation of a vigilantly good officer and I think is greatly improved by the exhibition. Your brother Thomson has lately returned from a Tour of Militia Duty upon James River [in Virginia], he commanded a platoon, in a pretty close action at Williamsburg & behaved with proper coolness and Integrity. The enemy's fleet commands our Rivers, & puts it in their power to remove their Troops from place to place, when, & where ... without opposition.... Our Militia turn out with Great Spirit, & have in

several late Actions, behaved bravely, but they are badly armed & appointed.[44]

In news of local import, Benedict Arnold had attacked in nearby Portsmouth, Virginia, having prepared large numbers of "Rat-bottomed" boats for plundering tobacco warehouses and homes along the rivers of Virginia and Maryland.[45] The war was now real and menacing for Mason and his family.

Mason's neighbor and friend Martin Cockburn had come to Gunston Hall, bearing news of an imminent attack. A British schooner was sailing their way. Cockburn had told Mason that he was taking everything he could and retreating further into the backcountry. He implored Mason and his family to do the same and asked him to come across the river with him over to Maryland. As British soldiers moved into the Northern Neck of Virginia, Mason worried that they would burn Gunston Hall, writing to George that "we are in daily expectation of sharing the same Fate with our Neighbours upon this, & the other Rivers; where many Familys have been suddenly reduced from Opulence to indigence ... the enemy taking all the Slaves, Horses, Cattle, Furniture, & other Property, they can lay their Hands on; and what they can't carry away they wantonly destroy."[46]

A few days earlier Mason had written Pearson Chapman, his friend and neighbor across the Potomac in Maryland, to ask permission to store his furniture at Chapman's home until it could be moved to the plantation of his son William at the head of Mattawoman Creek. "Lord Cornwallis with the main body of the British army was at Hanover Court House (fifty miles from Fredericksburg) on Tuesday morning ... I think if the winds permit we may expect their fleet up this river in a few days." Mason's letter to Chapman ended on a note of ominous foreboding: "Our situation in Virginia is truly critical and dangerous; a very few weeks, unless the enemy can be checked, will place Maryland in the same predicament. Nothing can speedily extricate the two states but the arrival of a strong French fleet which there is reason to expect every day ... I beg the favour of you to let your people and cart assist my people in carrying up the things from the landing to the house that the boat may return as quick as possible; and am dear sir Your most obedient servant, George Mason."[47]

Mason's spirits probably reached their lowest ebb in that June of 1781—it was the same month Governor Jefferson had to escape Charlottesville to avoid capture by cavalry under British Colonel "Bloody" Banastre Tarleton, bent on capturing the leading revolutionary figures in Virginia. Jefferson had called Tarleton "the most active, enterprising and vindictive officer who has ever appeared in Arms against us."[48]

As the war stormed through Virginia, the legislature, with Governor Thomas Jefferson's consent, decided to transfer their operations from Williamsburg to Charlottesville, which they thought was deep enough in Virginia's interior to be immune from British attack. Jefferson himself took his wife Martha and their children to nearby Richmond and joined the lawmakers in the city. Little more than a month later, a British raid, led by the traitor Benedict Arnold, now a British brigadier general, sailed boldly up the James River. Jefferson and his family were forced to flee from Richmond, this time in foul winter weather, while Jefferson frantically tried to rally the state's militia. Barely two hundred men turned out, while "Jefferson had to sit helplessly on his horse on the south side of the James River and watch Arnold burn millions of dollars' worth of cotton, tobacco, and other property in Richmond."[49] Even with more than fifty thousand militiamen on its rolls, Virginia was unable to stop 180 British dragoons from raiding into the heart of the state. No one had fired a shot at them.

Mason told George, now settled in Europe, "Our Affairs have been, for some time, growing from bad to worse."[50] Mason ended the June 3 letter to his son with doubtful hopes for victory in the war: "If our Allies had a superior Fleet here, I should have no doubt of a favourable issue to the war; but without it I fear we are deceiving both them & ourselves, in expecting we shall be much longer able to keep our people firm in so unequal an opposition to Great Britain. God bless you, my dear child! and grant that we may meet again in your native Country, as Freemen; otherwise, that we may never see each other more, is the Prayer of Your affectionate Father."

In the end, Gunston Hall was not burned. Colonel Fitzgerald and his small army made such a bold show that the British did not land and, although Fairfax County remained the "scene of war" a little longer, the Masons suffered no loss from enemy attack. Still, responding to repeated rumors about troop movements, Mason moved his furniture back and forth across the river so many times that he damaged it nearly as much as an actual raid on Gunston Hall might have done.[51]

And Mason remained on edge. He wrote a letter describing the desperate situation in Virginia to the Commonwealth's delegates in Congress at Philadelphia and lamenting "What may be the fatal consequences not only of disabling many thousands from paying their taxes and contributing to the support of the common cause, but of throwing them also as a dead weight on the rest of the community, or how few of them may have public virtue enough to withstand the terrors of poverty and ruin are topics which, however, disagreeable, deserve the most serious reflections that if possible the evil may be averted."[52]

Still doing all he could in the war effort, Mason assisted the provisional troops as they marched toward a decisive battle in Yorktown with British General Cornwallis. Though Gunston Hall was spared destruction, Britain brought the war to many Virginians' front doors. In addition to routing and burning their state capital and wrecking their economy, British military forces destroyed Virginians' crops, slaughtered their livestock, and threatened lives. A despondent James Madison wrote a friend of his sharp appraisal of the war: "No description can give you an adequate idea of the barbarity with which the Enemy have conducted the war in the Southern States ... Desolation rather than conquest seems to have been their object. They have acted more like desperate bands of Robbers or Buccaneers than like a nation making war for dominion."[53]

Raiding almost at will throughout Virginia, Cornwallis had terrorized the civilian population and disrupted state government without winning a decisive military victory. But in August 1781 Cornwallis withdrew to Yorktown and allowed himself to be trapped between a Franco-American army and de Grasse's French fleet. His surrender to Washington made independence inevitable.[54] When the news of the American victory reached Gunston Hall, Mason sensed that the surrender of Cornwallis's eight-thousand-man army would "lay the Foundation of a safe & lasting peace."

Washington announced the cessation of hostilities between America and Great Britain, recording that "the almost infinite variety of scenes thro[ugh] which we have passed with a mixture of pleasure, astonishment, and gratitude." The normally reserved Washington spoke ebulliently, declaring of his patriotic cause and kinsmen that "happy, thrice happy shall they be pronounced hereafter ... in erecting this stupendous fabric of freedom and empire on the broad basis of independence ... and establishing an asylum for the poor and oppressed of all nations and religions." The General ended on a theatrical, and possibly prophetic, note: "Nothing now remains but for the actors of this mighty scene to preserve a perfect union."[55]

CHAPTER NINE

A New Constitution for a New Country

The revolt from Great Britain and the formations of our new governments at that time, were nothing com- pared to the great business now before us....

—GEORGE MASON to his son George (1787)

Perhaps the most momentous event in Mason's life toward the end of the war was his second marriage. Nearly eight years after his beloved Ann's death, Mason had recovered enough to jest about the prospect of remarriage. He lamented to James Mercer that "I find cold sheets extremely disagreeable," and wrote that the "cold weather has set all the young Folks to providing Bedfellows." He listed his specific criteria for another wife in a letter: "She must be tolerable Handsome tho' good-natured and Sensible."[1]

More important, Mason had finally come to the realization that his children needed a mother. Life at Gunston Hall did not stand still during these years, and the domestic burdens upon him were heavy, raising nine children by himself in the middle of a bloody war. On April 11, 1780, he married Sarah Brent of Stafford County, whom he had known for years. She was the fifty-year-old daughter of his old family friend George Brent. The relationship between the Brents and the Masons was of long standing, with Mason likely considering the Brents as old family friends. The Brent-Mason connection comes up in at least one eighteenth-century record preceding the marriage in 1780. In 1760, Mason sent to George Washington a survey he had conducted of land originally owned by the Brents. Mason's father had purchased some of this property from the Brents years earlier, and Washington was buying some of it to add to his holdings at Mount Vernon.

Sarah and George Mason wed about two years after her father's death. It was her first and only marriage—unusual for a woman of her age and gentry status. Virtually no details of Mason's second marriage have survived, but it seems unlikely that he grew as emotionally close to Sarah as he had been to Ann. Mason found a small gathering place for his second marriage at the home of a Mr. and Mrs. Graham in Dumfries, Virginia. George and Sarah Mason stood before the fireplace in the drawing room and greeted the members of their families and the few intimate friends who had come to see them married. The following week found them all back at Gunston Hall, with Sarah already starting a beneficent reign with the younger children. The quiet house received its new mistress with little commotion. Sarah, with her needlework and gentle manner, seemed constantly aware of the family's needs, cleaning the boys' room and making it warm with a blazing fire on the hearth.[2]

Oral tradition held that Sarah was "small and colorless and without great charm," but she seemed just what the Mason family needed at that time. And she was of upper-class stock. The details on Sarah are somewhat vague. The information that can be gleaned from various public records, letters, and documents is almost exclusively from male family members. Like Mason, Sarah traced her family roots to England. She had taken over the management of the Brent household when her mother died in 1751. Twenty-one at the time, the new mistress of Woodstock was not much older than Nancy Mason, eldest daughter of George Mason, when she began to oversee the house and family at her mother's death. The industrious Sarah had headed the Woodstock household for twenty-seven years until her father's death in 1778. Interestingly, her sister Elizabeth was likely at home as well, since family records shows her dying unmarried in 1783. But it was Sarah whom her father remembered in a special way in his will, executed the year of his death. George Brent bequeathed Sarah a silver tankard, salver, and two porringers that had belonged to her grandmother as a "lasting monument of the sense I have of her merit and the care she has taken of me."[3]

It is likely that Sarah was a practicing Roman Catholic, like her father and the whole Brent family. But Sarah and George were married by Reverend James Scott of the Anglican Church. Like her stepdaughter Nancy Mason, Sarah was more mature than most eighteenth-century women marrying for the first time. She was fifty years old and George Mason was fifty-five. In an arrangement not typical for the eighteenth century, George and Sarah signed a marriage agreement (like a modern-day "pre-nuptial") several days before the wedding, protecting Sarah's property. Under the terms of this contract, Sarah gave ownership of her slaves to Mason for the length of the marriage but regained possession of them should her husband die if there were no children of the marriage. Under this agreement, Sarah received as dower four hundred acres of Mason's land at Dogue's Neck. Some historians take this agreement as evidence that the marriage was more a business arrangement rather than a romantic marriage. But it can also be interpreted as a practical arrangement between two mature people in their fifties who, not unreasonably, wanted to safeguard their property for their heirs—Mason for his children, and Sarah for the sons and daughters of her sister Jean in Dumfries. In Sarah's 1794 will, she bequeathed the slaves she regained upon Mason's death to those children.[4]

Sarah brought to the marriage and to Gunston Hall her ten-year-old nephew, George Graham, eldest son of her sister Jean. George was the same age as Mason's youngest son Thomas, and he was eventually sent away to school with Thomas and John. It may appear unusual that George Graham moved from his own home to that of his aunt. But gentry families of the eighteenth century often made similar arrangements, including long periods of time spent with trusted relatives, to acquire an education for their sons.

Signs indicate that the marriage between George and Sarah was an amiable if not a romantic one. She did not have to marry for financial reasons, since her father's will had provided her with a fine estate and an annual allotment of twenty-five pounds for as long as she remained single. In 1783, Mason wrote to his son George in France, thanking him for obtaining a watch for his stepmother. While at the federal Constitutional Convention in Philadelphia, George kept in touch with Sarah, enclosing at least one letter for her in his letter to his son. When Sarah fractured her leg, George offered an update on her health, writing to his son that Sarah is "still unable to walk a step, 'tho—I think she begins to gain her strength in her leg and foot."[5]

By all accounts Sarah wore the mantle of mistress of Gunston with grace and dignity. With the children, she seemed never intrusive, cognizant of her role as stepmother, not mother. But she was always available, and they turned to her for advice and guidance with increasing frequency. And the household ran smoothly. Sarah had brought contentment, and she seems to have been well liked both by the children and by the servants. And it is important to note that Sarah accompanied Mason through some of the hardest trials and tribulations of his life. They were together during the final period of the

American Revolution, when fighting in Virginia led Mason to move his family, including Sarah and the younger children, across the Potomac River, for safety. And it was Sarah who consoled George after his defeat in the Constitutional debates in Philadelphia, and again after the Ratification Convention in Richmond and during the final years of Mason's life.[6]

With the bloody Revolutionary War at an end, Mason dropped out of public affairs for a time. His intermittent attacks of gout made him an uncertain member of the Virginia Assembly, and he had seemingly retired to live the life of a quiet country gentleman. The passage of time after the war brought some easing of Mason's domestic responsibilities. By this time his second daughter, Sally, had married the son of his neighbor Daniel McCarty. Nancy, Mason's eldest daughter was still at home; she had served as "Mistress of my Family, and manage[d] my little domestic Matters, with a Degree of Prudence far above her Years," until his second marriage.[7] During these years his daughter Betsy fell in love and became engaged to William Thornton. John and Thomas, the unmarried sons, were still only seventeen and twenty-one. As his children entered adulthood, he described them proudly as "free from Vices, good-natured, obliging & dutiful."

But Mason watched the progress of post-war events with anxiety. These were not only "the times that try men's souls" in the words of Thomas Paine, they were also the times that tested Americans' political skills in creating a strong national government.[8] For every period of history, as historian Pauline Maier has pointed out, there is some problem that seems to attract the talents of the greatest minds of the age. In the eighteenth century, the question of the age was government—how to create an enduring political structure that would protect liberty. George Mason knew that it was one thing to win a Revolution. It was quite another to avoid a dictatorship and create a system of government that would preserve the freedoms for which the people had fought. This was now the problem facing the thirteen "United States." To fight the war, they had joined together somewhat reluctantly into a loose "Confederation." All real power—the power to tax, to raise armies, to enforce treaties—rested not with the Continental Congress, but with the states.[9]

It was not clear whether the states were going to be part of a perpetual union. Some were talking in terms of two or three different confederations, perhaps, or no confederations, just thirteen separate governments. During the years before the Constitutional Convention in 1787, this major question loomed: Thirteen "countries" or one consolidated nation? Mason knew it would be the last battle of the American Revolution—fought not with bullets and swords, but with words.

There was general dissatisfaction with the Articles of Confederation. The Continental Congress had adopted the Articles of Confederation, the first Constitution of the United States, in 1777, though the states had not ratified them until 1781. The Articles created a loose confederation of states and an anemic central government, leaving most of the power with the states. Once peace prevailed after the war, the weakness of the Articles became apparent. The states had stood together for a common cause, but now they were beginning to pursue their own agendas.[10]

Mason recognized the limitations of the Articles of Confederation. He felt strongly that the government under the Articles was "approaching to Dissolution" and that "some of its Principals have been found utterly inadequate to the Purposes for which it was establish'd...."[11]

And that opinion was widely shared among the other prominent Virginians. As early as a March 4, 1783, in a letter to Virginia governor Benjamin Harrison, Washington had complained, about the Articles of Confederation, "that if the powers of Congress are not enlarged, and made competent to all general purposes, that the Blood which has been spilt, the expense that has been incurred, and the distresses which have been felt, will avail us nothing; and that the band, already too weak, which holds us together, will soon be broken; when anarchy and confusion must prevail."[12]

Later in the same year, James Madison stopped in at Gunston Hall on his way back to Montpelier, his estate in Orange County, and tried to enlist Mason in the nationalists' drive for a new and stronger federal government and Constitution to revise or replace the Articles. Madison wrote to Jefferson of his meeting with Mason: "I found him much less opposed to the general impost than I had expected. Indeed he disclaimed all opposition to the measure itself but had taken up a vague apprehension that if adopted at this crisis it might embarrass the defence of trade against British machinations. He seems upon the whole to acquiesce in the territorial cession but dwelt much on the expediency of the guaranty. On the article of a convention for revising our form of government he was sound and ripe and I think would not decline a participation in the work. His heterodoxy lay chiefly in being too little impressed with either the necessity or the proper means of preserving the confederacy."[13]

The federalists, including Madison and Washington, would try for nearly a decade to allay Mason's fears, to no avail. As early as in 1786, Madison knew it would be difficult to cure Mason of his parochial views and make him a "nationalist." As he wrote to Jefferson, "Among the many good things which may be expected from Col. Mason we may reckon perhaps an effort to review our Constitution.... I am not without fears also concerning his federal ideas. The last time he seemed to have come about a good deal towards the policy of giving Congress the management of Trade. But he had been led so far out of the right way that a thorough return can scarcely hope for." On that same day Madison wrote to James Monroe, recently defeated in his own election for the Virginia Assembly, but a rising young political star. "Col. Mason will be an inestimable acquisition on most of the great points ... I am somewhat apprehensive likewise that Col. Mason may not be fully cured of his Antifederal prejudices."[14]

In any case, Mason was still not ready to return to active participation in the political realm. He complained to his friend and neighbor Martin Cockburn, "I have been lately informed that some People intend to open a Pole for me at the Election to-morrow for this County. I hope this will not be offered; for as I have repeatedly declared that I can not serve the County, at this time, as one of its Representatives, I shou'd look upon such Attempt, in no other Light than as an oppressive & unjust Invasion of my personal Liberty; and was I to be elected under such Circumstances, I should most certainly refuse to act."[15]

But Mason's concerns with commercial restrictions on Virginia would lead him back into political life. The inability of the Confederation Congress to regulate commerce between the states led to the convention of two conferences—one at Mount Vernon and the other at Annapolis—that would in turn lead to the calling of a federal Constitutional Convention in Philadelphia.[16] Madison and Washington were deeply involved in both interstate conferences, and they insisted on including Mason as a delegate. While Mason did take part in the conference at Mount Vernon, Virginia governor Edmund Randolph expressed concern in a June 12, 1786, letter to Madison that Mason would not be attending in Annapolis: "I have never received any notification from Colo. Mason, that he accepts his appointment. Indeed, a journey from home ex gratia seems not to be a hobby-horse of his."[17] Monroe urged Madison on September 5, "Prevail I beg of you on Colo. Mason to attend the convention. It will give him data to act on afterwards in the State." Mason attended neither the conference in Annapolis nor the Virginia Assembly that year due to "the longest & most severe Fit of the Gout, I ever experienced."[18]

Then, at the end of 1786, George Mason's life seemed to be thrown into turmoil when Madison informed him that the Virginia legislature planned to name him one of the state's seven-man delegation to the forthcoming "federal convention" in Philadelphia, along with Washington and Madison. Governor Randolph pleaded with Mason to accept: "Give me leave to call to your mind the tottering condition of the United States, and to press you into this Service, if your health should permit." Madison told Jefferson that Mason "will pretty certainly attend."[19]

But Mason had never ventured out of his native Virginia in his life. While men like Madison and Jefferson yearned for higher political offices, Mason, secure in his land and his family's reputation—and his own—preferred whenever possible to remain at Gunston Hall. And the chronic illness that had begun in his thirties made attendance at meetings difficult. Intermittent attacks of gout affecting his hands, feet, and stomach and lasting for weeks often kept him at home. Fatigue, no doubt, caused Mason's equally chronic impatience with oratory, political maneuvering, and colleagues who acted with less intelligence than he did.

As he wrote to Washington, Mason preferred to "sit down at his Ease under the Shade of his own Vine, & his own fig-tree, & enjoy the Sweets of domestic Life!"[20] It would take extreme urging from his friends and family to persuade him to accede to their wishes. Holding himself aloof, he had learned to set a high price on his participation, yielding only with reluctance.

Literal money concerns also made the frugal Mason hesitant to travel to Philadelphia. In April 1787 Mason wrote Governor Randolph to request an advance against the £100 the assembly had appropriated for his travel expenses. Mason's tobacco sales had been sadly disappointing that season, and the advance was "of such Importance to me, that without it, I could hardly have attended."[21] Acknowledging receipt of the money a few days later, Mason explained his financial concerns: "Considering the Number of Deputies from the different States, the great Distance of some of them, & the Probability that we may be obliged to wait many Days, before a full Meeting can be obtained, we may perhaps be much longer from Home than I at first expected."[22]

Mason would go to Philadelphia, though reluctantly. The crisis was real, as the November 23, 1786, Act of the Virginia Assembly endorsing the call for the Convention and authorizing the election of delegates had made clear. In one historian's summary, "The act, which Governor Randolph forwarded to the other states as well as to Washington, said the crisis had arrived when 'the good people of America' had to decide whether they were to reap the fruits of independence and a union 'cemented with so much of their common blood' or give way to 'unmanly jealousies and prejudices, or to partial and transitory interests,' and 'renounce the auspicious blessings prepared for them by the Revolution.'"[23]

Although Mason was always hesitant to leave Gunston Hall, he felt the call of duty this time. As he had written to his friend Martin Cockburn three years earlier, "If ever I shou'd see a Time, when I have just Cause to think I can render the Public essential Service, and can arrange my own Domestic Concerns in such a Manner, as to enable me to leave my Family, for any Length of time, I will most cheerfully let the County know it."[24] This was that time. Once again George Mason would render "essential Service" to "the Public."

George Washington, like George Mason, was among the seven delegates chosen by a joint ballot of the House of Delegates and Senate of the Virginia General Assembly on December 4, 1786, to attend "a Convention proposing to be held in the city of Philadelphia in May next, for the purpose of revising the federal constitution."[25]

Washington initially wrote to Governor Randolph declining the appointment to the Convention. At that time he secretly hoped his

Virginia associates would drop the matter. But when Madison learned of Washington's decision, he asked the General to keep the door ajar "in case the gathering clouds should become so dark and menacing as to supersede every consideration but that of our national existence or safety."[26] For weeks, Washington wrestled with indecision. "My name is in the delegation to this convention," Washington told Jay, "but it was put there contrary to my desire and remains there contrary to my request."[27] Washington encouraged the perception that he was following rather than leading events. Henry Knox sent Washington a letter saying that he took it for granted that Washington would be elected president of the Convention. If the Convention still faltered and produced only a "patchwork to the present defective confederation, your reputation would in a degree suffer." But if the Convention forged a vigorous new federal government, Washington would be hailed a hero once again.[28]

Washington, as was his style, sought out the advice of friends such as Mason to resolve his dilemma. Both Washington and Mason continued to allow the issue of attendance to percolate for months. Basically, the two men agreed: if you go, I will go. For years, Washington had relied upon Mason's skills and knowledge for political acumen and theory. Mason's agreement to attend the Convention was a deciding factor for Washington. On March 28, the General wrote to Randolph and agreed to attend the Philadelphia Convention. He made it clear that he was submitting to the entreaties of friends. Washington acknowledged that his attendance would have "a tendency to sweep me back into the tide of public affairs." Knox was pleased with Washington's decision. "Secure as he was in his fame," he wrote to Lafayette, "he has again committed it to the mercy of events. Nothing but the critical situation of his country would have induced him to so hazardous a conduct."[29]

Patrick Henry had also been chosen, but he would not attend. Henry had recently declined a third term as governor and left

Richmond for retirement. "My wife and self [are] heartily tired of the bustle we live in here," Henry had written in October. "I shall go to Hanover to land I am like to get of Gen. Nelson, or if that fails, towards Leatherwood again."[30] Governor Randolph wrote to Henry at Leatherwood, urging him to accept appointment to the Convention. Matters had grown so perilous, Randolph said that "those who first kindled the Revolution" must now come forward again to devise the means of saving it. "The neglect of the present moment may terminate in the destruction of Confederate America," Randolph implored. Nearly three months passed without a reply from Henry. Finally, in mid-February 1787, writing from yet another new "seat"—this one in Prince Edward County—Henry politely declined the invitation. He offered no reasons, and only later commented famously that he had not ventured to Philadelphia because he "smelt a rat"—prophetic words.[31]

George Washington, James Madison, Edmund Randolph, George Wythe, James Blair, and George Mason would represent Virginia at the Constitutional Convention in Philadelphia. Next to Pennsylvania, Virginia would have the largest delegation. The Assembly had authorized the delegates to consider "all such Alternations and farther Provisions as may be necessary to render the Federal Constitution adequate to the Exigencies of the Union."[32]

George Mason's trip to Philadelphia would be the geographical adventure of his life and the culmination of his intellectual and political experience. The one hundred and forty miles he would travel to Philadelphia was the farthest trip in his life. He certainly had no desire to leave his comfortable estate or family simply to become the leader of the opposition leader to a new federal Constitution. On the contrary, Mason went to Philadelphia with every intention of imparting his best advice for its preparation.

According to scholar Josephine Pacheco, Mason "did not want to see the Revolution destroyed. He had been one of the leaders in precipitating the War for Independence. Like many Americans in the 1780s, he feared that the United States might disintegrate; what he wanted was a strong, united country. How could he stand by and see his efforts come to nothing?"[33]

In addition, there was the issue of trade, which had led to the conferences at Mount Vernon and Annapolis. Mason owned extensive agricultural property on the Potomac River. The Potomac provided Gunston Hall with access not only to the Maryland shore but to the rest of the United States. Mason became concerned about the establishment of his trade patterns, and the difficult relations among the states and with foreign countries in the years after the Revolution.[34] "Hoping to reverse this pattern," according to Pacheco, "he, along with Archibald Henderson, represented Virginia at the Mount Vernon Conference of 1785, which developed an effective agreement with Maryland on the use of the Potomac and other waterways.... Mason was looking beyond Virginia for ways to strengthen the new nation."[35] As he told his son George, he had a responsibility to "millions yet unborn."[36]

But something more than a desire to improve trade conditions and establish a firmer union of the states motivated Mason to leave his beloved Gunston Hall, travel outside his native Virginia for the first time in his life, and undertake a grueling journey despite his chronic ill health. Had he not answered the call, he would have felt that his mission to safeguard the liberties of his new country for which he had fought so hard was incomplete. According to historian Jeff Broadwater, "Mason went to Philadelphia because he believed the convention would do important work, because a near consensus existed among America's political elite that Congress needed new powers, and because he saw a stronger central government as a possible check on the state legislatures."[37]

Hence, on May 9, 1787, as dawn broke cool over Gunston Hall's fields, George Mason's servants harnessed the steaming horses to his coach in the morning chill. Shortly after sunrise Mason, his son John, and his slave James set off for Philadelphia on the rutted trails Virginians called their "High Waies." Farm wagons and gentry coaches alike struggled across the hilly, broken ground through long stretches of pine forests separating the tobacco and wheat fields and the peach, pear, and apple orchards.

During the long journey, his gout abated, but Mason was beset by other ailments, including a violent headache and an upset stomach—perhaps the somatic expression of his anxiety about the pending Convention.[38] As Mason left his beloved farm and family behind, no doubt he pondered the postwar world and wondered how to secure Americans' freedoms. He seemed well equipped to play a large part and have a major effect on the outcome. Washington had never taken a leading role in drafting political documents. Adams and Jefferson were off on diplomatic assignment in Europe. Benjamin Franklin was now over eighty years old. Hamilton and Madison were too junior to assume leadership roles.

Mason travelled to Philadelphia by way of Baltimore, where he wrote letters to his sons William and Thomson. When he and John finally arrived at the Indian Queen Inn, the fashionable Philadelphia tavern, Mason wrote a long letter to his son George saying, "The expectations and hopes of all the Union centre in this Convention. God grant that we may be able to concert effectual means of preserving our country from the evils which threaten us."[39] He had arrived on "Thursday evening," which would have been May 17, 1787.

Sumptuous comfort abounded at the Indian Queen, for here a proud city entertained its honored guests. Not all the delegates were there. Washington was the houseguest of Mr. Robert Morris, and delegate Elbridge Gerry of Massachusetts rented a house so that his young wife and baby could be with him.[40] But the guests staying with Mason at the Indian Queen were some of the most distinguished visitors: James Madison, Charles Pinckney of South Carolina, Governor Alexander Martin and Hugh Williamson of North Carolina, Richard Bassett of Delaware, Alexander Hamilton of New York, and Nathaniel Gorham and Caleb Strong of Massachusetts. Wearing the colorful dress of their day and waited upon by liveried servants, the delegates bustled in and out of the Indian Queen from the latter part of May until September 17, 1787. The delegates arrived slowly, for travelling was difficult, and many of them had come far. Those were not days of haste or impatience, however, and the earlier arrivals made use of their time by discussing the grave matters before them.

Mason was one of the last of the Virginians to reach Philadelphia. Although travel was very expensive—eight or nine dollars a day—lodgings in Philadelphia were inexpensive. At the Indian Queen, Mason paid twenty-five shillings, Pennsylvania currency, for adequate accommodations, including his servant and horses, but not his beloved Madeira. Upon arrival, Mason wrote that the Virginia delegates met for "two or three hours every day and there was a general meeting of all the deputies who had arrived, every afternoon at three."[41] Officers of the Society of the Cincinnati (former Revolutionary Army officers) were also meeting in Philadelphia, which meant even more mingling, debating, and dining together.

The Convention would hold its deliberations in secret. Mason was sorry that his young son John would not be able to hear the most important parts of the debates. But in another letter to his son George, he defended the private deliberations: "It is expected our doors will be shut and communications upon the business of the Convention be forbidden during its sitting. This I think myself a proper precaution to prevent mistakes and misrepresentation until the business shall have been completed, when the whole may have a very different complexion from that in which the several crude and indigested parts might in their first shape appear."[42]

George Mason's life and reputation were about to be changed forever.

CHAPTER TEN

The Philadelphia Convention

I am truly conscious of having acted from the purist motives of honesty and love to my country, according to that measure of judgment that God has bestowed on me. I would not forfeit the approbation of my own mind for the approbation of any man, or all the men upon earth.

— **GEORGE MASON** to his son John (1789)

In 1786, a year before the Constitutional Convention began, Thomas Jefferson visited John Adams in London. Adams took him to the Royal Palace and introduced him to George III. The king had been more than cordial to Adams when he presented himself as the American ambassador. But His Majesty purposely turned his back on Jefferson, the author of the insult-riddled Declaration of Independence. Deeply offended, Jefferson would later tell the Virginia delegates to the federal Convention in Philadelphia that the English would have to be "kicked into common good manners."[1]

Ten years after the Declaration of Independence, Americans were not free of the specter of kingly tyranny. George Mason, for one, feared that any proposed strong national government would quickly turn into a sanitized version of a monarchy.

Mason joined his fellow Virginia delegates in the Convention, and almost immediately, George Washington was unanimously elected its president. The thirty-six-year-old James Madison became the official notetaker. Mason could have no idea that after the Convention was over, both men would be his bitter political enemies.[2]

The diminutive Madison, hair brushed forward to conceal his receding hairline, habitually followed the General to the front of the room. Wearing the sober black he favored—black breeches, black silk stockings, and three-pointed black hat—Madison chose "a seat in front of the presiding member, with the other members on [his] right and left hands."[3] From that vantage point facing the delegates, which only he and Washington had, he would take detailed notes for the next four months. "I was not absent a single day, nor more than a casual fraction of an hour in any day," Madison would boast.[4] Although Madison was a physically small man and spoke softly, he was a rigorous political theorist with a sharp intellect.

Washington and Madison were not only colleagues but also personal friends. Washington had a paternal affection for Madison. Yet the erect, soldierly Washington and the slim, slight Madison were an unlikely pair. Shy and socially awkward, Madison did not charm the ladies like the handsome Alexander Hamilton. He was neither cosmopolitan like the rakish Gouverneur Morris nor flamboyant like Patrick Henry. The thirty-four-year-old congressman from Orange County was nineteen years younger than the gray-haired General Washington. Whereas Madison seemed to be humble and soft-spoken, Washington's stoic manner could be forbidding. No one who saw Washington's rage ever forgot it. The combination of steely discipline and powerful drive generated a charisma so compelling that, by one account, every king in Europe "would look like a valet de chambre by his side." Washington's blue eyes seemed judgmental, yet they could sparkle with delight, especially to an admiring woman.[5]

The bookish Madison, in contrast, just thirty-four years old, was described as "prematurely aged, with thinning hair combed flat atop his head. His dark, intense eyes stared from a pale face with heavy eyebrows. Only five foot four and plagued by delicate health, he was abstemious in his habits. To some, he seemed an austere personality. The wife of one Virginia politician called him 'a gloomy stiff creature,' while another woman found him 'mute, cold, and repulsive.' He was wont to croak and mumble, could scarcely be heard during speeches, and was painfully retiring at first meeting."[6]

Mason seemed pleased to see so many "gentlemen of competent years" at the Convention. And the feelings were mutual. The men who met Mason in Philadelphia—and points north—were impressed. John Jay met Mason for the first time when Mason traveled up to the city of New York with his son John during a recess in the Convention. Jay described Mason as "a man of talents and an agreeable companion. There are few with whom you so trust on an acquaintance. I have been so much pleased and I regret that it was not convenient to him to have remained longer in this city." A fellow delegate, William Pierce, seemed even more impressed with Mason: "Mr. Mason is a Gentleman of remarkable strong powers, and possesses a clear and copious understanding. He is able and convincing in debate, steady and firm in his principles, and undoubtedly one of the best politicians in America. Mr. Mason is about 60 years old, with a fine strong constitution."[7]

Governor of Virginia and fellow delegate Edmund Randolph, thirty years Mason's junior, was also captivated with Mason's intellectual capacity: "Among the numbers who in their small circles were propagating with activity the American doctrines was George Mason in the shade of retirement. He extended their grasp upon the opinions and affections of those with whom he conversed. He was behind none of the sons of Virginia in knowledge of her history and interest. At a glance he saw to the bottom of every proposition which affected her. His elocution was manly sometimes, but not wantonly sarcastic."[8]

The stakes in Philadelphia in the summer of 1787 could not have been higher. As Mason saw it, "The Revolt from Great Britain, & the Formations of our new Governments at that time, were nothing compared with the great Business now before us."[9] Mason believed the Convention was momentous because of what the outcome would mean for future generations. "The Influence which the Establishments now proposed may have upon the Happiness or Misery of Millions yet unborn," Mason wrote, "is an Object of such Magnitude, as absorbs, & in a Manner suspends the Operations of the human Understanding."[10]

Over the next months, rumors of dissension at the Convention spread. Washington's dour expression as he left the Convention hall one day prompted a report that the delegates were in disarray. Some patriots on the outside were convinced that the delegates on the inside were up to no good. As the Convention plodded on during the sweltering summer, the thermometer topped 90 degrees with a drenching humidity that began to exhaust Mason and his colleagues. Blinds covered the Convention hall's windows and kept out the sun, the noise—and the fresh air. But when they were opened, flies swarmed in.

Both Mason and Washington greatly missed their homes and family, complaining when letters from Virginia failed to arrive, since that denied them "the consolation of hearing from home, on domestic matters."[11] Washington so loved his estate that once as his army had marched toward Yorktown during the war, he had ridden his horse a hard sixty miles for a brief visit to Mount Vernon. Now, in the words of one scholar, he "dreamed of the day when he could join those who, in the words of the prophet Micah, had beaten their "swords into plowshares" and he too could sit at peace "under his vine and under his fig tree" with no pressing political affairs.[12] George Mason felt exactly the same way.

In between meetings over the next three months, the delegates did what they could to assuage boredom. Some had their portraits made by an apparatus which produced an exact silhouette of a person's features. Thus there are actual images of Madison, Franklin, and Washington from fifty years before the invention of photography, actual shadows captured from another era.[13] Mason's doings in Philadelphia reflected his far-ranging interests. It is probable that surgeon Abraham Chovet gave Mason and Washington a private tour of his Anatomical Museum, with its displays of human figures. The two Virginians may also have enjoyed the theater, by attending plays at the Southwark Theater, located just outside of Philadelphia because of the law banning theater performances in the city. Mason also took advantage of his leisure time to do some shopping in the bustling city, buying furniture for Gunston Hall: two sets of "Windsor" side chairs (chairs without arms) made in Philadelphia, which were remarkably different in style and shape from the Windsor chairs made in Virginia. Mason also purchased other household furnishings for his son John.[14]

While in Philadelphia, as throughout his life, Mason exhibited an irenic spirit in matters of faith. On his first Sunday at the Convention, Mason and the other Virginia delegates, except for Washington, actually went to a Catholic Mass, "more out of Curiosity than compliment." One can visualize Mason walking through the oak-carved doors and kneeling in front of the altar. The scent of slow-burning white candles and freshly cut flowers might have filled his nose. Mason commented on the large congregation, but seemed put off by "an indifferent Preacher." The music and "the Air of Solemnity" that filled the chapel impressed the Virginian, although "I was somewhat disgusted with the frequent Tinkling of a little Bell, which put me in Mind of the drawing up [of] the curtain for a Puppet-Shew."[15] According to one scholar's assessment, "More important perhaps than his critique of the service was Mason's willingness to attend, given the anti-Catholicism that pervaded English republicanism and much of American society. Mason's republicanism had never embraced religious prejudice."[16]

Through that scorching summer, some delegates attended the Convention with mismatched shoes and soiled underwear. Some fell asleep during debates, and some drank too much in the evenings and arrived with hangovers the next morning. And some gambled recklessly, both on cards and female companionship, while others, like Mason and Washington, pined for distant loving wives and the comforts of home.[17] Meanwhile, reporters tried to pierce the veil of secrecy to discern what the delegates were doing.[18] To guarantee confidentiality, William Jackson, the Convention secretary, burned all loose scraps of paper and entrusted the official journals to George Washington's care—another act of tremendous faith in Washington's integrity.[19] The press sensed that something significant was afoot behind locked doors. Two of the three delegates from New York State had already gone home in protest of the secret meetings of the Convention. The Convention's confidentiality rule had stimulated candor in the deliberations behind closed doors, but it had also led to conspiracy theories from the outset. "I am sorry they began their deliberations by so abominable a precedent as that of tying up the tongues of their members," Jefferson complained to John Adams.[20]

After weeks of exhausting debates, the delegates would emerge with a plan that would completely erase the Articles of Confederation. They were writing a blueprint for a new nation.[21] Mason and his colleagues were addressing the issue of political power in an entirely new way. They were making a revolution in political thought. Mason put forward the idea that only in a large democracy with an extensive system of checks and balances could the rights of the people be protected from potential tyranny by the majority. Yet at the same time, from almost the beginning, Mason seemed skeptical of too much concentrated power in a centralized government. "These men had just come out of the war," comments historian Carol Berkin: "They had risked their lives to fight for no taxation without representation, and the power of local government, and all men are created equal. Within a few short years, what is being proposed but the creation of a central government that looks suspiciously to them just like the British government that they had been fighting against?"[22]

By the end of July, Mason, who had spent sweltering weeks and spoken 136 times on the Convention floor, knew that the Constitutional Convention had come to a crucial crossroad. He confided to a friend that "two or three days will probably enable us to judge— which is at present very doubtful—whether any sound and effectual system can be established or not."[23] Acutely disillusioned with the emerging Constitution, Mason would often write late into the night in the elegant apartments that had given the Indian Queen Inn its worthy reputation. Mason's tavern had come to serve as the unofficial nest of the Convention, hosting many lively debates among the delegates well into the evening.

The Convention faced many monumental issues. But none was more contentious than the nature and power of a republican "president." As an exercise in political theory, the formation of the office of the presidency may have been the most difficult task that Mason and his fellow delegates faced.[24] The fear that the presidency would evolve into a monarchy was real and palpable to Mason. His fledgling country had broken ties with a tyrannical king ten years earlier, and

Mason was extremely apprehensive of power concentrated in a single chief executive. According to presidential scholar Martin Sheffer, the political system Mason was adamant to design would accomplish two things: "ensure that the exercise of arbitrary, excessive, and dictatorial power would be prevented (and/or controlled) by the use of institutional and auxiliary constraints; and that every generation of the American people would be watchful and alert to the potential abuse of executive power. Executive power was never denied to the presidency; only its arbitrary, unconstitutional use was seen as dangerous to the principles of constitutional democracy."[25]

Mason's beliefs dictated that government must not be monolithic, or it would overwhelm individual liberties. He vigorously favored a separation of powers, with checks and balance. He could accept only a restrained presidential power, which he believed would be compatible with limited government.

When Mason rose as the first speaker on Thursday, July 26, he injected himself eagerly into the vigorous debate surrounding the presidency. After two months in Philadelphia, Mason was now comfortable in this larger arena. He was ready to do more. In the Convention's first days Mason had given speeches but he had not tried to control the debate agenda. Delegates like Madison and John Rutledge had framed most issues. On this day, however, with a heavy rain drumming against the windows of the State House, Mason posed important questions about the presidency: How should the president be chosen? How long should he serve? Should he be eligible for more than one term? The issues about the presidency seemed straightforward to the blunt George Mason, but were more complicated when studied closely. Most of Mason's colleagues, frustrated with the weakness of the government under the Articles of Confederation, wanted a presidency with vigor and vitality.

But the president should not be too strong, Mason warned again and again. That would risk monarchy and oppression. The goal was easily stated, Mason argued, but difficult to achieve. Mason pointed out that in many states, the legislature made the choice of the chief executive, but several allowed the people to elect the governor directly. Pennsylvania used a more complicated method, having the people vote for members of an Executive Council, with the Assembly selecting a president from that council.

One overriding personality loomed over the discussions about the presidency: George Washington. Every delegate, including Mason, assumed that the man who presided over them would be the first president under the new Constitution because of his war leadership and national stature. The intellectual challenge was imagining the successor to Washington. Mason and his colleagues had to design the presidency for the next man, who might not be a hero. A North Carolina delegate touched lightly on this point. Though current Americans, he said, knew the "distinguished characters" who might serve as president, in the future "this will not always be the case." Agreeing with Mason, Major Pierce Butler of South Carolina thought the delegates would grant the president too much power because they cast their eyes towards General Washington. The delegates, he feared, would shape the powers to be given to a president by their opinions of Washington's stature—trusting that whatever temporary defects might be written into the office of the presidency would be remedied by his monumental moral character. But after Washington transferred power to a successor, Mason asked, how could the delegates prevent the office from becoming an instrument of tyranny?[26]

As Convention president, Washington sat through extensive discussions of what would soon be his own job description. With his stoic image before their eyes, some delegates seemed governed by their hopes instead of their fears. And the delegates were on the horns of a dilemma: How could the Constitution restrict the presidency without giving affront to Washington, and perhaps even alienating him from the new government? George Mason's reiterated proposals for a three-person executive, for example, may have been voted down because the delegates feared that Washington would not be willing to serve under those conditions. As one historian has concluded, "Washington might not have accepted the presidency if it had consisted of a three-member executive committee, as Mason proposed."[27] The fact that most delegates overcame their dread of executive power and created a formidable presidency can be traced directly to Washington's intimidating presence. Still, with memories of the Revolution fresh in all their minds, Mason prevailed on the delegates to reserve significant powers for Congress, endowing it, for instance, with the authority to declare war, thereby avoiding the British precedent of a monarch who retained this awesome power.

But the Convention would resist most of Mason's proposals for limiting the president's powers and made the new chief executive so strong, so kinglike, precisely because the delegates expected Washington to be the first president. Indeed, George Washington was the only American in 1787 who possessed the dignity and reputation for republican virtue that the untried office of the presidency needed. Both Mason and Jefferson expected that Washington might be president for life, that he would be a kind of elective monarch.[28] Actually, Mason's fear of the executive turning into a king was not far-fetched. From the outset, according to prominent historian Gordon Wood, Washington's behavior often seemed regal in nature. "For example, his journey from Mount Vernon to the capital in New York in the spring of 1789 took on the air of a royal procession. He was saluted by cannons and celebrated in elaborate ceremonies along the way, as he was in the Philadelphia Convention. Everywhere he was greeted by triumphal rejoicing and acclamations of 'Long live George Washington!' James McHenry of Maryland told Washington in March 1789, 'you are now a King, under a different name,' and wished that the president 'may reign long and happy over us.'"[29] According to Wood, "It was not surprising therefore that some people referred to Washington's inauguration as a 'coronation.' So prevalent was the thinking that Washington resembled an elected monarch that some even expressed relief that he had no heirs."[30]

Even with the near certainty that Washington would be the first president, Mason was insistent upon restraining presidential power. He wanted to delete the power of the president to issue pardons for treason, "which may be sometimes exercised to screen from punishment those whom he had secretly instigated to commit the crime, and thereby prevent a discovery of his own guilt." He advocated that Congress should have not just legislative but "inquisitorial powers," which he said could "not safely be long kept in ... suspension." He attacked the Supremacy Clause because the House of Representatives had no role in making treaties, which meant that the people would be bound by treaties with the force of law even though the people's only elected representatives had not consented to them.[31]

In his argument for restricting the powers of the executive, Mason drew on his constitutional expertise and his knowledge of philosophers through the ages. From Aristotle Mason gained the rudiments of the political motives of man; Machiavelli gave him the theory of Realpolitik that made expediency the center of executive action; Hobbes instilled the notion in Mason of executive power as an attribute of sovereignty; Montesquieu contributed the theory of separation of powers and checks and balances. Mason had read Montesquieu thoroughly, perhaps more than any other philosopher.[32] A practical man, Mason viewed executive power as "capable of penetrating the remotest parts of the Union," while simultaneously bringing assistance to the states (a lesson he learned from Shays' Rebellion) during domestic unrest. But this new executive power had to exist in the face of widespread trepidation of monarchy. How could executive power be established to accomplish these purposes while being made safe for popular liberty?[33]

Throughout the Convention, Mason was concerned with correcting the deficiencies of the Articles of Confederation, but also with preventing tyranny. Under the Articles, Congress exercised both legislative and executive powers, in what was in effect a parliamentary government without the leadership of a prime minister. What he had learned from the defects of the Articles led him to favor more executive leadership, while what he had learned from a tyrannical king led him to favor less centralization of executive power. Thus Mason was determined to fashion a perfect compromise—a strong, but strictly limited, presidency.[34]

Mason's novel ideas concerning the chief executive, and its powers, duties, and role in the new central government were not only thought-provoking for his time. They are still extremely relevant some 250 years later.

He led a small band of dissenting delegates who had difficulty conceiving of a mighty presidency that did not look suspiciously like a monarchy. The very idea of a separate executive branch with a president independent of the legislature and able to veto its laws was regarded as almost heretical by Mason. Indeed, Benjamin Franklin agreed in principle with Mason, and so distrusted executive power that he advocated for a small "executive council" instead of a president. In advancing this idea, Franklin, with a figurative nod toward Washington, remarked that the first president would likely be benevolent. But Mason feared despotic tendencies in Washington's successors. He had felt the abuse of executive power and tried to stem it long before the Revolutionary War. An earlier period of executive dominance in the colonies had lasted until the French and Indian War, when the colonial legislatures brought the royal governors under legislative control through their management over supplies, money, and the armed forces. Leading up to the Revolution, Mason's experience—and that of Americans in general—was that the true ally of political liberty was the legislative branch, while its natural enemy was unbridled executive authority.[35]

So in most of the early state Constitutions, the governor was stripped of most of the prerogatives of his royal predecessor. And to further weaken executive power, most states required annual elections of the governor by the state legislature. The executive functions that remained were then restrained by a legislative council. Mason's Virginia Constitution of 1776 is a classic example of this constitutional structure.

In yet another check on "the executive powers of government," they were to be exercised "according to the laws" of the Commonwealth, and no power or prerogative was ever to be claimed "by virtue of any law, statute, or custom of England." In short, Mason held that executive power should be left to legislative definition and cut off from English constitutional usage and the resources of the common law.[36]

As his previous authorship of Virginia's Constitution makes clear, what Mason feared most in a central government was a too powerful executive. Suspicion of power, and most particularly of power concentrated in the hands of a single figure, was a central feature of Mason's thinking on the presidency.

Thus he made several innovative proposals to restrict executive authority in the course of constitutional debates: three men could compose the executive instead of a single person; the president could be appointed by the legislature or by the judiciary and subject to recall; veto power could be withheld from the president; the states could be vested with impeachment powers; the president might not be named commander-in-chief of the nation's military, nor be accorded a major role in setting foreign policy; the president could be limited to a single term.

While some other delegates were concerned that, in the words of South Carolina delegate John Rutledge, "we are leaning too much towards Monarchy," in the end, most of Mason's bold and unique ideas for curtailing executive power would be voted down by the Convention. But opposition did not deter his dogged determination to limit centralized power vested in the executive.

Mason would rise more than a hundred times to voice his opinion and offer cogent advice on the powers of the presidency before the Convention wrapped up its work nearly three months later in September 1787, as cooler weather finally trickled into Philadelphia. For him, it all came back to one constitutional question: How do you prevent a chief executive, a president, from evolving into a king?

Strange as it may seem to us today, the single-person executive was not a foregone conclusion. In fact, when delegate James Wilson moved that "the executive consist of a single person," the delegates sat speechless in their chairs. "A considerable pause ensuing," noted Madison, "and the chairman asking if he should put the question, Dr. Franklin observed that it was a point of great importance and wished that the gentlemen would deliver their sentiments on it before the question was put." A lively debate began immediately and revealed two things: The delegates agreed that a republican executive could not be modeled on the British monarchy, but the majority of delegates were more influenced than Mason by factors such as efficiency and responsibility that required a single-person executive. Mason led the dissenters, who variously favored either a plural executive, a kind of government by committee, or some form of ministerial government akin to the British cabinet. Indeed, fully twelve delegates, more than 25 percent of the total present when the issue was finally decided, so feared executive power that they sought to diffuse it among several persons.[37]

Time and again Mason voiced his fear of the power of a solitary official equipped with the power to veto legislation and to appoint federal officeholders. The president could use his patronage to corrupt Congress, Mason argued, the way the British monarchy had used a similar power to manipulate Parliament. According to the notes he made for himself in the course of the debates, Mason believed, "If strong extensive powers are vested in the Executive, and that executive consists of only one person, the government will of course degenerate (for I will call it degeneracy) into a monarchy."[38] Mason habitually proposed his three-person executive as a partial remedy for the lack of a "council of revision," which he had envisioned as an advisory panel of elder statesmen who could serve as a check on the executive. Mason knew that such councils had been common in the colonial governments. Internal competition within the three-person executive would be a means of "checking and counteracting the aspiring Views of dangerous and ambitious Men," so that the government would be grounded in "the invaluable Principles of Liberty."[39]

Interestingly, Mason's three-member presidency would have consisted of representatives chosen by region—one each from the Northern, Middle, and Southern states—thus guaranteeing a sectional balance. This would have ensured that the government could receive exact information on sectional interests. Mason's proposal for a multiple executive is evidence of his sensitivity to sectional differences. From the very beginning of the Convention, he feared that Southern interests would not be protected in the new government.[40]

The delegates generally seemed to consider a single executive to be the best and most efficient means of enforcing the laws of the Union, and the most secure way of ensuring accountability in the executive branch. Nevertheless, Mason was relentless in favoring a presidency by committee. He reasoned that a single executive would be controlled by his "Minions & Favorites."[41] And, while not a king, each successive president would arrogate tremendous power to the executive branch. He did have some support. Edmund Randolph favored a similar arrangement. Hugh Williamson of North Carolina was apparently the first delegate to raise the issue on the record when he proposed that "the Executive power ... be lodged in three men taken from districts into which the States should be divided."[42] Perhaps the idea was discussed informally among the delegates over dinner at the Indian Queen tavern. Neither Williamson's suggestion nor Mason's attracted much support among the delegates.[43]

Mason also considered a three-man council of advisors to the president to be an essential safeguard for the people and the states. In fact the lack of a council was one of the principal defects he would point to in his famous and widely circulated Objections to the Constitution: "The President of the United States has no Constitutional Council, a thing unknown in any safe and regular government. He will therefore be unsupported by proper information and advice, and will generally be directed by minions and favorites; or he will become a tool to the Senate—or a Council of State will grow out of the principal officers of the great departments; the worst and most dangerous of all ingredients for such a Council in a free country. From this fatal defect has arisen the improper power of the Senate in the appointment of public officers, and the alarming dependence and connection between that branch of the legislature and the supreme Executive."[44]

Mason also argued for limiting the length of time the executive would hold office. Initial proposals ranged from three years, to Mason's proposal of a single seven-year term with no possibility of reelection, to Hamilton's advocacy for a lifetime appointment. The final provision of the Constitution establishing a four-year term with the prospect of reelection was a significant compromise at the Convention. "The Executive Magistrate is now re-eligible," Roger Sherman wrote, ".... If he behaves well he will be continued; if otherwise, displaced on a succeeding election."[45] Making the president ineligible for reelection, argued Gouverneur Morris, would "destroy the great motive to good behavior, the hope of being rewarded by a reappoint-ment." An executive who was not eligible for reelection, he continued, would be tempted to "make hay while the sun shines," whereas desire for reelection would be an incentive to good behavior.[46]

On the other hand, "how could the executive be expected to discharge his duties conscientiously, free from improper legislative influence, unless he were made ineligible for reelection"?[47] And the possibility of reelection posed other dangers as well. A year later, in the Virginia Ratifying Convention, Mason would remark, "Mr. Chairman, there is not a more important article in the Constitution than this. The great fundamental principle of responsibility in repub-licanism is here sapped. The President is elected without rotation. It may be said that a new election may remove him, and place another in his stead. If we judge from the experience of all other countries, and even our own, we may conclude that, as the President of the United States may be reelected, so he will. How is it in every govern-ment where rotation is not required? Is there a single instance of a great man not being reelected? Our governor is obliged to return, after a given period, to a private station. It is so in most of the states. This President will be elected time after time: he will be continued in office for life."[48]

Mason vigorously opposed the proposal of one of his own Vir-ginia colleagues, James McClurg, that the executive should serve "during good behavior," calling it "a softer name only for an execu-tive for life … an easy step to hereditary monarchy." McClurg's reasoning was that "it was an essential object with him to make the Executive independent of the Legislature; and the only mode left for effecting it … was to appoint him during good behavior." Mason countered that it would be impossible to define "misbehavior" in such a way as to bring the executive to trial, nor would it be possible to compel such a person to submit to trial.

Mason's arguments about the all-too-powerful presidency fell on mostly deaf ears. The Convention voted seven states to three to establish "a single Executive." The divisive issue split the Virginia delegation: Mason, Randolph, and Blair voted against it; Madison, Washington, McClurg, and Wythe (who had already left the Convention and who cast a vote by proxy) supported it. The delegates did vote to limit the president to a single term of seven years, then later in the summer reduced the executive's term to six years but lifted the ban on a second term. When the Convention returned to the issue on July 26, Mason moved to reinstate language limiting the executive to a single seven-year term. Having for his primary object the preservation of the rights of the people, he argued that unlimited power in the executive was "an essential point." He feared that "the very palladium of Civil liberty" could "become an engine of imposition and tyranny."[49] In the end the delegates decided the president would serve four-year terms and be eligible for reelection.[50]

The office of presidency was fiercely controversial, producing heated polemics on both sides, not only at the Philadelphia Convention but in the battle to come over ratification of the Constitution. When Jefferson, still in Paris at the time, wrote to Adams, he asked, "how you do like our new constitution? I confess there are things in it which stagger all my dispositions to subscribe to what such an assembly has proposed." The details of the presidency troubled him for the same reasons as they troubled George Mason. "He may be reelected from 4 years to 4 years for life," Jefferson wrote: "Reason and experience prove to us that a chief magistrate, so continuable, is an officer for life. When one or two generations shall have proved that this is an office for life, it becomes on every succession worthy of intrigue, of bribery, of force, and even of foreign interference."[51] When he finally read the entire Constitution, Thomas Jefferson called the presidency "a bad edition of a Polish king."[52] William

Short, Jefferson's executive assistant, also viewing the new Constitution from Paris, did not sense immediate danger in the power concentrated in the executive. But he thought that "the President of the eighteenth century" would "form a stock on which will be grafted a King in the nineteenth."[53]

Mason and Jefferson would have a powerful ally in their skepticism over the new presidency: Patrick Henry. A president eligible for reelection as long as he lived, Henry argued, could easily become a despot, especially since he was given command of the army. Ordinary citizens needed protection against a government of such size and complexity. Moreover, they had a right to be suspicious of it. Henry predicted that if the Constitution were ratified, the president would use his constitutional powers to make himself king and "enslave America."[54] In short, Henry thought that, though Congress had the war-initiation power, the president was dangerous domestically because he commanded the army. Henry's fear was not that the president would order the army to attack a foreign nation, but that the president would order the army to overthrow the U.S. government.[55]

Unlike Mason, most delegates eventually agreed that their new country needed a strong executive leader with "the vigour of Monarchy" while the "manners ... are purely republican," in the words of Pennsylvania delegate James Wilson. Yet they were uncertain what powers should be delegated to the executive. Mason himself wanted the president to have the power to achieve what James Wilson characterized as "vigorous execution of the Laws."[56] But he never let go of his fear of an evolving monocracy.

During the remaining six weeks of the Convention, the debates became more rushed and more focused, and far and away the most momentous changes the delegates made were to the powers of the executive. It was not until the end of the Convention that the delegates finally delineated the powers of the executive and distinguished them from those of the legislature. Congress would have the commercial powers (taxation and regulation); the naturalization power; the power to establish courts; and the power to declare war, raise armies, build and equip navies, and "provide for calling forth the Militia to execute the Laws of the Union, suppress Insurrections and repel Invasions."[57] All of these powers were assigned to the legislature. In the final report of the Committee of Detail, the major duties of the president were to see that the laws were "duly and faithfully executed" and to serve as commander-in-chief of the armed forces.[58] The president would also enjoy a limited veto over Acts of Congress. The president was given the power to make treaties and appoint ambassadors and judges with the Senate's approval. He was given unlimited authority to grant pardons and reprieves and receive ambassadors.

Interestingly, Mason strongly advocated that two of the powers of the presidency be left to the Senate: the power to make treaties, and the power to appoint ambassadors and justices of the Supreme Court. Giving war powers to the president also troubled Mason, though to Hamilton it seemed like the self-evident choice, as he explained in a condescending rebuke of Mason, summarily dismissing arguments against the president's role as commander-in-chief: "The President of the United States is to be Commander in chief of the Army and Navy of the United States, and of the militia of the several States when called into the actual service of the United States. The propriety of this provision is so evident in itself; and it is at the same time so consonant to the precedents of the state constitutions in general, that little need be said to explain or enforce it."[59] Mason vigorously continued to oppose executive war powers, declaring that he "admitted the propriety of his [the president] being commander-in-chief, so far as to give orders and have a general superintendency, but he thought it would be dangerous to let him command in person, without any restraint, as he might make a bad use of it."[60] Mason believed Congress should be required to authorize personal command of the military, for, as he reminded his fellow delegates, "so disinterested and amiable a character as General Washington might never command again." As one scholar has concluded, "Mason ... wanted safeguards against the possibility of a military dictatorship."[61] The liberty of the people, Mason declared, had frequently been destroyed by military commanders. According to one historian, Mason recognized the danger of "the junction of great civil powers to the command of the army and fleet. Although Congress was to raise the army, said Mason, 'no security arises from that; for, in time of war, they must and ought to raise an army, which will be numerous, or otherwise, according to the nature of the war, and then the President is to command without any control.'"[62]

Mason won few victories in his vigorous battle against what he saw as too much power concentrated in the executive. The majority of the delegates apparently found the safeguards in the Constitution sufficient. As Alexander Hamilton pointed out, the president would not be the chief legislator, would not have unchecked power over the military or foreign policy, could not rule by decree, and would have no control over "the commerce or currency of the nation." According to Hamilton, the Constitution actually gives the president few and defined powers. [63]

Perhaps Mason's greatest contribution to the debate over the presidency was his addition to the Impeachment Clause. Of paramount importance to Mason was how to remove a bad president. He personally added the immortal words "high crimes and misdemeanors" to the Constitution. Mason and Franklin successfully argued for removal of the president by legislative impeachment, an English practice for discharging the king's ministers. Franklin thought the power of impeachment would not only preserve republican government, but would be "favorable to the executive": "It would be the best way there-fore to provide in the Constitution for the regular punishment of the Executive when his misconduct should deserve it, and for his honorable acquittal when he should be unjustly accused." And Elbridge Gerry of Massachusetts (who would serve as vice president under Madison) in blunt fashion, added, "A good magistrate will not fear them [impeach-ments]. A bad one ought to be kept in fear of them. He hoped the maxim would never be adopted here that the chief Magistrate could do [no] wrong."[64]

Having no political ambitions and little concern about offending Washington, Mason put the matter frankly: "Shall any man be above justice? Above all, shall that man be above it who can commit the most extreme injustice?" Without impeachment, Mason urged, the only way to remove an unjust leader was assassination. Impeachment would permit "regular punishment" or "honorable acquittal." Impeachment should be available to curb abuses of executive power, Mason wrote, but it should not be so easy as to provide Congress with a device by which it could dominate the president.[65]

Gouverneur Morris thought only "treachery" or "bribery" and corruption should be grounds for impeachment, but Mason believed those grounds were too limited. He suggested that "Mal-administra-tion" should be a sufficient a basis for removal from office, but when he failed to persuade the delegates, he suggested the now famous term "high crimes and misdemeanours" as an alternative. Borrowed from English law, the phrase went into the Constitution, and into history. Madison went so far as to advocate that acts of a purely partisan nature could be "misdemeanors."[66]

Interestingly enough, Mason believed federal judges would be called upon to decide impeachment cases, and, in part to maintain their independence, he opposed presidential appointment of the fed-eral judiciary. He would have allowed Congress to pick judges.[67]

In Mason's view, the method by which the president could be removed from office was connected to every other crucial question at the Convention. If the president's term in office was long, should he be confined to one term? If he could serve multiple terms, should not the selection process protect against corrupt scheming for extra terms? The answers to these questions were interconnected, so changing one answer could change the answers to others.

The two remaining items to be resolved at the Convention were the reworking of the executive power clause—into its present, open-ended form—by Gouverneur Morris and the Committee of Style, and deciding on a method of presidential election. Having decided how to remove a president, the delegates struggled with how to choose one. After long and tedious debates, Pierce Butler's Committee of Eleven was appointed to resolve all unsettled questions. The Committee finally settled on the indirect Electoral College system, which was a modification of the method earlier suggested by James Wilson.[68]

The existence of the Electoral College is evidence of how far the delegates were prepared to go to prevent a direct popular majority from choosing a potential tyrant. Nothing else so clearly reveals their distrust of direct democracy.[69] The Framers, and Mason in particular, feared that a scattered population could never "be sufficiently informed of characters" to choose wisely among what the delegates assumed would be a large field of candidates. Believing that popular election was impractical, many of them at first saw no alternative to having Congress choose the executive. But this raised other objections. Mason, who had strong objections to popular election of the president, also feared collusion between the Senate and a presidential candidate. An election by Congress would be "the work of intrigue, cabal, and of faction," Gouverneur Morris asserted. "Real merit" would be passed over.[70]

As the debates went on, Mason's opposition to popular election seemed to harden. In a country the size of America, the people would know too little about candidates for national office. A popular election would be dominated by the nation's only organized interest group, former Continental army officers, he argued: "A popular election in any form … would throw the appointment into the hands of the Cincinnati, a Society for the members of which he had a great respect; but he never wished to have a preponderating influence in the government," Mason declared. The example struck uncomfortably close to Washington, who had recently headed that organization of former army officers. Most of the delegates agreed with Mason, but they struggled throughout the Convention to find an alternative to direct elections.[71]

Mason's views and language on the election of the president were sharp. As Jefferson observed, his words were "strengthened by a dash of biting cynicism when provocation made it seasonable." Eventually, on this topic, Mason felt provoked. Noting the "difficulty of the subject and the diversity of the opinions concerning it," he insisted that presidents should be selected by those who know the candidates best, whereas popular election would assign it to "those who know least." He complained that "it would be as unnatural to refer the choice of a chief magistrate to the people, as it would, to refer a trial of colors to a blind man." The Convention appointed a new committee to consider, among other items, what James Wilson called "in truth the most difficult of all [the questions] on which we have to decide," the process for electing the president. The chief justice of the New Jersey Supreme Court, David Brearly, reported for the Committee on September 4. The plan the Convention finally adopted, proposed by delegate Oliver Ellsworth, was for election of the president by an "Electoral College." Two Electors would be chosen by the legislature of each state to cast two votes each for president, at least one of which would have to be for a

Portrait of George Mason at age twenty-four. By Dominic W. Boudet, after John Hesselius's original painting, which is now lost. *Gunston Hall*

Portrait of Ann Eilbeck, George Mason's first wife, at age sixteen. By Dominic Boudet, after John Hesselius's original painting, now lost, commemorating their marriage. *Gunston Hall*

George Mason's portable writing desk, open as he would have used it for writing. Language that would be adopted in the founding documents of the United States and protect Americans' rights for over two centuries was almost certainly drafted on this surface.

The numerous large eighteenth-century Mason plantations (marked by red squares) in Virginia and Maryland, in relation to other major estates nearby (marked by blue squares). As George Mason's son John would write, "At that time, all the best families of the state were seated on the tidewater of the rivers." *Gunston Hall*

Gunston Hall, the house George Mason built in the 1750s on "Dogue's Neck," now "Mason's Neck." View from the Magnolia Avenue. *Gunston Hall*

Inside Gunston Hall. The entrance hall and the carved staircase to the second floor. In the musicians' gallery at the head of the stairs, fiddlers played while planters and their ladies danced to measured minuets. Much of Gunston Hall was built by slaves, including both unskilled laborers and skilled craftsmen, but this balustrade was probably carved by convicts from England under the supervision of English architect William Buckland, who, as Mason wrote on the back of Buckland's indenture, "had the entire Direction of the Carpenters and Joiners work" of Mason's "large house." *Gunston Hall*

The formal dining room at Gunston Hall. This "Chinese Chippe Room," the only one of its kind in Virginia and the earliest known use of Chinese motifs in colonial architecture. The cornice designs may have been inspired by reversed scallops on the canopy of a Chinese sofa in *Chippendale's Director*, an architectural pattern book owned by Gunston Hall architect William Buckland. The yellow of the paint on the high Palladian windows was the most expensive imported pigment, even more costly than the green at George Washington's Mount Vernon. *Gunston Hall*

The Masons' informal family dining room, which doubled as George Mason's study. His sons and grandsons heard him say that he used this walnut writing table when he wrote the Virginia Declaration of Rights. *Gunston Hall*

Gunston Hall's Palladian parlor. In this room with its intricately carved chimney breast, gilded beaufats, broken pediments, and sweeping view of the Potomac riverfront, George Mason entertained guests, including George Washington. *Gunston Hall*

The modest master bedroom at Gunston Hall, with closets where the Masons kept sweets and other delicacies, the family's clothes, and "the Green Doctor," a riding crop used sparingly to spank the children. *Gunston Hall*

George Mason V, the son of our George Mason. He built a plantation house named Lexington after the battle that started the Revolutionary War, suffered from ill health all his life, and died just four years after his father. *Gunston Hall*

John Mason, George Mason's son and the author of *The Recollections of John Mason: George Mason's Son Remembers His Father and Life at Gunston Hall*. John was probably the closest to his father of all George Mason's children. *Gunston Hall*

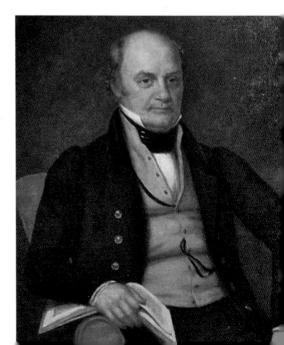

View of the Potomac, Virginia. Engraved by J. Jeackes, after a painting by W. Roberts. In the years leading up to the Revolutionary War, Mason's experiences with the Ohio Company, in an attempt to add Western lands to his holdings, was one factor in his growing frustration with British governance. *Library of Virginia*

Depiction, by an unknown artist, of George Mason and a slave at an Alexandria tavern. *Library of Congress*

This silver Monteith or bowl for chilling wine glasses was made around the year 1700 and served as the Mason family christening bowl for generations. George Mason's last will and testament instructed that it "remain in the family unaltered for that purpose." *Gunston Hall*

The grave of George and Ann Mason in the family burying ground at Gunston Hall. *Gunston Hall*

candidate from another state. If no candidate received a majority of the electoral votes, the Senate would select from among the top five vote-getters. The first runner-up would become vice president.[72]

In the end, the Electoral College was one of the most complex and controversial provisions of the Constitution. It was viewed as the ideal compromise, and Mason finally acquiesced. The states were the critical element in the Electoral College, argued Mason. That was how the institution should be viewed, as an agent of the will of the people of the states.[73]

The debate over the Electoral College created strange bedfellows. Mason, the great critic of centralized power, agreed with the nationalist Gouverneur Morris that, because the electors would vote in their home states, "the danger of cabal and corruption" had been greatly reduced.[74]

The key discussions during the final months of the Convention that led to the adoption of the Electoral College took place within the secrecy of the "Committee on Postponed Parts." Very little is known about what was said during its debates, but some idea may be gleaned from its final report, read on September 4. In the report, the office of the president suddenly enjoyed significant responsibility for foreign affairs and the power to appoint ambassadors, judges, and other officials, with the "advice and consent" of the Senate. At the same time, the president's election by an Electoral College promised to make him politically independent of Congress. The report also specified a four-year term and eligibility for reelection. It was assumed that the large states would enjoy the advantage in promoting candidates for the presidency. But if an election failed to produce a majority—as many delegates thought it usually would—the election would fall to the Senate, where the small states would have greater influence.

Of all the men fighting for limited executive power in the Constitution, George Mason was paramount. He made the American presidency a powerful but limited office that combined the symbolic authority of an elected monarch with the substantive role of prime minister responsible for overseeing domestic and foreign policy. Mason had applied the prism of broad knowledge and deep thought on constitutional matters to the office of the presidency. In so doing, he served as midwife to the true spirit of liberty in America: liberty of thought, speech, and religion, liberty for self-government balanced and coexisting with executive leadership. Mason and the other Framers were patriotic men of varied capacities who rose above their passions and self-interest to forge a grand document. But, as one historian has written, "they left Philadelphia viewing the Constitution as a hopeful experiment whose results and meanings would be made known only through time."[75]

Delegate William Pierce of Georgia aptly described Mason's contributions throughout the Convention as those of a man "of remarkable strong powers" with a "clear and copious understanding," who was "able and convincing in debate, steady and firm in his principles, and undoubtedly one of the best politicians in America."[76] As historian Carl Becker put it, Mason believed that "the only thing to do with political power, since it is inherently dangerous, is to abate it."[77]

CHAPTER ELEVEN

Objections

—

At the Philadelphia Convention Mason took an active
part in all the proceedings and was unquestionably
one of its most useful members, although he finally
refused to sign.... Of all the opponents of the Con-
stitution either in Virginia or any other state, he was
beyond doubt the ablest constructive statesman.[1]

— **JAMES MONTGOMERY BECK,** Pennsylvania Congressman (1933)

A t the start of the Convention, Mason had acted hand in
hand with delegates who wanted to create a more cohesive
central government. Over the next three months, however,
he became increasingly wary about the emerging Constitution.
Mason recognized a dangerous trend: power and sovereignty
shifted from state and individual rights to the federal level. Despite
his commitment to representative democracy, Mason took a jaded
view of majorities.

Mason's deep skepticism of unchecked federal power soon began
to show through. He demanded that the delegates "attend to the
rights of every class of the people." Mason said that he "had often
wondered at the indifference of the superior classes of society to this
dictate of humanity."[2] Yet more and more of his colleagues favored
giving additional power to a centralized government, with little
authority left to the states, and little protection for the rights of the
people. This was alarming to Mason, and he finally vented his

mounting frustration on paper. Mason's seventeen "Objections" to the nearly completed federal Constitution became, arguably, one of the most famous and influential political dissents in American history.

George Mason was not a rebel by nature. But near the end of the Convention, Mason stayed up well past midnight and penned seventeen "Objections" to the nearly complete Constitution. He wrote them on the back of the Committee of Style report. His words were clear. The most comfortable arena for Mason was a study, and his most natural podium, his writing desk. Ever since his early days reading law and history in his Uncle's library, Mason had spent a great deal of his time alone, reading and taking extensive notes on what he read. He would copy passages from Coke on the law. Solitary study allowed him to work out his perspective. Mason was a philosopher, a ceaseless striver at work with a quill pen and analytical mind, suffused with Enlightenment ideas about the individual rights of man versus governmental intrusion. The document he now wrote on a small wooden desk flowed naturally both from his character and from his deep-seated convictions.[3]

Over the last three months George Mason had endured blazing sun, bitter debates, intellectual fights, compromises, and the betrayal of allegiances. Now, in the final weeks of the Convention, Mason longed for the comfort of his family back home at Gunston Hall. The slow pace and acrimony of the summer had taken its toll on Mason— and not only on him. Attendance at the Convention began to wane, with delegates leaving for home early. Among the first to leave from the Virginia delegation had been George Wythe, Jefferson's law tutor, who left to go home and care for his ailing wife. Wythe's departure left Mason as the only member of the Virginia House of Delegates who was also serving in the Convention. He worried that when the time came for a report to the state legislature, "the whole weight of explanation must fall upon me."[4]

But the domestic Mason, notoriously averse to public service away from home, stayed in Philadelphia. He would make a stand for the rights of the people and against the encroachment of government power. He would argue in pointed language, bringing to bear his wide, deep knowledge of history and political philosophy, for Americans "yet unborn."

Some of the delegates had already been on the receiving end of Mason's blistering lectures on historical precedents and constitutional government. Gaining confidence as he repeatedly rose to his feet throughout the Convention, Mason evolved into a rhetorical force, part actor, part preacher in the pulpit. He could go on for hours at a time without notes, always casting a spell. He had already lost some friendships.

But the one thing Mason had not lost was the respect of his colleagues. In fact, he had gained a modicum of admiration from many adversaries in the Convention. Though not as tall as Washington, Mason commanded attention with his erect posture, formal manner, and sharp insights. His years gave weight to his views, which were also reinforced by his candor and lack of political ambition. When Virginia governor Edmund Randolph first met Mason, he commented on the older man's "indifference for distinction ... his hatred for pomp."[5] A Georgian at the Convention shared Randolph's high opinion of Mason: "Mr. Mason is a gentleman of remarkable strong powers and possesses a clear and copious understanding. He is able and in debate, steady and firm in his principles."[6]

But peers and friends would soon desert the sixty-one-year-old patriot. To the alarm of his Virginia colleagues, especially George Washington, Mason boldly wrote out his most powerful objections to the emerging Constitution: First, he pointed out, "There is no Declaration of Rights." His second point was a scathing indictment of the new presidency. The recurring theme throughout all of Mason's specific objections was simple—the proposed Constitution placed far too much power in a national government. This, Mason reasoned, was the principal weakness in the newly formed document: too much power, and uncertain control of it. These two central and inextricably linked criticisms of the document would consume Mason's life over the next two years. His writing, speaking, and debating about these would cost him greatly, both personally and professionally. The list of objections that Mason wrote on the back of the Committee of Style report in the last two weeks of the Convention would become a platform for critics of the Constitution.

First and foremost, Mason wrote, the Constitution did not include a "bill of rights," or a "declaration of any kind" for preserving liberty of the press, trial by jury in civil cases, or defending against "the danger of standing armies in time of peace." As Mason wrote bitterly, "Here is no declaration of rights, and the Laws of the general Government being paramount to the Laws & Constitutions of the several States, the Declarations of Rights in the separate States are no Security. Nor are the People secured even in the Enjoyment of the Benefit of the common Law."[7] He wanted a "declaration of rights" to sharply define the line between the federal and state governments in order to prevent "that dangerous clashing of interest and power, which must, as it now stands, terminate in the destruction of one or the other." Without a Declaration of Rights, the federal judiciary in particular, Mason suggested, threatened the state governments. He was not willing to sign without a Bill of Rights, but with amendments that protected the states he would "most gladly" put his hand to the Constitution. The amendments, he implied, would have to come before its adoption.

No one doubted Mason's sincerity, for his reputation as a champion of rights was well known before the Convention. Most delegates knew that he was a scion of a wealthy planter family, and that the sixty-two-year old had authored his own state's Declaration of Rights, making Virginia the first state to guarantee freedom of the press, tolerance of religion, protection from unreasonable searches, and the right to a fair and speedy trial. Yet Mason had only two staunch allies in his quest for a "declaration of rights"—his Virginia colleague Governor Edmund Randolph, and wealthy Massachusetts delegate Elbridge Gerry, a member of the "codfish aristocracy" north of Boston. In one author's assessment: "Gerry was a strange ally for George Mason. A New Englander, slender and of average height, with a broad forehead and a long, sharp nose, he was nineteen years younger than Mason, and a college man to boot (Harvard 1762). But Gerry, unlike Mason, had no family to leave behind. Gerry came from the town of Marblehead, on the coast north of Boston, where his father had made a fortune shipping."[8]

Mason's Virginia colleague Richard Henry Lee opposed a formal Bill of Rights, arguing that the rights of the people were so well understood that it was "not uncommon for the ablest men" to assume they did not need to be "constantly kept in view ... in [a] bills of rights.[9] So did George Washington.

Mason vainly tried to persuade his old friend of the need to include a Declaration of Rights in the Constitution. Washington, staid and austere in his demeanor as chairman of the Convention, rebuffed his former mentor, deeming a Bill of Rights superfluous.[10] To Mason's chagrin, Washington was greatly influenced by James Madison. Under Madison's political guidance, Washington was concerned that critics would subvert the new political system by "attempting premature amendments." Even two years later, when aide David Humphreys drafted President Washington's original inaugural speech, the General was still worried that agitation for a Bill of Rights was being exploited by forces opposed to the new federal government under the Constitution: "I will barely suggest whether it would not be the part of prudent men to observe [the Constitution] fully in movement before they undertook to make such alterations as might prevent a fair experiment of its effects?" [11]

Madison emerged as the voice of fierce opposition to Mason's call for a formal Declaration of Rights. Next to Mason, Madison was the best prepared of all the speakers at the Convention. Madison attended all the debates in Philadelphia, and he possessed the most complete set of notes. "To prepare for the Federal Convention," one historian has observed, "Madison plowed through an entire 'literary cargo' of books that Jefferson forwarded from Paris. A skillful legislator, secretive and canny, he exerted his influence in mysteriously indirect ways. Political foes who underrated James Madison did so at their peril."[12]

In response to Mason's call for a Bill of Rights, Madison insisted that the Constitution itself was a Bill of Rights, for it declared and specified "the political privileges of the citizens in the structure and administration of government." The Constitution created a government of only limited powers, and American citizens would retain all rights that they did not expressly renounce in the Constitution. To affix a Bill of Rights to the Constitution, Madison argued, would even be "dangerous" because it would contain "various exceptions to powers not granted ... and would afford a colorable pretext" to claim the very powers upon which restraint was sought. "Why declare that things shall not be done for which there is no power to do?" asked Madison.

But as Mason reasoned, clouds of construction and inference had obscured the people's rights in the past, and could do so again in the future. From classical political study he knew that protection for popular liberty had remained uncertain in England until the Bill of Rights of 1689 spelled out rights that had only been implied. Mason believed that the colonists had successfully opposed this "constructive power" of Great Britain in the Revolution, and now "the most important thing that could be thought of was to exclude the possibility of construction and implication" by making "a bill of rights." No one in 1776, Mason emphasized, had been satisfied to leave their rights to the vagaries of political interpretation, and neither should they now.

Hence a formal Bill of Rights was "indispensably necessary" before Mason could give his seal of approval to the Constitution. "A general positive provision should be inserted in the new system," Mason proposed, "securing to the states and the people every right which was not conceded to the general government" and doing away with "every implication."

As Mason well knew, a volatile alliance of aristocrats and commoners had made the Revolution successful. Each faction claimed "liberty" as its polestar and presented itself as the faithful guardian of Revolutionary values. Mason's struggle with Madison and Washington over the powers in the Constitution was a fight over the meaning of political liberty—and the last real battle of the Revolution. Mason was convinced that the fundamental principles of the Revolution stood in jeopardy.

The man from Gunston Hall regarded the people's rights as too sacred and important to be left to "implication." Why not exclude "the possibility of dispute" by stating them explicitly—especially if doing so suited the "genius" of the people?[13] "A Declaration of Rights would give great quiet to the people; and with the aid of the state declarations, a bill might be prepared in a few hours." He thought a compromise could be reached before the end of the Convention—that a "general principle laid down on this and some other points would be sufficient."

Mason mentioned "some other points" because the lack of a Declaration of Rights was not his only objection to the Constitution. Mason objected to the principle of a consolidated, all powerful government and insisted that it violated the spirit of the Revolution.

He wrote to his old associate, the fiery orator Patrick Henry, with whom Mason said he had "long toiled in the vineyard of liberty," that he had made "a common insistence upon amendments—especially a bill of rights—prior to ratification. Otherwise the powerful new government would be, from the outset, an elective despotism."[14] Patrick Henry, who had declined to serve in the Constitutional Convention, would agree wholeheartedly with Mason's insistence on an explicit Declaration of Rights. He echoed Mason's argument that a state Declaration of Rights would not protect against the power of the new federal government: "You have a Bill of Rights to defend you against the State Government, which is bereaved of all power; and yet you have none against Congress, though [it is] in full and exclusive possession of all power! You arm yourselves against the weak and defenseless, and expose yourselves naked to the armed and powerful."[15]

And Patrick Henry was not the only rhetorical hero of the Revolution who would be appalled by the Constitution. After the Convention, Madison would send Jefferson, then in Paris, an outline of the Constitution, not knowing that Jefferson had already received a copy from John Adams. The author of the Declaration of Independence was made livid by what he read. "How do you like our new Constitution?" he asked Adams. "I must confess there are things in it which stagger all my dispositions to subscribe to what such an assembly has proposed." Jefferson had expected only a few new amendments to be added to "the good, old, and venerable fabrick" of the Articles of Confederation."

Jefferson's view echoed Mason's: first and most troubling to him was the omission of a Bill of Rights, which would guarantee freedom of religion, habeas corpus, trial by juries, freedom of the press, and protection against standing armies. "The people are entitled to a bill of rights against every government on earth," Jefferson insisted to

Madison. Madison responded that he thought a Bill of Rights was unnecessary. Madison conceded that he and Jefferson seemed to be on different pages. While he was not opposed to the idea of a Bill of Rights in principle, "I have never thought the omission [of a Bill of Rights] a material defect, nor for any other reason than it is anxiously desired by others.... I have not viewed it in an important light." All Bills of Rights, Madison thought, were "parchment barriers," easily ignored and violated "by overbearing majorities in every state."[16]

As the Convention moved to conclusion and the Constitution took its final shape, Mason, Gerry, and Randolph formed a "dissident caucus." When the other delegates rejected Mason and Gerry's plan to preface the Constitution with a Bill of Rights, "it was the final straw," Mason complained. Not mincing words, he insisted "that he would sooner chop off his right hand than put it to the Constitution as it now stands." If his objections were not satisfied, his "wish would then be to bring the whole subject before another general Convention." Mason charged that the Convention had violated the basic tenet of republican government: "This Constitution has been formed without the knowledge or idea of the people. A second Convention will know more of the sense of the people, and be able to provide a system more consonant to it. It was improper to say to the people, take this or nothing."[17]

In September, with the Convention almost over and the Constitution largely complete, it seemed too late for major changes. Yet a North Carolina delegate raised an issue. Although the Constitution guaranteed trial by jury in criminal cases, it was silent about juries in civil trials. Mason sensed a larger opportunity: agreeing that civil jury trials should be guaranteed, he again took up the argument for the addition of a formal Bill of Rights. Gerry made the motion and Mason provided the promised second. They knew a Bill of Rights could be written quickly. Luther Martin, a lawyer

and delegate from Maryland, had drafted one before leaving Philadelphia the week before, though it had not been presented to the
Convention. Roger Sherman of Connecticut spoke against the
motion. He supported "the rights of the people," he said, but he was
sure that the state constitutions adequately protected them. Mason
responded with the observation that the "Laws of the U.S. are to be
paramount to State Bills of Rights."[18]

Mason's assurance that a Bill of Rights could be drafted quickly
fell on deaf ears. No doubt Mason could have drafted a Bill of Rights
within a matter of a day or even hours, but how long it would have
taken the delegates to agree on a draft would have been another matter. The Convention had already lasted longer than most delegates
had anticipated, a grueling four months. The room was saturated with
exasperation. The delegates knew from their experiences over the last
three months that nothing at the Convention was done quickly. A
nightmare vision arose of days, if not weeks of heated debate. What
rights would they agree to include? How could they be certain these
were the most deserving of protection? Did the inclusion of some
rights mean the exclusion of all others? There was furious opposition
to Mason's proposal.

Pennsylvania's Gouverneur Morris resisted any further editing or
refining of the Convention's work, and with no more debate, every
state delegation voted against Mason's proposed Bill of Rights.[19] After
four long, sweltering, and acrimonious months, the omission of a Bill
of Rights may have owed as much to the delegates' desire to return to
their homes and families as it did to political theory. The scorching
weather continued to make the delegates anxious to end their business. "At each inhaling of air," wrote one visitor to Philadelphia, "one
worries about the next one. The slightest movement is painful." Many
of the delegates from nearby states had taken the opportunity to
return home, while those from farther away fled to the countryside.

Washington, in his usual taciturn style, recorded in his journal, "In company with Mr. Govr. Morris and in his Phaeton with my horses, went up to one Jane Moore's (in whose house we lodged) in the vicinity of Valley Forge to get Trout."[20]

Toward the end, the delegates became less tolerant of civil discussion. Connecticut's Oliver Ellsworth was dubbed "endless Ellsworth" for his prolific speeches. Ellsworth, who had been expelled from Yale for hijinks such as poisoning the communal bread, employed a heavy-handed mockery in the final debates, referring to one delegate as a liar and another as subject to insanity.

Tempers were short. Ironically, it was Alexander Hamilton who prevented a duel between a Georgia delegate and a merchant. When Hamilton presented the merchants' apology, the delegate professed himself satisfied and withdrew his challenge. Although Hamilton enjoyed an intellectual fight, even he seemed surprised at the personal vitriol on display at the time of the final Convention debates. He read a pair of New York newspaper articles with the byline "Inspector" that portrayed Hamilton as "Tom Shit," a bastard of mixed racial origins, and referred to Washington as his "immaculate daddy." Both charges were completely false, but they haunted Hamilton for the rest of his life.

As the delegates edged toward final, frantic agreement, Madison thought of only one way to describe the outcome of their hundreds of hours of often abrasive argument: it was a miracle. He tried to explain Mason's opposing attitude: "A number of little circumstances arising in part from impatience which prevailed towards the close of business conspired to whet Mason's acrimony."[21] Rancor turned into warning when Mason concluded his written Objections with this prophecy: "This government will commence in a moderate aristocracy; it is at present impossible to foresee whether it will, in its operation, produce a monarchy or a corrupt oppressive aristocracy: it will

most probably vibrate some years between the two, and then terminate in the one or the other."

George Mason struck the most damaging blow to the Constitution as it went to the states for ratification. His one-sentence alarm,
"there is no Declaration of Rights," filled "Anti-Federalist" newspapers—a term that would soon take on a negative connotation.[22]
Critics of the Constitution began to talk about the need for "necessary amendments" or even "for a second Convention" to correct the
Constitution's errors. In retrospect, some historians have called the
omission of a Bill of Rights "the greatest blunder" in the Constitutional Convention.

Mason's seventeen objections to the Constitution would, in prac-
ticality, have required a significant recasting of the document to meet
some of his most grave concerns. He would continue to insist that the
people and their chosen representatives should be able to "amend"
the Constitution to their wishes before it went into effect.

George Mason had endured punishing fatigue and lonely times
during the last days of the Convention. With the finish line in sight,
the delegates became less tolerant of his protestations. Mason now
stood apart from the three dozen colleagues with whom he had
worked for months. He, Gerry, and Randolph were dissenting from
an overwhelming consensus supported by America's greatest national
heroes, George Washington and Benjamin Franklin. Would Americans honor the dissenters for their principles, or would they be seen
as vain and egotistical?

On Wednesday, September 12, 1787, the Convention's task seemed
largely complete. A five-man Committee of Style had delivered the final
draft of the new Constitution. Gouverneur Morris, the flamboyant and
talented delegate from Pennsylvania, had worked on the cover letter to
Congress that would accompany the new charter.[23] For Mason and the
other delegates most skeptical of the draft Constitution, a sense of dread

mounted near the end. Elbridge Gerry shared with his wife his prophetic fears. "I am exceedingly distressed at the proceedings of the
Convention," he wrote, "and almost sure they will if not altered mate-
rially lay the foundation of a civil war." He predicted, "the sovereignty
or liberty of the states will be destroyed." Gerry remained in Philadelphia, he explained, only "to prevent my colleagues from saying that I
broke up" the Massachusetts delegation. Randolph echoed Gerry,
declaring the Constitution "would end in tyranny," while as we have
seen Mason could not decide between two disastrous outcomes: aristocracy or monarchy.

In the final analysis, most delegates had lingering objections to
the Constitution but assented to the document. As historian Pauline
Maier, concluded, "[Hamilton] would sign the Constitution despite
his misgivings … because the alternatives were "anarchy and Convulsion on the one side," and, on the other, a remote chance that the
Constitution would do some good. Gouverneur Morris, who was
Washington's fishing partner and one of the most influential nationalists in the Federal Convention, said he also had objections but
would support the Constitution "with all its faults" as "the best that
was to be attained."[24] And Benjamin Franklin, at eighty, the oldest
delegate and, because of his achievements in science and diplomacy,
the only one who rivaled Washington in reputation, confessed that
there were "several parts of this constitution which I do not at present
approve." He thought, however, that he might change his mind in the
future, as he so often had over his long life, on account of "better
information, or fuller consideration." Franklin consented to the
Constitution "with all its faults, if they are such," because the country needed a general government and he doubted that another Convention could produce a better one.[25]

On Saturday, September 15, the Convention's last day of substantive business, Franklin addressed a final plea for unity to Mason. He

pushed his bifocals onto the top of his head and said, "I cannot help expressing a wish that every member of the Convention who may still have objection to [the Constitution] would with me, on this occasion, doubt a little of his own infallibility—and to make manifest our unanimity, put his name to this instrument."[26]

Gouverneur Morris had contrived a stratagem to secure those last signatures, making the support for the new Constitution look unanimous. Rather than have the signatories attest that they personally agreed with the Constitution, Morris drafted the following statement to appear above the signatures: "Done in Convention, by the unanimous consent of the states [not, that is, of the delegates] present.... In witness whereof we have hereunto subscribed our names." In this way, the signers affirmed only that the states had voted for the Constitution, as indeed they had. This was partly successful. A North Carolina delegate who had originally refused to sign "was relieved by the form proposed" and agreed to sign it. But even after James Wilson read a long, eloquent speech by Franklin calling on the reluctant delegates to sign the Constitution, Randolph refused. He wrote that this, "might be the most awful [decision] of his life, but it was dictated by his conscience." Gerry also refused, responding dramatically that he feared the Constitution would only aggravate the division in Massachusetts between "two parties, one devoted to democracy, the worst of all political evils, the other as violent in the opposite extreme."[27]

The principal target of the plea—George Mason—remained unwavering. He had come to Philadelphia with every intention of forming a new but properly limited national government. The Convention had come into existence for "the protection, Safety & Happiness of the people," he said. When it had appeared that the Convention might end abruptly, Mason had written that although it was tiresome for him to remain in Philadelphia, he "would bury his bones in this City rather than expose his Country to the Consequences of a dissolution of the Convention without any thing being done."[28] But he could not put his signature to a Constitution that he believed failed to safeguard the rights of the people, gave too much power to the federal government, and was bound in the long run to create some kind of tyranny. With tremendous personal courage and fortitude, George Mason refused to sign the Constitution.

On September 17, 1787, the crisp air announced the arrival of fall. As president of the Convention, Washington signed first, placing foremost on the paper the name that Americans most wanted to see. After the Convention decided to entrust its journal and papers with Washington, the other delegates proceeded to sign the document. After almost four months of hard-fought battles, the Convention ended when thirty-nine delegates from twelve states signed the Constitution. As the last delegates signed, Franklin made his famous observation about the sun painted on Washington's chair: "I have, often and often in the course of the session, and the vicissitudes of my hopes and fears as to its issue, looked at [the sun] behind the President without being able to tell whether it was rising or setting: But now at length I have the happiness to know that it is a rising and not a setting sun." Legend claims that as he left the State House, Franklin met a young woman, Elizabeth Powel, who asked about the form of the new government created by the delegates. "A republic, madam, if you can keep it," Franklin replied. Powel later claimed that she had no recollection of the famous retort, but she did say that "the most respectable, influential members of the convention" had gathered at her house and that "the all important subject was frequently discussed" there.[29]

Washington recorded in his diary on Monday, September 17, 1787, that "the Constitution received the Unanimous assent of 11 states and [Colonel] Hamilton's from New York (the only delegate from thence in Convention)," and was signed by every member present except Virginia's Governor Edmund Randolph, George Mason, and Elbridge Gerry of Massachusetts. A farewell dinner took place in the high-ceilinged space of the Rising Sun Tavern. The toasts and camaraderie were genuine. After sweltering through the summer, the delegates warmed themselves before roaring fires on the coldest day of the Convention. After dinner with the delegates, Washington returned to Robert Morris's house and wrote a letter to the Marquis de Lafayette, who he sometimes called his "adopted son," about the success of their Convention. After describing the contents of the Constitution, he told Lafayette: "I do not believe that providence has done so much for nothing."[30]

Of the three holdouts, it is ironic that two—Edmund Randolph and George Mason—came from Washington's home state, Virginia, and were his close friends. As heir apparent to the presidency, Washington took offense at Mason's declaration that the new government "would end either in monarchy or a tyrannical aristocracy." Their thirty-year friendship would not survive their split over the Constitution. "Col. Mason left Philad[elphi]a in an exceeding ill humor," Madison reported to Washington. "He returned to Virginia with a fixed disposition to prevent the adoption of the plan if possible. He considers the want of a Bill of Rights as a fatal objection."[31]

Tired and nursing wounds both political and psychological, Mason was glad to be headed home to his farm and family in Virginia. Deeming the new Constitution defective, he had been unable to sign. But former friends and colleagues would attribute his refusal not to principle, but to pique. His opposition provoked a caustic, prophetic response from Washington: "Pride on the one hand and want of manly candor on the other will not, I am certain, let him acknowledge an error in his opinions ... though conviction should flash on his mind as strongly as a ray of light."[32] Mason's deep frustration shown through, as he later wrote about the Convention with his customary bluntness:

"You may have been taught to respect the characters of the members of the late Convention. You may have supposed that they were an assemblage of great men. There is nothing less true. From the Eastern states [New England] there were knaves and fools and from the states southward of Virginia they were a parcel of coxcombs and from the middle states office hunters not a few."

On September 28, 1787, as the last red ember of the sun glowed on the Virginia horizon, George Mason finally arrived home at Gunston Hall. He had suffered a carriage accident en route to home. He promptly submitted his expense account to the Virginia General Assembly for service at the Constitutional Convention: it consisted of 138 grinding days of work from May 13 to September 27, travel time included, and it totaled £248 and eight shillings. Yet his true work had just begun. Mason had already decided to actively oppose the Constitution at the forthcoming Ratifying Convention in Richmond. There he would have a second chance to air his "Objections"—and hope, this time, to prevail.

Mason knew that the first phase of the American Revolution had concentrated on resistance to governmental power. The second phase would be about controlling it. In refusing to add a Bill of Rights, the men who supported the Constitution had handed Mason the most powerful weapon in his arsenal. And Mason would soon find himself immersed in the most profound political and personal battle of his life. The greatest political debate in American history was about to explode across the country.

CHAPTER TWELVE

A Slow Poison

Every master of slaves is born a petty tyrant.
—GEORGE MASON at the Constitutional Convention (1787)

S lavery was one of the most divisive issues at the federal Constitutional Convention in Philadelphia.[1] And it was the proverbial straw that broke Mason's back—one of the principal reasons that he refused to sign the new Constitution. In correspondence with Jefferson, Mason observed that the turning point for him at the Convention was the "deal" over the slave trade.[2] Until then, according to Jefferson's notes, Mason would have "set his hand and heart" to the Constitution. During the Convention, Mason passionately condemned not only the slave trade but slavery itself, as an institution that "retarded industry, discredited labor, and fostered tyrannical habits in owners. Slavery was a moral evil," and "providence punishes national sins," he predicted, "by national calamities."[3] The clause in the Constitution allowing the slave trade to continue another twenty years "created more dangers than any other." The trade was "diabolical in itself, and disgraceful to mankind."[4]

Mason lost on the issue of the slave trade. The "deal" that he
alluded to was the alliance between New England and South Carolina allowing the continuance of the slave trade for another twenty
years. Madison had tried to persuade Mason that "the Southern
States," by which he meant Georgia and South Carolina, would not
agree to the Constitution without that temporary continuation of
the slave trade. "Mason was ready to leave those states out of the
Union," in one historian's view, "unless they agreed to discontinue
'this disgraceful trade,' but Madison disagreed. 'Great as the evil
is,' he said, 'a dismemberment of the Union would be worse.' Since
the Constitution allowed Congress to end the slave trade after
twenty years, which it could not do under the Articles of Confederation, it was a step forward."[5] But for Mason, this fundamentally
changed "the great principles of the Constitution."[6] More than a
century later, President Theodore Roosevelt would praise the "high-
minded" Mason, who he said had battled against the slave trade and
predicted a civil war if slavery should continue. Roosevelt lauded
Mason "in shameful contrast" with "many of the northerners; in
particular, Oliver Ellsworth of Connecticut, whose name should be
branded with infamy because of the words he then uttered" in
defense of slavery.[7]

Yet Mason's words and deeds on slavery were contradictory, and
arguably remain a blemish on his record. We have no idea how much
Mason wrestled inwardly with the issue of slavery. Regarding the
trade in slaves, many established plantation owners in the Tidewater
region—as Mason certainly knew from his time in the House of
Burgesses—sanctioned an end to slave imports only because their
own estates were already filled with slaves. Any new arrivals would
only reduce the market value of their own enslaved people. In any case
Mason knew that ending the slave trade was not in any way synony-
mous with ending slavery. But at the Constitutional Convention,

George Mason emerged as an opponent not just of the slave trade, but of slavery itself.

Mason himself was a major slave owner. One of the most precise descriptions of slavery at Gunston Hall comes from the *Recollections* of Mason's son, John. John described the specialized skills of different slaves, portrayed the extensive farm economy supported by a slave labor force, and discussed the heavy domestic burden shouldered by numerous "house servants"—the preferred term for slaves working within the mansion. But throughout John's writings, only one individual slave is mentioned by name: James, his father's personal servant. Many documents—wills, inventories, tax records, and letters—also give information about slaves owned by the Mason family. Searching these documents and piecing together details about individuals, work, skills, and values yields a sketchy but informative picture about the dynamics of slave life on the Gunston Hall plantation.[8]

John Mason's *Recollections* captures both the mood and the essence of Southern plantation life, as well as the centrality of slavery as its life blood. There was a slave for every job at Gunston Hall: "Carpenters, Coopers, Sawyers, Blacksmiths, Tanners, Curriers, Shoemakers, Spinners, Weavers & Knitters, even a Distiller."[9] Luxury goods such as wines, broadcloth, silk dresses, and jewels for Ann were imported. But Mason had little need to go outside his own estate for food and other goods when his slaves were taught all the useful trades to produce them right on the premises. According to Mason's first biographer, "George Mason in his peninsula principality was a fair type of his class in colonial Virginia. With his village of Negro artisans, his flocks and herds and broad, teeming fields, he led a busy life. And his wife with her spinning-women, knitters and weavers."[10]

Through grueling labor, Mason's forests were harvested into lumber that some slaves cut from the fields and made into barrels that others packed with tobacco. "His field slaves," in the description of one historian, "cultivated cotton for their own clothes and raised sheep and cattle for their food. And, as John Mason recalled, his father's 'carpenters & sawyers built and kept in repair all the dwelling houses, barns, stables, ploughs, harrows, gates, &c.'"[11] According to numerous written accounts and oral histories of Gunston Hall, "Scores of slaves worked Mason's fields, and the Mansion slaves lived within earshot of Gunston Hall, called at any time, day or night."[12] Mason so took for granted the slave labor that permeated his life that it was a point of pride that he always shaved himself, instead of relying on his servant, James.[13]

In the 1780s nearly one hundred enslaved men, women, and children lived and worked on Mason's four farms (or quarters, as they were called) and the Gunston Hall mansion house that comprised Mason's estates. Many were sons, daughters, grandsons, or granddaughters of approximately thirty-two slaves that Mason had inherited in 1735. Other slaves came into Mason's possession as wedding gifts (or dowry), when he married Ann in 1750, and as inheritance from her parents. The majority of the Gunston Hall slaves were born into slavery under Virginia's harsh legal code: a child born to a slave woman was a slave for life. Thus slavery in Virginia was perpetuated by "natural increase."[14]

Skill levels at Gunston Hall varied. Field slaves, who were generally unskilled men, women, and children, tended fields of tobacco, corn, and wheat, also caring for cattle and sheep. Domestic servants cooked, cleaned, laundered, served at table, and attended the family and guests. A few served as personal attendants to individual Mason family members. Other slaves with specific skills, such as carpenters and blacksmiths, provided a considerable work force that lived and worked primarily near the mansion house.[15] Carpenters or blacksmiths might travel to outlying quarters to do repairs, or a midwife might deliver slave babies throughout the slave neighborhoods. But at harvest time all slaves were needed in the fields, regardless of their skill level or daily job.[16]

Slave quarters on estates such as Gunston Hall, Mount Vernon, and Monticello were designed to be hidden from view of the house. According to John Mason, the household slaves' quarters were "skirted by a wood, just far enough within which, to be out of sight." At Gunston Hall, the slaves lived near where they worked. Field slaves lived on the quarter where they tended crops or animals. The houses at the quarters, usually made of wood (clapboard or logs with mud chinking to keep out the air) would be single or double family structures. Dirt floors and wood-shuttered windows were typical features. Domestic slaves who worked in or near the mansion (for example in the kitchen or laundry) lived in cramped cabins. Loft spaces above the work areas provided small living areas for several slaves in each building. All these buildings would have had painted or whitewashed walls, wood or brick floors, and glass windows because they were visible to the family and guests.[17]

Mason's plantation also had one slave housing area known as "Log Town, so called because most of the houses were built of hewn pine logs."[18] This village of buildings was home to James, Mason's personal servant, his family, and some of the carpenters and their families.[19] Log Town was situated behind a wooded area, out of sight of the mansion house. Its residents enjoyed a modicum of comfort and privacy within their own slave community. Living in Log Town provided some intimacy for the slave families who lived there, away from where most of the other domestic slaves lived and worked. The slave families privileged enough to live in Log Town could talk without being overheard by their master or by other slaves. They could socialize, sing, dance, and have some sort of family life.[20]

Slavery was woven into every aspect of Gunston Hall life, even for Mason's visitors. "Everyone felt himself at home and had a negro servant to wait on him and supply his wants," wrote an admiring English visitor.[21] "Each of the Virginia presidents kept slaves as attendants and laborers," notes historian Lorri Glover, "using them for state dinners, construction projects, childcare, personal grooming, and anything else that arose." Glover relates one famous anecdote of the slave Paul Jennings: "Paul Jennings was among the last people to leave the White House in 1814 as British forces advanced on the nation's capitol. He was setting the table when a frantic rider called out the warning to 'clear out, clear out!' Later he learned that invading British soldiers ate the very meal he set out. Jennings also held the ladder that several men, including other slaves, climbed to cut down George Washington's portrait (though Dolley [Madison] is usually given credit for saving it). And he watched the federal city go up in flames. Given the centrality of slaves to every part of rich slaveholders' lives, it was not surprising that men like Jefferson and Washington thought about their bondsmen and women as being part of their families. This was not simply rhetoric."[22]

By all historical accounts, Mason was a benevolent master, never cruel to his slaves. He wanted to think well of himself and believed he was a merciful master even as the inherent brutality of the system forced him to question that belief. Under Virginia law, Mason could have abused his slaves as punishment for misconduct and avoided legal consequences. Like Mason, Washington believed that, as one scholar has written, "whipping slaves was counterproductive," so he "tried to restrain such brutality."[23] As he lectured one estate manager, it "oftentimes is easier to effect [change] by watch-fulness and admonition than by severity and certainly must be more agreeable to every feeling mind in the practice of them."[24] In fact, Washington's overseers were specifically required to issue warnings to runaway slaves before whipping them. "General Washington has forbidden the use of the whip on his blacks," a French visitor to Mount Vernon later averred, "but unfortunately his example has been little emulated."[25]

One Washington biographer notes, "However horrifying it seems to later generations, abominable behavior toward dark-skinned people was considered an acceptable way of life. In 1767, when four slaves were executed in Fairfax County for supposedly colluding to poison their overseers, their decapitated heads were posted on chimneys at the local courthouse to act as a grim warning to others. Nobody protested this patent atrocity. At the same time, slave masters in the eighteenth century seldom rationalized or romanticized slavery as a divinely sanctioned system, as happened before the Civil War."[26]

During one bitterly frigid winter, Washington refused to cancel any slave activities or the arduous field work. On January 3, 1788, Washington noted the twenty-five-degree cold, as he made the chilly rounds on horseback: "Nevertheless everyone was outdoors working. At Dogue Run, he wrote, 'the women began to hoe the swamp they had grubbed in order to prepare it for sowing in the spring with grain and grass seeds.' At Muddy Hole, 'the women, after having threshed out the peas, went about the fencing.' And at another farm, 'the women were taking up and thinning the trees in the swamp, which they had before grubbed.' It is hard to imagine more brutal manual labor than women pulling up tree stumps in icy swamps in record-setting cold, but Washington seems not to have found this inhuman scene objectionable."[27]

Summer on a plantation could be even worse. During a July 1793 heat wave, for instance, Madison wrote Jefferson that the corn crop was burning up, the dire situation made worse by the fact that heavy spring rains had preceded the blistering summer sun, baking the soil "into Brick."[28] It was slaves, not their masters, who plowed the hard earth, worked outdoors in the scorching Virginia heat, and suffered from the lost crops.

Like other slaveholders, both Mason and Washington spoke about slaves in general terms as merely another form of property.

Washington could "especially be cold-blooded in specifying instructions for buying slaves, telling one buyer, as if he were purchasing a
racehorse, that he wanted his slaves 'to be straight-limbed and in every
respect strong and likely, with good teeth.'"[29] George Mason seldom
spoke or wrote the word "slavery" or "slaves," preferring euphemisms
such as "servants," "Negroes," "my people," or "my family."

Yet Mason's behavior was relatively humane, within an inhumane
system, as evidenced by his refusal to separate slave families. More
important, the slaves at Gunston Hall could move about without
supervision, while slaves were controlled by the threat of whips and
chains at other plantations. Although slave marriages were not sanctioned by Virginia law, Mason recognized them as binding. In time,
he refused to sell slaves if it meant the breakup of a slave family. Slaves
who wished to marry slaves from other plantations needed the owner's permission, and there is no evidence Mason ever denied it. Yet the
most malignant aspect of Mason's ownership of his plantation was
that the tobacco culture was extremely strenuous, making it a natural
match for slavery. Growing tobacco as a cash crop kept George Mason
entangled with the repugnant slave system. "Slaves were ubiquitous
in this rich, populous colony," comments one scholar, "making up 40
percent of Virginia's population. In fact, slavery had acquired such a
firm grip on the colony that one minister maintained in 1757 that "to
live in Virginia without slaves is morally impossible."[30]

And there is no doubt Mason's field slaves lived extremely hard
lives working the demanding farm. Watt was a slave of George
Mason's who ran away, but later returned. He did arduous work in
the fields on the Hallowing Point Quarter, along with many other
men and women. Two women, Dinah and Winny, were older than
Watt, but all three of these individuals received respect as "elders" in
this community. "The elders passed on the history and memory of
people and events," observes one scholar, "such as the middle passage

across the Atlantic of the first generation of Africans forced into Virginia slavery.... A description of Watt appeared in the Alexandria newspaper in 1786 after he had run away and George Mason placed this ad for his return. 'WATT, a stout Negro fellow, remarkably black ... has lost some of his foreteeth, which in some measure affects his voice ... is an artful fellow, has a down look, and seems confused when examined.' Watt ... was discovered and returned to Virginia. Watt did not attempt to run again. Surely as an 'elder,' he told the story of his runaway experience (and likely subsequent punishment) to all the children in the quarter."[31]

Each slave at a plantation such as Mount Vernon or Gunston Hall received one set of new clothes per year—a woolen jacket, a pair of breeches, two shirts, a pair of stockings, and a pair of shoes. Slave women received an annual petticoat and smock: "Some slaves also had Sunday outfits of dark coats with white vests and white breeches. Every day the slaves received approximately one quart of Indian cornmeal, and every month twenty salted herrings, which sounds like a terribly meager ration. 'It is not my wish or desire that my Negro[e]s should have an ounce of meal more, nor less, than is sufficient to feed them plentifully,' Washington told his estate manager."[32]

James, the one individual slave mentioned by name in John Mason's *Recollections*, held a prized and envied position. He not only attended Mason but served as a butler and valet for the mansion. James wore a uniform as he greeted guests and family at Gunston Hall. James, who had Mason's personal authority and trust, would escort family and friends directly inside the mansion, but a traveler on business would be made to wait on the porch.[33] In the hierarchy of servants, James also had the greatest personal freedom of movement. He traveled with Mason to Williamsburg, Richmond, and later to Philadelphia. His experiences in other cities probably filtered back into the slave community at Gunston when he returned. Working inside the mansion, James would also be able to overhear confidential conversations among the family and their guests. Although he worked during the day, at night James returned to Log Town where he could live in a modicum of freedom with his family.[34]

"My father kept no stewart or clerk about him," John Mason recorded in his memoirs, "he … superintended, with the assistance of a trusty slave or two … all the operations at or about the home house."[35] Nace, who acted as a semi-manager on the plantation, was one of those trusted slaves. An overseer's job required that he supervise the tasks assigned by the master. Usually, this position fell to a paid white overseer. Slaves in this position were rare and may have been in an awkward situation in plantation society. Nace may have had to supervise and enforce work orders on other slaves, as well indentured servants. Thus, "Nace had to find a means to convince everyone to work together for the good of all," according to one historian: "Second, Nace had authority over others in the community that was given by the master, but he had to earn the respect of everyone in the slave community also. If Nace misused or otherwise lost that respect among the other slaves, they could shun or isolate him and his family in retaliation. Additionally, the 'remuneration' for a slave in this position might be more clothing or extra food for his family, things that others in the slave community might resent. Consequently, as a 'middleman' on the quarter, Nace had to carefully juggle responsibility to the master and his place in his community."[36]

Nace had an additional skill that Mason respected, the training and breaking of horses. Mason demonstrated his admiration for Nace's ability in a letter he wrote to John: "I have ordered Nace to take your sorrell Horse into his charge; he will fare much better with him, than with our careless Rascals at Gunston." Nace also earned money with this skill. Occasionally Mason's neighbor Martin Cockburn paid Nace for "breaking a colt" or "breaking a young horse."

Of all the Mason slaves apart from James, Nace held the highest skill level and greatest position of responsibility.[37]

The slave known as "Gunston Nell" (or House Nell) was probably one of the enslaved women who came to Gunston Hall after Ann Eilbeck's marriage to George. Nell served as a "nurse" to the young Mason children, tending to their daily needs until they were old enough to begin lessons with the governess. But most important, Nell specialized in midwifery, and would have traveled to deliver babies, although it is unlikely that she assisted in the birth of Mason family babies. But it would have been comforting for the Masons to know that Nell could be relied on if their personal doctor, Dr. Craig, was not available. And Nell, like Nace, earned money with her skills, and was paid by Martin Cockburn for her services. Nell had at least two children of her own, Jack and Nell.[38]

No aspect of George Mason's life is more problematic in modern times than his ownership of slaves. At the Constitutional Convention, he expressed staunch opposition to slavery. What transformed Mason, slave owner all his life, into a vigorous critic not only of the slave trade, but of slavery itself?

Mason's opposition to slavery was the product of a gradual awakening over many years. During the Stamp Act crisis, more than twenty years before the Constitutional Convention, Mason had condemned slavery as "an Evil." He believed that slavery had a terrible effect on the "Morals & Manners of our people." As early as 1765, Mason had complained of the insidious effects of slavery in Virginia: "One half of our best Lands in most Parts of the Country remain unsettled, & the other cultivated with slaves; not to mention the ill effect such a Practice has."[39]

Mason was far from the only slave-owning Virginian to take an anti-slavery position. His friend and neighbor George Washington expressed his distress over slavery in 1786: "There is not a man living who wishes more sincerely than I do to see a plan adopted for the abolition of slavery."[40] In 1781 Jefferson wrote grimly of the evil of slavery: "I tremble for my country when I reflect that God is just."[41] And as early as 1773, Patrick Henry condemned slave-holding as an "abominable practice" that Christians should feel ashamed to tolerate. He judged slaveholding "a species of violence and tyranny" antithetical to the teachings of the Bible, to political principles, and to basic humanity. He conceded that he could manufacture no valid excuse for the fact that he owned slaves: "I will not, I cannot justify it."[42] Henry pointed out, "What adds to the wonder, is that this Abominable Practice has been introduced in the most enlightened Ages.... [An era that] boasts of high Improvements in the Arts, Sciences, & refined Morality [has] brought into general use & guarded by many Laws, a Species of Violence & Tyranny, which our more rude & barbarous, but more honest Ancestors detested ... when the Rights of Humanity are defined & understood with precision ... we find Men, professing a Religion the most humane, mild, meek, gentle & generous; adopting a Principle as repugnant to humanity as it is inconsistant with the Bible and destructive to Liberty.... Every thinking honest Man rejects it in Speculation, how few in Practice from conscienscious Motives?[43] George Mason's rhetoric was as critical of slavery as Patrick Henry's.

The opening words of Mason's Declaration of Rights provoked throbbing conflict among Virginia slaveholders: his original unqualified statement that "all men are born equally free and independent, and have certain inherent natural rights" was so offensive to defenders of slavery that it created the danger of—as one delegate warned prophetically—"civil convulsion."[44] So Mason's claim that all men are born free, with natural rights was edited to include a key restriction: "when they enter into a state of society."

Mason led the charge against the slave trade at the Constitutional Convention in Philadelphia, rallying the anti-slavery delegates to oppose the clause forbidding the new federal government from out-lawing the slave trade for twenty years. By the time of the Philadel-phia Convention, Mason had honed his fiery anti-slavery rhetoric. Slavery "discourages arts & manufactures," Mason complained, and by undermining immigration imperiled stability and prosperity. In time, Mason warned, Americans would pay for their unjust enslave-ment of men and women. His dire warning foreshadowed the Civil War: "Slaves bring a judgment of heaven on a country. As nations cannot be rewarded or punished in the next world, they must be in this. By an inevitable chain of causes and effects Providence punishes national sins, by national calamities.[45]

Mason was one of a precious few delegates determined to pre-serve the dignity of mankind, including even that of slaves. During the Convention, Mason and several colleagues would slip out of their rooms late at night and hold "secret meetings" to devise means to channel the onrushing tide of concentrated governmental power to eliminate the slave trade. Connecticut delegate Oliver Ellsworth was anxious to do a deal: South Carolina and Georgia would get the continuation of the slave trade for twenty years, and New England would be allowed a monopoly in the trade. Ellsworth became some-thing of a peeping Tom, shadowing Mason and his band of patriots at their meetings to strategize on the slavery issue. Delegate Luther Martin described Ellsworth as one with "a heart which would dis-honor the midnight assassin."[46]

Slavery had crept into the Convention at its very beginning when the "Virginia Plan" for the Constitution proposed to apportion leg-islators based on "the number of free inhabitants."[47] Mason and Madison had moved to strike that phrase. One historian has power-fully synthesized the Framers' moral dilemma over slavery: "Aware that history, as well as their creator, would judge them harshly, James Madison and the Philadelphia delegates representing the southern states were careful to keep the words 'slave' and 'slavery' out of their crowning achievement, the US Constitution, even as they made absolutely certain that the federal government would protect slaveholding. Twenty-five of the fifty-five men gathered in Philadelphia owned slaves, and three-fourths of those were dependent on slave labor for their economic well-being. Most delegates were determined to protect slavery in the new government, and most of those were ashamed of themselves for it."[48]

Mason continued to speak out strongly and repeatedly against slavery in the debates at the Convention. He opposed the provision to count slaves "for purposes of determining [congressional] representation 'notwithstanding it was favorable' to Virginia."[49] He went on to declare, "I cannot express my detestation of [the slave trade]," and objected that the proposed Constitution did not utilize its "power to prevent the increase of slavery."[50]

And, as we shall see, Mason continued to pound on the slavery issue in the Virginia Ratifying Convention, using the inhuman protection of the slave trade for twenty years as an argument against the adoption of the Constitution.

And yet, despite his stirring rhetoric from the time of the controversy over the Stamp Act of 1765 through the debates over the new federal Constitution in the Virginia Ratifying Convention of 1788, Mason did nothing to free his own slaves, or propose a plan for emancipation. Thus Mason himself embodied the contradictions of the American founding. On one hand, he affirmed the inborn freedom and natural rights of all men and denounced the Constitution for allowing the "detestable trade" of slaves to continue for the next twenty years, but on the other, he continued to be a slave owner enjoying the benefits of wealth and position that accrued to him from slave labor.[51]

As a fourth-generation Virginian, Mason had been brought up among slaves and he was dependent on their labor at his working plantations. Over time and with maturity, Mason came to believe that slavery was morally and politically wrong on every level. Yet he continued to benefit from it. Mason agonized over slavery and how to end it—as did many of his Virginia colleagues. Washington believed that the cure for the cancer of slavery must be gradual: "to get slaves afloat at once would I believe be productive of much inconvenience and mischief; but, by degrees, it certainly might and assuredly ought to be effected, and that, too, by legislative authority."[52] Jefferson wrote that "there is nothing I would not sacrifice to a practicable plan of abolishing every vestige of this moral and political depravity."[53] But then he added a caveat: "But as it is, we have the wolf by the ear, and we can neither hold him nor safely let him go. Justice is in one scale and self-preservation in the other."[54] Madison also expressed his abhorrence of slavery, lamenting that "we have seen the mere distinction of colour, made in the most enlightened period of times, a ground for the most oppressive domination ever exercised by man over man," and writing that the "magnitude of this evil [slavery] among us is so deeply felt and so universally acknowledged that no merit could be greater than that of devising a satisfactory remedy for it."[55]

But no one seemed to be able to. Slavery would fracture the Constitutional Convention—and, eventually, the Union. Although many of his contemporaries addressed the issue of slavery, arguably no one was more relentless than George Mason in his attacks upon slavery and the slave trade. His original draft for his "Scheme for Replevying Goods & Distresses" in protest of the Stamp Act had contained an antislavery preamble. He faulted the British for not encouraging the "importance [that is, the import] of free people" and not discouraging the slave trade. Slavery not only discouraged settlement by free people; Mason blamed it for the fall of the Roman Empire: "One of the first signs of the decay, and perhaps the primary cause of the destruction of the most flourishing government that ever existed was the introduction of great numbers of slaves—an evil very pathetically described by Roman Historians...."[56]

As early as 1773, Mason condemned slavery in the strongest terms: "That slow poison ... is daily contaminating the minds and morals or our people. Every gentleman here is born a petty tyrant. Practiced in acts of despotism and cruelty, we become callous to the dictates of humanity, and all the finer feelings of the soul. Taught to regard a part of our own species in the most abject and contemptible degree below us, we lose that idea of dignity of man which the hand of nature has implanted in us for great and useful purposes."[57]

Time and again throughout his life, Mason would return to two themes that underlay his views on slavery: the dangers posed by slavery to a nation; and the way in which slavery affected the "morals and manners" of the people. His most famous speech at the Philadelphia Convention was an impassioned attack on slavery.[58] Mason launched an assault on the slave trade, which he called "that infernal traffic." He claimed that "the British government constantly checked the attempts of Virginia to put a stop to it." But Mason ended his speech with a stern caution: "This task must be accomplished gradually, with the good of the entire country kept constantly in mind. It must not be done suddenly. The Negro must be educated and helped to be self-supporting before he was cast upon his own resources and made to fend for himself. Otherwise he would suffer and become a burden on the whole community, which would suffer also."[59]

As Helen Hill Miller concludes in *George Mason, Constitutionalist*, Mason was the leader of a group at the Convention "composed of both Northerners and Southerners, who wished to treat slavery as a social institution, rather than as the raw materials of bargaining power."[60] Mason made an impassioned plea that the slave trade be discontinued: "It is lamentable that some of our Eastern brethren have ... embarked on this nefarious traffic. As to the states having the right to import, this is the case with many other rights, now to be properly given up. It is essential, from every point of view, that the general government should have power to prevent the increase of slavery."[61]

Mason's conversion from enthusiasm to active opposition toward the Constitution occurred when the Convention adopted the specific provision allowing the slave trade to continue for another twenty years. Although the new charter empowered Congress, in Article 1, Section 8, "to regulate Commerce with foreign Nations, and among the several States," Section 9 placed a restriction on that power: "The Migration or Importation of such Persons as any of the States now existing shall think proper to admit, shall not be prohibited by the Congress" before the year 1808.

At the end of Mason's infamous Objections to the Constitution, he complained that "the general legislature is restrained from prohibiting the further importation of slaves for twenty odd years; though such importations render the United States weaker, more vulnerable, and less capable of defense." Those appear, at least to historian Helen Hill Miller, to be the greatest obstacles to Mason's approval of the Constitution. "The objections between the first and last might have been compromised," according to this rendition. "But the first and last objections concern liberty. On that there is no compromise. You are free, or slave."[62]

There is no consensus among scholars on Mason's record on slavery. Miller concluded that, "After the navigation-act-slave trade bargain was made known ... Mason began to have reservations about the Constitution." She acknowledged the importance of "the deal on commercial regulations and the slave trade." As she wrote, "Mason lost on both counts, and the double defeat was reflected in his attitude thereafter."[63] Scholar Lance Banning agreed, contending that "this bargain was unquestionably the act" that explains Mason's turn against the Constitution.

But historian Robert Rutland has a different perspective. He has contended that Mason showed only "belated concern over the personal rights of citizens." Rutland observed that Mason had economic as well as moral reasons to be troubled over slavery and the slave trade. Virginia planters, among them Mason's father, had welcomed the trade. "But natural increase supplied new generations of recruits to the plantations, and the Revolution brought social turmoil, military invasion, and economic disruption. Moreover, slaves malingered, ran away, and rebelled. They promised too little profit, threatened too much danger, and, by their mere involuntary presence, challenged planters' and politicians' notions of natural rights in a white republic."[64] In Rutland's opinion, Mason was ultimately ambivalent about slavery and the slave trade, notwithstanding his passionate speech in the Convention and his antislavery rhetoric.[65]

In charting Mason's conflicting words and deeds about slavery, one begins to sense that he had developed a split personality on the issue. On the one hand, he was still a Southern planter with an acquisitive business personality, living and prospering in a culture that had few moral qualms about slavery. On the other hand, Mason was an Enlightenment intellectual with a capacious knowledge of political history and a commitment to the natural rights of mankind. With Jefferson, Madison, Henry, and Wythe, he inflamed Revolutionary ideals he had honed in countless conversations with his illustrious colleagues.

Thus the dilemma of what to do with his slaves dogged Mason—and Washington, and Jefferson, and Madison—for the rest of their lives. Mason's public statements on slavery at the Convention make it plain that guilt tugged at his mind. But Virginia still lacked a free labor force, and Mason could not farm without slaves. However much he admired the economies of the New England and Mid-Atlantic States, he did not see how he could re-create that free world at his home.

But if Mason had lived longer—he died in 1792, at age sixty-seven—might he have, perhaps in conjunction with Jefferson[66] or Madison, devised a practicable plan of slave emancipation and abolition that possibly could have avoided the Civil War? The historical record, Mason's character, tenacity, stubbornness, and political courage allow us to answer that question with a qualified "yes." Had Mason lived ten, perhaps fifteen years longer, his speeches and correspondence support the proposition that, especially given his intense interest in Western lands, he might well have devised a very different plan to resolve the tensions that were eventually addressed in the ultimately unsuccessful "Missouri Compromise"—if he had not already: a plan of emancipation.[67]

Any plan for abolition that Mason might have offered would likely have looked similar to the one proposed by St. George Tucker, a protégé and colleague of Mason's.[68] Tucker, a lawyer and law professor in Virginia, was an admirer of Mason and Thomas Jefferson, who were both his mentors. And just three years after Mason died, Tucker advanced a specific plan for the emancipation of the slaves. Tucker had met and visited with Mason in Williamsburg on numerous occasions, and he had certainly heard Mason's speeches on liberty and natural rights in the House of Burgesses and the Virginia Conventions over the years. In fact, one of Tucker's sons, St. George Tucker Campbell, married Mason's granddaughter, Sarah Elizabeth Mason, at "Colross," in Alexandria, on November 17, 1841. Hence, it is not a historical leap to believe that over the years the two men discussed the issues of natural rights, slavery, and emancipation. So George Mason may very likely have inspired or at least influenced St. George Tucker's emancipation plan. And surely, given his disgust with the slavery compromise at the Constitutional Convention, Mason would have embraced it if he had lived to see it.

Tucker was born and raised in Bermuda, where half the population was enslaved. He moved to Virginia in 1772 at age nineteen to attend the College of William and Mary and study law under the direction of George Wythe, a Mason colleague and one of the colony's foremost legal minds. In 1790, he took up Wythe's law professorship, while maintaining a position on the bench.[69] Tucker began to research and draft his *Dissertation on the Abolition of Slavery* in 1795, and it took him more than a year to complete. From the scant historical records, it would appear that he began by corresponding with Jeremy Belknap of the Massachusetts Historical Society, a clergyman and historian Tucker hoped could tell him how Massachusetts had managed the peaceful abolition of slavery. Belknap passed along the professor's questions to some prominent correspondents, several of whom noted that the end of slavery in Massachusetts had come not with a formal decree, but with the interpretation of the Massachusetts Constitution of 1780. That document directly quoted the language of George Mason's own Declaration of Rights, declaring, "All men are born free and equal, and have certain natural, essential, and unalienable rights, among which may be reckoned the right of enjoying and defending their lives and liberties." Belknap synthesized the various responses he had received in a report for Tucker. In his reply, Tucker provided a draft for his *Dissertation on Slavery*, including a plan of abolition that he thought his fellow Virginians might accept. By proposing a plan for gradual emancipation, Tucker hoped that he could convince the world—as he wrote to Belknap in 1795—"that the existence of slavery in this country is no longer to be deemed a reproach to the present generation."[70]

Tucker began the essay by paraphrasing Mason's language from his many speeches on freedom. Both pointed out the "incompatibility" of slavery with the natural rights principles of the American Revolution and therefore found it impossible to justify the enslavement of black people "unless we first degrade them below the rank of human beings, not only politically, but also physically and morally." Unwilling to take this step, Tucker argued, in language similar to Mason's, that the time had come to accept the "moral truth" of the depravity of slavery.[71] He noted that mass abolition had proven successful only in those states with a low ratio of slaves to free people. According to Tucker, Virginia had too high a ratio of slaves to free people immediately. In some parts of the state, "it is probable that there are four slaves for one free white man." He argued that under such conditions immediate full-scale emancipation would produce famine at best and a race war at worst.[72] With these considerations in mind, Tucker set forth a complex plan of gradual emancipation—a revised version of the gradual emancipation plans that had been used in several Northern states. First, all females born to slaves would serve twenty-eight-year indentures, after which their owners would give them twenty dollars and two suits of clothes. If the master refused to pay freedom wages upon the arrival of the twenty-eighth year, he would have to pay the court a five-dollar fee. Children born to those serving such indentures must "be bound to service by the overseers of the poor, until they shall attain the age of twenty-one years." This same agency would receive 15 percent of their wages when they were hired out for the short term, and 10 percent of their wages if they received an apprenticeship lasting for a year or more.[73]

Tucker saw the right to property as a natural right, but he doubted that the slave owner had a "property" right to an unborn child. Tucker thought that his scheme could win over skeptical slave owners. He pointed out features of the plan that might surprise and persuade them: "the number of slaves will not be diminished for forty years after it takes place; that it will even increase for thirty years; that at the distance of sixty years, there will be one-third of the number at its first commencement; that it will require above a century to complete it; and that the number of blacks under twenty-eight, and consequently bound to service, in the families they are born in, will always be at least as great, as the present number of slaves."[74]

It should be noted that Tucker's plan denied freed slaves basic civil liberties, including the right to keep weapons, to serve on juries, to testify against or marry white people, or even to write a will. It is difficult to believe that Mason would have agreed with this proposal. Tucker justified this course of action in the same way he justified the continuance of slavery during the gradual emancipation he proposed: by arguments from the philosophy of natural rights and from the violence against white people committed by slaves in the Haitian Revolution. Tucker argued that when dealing with people entering "into a state of society," those already in the society have a right to "admit or exclude" anyone they wish. Thus, he found it consistent with natural rights to deny freed slaves the basic rights of citizens. He argued that the "recent scenes transacted" in Haiti were "enough to make one shudder with the apprehension of realizing similar calamities in this country." Finding it impossible to propose a plan of emancipation that did not "either encounter, or accommodate [it]self to prejudice," Tucker proposed a course that would negotiate what he saw as an acceptable mean between the evils of slavery and a mass emancipation that would "turn loose a numerous, starving, and enraged banditti upon the innocent descendants of their former oppressors."[75]

By restricting the civil liberties of freed slaves, it seems Tucker hoped that he might encourage them to leave the state altogether, a sentiment shared by Jefferson. "There is an immense unsettled territory on this continent more congenial to their natural constitutions than ours," he writes, "where they may perhaps be received upon more favourable terms than we can permit them to remain with us."

Tucker sent a copy of his *Dissertation* to Jefferson. The future president agreed with Tucker on both the urgency of the question and the plan for emancipation, and no doubt Mason would have as well. According to Jefferson, history would decide the question of emancipation, regardless of the answer given by the slave owners. Jefferson believed that the consequences of failing to plan for emancipation would be disastrous. He noted that only the Southern states had to concern themselves with slave uprisings, which "a single spark" could produce at any time. If such an uprising were to come, Jefferson held out little hope that the other states would be of any assistance in putting it down.[76]

It is probable that Mason, had he lived another five or ten years, would have either embraced St. George Tucker's *Dissertation* for emancipation and abolition, or advanced his own plan. Given the historical record, including Mason's fervent protests of slavery and the slave trade, his political courage and tenacity in refusing to sign the Constitution, and his firm adherence to the notion of natural rights, it seems probable that he would have welcomed such a plan.

What exactly is George Mason's legacy on slavery and the slave trade? In the end, his record is a mixed bag. Assessments of Mason on the slavery issue have ranged from moral outrage at his rank hypocrisy to kudos for his political courage in speaking out against slavery and refusing to sign a Constitution that continued the slave trade. Is there a middle ground? As one scholar has noted, "Few of us entirely escape our times and places."[77] Mason certainly knew slavery was morally wrong, but he did nothing tangible to lead the way to emancipation for his own slaves, or to the abolition of slavery in Virginia. Slavery appears to be the only contradiction in Mason's seemingly virtuous life. But that contradiction is significant. Mason hoped and expected that his son's generation would abolish slavery, yet he never freed one slave in his lifetime or at his death.

Family biographer Kate Mason Rowland, a sympathetic white
Southerner writing during the heyday of Jim Crow, denied emphatically
that Mason was "an abolitionist in the modern sense of the term."
Rowland even asserted that Mason "insisted that the rights of his section in this species of property should be protected, and he wished for
a guarantee in the Constitution to protect it," which is apparently a
reference to Mason's observation at the Virginia Ratifying Convention
of 1788 that the Constitution did not explicitly protect the slave owner's
investment. Yet, "in the hands of recent historians," biographer Jeff
Broadwater has written, "Mason has become an abolitionist, an 'openly
and urgently abolitionist,' no less. Openly perhaps, but not urgently.
Mason consistently voiced his disapproval of slavery. His 1787 attack
on slavery echoes a similar speech to the Virginia Convention of 1776.
His conduct was another matter. Washington freed his slaves in his will.
Jefferson freed a few. Mason freed none, either during his lifetime or
in his will."[78] Yet Mason never seemed defensive about this glaring
inconsistency: "He made no excuses, and he expressed no remorse. In
all likelihood, Mason believed, or convinced himself, that he had no
options. Mason would have done nothing that might have compromised the financial futures of his nine children. Racial prejudice reinforced economic self-interest."[79]

It is reasonable to assume that Mason shared the belief of Jefferson and others that "miscegenation," the mixing of the races, could
never be practicable in their lifetimes. According to Broadwater's
interpretation, "emancipation could not proceed until a way acceptable to whites could be found to segregate the two races. Mason could
rise above interest and prejudice, which was a feat in itself, to see the
evil of slavery, but he could not rise far enough to move effectively
against it."[80]

Thus the sting in Dr. Samuel Johnson's mortifying question
remains: "how is it that we hear the loudest yelps for liberty from the

drivers of Negroes?"[81] This is certainly fair moral criticism of Mason, but is it the final analysis? "Slavery and discrimination cloud our minds," declared one historian, "in the most extraordinary ways, including a blanket judgment today against American slave owners in the 18th and 19th centuries. That the masters should be judged as lacking in the scope of their minds and hearts is fair, indeed must be insisted upon, but that doesn't mean we should judge the whole of them only by this part."[82]

The protection of slavery in the Constitution seemed a betrayal of Mason's treasured commitment to the natural rights of mankind. This was a major reason for his refusal to sign the document. But, as one historian has observed, "in a pattern to be replicated again and again, he changed course, afraid to "expose our Weakness by examining this Subject too freely.'"[83] On one hand, he denounced the Constitution for allowing "this detestable trade" of international slave trafficking to continue for at least twenty years. On the other hand, he complained at the Virginia Ratifying Convention that nothing would "prevent the Northern and Eastern states from meddling with our whole property of that kind."[84] Mason drew an intellectual line between the international slave trade (which he tried to end) and the ownership of slaves (which he deplored, but never fully rejected).

One historian has rightly castigated the Founders, including Mason: "Whatever aversion or ambivalence they felt, Mason, Henry, Jefferson, Washington, and Madison owned slaves until the day they died.... When asked in 1823 if there was in Virginia any plan for general emancipation, James Madison answered, uncharacteristically, with a single syllable: 'None.' Each of Virginia's leading founders knew that slavery was antithetical to his political principles. Though some were more publicly vocal than others, their own writings provide a litany of blistering rebukes of their hypocrisy of perpetuating racial slavery in an ostensibly free republic."[85]

The Marquis de Lafayette pointed out the Founders' hypocrisy in allowing slavery to thrive not only in Virginia but inside their own homes. For Lafayette, the notion that an independent America would tolerate slavery was more than a contradiction in terms: it was anathema to everything he believed.[86] As he wrote to British abolitionist Thomas Clarkson, "I would never have drawn my sword in the cause of America if I could have conceived that thereby I was founding a land of slavery."[87] As early as 1783, Lafayette made it clear to Washington that the General could not escape this subject: "Permit me to propose a plan to you which might become greatly beneficial to the black part of mankind. Let us unite in purchasing a small estate where we may try the experiment to free the Negroes and use them only as tenants."[88] If Washington took that bold stand, Lafayette hoped it "Might Render it a General Practice."[89]

When Lafayette visited James Madison, the French general was preoccupied by three issues: the French-American alliance, the unity of the thirteen states, and "the manumission of the slaves." Madison wrote to Jefferson that Lafayette's position on slavery "does him real honor, as it is a proof of his humanity." Yet, as historian Ron Chernow concluded, "After the Revolution it was unquestionably fashionable to utter such high-minded sentiments, but talk was cheap and direct action was quite another matter."[90]

Mason was certainly aware that other men had taken direct action on slavery. For example, Robert Pleasants, a Quaker merchant from Henrico County and well known to Mason, freed his slaves in the wake of the Revolutionary War. He also issued a prophetic warning to both Washington and Madison that they jeopardized their legacy by perpetuating slavery. And as scholar Lorri Glover notes, "In 1791, Robert Carter, one of Virginia's richest planters, likewise followed his convictions and emancipated more than five hundred slaves—perhaps the largest private manumission in America before the Civil War."[91] Also, according to Glover, "John Randolph numbered among those who committed to manumission: he freed hundreds of slaves in his will and bequeathed them money to purchase land. And Edward Coles, President James Madison's personal secretary (and brother to Isaac Coles, Jefferson's secretary), left Virginia for Illinois and freed his slaves after fairly begging, unsuccessfully, both Jefferson and Madison to set an example of manumission. Coles frankly informed Madison that it appeared to him 'repugnant to the distinctive & characteristic traits of your character ... not to restore to your slaves that liberty & those rights which you have been through life so zealous and able a champion.'"[92]

Some mid-Atlantic and Northern states had commenced gradual emancipation programs starting in the 1770s. Pennsylvania, where some of the Founders gathered and even lived for months at a time, took the lead: the first antislavery society was founded in Philadelphia in 1775.[93]

Thus, Mason was not without models for a way out of the slavery dilemma. And he certainly realized that slavery could not be reconciled with the values of the Revolution, that it was morally bankrupt and perverted the character of masters and their children.[94] "Something clearly mattered more to Virginia's leading founders," one historian has written, "than practicing their political principles. What greater harm did they fear? What led them to perpetuate a 'moral and political depravity'"?[95] During the 1788 Virginia ratification debates, Mason could only muster a tepid explanation of why he failed to free his slaves or act for emancipation. "It is far from being a desirable property," he allowed. "But it will involve us in great difficulties and infelicity to be now deprived of them."[96] Slave mastery had been, and was, the foundation of the Virginia gentry, and to abolish it would have severely disrupted gentry society as the planters knew it. "White slaveholding families before the Revolution," observed one historian, "had been genteel, leisured, wealthy, and powerful because of racial slavery, and they remained so afterward. George Washington could spend his retirement riding across Mount Vernon ... because he commanded scores of slaves. Jefferson could open Monticello and James Madison Montpelier to droves of visitors, who marveled at their dinner parties and beautifully appointed homes, because slave labor bought those lifestyles. George Mason and Patrick Henry could educate their sons and endow them with thriving estates because their slaves turned handsome profits on their plantations."[97]

Owning slaves was an elemental part of Mason's life and his identity as a family farmer. "Had letting go of slavery been simply a matter of convenience," declares one historian, "these founders would surely have followed their consciences. They sacrificed so much for the revolutionary cause that it seems highly improbable that a mere 'infelicity' would have made them cling to what James Madison called 'the most oppressive dominion ever exercised by man over man.'"[98] As Lorri Glover has argued, the failure of these influential Virginia political leaders to act during their lifetime was "a glaring reversal of their courageous and principled conduct during the Revolution. Instead, they codified this institution in their new governments and upheld it in their homes. In time, each man retired from public life to a splendid family estate of white leisure and black labor, unable to see the Revolution through to fruition because they were unwilling to sacrifice the status of their white families and violate their duties as fathers."[99]

Mason must have realized two contradictory truths. First, slaveholding violated his republican principles. And second, his family status and economic security depended on slavery. So the patriot leader was on the horns of a dilemma: to be either a principled founder or a dutiful father. In the end, Mason was not about to sacrifice what

Jefferson called his "indoors" family for his "outdoors" family. Fatefully, Mason, like Washington, Jefferson, and Madison, chose family over political principles.[100]

But to judge George Mason definitively on his lack of action on the slavery question is to paint an incomplete picture of Mason. The fact is that slavery was not an evil introduced by the Founders. Slavery was introduced in America nearly two centuries before Mason was born. In fact the Revolution was a pivotal turning point in the national attitude about slavery—and it was George Mason who contributed greatly to that change and intellectual debate. After all, one of the reasons given by Mason and Jefferson for the separation from Great Britain was a desire to rid America of the evil of slavery imposed on them by the British.

Author and historian R. Carter Pittman made the ambitious assertion that "had George Mason had his way the Federal Constitution would have emancipated slaves and there would have been no civil war."[101] Overblown statements of this sort go back at least to 1919, when Robert C. Mason, a Mason descendant, published a distorted celebration of his ancestor. Mason was "the wealthiest man in Virginia, owner of a thousand slaves," he wrote. "Nonetheless, he came to recognize that freedom and slavery were incompatible foundation stones upon which to erect the cardinal principles of our government." Thus, "he began to advocate the curtailment of slavery by restricting the slave traffic." In fact, "he agreed to free his own slaves and, therefore, was the first known abolitionist."[102] The last statement is just factually wrong. What is true, though, is that Mason "refused from conscientious motives" to sign the Constitution.[103] And one of his most important "motives" for withholding his signature was his objection to the abhorrent slavery "compromise." Historian Winthrop D. Jordan concluded that George Mason was "a vigorous opponent of slavery. Mason employed vigorous language, language that sounded antislavery, but he aimed it most directly at the slave trade. He denounced it as 'this detestable trade,' 'that nefarious trade,' and 'this infamous traffic' and declared that 'such a trade is diabolical in itself, and disgraceful to mankind.' Mason's reservations about slavery were numerous, his language passionate."[104]

Mason never stopped condemning slavery in his speeches and writings. If slavery was American's original sin, as it has often been called, Mason's record of complicity in its continuance is no doubt a stain on his legacy.[105] Joseph Ellis has argued that slavery was the most blatant contradiction of everything the American Revolution and Constitution stood for. "It required herculean feats of denial not to notice that 20 percent of the American population, about 500,000 souls, were African Americans, and that fully 90 percent of them were slaves, the vast majority residing south of the Potomac."[106] In fact, Ellis noted, "Adams had received requests to place this glaring anomaly on the agenda of the Continental Congress: that failure to address this issue would expose the entire case against British tyranny as fraudulent and hypocritical. An anonymous petitioner from Virginia put the problem most succinctly: 'Is it not incompatible with the glorious Struggle America is making for her own Liberty, to hold in absolute Slavery a Number of Wretches.'"[107] Another historian has bluntly concluded that both the Constitutional Convention and the Revolution itself "failed to free the slaves, failed to offer full political equality to women … failed to grant citizenship to Indians, [and] failed to create an economic world in which all could compete on equal terms."[108] But even though the Constitutional Convention in Philadelphia rejected Mason's arguments and in effect sustained slavery, Mason had helped put the corrosive and divisive issue on the national political agenda for the first time, in a way in which it had never been discussed before.

And to be fair, all efforts to wrench Mason out of his own time and place on the issue of slavery are futile and "invariably compromise the integrity of the historical context that made him what he was," in the words of prominent historian Joseph Ellis.[109] Yet neither Mason nor his Virginia colleagues went nearly far enough in deeds. Perhaps historian David Stewart was right when he wrote elegantly of Mason and the other Founders' historical legacy on slavery: "For all they have been celebrated, the delegates bear responsibility for having entrenched slavery ever deeper.... They created a government so entwined with slavery that in 1859 the abolitionist John Brown could write in his gallows statement that 'the sins of this guilty land can only be purged with blood.'"[110]

In the end, slavery was their most profound failure, leaving a festering racial wound that still has not healed.[111]

CHAPTER THIRTEEN

The Virginia Ratifying Convention

I believe there are few men in whom [Washington] placed greater confidence; but it is possible my opposition to the new government, both as a member of the national and of the Virginia Convention, may have altered the case.

— **GEORGE MASON** to his son John (1789)

W eary and graying at sixty-two after the Philadelphia Convention, Mason went home to Gunston Hall and threw himself into improvements of his beloved estate. Mason retreated to the bosom of his devoted family, writing: "[A] t my time of life, my only satisfaction and pleasure is in my children, and all my views are centered in their welfare and happiness."[1] There is little doubt that during his time in Philadelphia Mason suffered political and psychological wounds that never completely healed. He was happy to be returning home, but the severe accident when his carriage overturned on the way back was perhaps an omen. Daniel Carroll, a delegate to the Convention from Maryland, wrote to James Madison chronicling Mason's accident. After leaving Philadelphia he had overtaken Mason and a traveling companion, James McHenry, on the road: "By the time they had reachd within 9 Miles of Baltimore, they had exhausted all the stories of their youth &ca. and had enterd into a discusn. of the rights to the Western World. You know they are champions on opposite sides of this question. The Majr. having pushd the Col. hard on the Charters of Virginia the latter had just wax'd warm, when his Char[i] oteer put an end to the dispute, by jumbling their Honors together by an oversett. I came up soon after. They were both hurt—the Col. most so—he lost blood at Baltimore, & is well."[2]

Mason himself described the accident in a letter to Washington shortly after his return from Philadelphia: "I got very much hurt in my Neck & Head, by the unlucky Accident on the Road; it is now wearing off; tho' at times still uneasy to me."[3] Washington mentioned the accident in his reply: "I am sorry to hear you met with an accident on your return. I hope you experience no ill effect from it. The family here join me in compliments and good wishes to you, Mrs Mason and Family. I am Dr Sir, Yr Most Obed. & Affecte Hble Servant."[4]

It is ironic, perhaps a foreshadowing, that Washington had also suffered misfortune on his way back from the Convention. Washington had set out for Mount Vernon from Philadelphia on the afternoon of September 18, 1787, along with fellow Virginia delegate John Blair. He was in such a hurry to return to his beloved estate that he refused to wait when heavy rains prevented the pair from crossing a ford at Elkton, Maryland. He attempted to send his carriage, loaded with baggage, over an old abandoned bridge. He and Blair got out of the carriage as a precaution against accidents— fortuitously, because the bridge collapsed. One of Washington's horses, still in harness, dropped fifteen feet, and the other came close to falling, which would have crushed Washington's carriage. Workers from a nearby mill managed with "great exertion" to save the horses and prevent further damage. Washington, exhausted and emotionally spent, finally arrived at Mount Vernon, "about Sunset after an absence of four Months and 14 days."[5]

The Convention, and the proposed Constitution, had bitterly divided the states almost immediately, drawing dramatically divergent opinions. According to historian Ron Chernow, "For all its gore and mayhem, the American Revolution had unified the thirteen states, binding them into a hopeful, if still restive, nation. The aftermath of the Constitutional Convention, by contrast, turned ugly and divisive, polarizing the populace."[6] In Chernow's telling, many Americans blanched in amazement at the finished document. This Constitution went far beyond Congress's instructions to rework the Articles of Confederation: it created a brand-new government. The old confederation had simply vanished. Marinus Willett, New York's sheriff, attacked the new Constitution as "a monster with open mouth and monstrous teeth ready to devour all before it."[7] Amid fierce debate, the country split into two groups. Those in favor of the new dominant central government were called "federalists." Opponents of the Constitution, who feared encroachments on state government, were termed "anti-federalists." The two sides predicted competing disasters if the other side prevailed. Yet each side claimed "liberty" as their polestar and presented themselves as the faithful curators of revolutionary values. One correspondent of James Madison articulated the bitter fracture: "Opinions have already been deliver'd, and that work [the Constitution], which was the production of much labour & time, has been in a few hours either damn'd or applauded, according to the wish, sentiments, or interest of the politician."[8]

To add insult to his physical injury, Mason was now being roundly attacked for his failure to sign the Constitution.[9] He became the victim of a goading, insinuating resentment from some colleagues, as was reported in the *Pennsylvania Journal*, on October 17, 1787:

"We hear from Virginia, that on the arrival of Mr. Mason at Alexandria, he was waited on by the Mayor and Corporation of that Town, who told him, they were not come to return him their thanks for his conduct in refusing to sign the Fœderal Constitution; but to express their abhorrence to it, and to advise him to withdraw from that town within an hour, for they could not answer for his personal safety, from an enraged populace, should he exceed that time."[10] In an acrimonious letter to Horatio Gates on November 20, Virginia attorney James Hughes wrote, "The Federal constitution is universally approved of here. Should Col. Mason offer himself he would hardly get twenty votes in the whole County for, he has made himself odious, by an illiberall abuse of the Commissioners of the Turnpike, & an attempt, to divide the Town, from the County."[11] The *Pennsylvania Gazette* denounced Mason: "We hear from Virginia, that George Mason has been treated with every possible mark of contempt and neglect, for neglecting to sign the Fœderal Constitution."[12]

But not all commentaries were critical of Mason. The *Philadelphia Independent Gazetteer* defended him: "A correspondent says that the brave Colonel George Mason, of Virginia, who nobly said that he would sooner cut off his hand than sign the new constitution, of the United States, deserves high praise; he should consider that time is only wanting to manifest the proposed constitution to be an odious system of tyranny, and therefore that his manly conduct will be attended with a growing fame; but if his conduct were not to be attended with the applauses which he is going to receive, he should consider that, as a celebrated poet expresses himself, 'One self approving hour, whole years outweighs, Of stupid Starers, and of loud huzzas.'"[13]

In stark contrast to the mostly hostile reception Mason received, Washington was again anointed a glowing hero after the Convention. The *Pennsylvania Herald* heaped praised on him: "The following instance of the influence of a good and great man, will, we presume, be acceptable to every reader who loves his country, and venerates its darling Hero.... general washington, rose, and spoke to the following effect.... Such was the magic force of this patriot's opinion! and it adds to the lustre of his virtues...."[14]

George Mason was not one to walk away from a political fight, or his convictions. Provoked by what he called "the precipitate, & intemperate, not to say indecent Manner" in which the Convention had acted during its last week, he became a zealous opponent of ratification. Though still recovering from his injuries on the road from Philadelphia to Gunston, Mason, warned to stay out of the city of Alexandria, accepted the challenge. He rode fearlessly into Alexandria and had the sheriff proclaim that George Mason was there to make a speech. As he warmed to the subject of the rights of men, a heckler yelled, "The people of Fairfax know that Colonel Mason is losing his mind!" Mason replied: "If you lose yours, no one will ever know it." When he finished his speech to a hushed audience, Mason mounted his horse and rode to Gunston Hall.[15]

Mason was truculent and despondent after the Constitutional Convention in Philadelphia. He wanted nothing more than to retire to his farm, his family, and his books. But he still entertained "hopes of proper & safe Amendments" to the Constitution. In the absence of those amendments, he would soon become a leading figure and fierce critic of the Constitution in the coming Ratifying Convention in Richmond, Virginia, to begin in June 1788. Mason was disappointed at the outcome in Philadelphia, but unapologetic about his convictions.

Mason traveled in Virginia, and perhaps as far away as North Carolina to oppose ratification. But while Mason denounced the Constitution and disseminated his objections to it, Washington rallied support for state ratification. Mason had written to the General on

October 7, 1787, not quite a month after the end of the Philadelphia
Convention, enclosing a copy of his Objections with his letter:

> I take the Liberty to enclose You my Objections to the new
> Constitution of Government; which a little Moderation &
> Temper, in the latter End of the Convention, might have
> removed. I am however most decidedly of Opinion, that it
> ought to be submitted to a Convention chosen by the people,
> for that special purpose; and shou'd any Attempt be made
> to prevent the calling such a Convention here, such a Mea-
> sure shall have every Opposition in my power to give it.
>   You will readily observe, that my Objections are not
> numerous (the greater part of the inclosed paper containing
> reasonings upon the probable Effects of the exceptionable
> parts) tho' in my mind, some of them are capital ones.
>   Mrs Mason, & the Family, here join in their Compli-
> ments to your Lady and Family, with dear Sir Your affecte
> & obdt Sert G. Mason.[16]

It was now painfully obvious to Washington that Mason would
be a fierce political foe of ratification.

Washington sent a letter with copies of the Constitution to all
three former Virginia governors—Benjamin Harrison, Thomas Nelson Jr., and Patrick Henry[17]—declaring his support for ratification:
"I wish the Constitution which is offered had been made more perfect,
but I sincerely believe it is the best that could be obtained at this
time—and as a constitutional door is opened for amendment hereafter—the adoption of it under present circumstances of the Union is
in my opinion desirable."[18]

Meanwhile, Mason dispatched a copy of the draft Constitution
(with his Objections) to Jefferson, still serving as Minister in Paris.

Benjamin Franklin sent one to Jefferson, too, and letters about the Constitution flowed into Jefferson's *Hôtel de Langeac*. John Adams, after reading a copy of the draft, told Jefferson that he thought it "seems to be admirably calculated to preserve the Union, to increase affection, and to bring us all to the same mode of thinking." But Adams also asked Jefferson, "What think you of a Declaration of Rights? Should not such a thing have preceded the model?"[19] As we have seen, Jefferson initially reacted to the Constitution just as critically as Mason. As author Jon Meacham explains, "Not only was there a lack of a bill of rights for citizens, but the details of the power of the presidency troubled Jefferson: 'He may be reelected from 4 years to 4 years for life,' Jefferson said. 'Reason and experience prove to us that a chief magistrate, so continual, is an officer for life. When one or two generations shall have proved that this is an office for life, it becomes on every succession worthy of intrigue, of bribery, of force, and even of foreign interference.'"[20] According to Meacham, Jefferson "blamed the British for features he did not like, arguing that the British press had exaggerated American instability for so long that the world has at length believed them."[21]

Washington, on the other hand, was committed to the Constitution. One historian has analyzed the motivation for the General's steadfast support of the new document: "In stark contrast to George Mason and Patrick Henry, George Washington operated on a national field from the early stages of the Revolution and never left it. His support for the Constitution, including its centralizing definition of country, was consistent with the views he first adopted during the Revolutionary War. From the outset of the military contest, George Washington prioritized the country—the United States—that chose him as its father."[22]

Washington and Madison shared their disappointment in the defection of Mason to the other side, which Madison found bizarre and Washington found unforgivable. Mason had been a long-standing friend, but all communication now ceased between Mount Vernon and Gunston Hall. According to author Joseph Ellis, "Washington had purchased an English translation of Don Quixote before leaving Philadelphia, and now considered his former friend the 'Don Quixote' of the ratification process. Moreover, Washington was outraged when his remarks on the Constitution—namely, that he was 'fully persuaded that it is the best that can be obtained at this time, and that it or disunion is before us'—were leaked to the press by Charles Carter, a correspondent he customarily consulted on agricultural matters. He chastised Carter for the indiscretion, claiming that he had played his last public role at the Constitutional Convention and now wished to retire to Mt. Vernon."[23]

If there was anything that set Washington's temper off, it was perceived disloyalty. Later, when he assumed the presidency, Washington would refuse to appoint anyone to the new government who had been hostile to the Constitution.[24] Some biographers have underestimated Washington's personal and political animosity toward Mason. But the comments of Tobias Lear, Washington's personal secretary and tutor to Martha Washington's grandchildren, surely reflect contempt that Washington must have expressed towards Mason and his Objections. "Some of them are raised upon so slender a foundation as would render it doubtful whether they were a production of Col. Mason's abilities." The personal letters of Lear shed additional light on Washington's dim attitude toward Mason after the Constitutional Convention, for Lear took his opinions directly from Washington's dinner table. On one occasion, the secretary wrote of Mason's Objections: "I enclose a copy of Colo. Masons objections to the Constitution. Some of his observations appear to be founded in truth, & their inconveniencies were undoubtedly seen by the Convention, but they found it necessary to make some issue upon the goodness of their cause. Others seem to be calculated only to alarm the fears of the people, and consequently raise objections in their minds which would not otherwise have been thought of.... Colo. Mason is certainly a man of superior abilities—he is sensible of it, & having generally felt his weight & influence in those public bodies where he has acted heretofore, he has contracted the idea of 'aut Caesar, aut nullus.'"[25]

The letters from Lear suggest that Washington saw Mason as a formidable opponent of the federalists. And the General himself would complain of Mason's powerful influence on others: "They are in the habit of thinking that everything he says and does is right and (if capable) they will not judge for themselves."[26]

Washington was politically astute enough to see what an effective weapon the Framers had put into Mason's hands by offering a Constitution with no Bill of Rights to the states for ratification. If Mason and his colleagues wielded that weapon cleverly, they might achieve their apparent goal: the defeat of the Constitution and the restoration of the autonomy and supremacy of state governments.

But the opponents to the Constitution were not just dangerous to the Constitution. They also used language that Washington found personally insulting. In a campaign speech for a seat at the Virginia Ratifying Convention, Mason made his opposition to ratification clear. But he also used the opportunity to provide a blistering portrait of the men who had been his colleagues in Philadelphia. "Fellow-Citizens," he said, "you have been often told of the wisdom and virtue of the federal convention, but I will now inform you of their true character—the deputies to that body from the states to the southward of us were Coxcombs; the deputies from Virginia you know pretty well; the majority of the deputies from the middle states were intriguing office-hunters; and those from the eastern states fools and knaves."[27] A George Nicholas—the apparent author of anonymous articles that would be published under the pseudonym "Decius" a few months after the Virginia Ratifying Convention—accused George Mason of having "vent[ed] his envy and hatred for Genl Washington" by claiming "in a public speech to the people of Stafford" that "'[s]peculators, place hunters, and horse jockeys composed that infamous body of traitors' who had drafted the federal Constitution."[28]

The assertion that Mason hated and envied Washington was incorrect. But Washington was coming to resent Mason: "The political tenets of Colo. M[ason] and Colo. R[ichard Henry Lee] are always in unison. It may be asked which of them gives the tone. Without hesitation I answer, the [former]; because I believe [he] will receive it from no one. He has, I am informed, rendered himself obnoxious in Philadelphia by the pains he took to disseminate his objections amongst some [of] the leaders of the seceding members of the Legislature of that State. His conduct is not less reprobated in this County."[29]

While Mason did not mean to insult Washington, his respected neighbor and lifetime friend, Mason's ridicule of the Framers ensured that the debate over whether Virginia should ratify the Constitution would turn personal and bitter. While Washington, for his part, had no personal vendetta against Mason or his family, he thought of himself as suffering a wound inflicted by a lifelong friend. The General perceived both a personal and political attack.

George Mason was always certain in his mind that his opposition to the Constitution stemmed from the highest motives, not personal animosity toward Washington—or anyone, for that matter. "I am truly conscious of having acted from the purest motives of honesty, and love to my country," Mason wrote his son John.[30] Whatever his opposition to the Constitution cost him, Mason was convinced that his conduct would "administer comfort to me in those moments when I shall most want it, and smooth the bed of death."

Scholars have debated Mason's real motivations. According to famed Jefferson biographer Dumas Malone, "George Mason's 'deep convictions,' caused him to assume a negative role and even to seem obstructive toward the new Constitution. Those deep convictions evolved a fundamental belief in the rights of human beings. The very reasons which led Mason to write the Virginia Declaration of Rights forced him to withhold his approval from an unlamented Constitution." Historians Samuel E. Morison and Henry S. Commager, on the other hand, have argued that Mason refused to sign the Constitution "largely because of wounded vanity, since some of … [his] pet projects were not adopted."[31]

Considering that the Bill of Rights was one of those "pet projects," perhaps Americans owe a debt of gratitude to Mason's vanity. In any case, whether he was acting out of pique or standing on the principles he had championed over the course of his public life, George Mason would hold rock solid in his opposition to the Constitution as it was written—without a formal Bill of Rights. He was simply continuing down the path he had set out on at the Philadelphia Convention, where, as Madison's notes recorded, Mason had insisted that "he would sooner chop off his right hand than put it to the constitution as it now stands."[32]

Mason would prove a formidable intellectual rival to the federalists, nearly turning the tables against Washington and Madison at Virginia's Ratifying Convention in Richmond in the summer of 1788. Mason launched the first of what would be many broadsides against the Constitution two weeks before leaving for Richmond. The first of his Objections—"There is No Declaration of Rights"—would become the rallying theme of the "anti-federalists" there, where Mason led the opposition to the Constitution in concert with William Grayson, who had served in the Continental Army and the House of Delegates, and the fiery Patrick Henry.

Henry's political base, unlike Mason's, lay in the counties of the Virginia backcountry south of the James River, including his own Prince Edward County. Patrick Henry was wealthy and connected. His "path toward fortune and fame" had begun "[o]nly when Henry took up the law," according to one scholar: "It is interesting to note that Jefferson thought Henry's reputation at that time was overblown, and considered Henry an undistinguished statesman. Jefferson, who was Henry's junior by seven years but whose political career ran parallel to Henry's for two decades, had no respect for his legal competence. After what Jefferson claimed was only six weeks of preparation, Henry arrived in Williamsburg in 1760, a man of twenty-four seeking a license to practice law."[33] Jefferson gossiped that Henry was a lazy lawyer. But Mason adamantly disagreed with Jefferson. Never given to effusive praise, Mason thought Henry was "by far the most powerful speaker I ever heard."[34] Patrick Henry's oratory dazzled even his sharpest critics.

In *Founders as Fathers*, Lorri Glover references Virginia's most prominent nineteenth-century historian, Hugh Grigsby, who pointed out some interesting differences between the leading proponents for the Constitution and its chief opponents. "The leading advocates" of the Constitution, "including Washington and Madison, were men of wealth, or held office by a life tenure, and that, though married, neither of them ever had a child"[35]—something that may explain why the leaders of the federalist cause "were willing to sacrifice Virginia's sovereignty to build a stronger, national country." The anti-federalists Henry and Mason, on the other hand "were men of large families.... With sons to launch, these men could not afford to subordinate state interests, particularly land claims, to a federal union. Washington and Madison might think of their duties to posterity in general terms, puzzling through the best interests of future generations of citizens, but Mason and Henry saw the faces of posterity at their dinner tables."[36] Mason and Henry's faithfulness to their state and their families "can better be understood as deriving from ... commitment to the duties of a traditional Virginia patriarch. Like most of [their] influential gentry friends and neighbors—including many who supported the Constitution ... [they] focused on Virginia interests."[37]

The one constant in both Mason and Henry's career was their abiding attachment to local interests, which would be on full display in the Richmond Convention. "Henry would fight ratification," according to one scholar, "with a ferocity that surprised even those who knew him well. Holding forth for hours at a time with blistering rebukes of the federal plan and its advocates, Henry insisted that the Constitution represented 'a revolution as radical as that which separated us from Great Britain.' 'This Government is not a Virginian but an American government,' Henry warned. And he wanted no part of it, like Mason."

Mason and Patrick Henry also had very different backgrounds from and vastly more life experiences than their nemesis, James Madison, also in attendance in Richmond.

It was May when Mason began his two-day trek to the Ratifying Convention. Worried about the heat and drenching rains of late spring in Virginia, Mason took the stagecoach, which would conveniently arrive on Sunday, June 1, the day before the Convention was scheduled to begin. The stagecoach company had promised to put extra coaches into service from Williamsburg and Fredericksburg if needed. The trip from Gunston Hall was not easy. The relatively uncomplicated fifty-mile trip by stage from Fairfax County to Richmond could take fifteen hours after a heavy rain. Delegates from western Virginia, including what would become Kentucky, had many more miles to travel, with dangerous mountains to cross.[38]

Richmond, Mason's destination, was a far different city from Philadelphia or Boston, where other state ratifying conventions were

meeting. The people of those port cities were in favor of a quick ratification of the Constitution, which they hoped would bring a needed
commercial influx of money into their cities. But Richmond was on
the upper reaches of the James River, in Virginia's Piedmont. It had
become Virginia's capital in 1779, during the Revolutionary War,
when the old capital, Williamsburg, was too close to the sea and thus
vulnerable to attacks. The legislature chose Richmond because it was
"more safe and central than any other town situated on navigable
water."[39] The arrival of some 170 Convention delegates and a "prodigious number of People from all parts of the Country" made the
little town "exceedingly crowded." One writer described the city,
spread out on two hills along the river, at that time:

> Richmond remained a small town in 1788 with about two
> thousand residents and fewer than three hundred wooden
> houses, mostly small with heavy shutters and chimneys
> built of short logs, along with taverns, shops, and tobacco
> warehouses. Goats and hogs wandered through its dirty
> streets, and yet as early as 1781 the Marquis de Chastelux
> found there a magnificent meal and comfortable lodgings.
> For diversion, elegantly dressed gentlemen and women
> could go dancing to the music of black fiddlers and banjo
> players. In 1788 the town even had a new "Academy,"
> otherwise known as the "New Theatre on Shockoe Hill,"
> a "Spacious and Airy Building" first conceived as a school
> for dancing, drawing, and foreign languages that was
> sometimes rented out for theater performances. [40]

The Convention would put the theater to effective use, moving
there from the old wooden statehouse on its second day, because it
had space for both the delegates and the throngs of people who

wanted to see the debate.[41] It was no mystery why spectators were flooding into Richmond. The Convention promised to be an epic oratorical contest among Mason, Patrick Henry, and the scholarly James Madison. The delegates included many of the political stars of Virginia, past, present, and rising. "Henry alone was a big draw," explains historian Pauline Maier, "and Mason would be at his side, opposing ratification of the Constitution in its current form. So would William Grayson, a fifty-two-year-old lawyer and former member of the Continental Army who had been a member of Virginia's House of Delegates. And the handsome, dark-haired James Monroe, only thirty years old but already an experienced public servant."[42] James Monroe had cut short his studies at William and Mary to fight in the Revolutionary War, then studied law with Jefferson and served in Virginia's House of Delegates.

Another delegate, Edmund Pendleton, had little formal education but had nevertheless become one of the most respected jurists in Virginia. Now in his late sixties, Pendleton had walked with crutches since 1777, after a fall from a horse. Given his infirmities, Pendleton was allowed to sit while presiding over the Convention. Governor Edmund Randolph was also in attendance, along with the rising lawyer John Marshall.[43] Some notable names were missing: Jefferson remained in Paris, Washington at Mount Vernon, and Richard Henry Lee at Chantilly, his home in Northern Virginia.

John Marshall would write that the official reporter of the Convention, David Robertson, did his best recording speakers such as William Grayson and James Monroe, who wrote out their speeches beforehand, or Mason, who spoke distinctly from "very copious notes." Randolph, "whose elocution was good," was also "pretty well reported." But Robertson did not fare as well with the soft-spoken Madison, who often spoke "too low to be understood." He fared even worse with the rapid-fire Henry, whom "no reporter could

correctly report." As for his own speeches, Marshall said that "if my
name had not been prefixed to the speeches I never should have recognized them." And yet Robertson succeeded in capturing the speakers' eloquence, and even their incoherence. "Used carefully along with
contemporary letters and newspaper reports," says Pauline Maier,
"[Robertson's] *Debates* preserve for posterity a historical record of
the convention that would otherwise have vanished."[44]

Mason met his old friend Patrick Henry at the Swan Hotel,
Richmond's finest place of lodging, on Broad Street behind the
handsome new Capitol. Nineteenth-century historian Hugh Grigsby
would describe Mason's daily walk to Shockoe Hill in Richmond,
and then to the Convention: Mason "was remarkable for the urbanity and dignity with which he received the courtesies of those who
passed by him."[45] Edmund Pendleton, who would be elected president of the Convention, had also taken rooms at the Swan, and,
according to one account, "he chirped greetings to all comers,
professing good health while he admitted the lack of an antidote for
the ailment of advancing age. The old judge had long since endorsed
the Constitution, and Henry and Mason had to find a private corner
to discuss their strategy."[46]

The federalists, including Washington and Madison, had tried
hard to divide these most prominent anti-federalists, portraying
Henry as an irresponsible demagogue while appealing to Mason, and
also to Governor Edmund Randolph, as moderate critics who might
soften their opposition in support of national unity. Mason had
appeared malleable in October of 1787, in the immediate aftermath
of the Philadelphia Convention, but the political and personal invec-
tives launched at him over the ensuing months had hardened his
opposition. He reacted emotionally to recurring charges that his
refusal to sign the Constitution had stemmed from personal anger,
rather than political principle.[47]

On Monday morning, June 2, 1788, Henry and Mason, wearing suits of deepest black, strode out of the Swan together and walked arm in arm down the hill to the clapboard meeting house that still served as the commonwealth's temporary Capitol. Inside the old assembly chamber, the hordes of eager spectators and the stifling heat quickened rumors of a surprise vote and early adjournment. But as it played out, the Virginia Ratifying Convention would last until nearly the end of June. It was "destined to become one of the most significant and consequential debates in American history. And the Virginia press, sensing the historical implications, had hired stenographers to record the words of all speakers, making it the most fully preserved of all the ratifying conventions."[48] Bernard Bailyn has gone so far as to call the ratification debates "the greatest outpouring of political thinking in Western history."[49]

The Richmond Convention came to appoint two committees, one to prepare a form of ratification and another to create a list of amendments that would be recommended to the new national Congress. The first committee consisted exclusively of delegates who would support ratification without amendments: Nicholas, Madison, Marshall, and Corbin. Edmund Randolph, the sitting Virginia governor, had been one of three delegates—along with George Mason and Elbridge Gerry—present in Philadelphia at the end of the Constitutional Convention who refused to sign the Constitution. But over the coming weeks, Randolph would eventually come over to the "pro" side for ratifying the Constitution. Patrick Henry took Randolph's change of position as high treason to the anti-federalists' cause. As Elbridge Gerry would write to James Warren on June 28, 1788, the day after the Ratifying Convention came to a close, "Patrick Henry has been brilliant in that convention, and very severe on [Randolph] who is reprobated for his duplicity and versatility."[50] Cyrus Griffin, a lawyer and judge who had served as president of the

Continental Congress, was also unimpressed with Randolph's performance at the Richmond convention. He wrote to Madison that
"the Governor by nature [is] timid and undecided."⁵¹ Jefferson would
be even harsher on Randolph, writing to Madison some years later,
"I can by this confidential conveyance speak more freely of R[andolph].
He is the poorest Cameleon I ever saw having no color of his own, &
reflecting that nearest him. When he is with me he is a whig, when
with H[amilton] he is a tory, when with the P[resident Washington]
he is what he thinks will please him. The last is his strongest hue,
though the 2nd tinges him very strongly.... I have kept on terms of
strict friendship with him hitherto, that I might make some good out
of him, & because he has really some good private qualities. But he
is in a station infinitely too important for his understanding, his firmness, or his circumstances."⁵²

The second committee, to prepare promised Constitutional
amendments, which would be chaired by George Wythe, included
nine critics of the Constitution, among them Mason, Henry, Grayson,
John Tyler, and James Monroe. Eventually the committee suggested
forty amendments, mostly from Mason's pen, including assertions of
rights that were taken largely from the Virginia Declaration of Rights
he had written twelve years earlier.

At first the Convention appeared evenly divided between federalists in support of ratifying the Constitution and anti-federalists who
opposed ratifying it without amendments. The coalition to derail
ratification was led by George Mason, Patrick Henry, and George
Wythe. Madison, the chief proponent of the Constitution, predicted
that Mason and Henry would do anything in their power to throw
sand into the gears of the new federal government.⁵³ (Henry and
Madison were sworn enemies. Indeed, Henry would later do his best
to keep Madison from being elected to Congress in 1789—in what

may be the first attempt in American history at what would later be called gerrymandering.)[54]

Mason and Henry would argue vigorously against ratification of the Constitution as it stood. The "anti-rats," as opponents of ratification were sometimes called, spoke out of fear for their country: fear of massive national power; fear of a national army; fear of the unfettered taxing power given to the new national government; fear of executive authority; and fear of a new aristocracy.

The debates began on the Convention's third day, June 4. Henry took the floor and effectively redefined the question that was before the delegates. One spectator recalled that Henry "involuntarily felt his wrists to assure himself that the fetters were not already pressing his flesh" when he spoke.[55] The public, Henry argued, was "extremely uneasy" over the proposed change in government. The people had been secure before the Constitutional Convention met, but its proposal had destroyed that security and put the republic in "extreme danger." The Constitution would set up a new government of nine states (the number required for ratification), annihilate treaties with foreign nations, and pose a grave threat to American liberty, Henry claimed. He asked why the members of the Convention had proposed a "consolidated Government, instead of a confederation. And what right had they to found its authority on "We, the People" instead of "Us, the States"? Even George Washington, Henry suggested, was answerable for his actions in Philadelphia. There had been "no dangers, no insurrection or tumult" in Virginia and no danger of sufficient magnitude to justify that "perilous innovation," the Constitution. The Federal Convention should have amended the Confederation, as instructed, Henry maintained. He warned that it was necessary "to be extremely cautious, watchful, and jealous of your liberty; for instead of securing your rights you may lose them forever."[56]

Mason took the floor after Henry's two-hour speech. At first he seemed to echo Henry, charging that the Constitution had created a national government instead of a confederation. But Mason then turned his attention to Congress's authority to lay direct taxes, which, he said, was "at discretion, unconfined, and without any kind of control." Would the people, Mason asked, "submit to be individually taxed by two different and distinct powers? Will they suffer themselves to be doubly harassed?" Since the "General Government" was superior to and more powerful than the states, the latter would necessarily "give way to the former," transforming "the confederation of States into one consolidated Government."[57] But no territory as large as the United States could be governed by a single government without destroying the people's liberty. Mason did not want to revert to the Articles of Confederation, whose "inefficacy" he recognized. Instead he proposed amendments to the Constitution to ensure that the people were more fully represented. Mason acknowledged that the people could not be represented fully in the general government; that would be "too expensive and too unwieldy." But only powers "absolutely necessary" should be granted to a government that was unavoidably defective in that way. The Constitution, Mason argued, would introduce the power of the federal government into every corner of the new country. He wanted the Constitution amended to define more sharply the line between the new general government and the state governments, and so prevent "that dangerous clashing of interest and power, which must, as it now stands, terminate in the destruction of one or the other." The problem was not confined to taxation. The judiciary also threatened the states. But with amendments to protect against the dangers he saw, Mason would "most gladly" put his hand to the Constitution.[58]

Mason, a "stalwart figure, attired in deep mourning, still erect, his black eyes fairly flashing.... His voice deliberate and full,"[59] pointed out that the Constitution spelled out the rights of government. But where, he asked, was a similar listing of the basic rights of individuals—a Bill of Rights protecting ordinary citizens against an all-powerful government. One's right to a jury trial, freedom of the press, freedom of assembly—these natural rights were the essence of liberty, Mason argued in Richmond. These inalienable rights that cannot be touched by any government. Without a guarantee that these inalienable rights could not be touched by the government, Mason contended, "we might as well just appoint ourselves a king and take lessons in the art of bowing low."[60]

Mason's objections were answered by federalists such as Madison and Noah Webster, who said, "I can understand a Bill of Rights to prevent kings and barons from encroaching on the rights of the people, but I don't see why we need a declaration of rights to protect us from our own elected legislature. In this new government, a Bill of Rights is absurd. It prevents what? Our own encroachments against ourselves?"[61]

The debate raged on into the summer heat of Richmond. One Virginia federalist concluded that Mason's chronic complaints about the Constitution had rendered him rather pathetic: "poor old man, he appears to have worn his judgment entirely thread-bare and ragged in the service of his country."[62] And yet Mason's "threadbare" "judgment" would be vindicated by history. He was the moving force behind our Bill of Rights, which would not exist without his tireless labors in the field of liberty.

First, at the beginning of the Revolution, before even the break from Britain, Mason called on his wide and deep knowledge of history and political philosophy to create the Virginia Declaration of Rights, which became the model for other states' declarations of rights, for the Declaration of Independence, and ultimately for the first ten amendments to the Constitution guaranteeing our rights to freedom of religion, freedom of speech and assembly, to jury trials, and to bear arms. His was nearly the lone—and certainly the chief— voice raised at the Philadelphia Convention in objection to a Constitution without a Declaration of Rights. And now, at the Virginia Ratifying Convention, he was still insisting on a Bill of Rights.

Mason's *Objections to This Constitution of Government*, which he had brought to Richmond with him and circulated among the delegates, began with the phrase, "There is no Declaration of Rights," yet just three of his sixteen paragraphs dealt with individual rights.[63] But the absence of a Bill of Rights was only one of many fatal defects Mason saw in the Constitution, as he made clear in Richmond. Day after day, Mason and Henry assaulted the document from all points of the compass, forcing James Madison to deal with their attacks. The strain brought on an attack of the "bilious fever" that had troubled Madison since his college days, when he had often studied to exhaustion. Madison missed three days of debate, and when he returned his voice was so raspy that he could not give speeches. The gap was filled by Virginia governor Edmund Randolph.

Although Randolph had refused to sign the Constitution in Philadelphia, he now declared himself in favor of ratification with no need for amendments or a second Convention. Without Virginia there would be no union, he argued. Raising his right arm in histrionics that rivaled Mason's and even Henry's, Randolph exclaimed he would rather "assent to lopping off this limb before I assent to the dissolution of the union."[64]

Madison wrote to Washington that Henry and Mason had "appeared to take different & awkward ground," and "the federalists are a good deal elated by the existing prospect." The Convention's outcome, however, remained uncertain, he told Washington. The opposition was privately using "every piece of address ... to work on the local interests and prejudices" of delegates from Kentucky and "other quarters." Madison knew that reining in Henry was impossible. He was a one-man show. But he had not given up on the sage from Gunston Hall.[65]

Madison and Washington were still not certain that Mason was forever lost to their cause. For several months after the adjournment of the Philadelphia Convention there was a strong movement afoot to summon a second national Convention to rewrite the Constitution. During the autumn of 1787, Mason played an active role in promoting it. He had helped change Virginia law to authorize the state Ratifying Convention to propose amendments that might become the agenda for a second national Convention. As long as it seemed possible to reopen the questions on which he had been defeated in Philadelphia, Mason indicated that he might ultimately accept an improved, even if still imperfect, Constitution. Madison and Washington had condemned the proposal for a second Convention, but even in its absence they held out hope that Mason might be persuaded to vote for ratification. They had had the identical hope for Governor Edmund Randolph, who had also refused to sign in Philadelphia—and in fact he did just as they wished.

The Convention went through the Constitution clause after clause, day after day. Nobody rivaled Mason's skill at a line-by-line analysis, but the task put enormous physical and emotional stress on him at age sixty-three. According to Pauline Maier, "Henry and Mason came down particularly hard on Congress's powers under Article I, Section 8, 'to raise and support armies,' to organize, arm, and discipline state militias, and to call up the militia 'to execute the Laws of the Union, suppress and repel Invasions.' When a country establishes a professional 'standing army,' Mason argued, 'the people lose their liberty.' It was better to rely on the militia, which was more closely connected with the people. And yet under the Constitution Congress could destroy the militia by failing to supply it with sufficient arms or making service odious. Mason wanted to require the consent of state legislatures before Congress could take a state's militia farther than a neighboring state. He also reasoned that militiamen should not be subject to martial law except in time of war."[66]

Mason then turned his critical eye on Article II, the executive, to which he raised multiple objections, as he had in Philadelphia a year earlier: the president's term was too long and, given the lack of term limits, he could be reelected indefinitely; a three-man executive council should advise the president in place of the Senate, whose advisory function violated the separation of powers; the office of vice president was unnecessary; the Senate should elect its own presiding officer; the president had too much power, Mason argued, which would make it worth the while of foreign countries to interfere in elections. And the Senate was an improper body to try impeachments on account of a blatant conflict of interest: since the Senate was charged with advising the president, "it would be his partner in crime."[67]

Next Mason expressed his grave concerns about the federal judiciary. He said that the judicial branch of the new federal government was "so constructed as to destroy the dearest rights of the community." Its jurisdiction was so broad that it left state courts impotent, and they would in effect be abolished. Federal courts would try all cases under the laws of Congress, whose power was basically unlimited. "Mason also questioned federal court jurisdiction in cases between a state and private citizens," one constitutional scholar explains: "'Is the sovereignty of the State to be arraigned like a culprit, or private offender?' he asked. 'Will the States undergo this mortification?' And what if they lost? A state's body could not be put in jail, and 'a power which cannot be executed, ought not to be granted.' Conflicts between citizens of different states should be left to state courts ... which were more convenient and whose members had the community's confidence. Since federal appellate courts had jurisdiction as to both fact and law, the problem was compounded. Even if a poor man who had suffered some serious injury received justice in an inferior court, what chance did he have on appeal? He might have to travel hundreds of miles at his own expense, and bring his witnesses."[68]

The specter of a new general government usurping the power of the states appeared again and again. In the pre-Revolutionary period, most powers had been enjoyed by the local organs of government. Mason charged that "these two concurrent powers cannot exist long together; the one will destroy the other."[69] James Monroe added, "If you give the resources of the several states to the general government, in what situation will the states be left. I therefore think the general government will preponderate." As usual, the last word went to Henry: "The whole history of human nature cannot produce a government like that before you.... [It] seems to me calculated to lay prostrate the states, and the liberties of the people."[70]

In response, the federalists charged Mason and Henry with taking too cynical a view of human nature. As Madison said, "I have observed, that gentlemen suppose that the [federal government] will do everything mischievous they possibly can, and that they will omit to do everything good which they are authorized to do. If this were a reasonable supposition, their objections would be good.... But I go on this great republican principle, that the people will have virtue and intelligence to select men of virtue and wisdom. Is there no virtue among us? If there be not, we are in a wretched situation."[71] And as John Marshall asserted, "I think the virtue and talents of the members of the general government will tend to the security, instead of the destruction, of our liberties."[72] Madison and Edmund Randolph did accept the need for vigilance, but they questioned the zealotry of the opposition. "I will agree," said Randolph, "in the necessity of political jealousy to a certain extent; but we ought to examine how far this political jealousy ought to be carried." Madison turned the anti-federalists' own arguments against them, claiming that their suspicions of the proposed federal government would keep it in line: "Another security is that ... I know this government will be cautiously watched. The smallest assumption of power will be sounded an alarm to the people, and followed by bold and active opposition. The fear of power also comprehended concern with the locus of that power, that is, the question of sovereignty, which is the question of the nature and location of the ultimate power in the state."[73]

The debate at the Virginia Ratifying Convention literally ended with a bang. A violent summer storm with wind, hail, and rain interrupted a speech by Francis Corbin, leaving the hall so "wet & uncomfortable" that the Convention adjourned. Edmund Pendleton stayed home the next day because his health could not endure the "extream dampness." Efforts to reopen the discussion failed: the delegates, it seemed, had had enough of Richmond, and the intense political bickering.

None of Madison's or Marshall's forceful arguments had persuaded Mason to vote for ratification. "A bill of rights may be summed up in a few words," he concluded. "What do they tell us?—that our rights are reserved. Why not say so? Is it because it will consume too much paper?" Mason and Henry would not yield an inch to the federalists. "My mind will not be quieted," Henry insisted, "Till I see something substantial come forth in the shape of a Bill of Rights." And as Mason argued, even if a Bill of Rights was not necessary in itself, it was "a favorite thing" with Virginians, as well as among the people of the other states. "It may be their prejudice, but the Government ought to suit their geniuses" or "its operation will be unhappy." Amending the Constitution with a Bill of Rights would "exclude the possibility of dispute."[74]

Mason agreed with the federalists on the need to amend the Articles of Confederation to establish a federal government on a firmer footing: In the end, the Richmond debates evidenced that the differences between the federalists and anti-federalists seemed more tactical than deeply strategic. "We acknowledge the defects of the confederation and the necessity of a reform. We ardently wish for a union with our sister states on terms of security. This I am bold to declare is the desire of most of the people. On these terms we will most cheerfully join with the warmest friends of this Constitution." Even Patrick Henry condescended to admit some common ground: "I acknowledge that licentiousness is dangerous, and that it ought to be provided against. I acknowledge also, the new form of government may effectually prevent it: yet there is another thing it will effectually do? It will oppress ... the people."

But neither Henry's rhetoric nor Mason's reasoning would triumph. The arguments of James Madison—though he was ailing and felt "extremely feeble"—finally won the day. As John Marshall said, "while Mr. Henry had without doubt the greatest power to persuade," it was "Mr. Madison" who "had the greatest power to convince."[75] Mason and Henry made a powerful case, but it was Madison who could close the deal. Washington's nephew Bushrod was also awed by Madison's talents, reporting to Mount Vernon that Madison had spoken "with such force of reasoning and a display of such irresistible truths that opposition seemed to have quitted the field."

The defection of Edmund Randolph to the federalist side also damaged the anti-federalists' chances. Mason believed that his former ally deserved censure for his handling of a May 8 letter from Governor George Clinton of New York to Randolph implying that New York would support a second Federal Convention. Randolph showed the letter to the council of state, which advised him to share it with the general assembly. The assembly was not in session at the time, and Randolph had procrastinated, not forwarding the letter to the legislature until the

Convention was winding down in late June. Incensed, Mason drafted resolutions calling for an investigation into what he considered Randolph's dereliction of duty in not making the Clinton letter public. Chastised by his colleagues in private, Mason decided against introducing the resolutions. Months later, Mason, still seething, referred to Randolph as "young A[rnol]d," comparing him with Benedict Arnold, traitor of the Revolution—the bitterest invective."[76]

On June 23, 1788, Virginia approved the Constitution by a slim ten-vote margin. "After weeks of passionate debate, the final vote was stunningly close: 89–79. Five votes swung the other way would have altered the course of the nation. But the Tidewater region (which included Washington's Fairfax County) ended the suspense with six straight votes for ratification. A change of six votes would have dispatched the Constitution to historical oblivion."[77] Four days earlier, New Hampshire had actually become the ninth state to ratify the Constitution, bringing the new federal government into effect. But the Virginia Ratifying Convention was unaware of the New Hampshire vote. And, in any case, the Constitution would probably not have succeeded if Virginia had not ratified.

"Technically any nine states could have ratified the Constitution," according to author Lorri Glover, "but in 1787–1788 everyone understood that, without Virginia, the Constitution would almost certainly fail: The state held one-fifth of the land in the United States, and one in six Americans lived there. And there was the not insignificant weight of recent history. More of the men who conceived the American Republic hailed from Virginia than any other state, arguably more than all the other states combined. If the home of George Washington and Patrick Henry was not to be in the United States, could there be a United States at all?"[78]

Some historians have criticized Mason's performance at the Richmond Convention as strident. And a speech he gave after it closed has met with condemnation on the same grounds. "Only one delegate left the convention with a tarnished reputation," according to Pauline Maier. "George Mason, who, according to Nelson, was said to have behaved with less good temper than Henry. On the evening after the convention adjourned, [Mason] assembled a substantial number of delegates who had voted against ratification on the pretense of issuing an address that would reconcile their constituents to the Constitution. Instead he proposed an inflammatory address to the public that prompted some men to leave the hall immediately. Others sat in stunned silence until, finally, Benjamin Harrison suggested that the meeting adjourn without doing anything. The opposition members had lost; now it was their duty as good citizens to submit to the majority. When other speakers supported Harrison, Mason withdrew his address and the meeting dissolved."[79] Harrison, John Tyler, and John Lawson objected to the sharp tone of what a contemporary newspaper called Mason's "fiery, irritating manifesto." Unintimidated, Mason would continue his fight.

Washington welcomed the triumphant Madison to Mount Vernon, but found him exhausted by the political war he had waged in Richmond. The Convention had been a draining ordeal for Madison, lasting twenty-six long, humid June days, with Mason and Henry orating throughout. Several of Henry's speeches lasted a full day. His and Mason's political assaults on the Constitution were shrewd and powerful. Washington saw at a glance how exhausted Madison was. For the first and only time, he showed his paternal feelings for this talented young man and urged Madison to "take a little respite from business and relax at Mount Vernon for a few days." The General advised a routine of "moderate exercise" and books only occasionally—books he could read for pleasure, "with the mind unbent." Madison took his paternal advice and spent four days at Mount

Vernon.[80] For Washington, the heavens were watching over "his" United States.

Mason had lost. He trudged home to Gunston Hall from Richmond, riding through oak trees touched with the red afterglow of the setting sun. As he exited his carriage, he was deeply disappointed and discouraged. His mandarin patience with the political process was at an end. He needed time to absorb his defeat, both emotionally and psychologically. The bitter political disagreement pulled Mason and Washington apart. Social contacts between the two men would virtually end after the Richmond Ratifying Convention. Writing about his relationship with Washington in March 1789, Mason would tell his son John, "I believe there are few men in whom he placed greater confidence; but it is possible my opposition to the new government, both as a member of the national and of the Virginia Convention, may have altered the case."

The battle had been lost—the Constitution had been ratified without Mason's sacred Bill of Rights. But the war over the nature and governing principles of the new government was far from over.[81] Mason's battle cry—"No Declaration of Rights"—was about to resonate throughout the country. The "anti-rats" had failed to block ratification, but they had succeeded in framing the ongoing debate. Soon there would be a groundswell for adding a Bill of Rights to the Constitution by amendments.

CHAPTER FOURTEEN

The True Father of the Bill of Rights

As a summary of the rights of men and of the principles of free government, it stands, and is destined to stand, without a rival in the annals of government.

— **DON P. HALSEY** on Mason's original Declaration of Rights[1]

I n George Mason's mind, the bitter political crisis in the fall of 1788 could be resolved only by more democracy. The core issue at stake—fundamental amendments to the Constitution— needed to be presented to the full citizenry for informed consent or rejection. In Mason's view, the proposed Constitution was a seismic political and psychological shift in the meaning of the American Revolution. He held fast to his belief that amendments to preserve the people's rights were absolutely necessary. Most of the arguments that Mason had made against the king in 1776 now applied to the government created by this new Constitution. And ratification of that Constitution by the state Conventions did not necessarily represent a clear statement of the will of the American people. As Joseph Ellis has written, "What ratification really represented was the triumph of superior organization, more talented leadership, and a political process that had been designed from the start to define the options narrowly." It was clear "that a shift of six votes in Virginia would have produced a shock wave that may have left four states—Virginia, New York, North Carolina, and Rhode Island—out of the union. It is difficult to imagine an American nation surviving in such a geographically splintered condition."[2]

Mason was so frustrated with politics after his harsh defeat at the Virginia Ratifying Convention that he reportedly exploded when the Virginia Assembly named him a United States senator in the place of William Grayson. He declined the offer on the grounds of his health. Lund Washington reported to his cousin George "that Colo. Mason either was or pretended to be vexd at his appointment saying that it was a ps. D-n'd impudence to send."[3] Vexed or not, Mason would undertake one more monumental political task. Bitter as the defeat on ratification was to Mason, he would soldier on— and ultimately play a pivotal role in the amendment of the Constitution to include our Bill of Rights. It would take almost three years for the Bill of Rights to be approved by Congress and then the States (1788–1791), but Mason would be a major influence on the process every step of the way.

Modern Americans know the Bill of Rights as the most important part of the Constitution, the touchstone, as Mason hoped it would become, of our shared inalienable rights and liberties. Along with the Declaration of Independence, these first ten Amendments— with their guarantees of freedom of religion, speech, the press, right to assemble, speedy trial, protection against unreasonable search and seizure, and the right to bear arms—announce to the world our national values and ideals.

Virginia's raucous Ratifying Convention had been only the opening gambit in Mason's campaign to formally insert these freedoms into the Constitution itself. "The battle moved to another field," according to scholar Pauline Maier, "either the first federal Congress or a convention called to propose amendments, as specified in Article V of the Constitution. From the perspective of some Federalists, that meant it was too early to declare victory. Washington regarded … a second convention to consider the amendments recommended by the states—as nothing less than a covert attempt to 'undo all that has been done.'"[4]

To George Mason, in contrast, amending the federal Constitution to include a formal Bill of Rights was an essential component in the creation of the new United States government. While federalists such as Washington and Madison believed that individual rights were fully protected by state and common law, Mason and his anti-federalist allies would never fully accept the new Constitution until amendments protecting the rights of the states and the people were passed. Amending the federal Constitution to include a Bill of Rights would be the essential compromise necessary to the creation of the United States government.

And yet today it is the federalist James Madison who is known as "the Father of the Bill of Rights." True, Madison steered the final passage of the first ten Amendments to the Constitution through the first national Congress. But it is more than a little ironic that Madison gets credit as "Father" of the Bill of Rights. As we have already seen, he opposed it vociferously from the time of the framing of the Constitution in Philadelphia through the debate in the Virginia Ratifying Convention all the way to ratification. Madison went so far as to argue that a Declaration of Rights in the Constitution would be worse than unnecessary—it would be dangerous.

And even after the Constitution was ratified and came into effect, Madison was at best lukewarm on amending it to protect the rights of the people and the states. In an October 17, 1788, letter to Jefferson, he claimed that he had "always" been for a Bill of Rights but admitted that "At the same time I have never thought the omission a material defect, nor been anxious to supply it even by subsequent amendment, for any other reason than that it is anxiously desired by others. I have favored it because I supposed it might be of use, and if properly executed could not be of disservice."[5] It would not be until Madison was running for Congress in the district that Patrick Henry had packed with anti-federalist voters that Madison saw the light and came out as a proponent of a Bill of Rights, in a campaign promise intended to steal the thunder from his anti-federalist opponent James Monroe.[6]

And even in his promise to the voters, Madison was still describing his support for a Bill of Rights in the most lackluster language:

> I freely own that I have never seen in the Constitution as it now stands those serious dangers which have alarmed many respectable Citizens. Accordingly whilst it remained unratified, and it was necessary to unite the States in some one plan, I opposed all previous alterations as calculated to throw the States into dangerous contentions, and to furnish the secret enemies of the Union with an opportunity of promoting its dissolution. Circumstances are now changed: The Constitution is established on the ratifications of eleven States and a very great majority of the people of America; and amendments, if pursued with a proper moderation and in a proper mode, will be not only safe, but may serve the double purpose of satisfying the minds of well meaning opponents, and of providing additional guards in favour of liberty. Under this change of circumstances, it is my sincere opinion that the Constitution ought to be revised, and that the first Congress meeting under it, ought to prepare and recommend to the States for ratification, the most

satisfactory provisions for all essential rights, particularly
the rights of Conscience in the fullest latitude, the freedom
of the press, trials by jury, security against general warrants &c.[7]

Madison's endorsement was tepid; he said amendments might
make the Constitution "better in itself, or without making it worse,
will make it appear better to those who now dislike it."[8] Essentially,
the supposed "Father of the Bill of Rights" had to be dragged kicking
and screaming into reluctantly supporting the addition of a Bill of
Rights to the Constitution.

In any case there is a much better candidate than Madison for
the title "Father of the Bill of Rights." In the first place, at the beginning of the Revolution, it was Mason's draft Declaration of Rights
for the newly independent state of Virginia—distilled from his ency-
clopedic knowledge of political philosophy and history—that provided the blueprint for the states' Declarations of Rights and the
United States' Declaration of Independence. Then Mason was the
chief proponent for a Bill of Rights at the Constitutional Convention
in Philadelphia. Then, when the Framers refused to include a Declaration of Rights, it was Mason's *Objections to This Constitution of
Government* that brought that omission to the attention of the people and kept the issue before the public. Again, at the Virginia Ratifying Convention, Mason was the leader of the anti-federalists arguing
for adding a bill rights to the Constitution before ratifying it—when
Madison was the leader of the federalists arguing against it. And
finally, after ratification of the Constitution, it was the arguments of
the anti-federalists—led by Mason's full-throated defense of the rights
of the people and the states, in sharp contrast to Madison's anemic
support for them—that kept the issue alive, eventually creating the
groundswell that would end in the first ten Amendments, our Bill of

Rights. And finally—in a truly astonishing reversal, considering how all along Madison had hung his objections to a Declaration of Rights on the notion that the enumeration of rights could endanger implied rights—Madison actually rose in Congress to oppose the adoption of the Tenth Amendment: "Mr. Madison objected to this amendment, because it was impossible to confine a Government to the exercise of express powers; there must necessarily be admitted powers by implication, unless the Constitution descended to recount every minutia."[9]

In the end, the Congress adopted twelve amendments to the Constitution, and the states ratified ten of them. In essence, all ten amendments (admittedly expertly edited and abridged by James Madison) had originally been written by George Mason. Mason regarded a Bill of Rights as the cornerstone of liberty, an absolutely necessary protection against governmental encroachment. The Bill of Rights added to the Constitution by amendment did not merely, like the famous English Bill of Rights in 1689, settle grievances against an existing power. Rather, it enunciated broad precepts and freedoms that should govern the exercise of any government power and laid specific prohibitions against the government in nascent formation. The original Declaration of Rights that Mason had drafted for Virginia had contained revolutionary language on natural rights. "All men are born equally free and independent," Mason had written, insisting that power was derived from the people. Mason's Bill of Rights had protected freedom of religion and speech and declared that as "one of the great bulwarks of liberty ... freedom of the press" could not be restrained. The bill had also affirmed the "sacred" right of trial by jury, forbidden the granting of general search warrants "unsupported by evidence," and contained guarantees of other fundamental liberties in criminal prosecutions: notice of the accusation, the right to confront witnesses and examine evidence, and protection against being compelled to give evidence.[10] It was precisely those rights which would be enshrined in the U.S. Bill of Rights.

The full story of how the Bill of Rights was negotiated in a complicated political process over three years is a tangled morass of history and personalities beyond the scope of this book. But at the center of the story is George Mason: his drafting of the Virginia Declaration of Rights, his advocacy for a Bill of Rights in Philadelphia and Richmond, his penning of amendments toward the end of the Virginia Ratifying Convention in Richmond—which formed the basis for the United States Bill of Rights—and his role in creating and stoking the public outcry that kept up the pressure on Congress to adopt them.

July 1788 at Gunston Hall, the month Mason returned home from the Virginia Ratifying Convention, was enlivened by terrible winds and rainstorms at the end of the month, which tore down some of Mason's corn and drowned a portion of his tobacco crop. August brought favorable political news. North Carolina had refused to ratify the Constitution until amendments proposed by Virginia were made part of it. It was rumored that Patrick Henry had engineered this stratagem. While New York had voted to ratify, the Convention there had hedged its ratification with various conditions, including a list of amendments that closely followed those proposed by Virginia—which must have been gratifying to George Mason. He had written the originals of those amendments.

The amendments that the Virginia Ratifying Convention had sent to Congress had come out of a committee consisting of eleven federalists and nine anti-federalists, including Mason, appointed by Convention chairman Edmund Pendleton to prepare a set of proposed "amendments" to the Constitution. George Wythe served as chairman. The Wythe Committee reported a "bill of rights" consisting of some twenty amendments, which reflected Mason's major influence. In fact, the ten Amendments that would become our Bill of Rights came almost verbatim from the amendments Mason wrote at the

Virginia Ratifying Convention and his previous 1776 Virginia Declaration of Rights.[11]

Pendleton had placed both Mason and Patrick Henry on the committee in charge of preparing these vital amendments because both
men had already proposed—unsuccessfully—that the Ratifying Convention consider "other alterations," and "refer a declaration of rights,
with certain amendments to the most exceptionable parts of the
Constitution, to the other States in the Confederacy [under the Articles of Confederation], for their consideration, previous to its ratification." Henry had assured the delegates that his amendments would
leave "the arm of power ... sufficiently strong for national purposes"
while securing the rights of the people. "The Government unaltered
may be terrible to America; but can never be loved, till it be
amended."[12] Amendments to confirm "the privileges of the people"
would give the new government a firmer hold on the affections of the
people, and so make it stronger than without those amendments.

These "other alterations" began with a clause that reserved to the
states all powers not expressly granted to Congress, which echoed
Article II of the Articles of Confederation. The next specified that
there "shall be" one representative for every thirty thousand people
until the House of Representatives had two hundred members. Henry
had drafted a third amendment stating that Congress could raise no
direct taxes or excises unless the revenue from import duties was
insufficient for public needs.

The amendments that Mason and Henry originally proposed
were the work product of an anti-federalist committee chaired by
Mason. Richard Henry Lee had written Mason before the Convention
had started, in May 1788, to suggest a meeting of a small group of
anti-federalist leaders to consider amendments. No record of any such
meeting exists, but shortly after the delegates assembled, the anti-
federalist caucus made Mason chair of a committee to draft

amendments. Mason prepared a rough draft of thirteen structural amendments to follow a Declaration of Rights. In the end, however, when Mason and his committee had completed their work, they proposed a twenty-article Declaration of Rights as structural amendments to the Constitution. About half of the new amendments came from Mason's draft of the Virginia Declaration of Rights, but the committee had made several additions. They recognized the rights of assembly and petition, prohibited the quartering of soldiers in private homes during peacetime, and permitted a conscientious objector to avoid military service "upon payment of an equivalent, to employ another to bear Arms in his stead."[13]

When Henry proposed the Mason Committee's amendments, James Madison immediately responded, declaring that Mason's and Henry's proposals consisted of "no less than forty amendments—a bill of rights which contains twenty amendments, and twenty other alterations, some of which," he added, "are improper and inadmissible." According to one account, "The delegates rose from their seats and pressed toward the lobby for the vote. They moved in two equally unruly clumps, and it took an agonizingly long moment for them to form in single files so that they might be counted by the doorkeepers. Each side looked anxiously to see where the doubtfuls now stood, but nothing certain could be known until the tally sheets were passed back to the chair and the delegates resumed their places. It was half past two o'clock before Pendleton solemnly announced that by a vote of eighty ayes and eighty-eight nays, Mr. Henry's motion had failed."[14]

And yet Mason's amendments would become the basis for the United States Bill of Rights. Though the proposals of Mason's antifederalist committee were voted down by the Virginia Ratifying Convention, they would become the basis for the amendments proposed by the Wythe Committee, approved by the Convention, and sent to Congress. As one historian has observed,

The bill of rights came almost verbatim from the Anti-
Federalist proposal of 24 June, with one noteworthy
change. Article 20 of the Mason committee's declaration,
which protected the free exercise of religion, also prohibited
discrimination in favor of any "particular religious Sect or
Society of Christians." The Wythe committee deleted "of
Christians." Likewise, the structural amendments repeated
the final draft of the Anti-Federalist caucus report with a
few minor additions that could not have been objectionable
to Mason. He failed in the Wythe committee to resurrect
his coveted executive council, but the committee revived a
proposal Mason had made on 11 June to prohibit Congress
from adopting regulations for congressional elections
"except when the legislature of any state shall neglect,
refuse, or be disabled by invasion or rebellion to prescribe
the same."[15]

It seems apparent that the Constitution would not have been
ultimately ratified by the states without the expectation that it would
be amended with a Bill of Rights. While it was not explicitly stated
as a condition of ratification, three of the most powerful States—Virginia, New York, and Massachusetts—all had sizeable enough minor-
ities with enough political muscle to block ratification had it appeared
that a Bill of Rights would not be adopted.[16]

It was only on account of Mason's long campaign for adding a
Declaration of Rights to the Constitution that Madison would
eventually agree that a Bill of Rights was necessary. Anxious to
avoid the second Constitutional Convention that the anti-federalists
were agitating for—and, as we have seen, under pressure from his
anti-federalist opponent James Monroe in the contest for a seat in
the First Congress—Madison came around to the position that the

first Congress should pass a Bill of Rights: "... it is evident that the change of situation produced by the establishment of the Constitution, leaves me in common with the other friends of the Constitution, free, and consistent in espousing such a revisal of it...." Far better that, than the second Constitutional Convention he dreaded. "It is, accordingly, my sincere opinion, and wish, that in order to effect these purposes, the Congress ... should undertake the salutary work."[17] Madison's motives for correcting the blunder that he had made by failing to provide a Bill of Rights in Philadelphia in 1787 appear more political than philosophical. "While we tend to regard the Bill of Rights as a secular version of the Ten Commandments handed down by God to Moses," asserts Joseph Ellis. "Madison saw it as a weapon to be wielded against opponents of the Constitution ... who were pushing the second convention proposal, which Madison regarded as a thinly veiled attempt to undo all that he and his fellow collaborators had accomplished."[18]

Madison only reluctantly "supported rights amendments," according to Pauline Maier, "to quiet the fears of the discontented, not because he thought they would secure the people's rights": "That became clear in the course of his extended correspondence with Thomas Jefferson, who in December of 1787 had said he saw two glaring defects in the proposed Constitution: It imposed no term limits for the president and did not include a bill of rights, which 'the people are entitled to against every government on earth ... and what no just government should refuse, or rest on inference.'"[19]

In response, Madison sent Jefferson a thirty-two-page pamphlet that included Mason's proposed amendments, as well as the others recommended by the various states. He conceded that "not a few" critics of the Constitution, "particularly in Virginia," argued for amendments "from the most honorable and patriotic motives" and that some of the Constitution's advocates also wanted "further guards to public liberty and individual rights." Seven state Ratifying Conventions, including Virginia, New York, and North Carolina, had formally asked that one be added to the Constitution.[20]

After the Virginia Ratifying Convention, Washington joined Madison and unenthusiastically advocated for amendments to the Constitution in his inaugural address. Mason, like many other antifederalists perceived that Washington and Madison's proposed amendments were a diversion from more substantial amendments in Congress or a second Constitutional Convention. Writing to his son, Mason called Madison's plan "a Farce": "You were mistaken in your Suggestion, that the Publication you saw of Mr. Madison's, was a certain Indication of proper Amendments to the Constitution being obtained. It was indeed, natural enough to think so. But the Fact was, Mr Madison knew he could not be elected, without making some such Promises. By them he carried his Election; and in Order to appear as good as his Word, he has made some Motions in Congress on the Subject, and to carry on the Farce, is now the ostensible Patron of Amendments. Perhaps some milk & Water Propositions may be made by Congress to the State Legislatures by Way of throwing out a Tub to the Whale; but of important & substantial Amendments, I have not the least Hope."[21]

The final amendments document adopted by the Virginia Ratifying Convention included Mason's language that "among other essential rights, the liberty of conscience and of the press" were sacrosanct. On June 27, 1788, the Convention approved the entire schedule of amendments proposed by the Wythe committee, largely written by Mason. The delegates ordered them engrossed on parchment, signed by Convention president Edmund Pendleton, then sent to Congress and to the legislatures of other states. The Wythe committee had recommended that the Convention "enjoin" their representatives in Congress to "exert all their influence and use all reasonable and legal methods" to enact Mason's Bill of Rights and an additional twenty amendments to the Constitution. Until then, all laws were to "conform to the spirit of these amendments as far as the said Constitution will admit." According to historian Pauline Maier, "the bill of rights which the convention approved without dissent, was a revised version of [Mason's] 1776 Virginia declaration of rights, including its affirmation of the right of trial by jury but without its opening statement."[22] And thus, after entrusting its journal to the archives of the state's Privy Council, ordering copies of the ratification and recommended amendments printed and sent to the counties, then thanking President Edmund Pendleton for his leadership, the Convention closed twenty-five days after its first meeting.[23]

Madison eventually proposed nine amendments to the first Congress, derived largely from Mason. Madison's provisions were a condensed, rearranged version of Mason's first three provisions of the Virginia Declaration of Rights, without its opening assertion that "all men are by nature equally free and independent." According to Madison, although "the perfect equality of mankind" was "an absolute truth," it was "not absolutely necessary ... at the head of a constitution."[24] He also modified Mason's radical assertion of the people's right to "reform, alter, or abolish" a government that failed to serve their happiness and safety; in Madison's formulation, they could only "reform or change" it. Next, Madison proposed to change the language in Article I, Section 2, paragraph 3, so that it would say "there shall be one representative for every thirty Thousand" until the House reached a certain size (unspecified), after which Congress would regulate the proportion so it fell within certain (undefined) proportions, although each state was guaranteed at least two representatives. Madison explained that he had "always thought this part of the constitution defective."[25] One of the last, but perhaps most important, changes Madison proposed involved "due process." He adopted the language proposed by the New York Ratifying Convention: no person could be deprived of life, liberty, or property "without due process of law," rather than Mason's language—"but by the law of the land"—as the Virginia Ratifying Convention had suggested.[26]

Due credit needs to be given to Madison for thoroughly reviewing the nearly two hundred recommendations made by seven ratifying conventions and for editing and pruning Mason's amendments. Madison limited himself to points he regarded as "important in the eyes of many and … objectionable in those of none." He wanted "nothing of a controvertible nature," because he sought measures whose passage would be absolutely assured. So there was nothing that looked like the grand charter of rights Mason had envisioned as a preface to the Constitution. Madison included Mason's rights to freedom of religion, free speech, free press, and trial by jury in both civil and criminal cases, and he proposed protections against arbitrary searches, excessive bail, and double jeopardy. Additional amendments stated that rights and powers not enumerated would belong to the people or states. Madison, who had originally wanted a national veto on state legislation, saw a new opportunity to promote uniformity, and he proposed that the states, as well as the federal government, be prohibited from infringing the fundamental rights of conscience, press, and trial by jury. ("The most valuable amendment on the whole list," Madison called it.)[27]

Madison submitted these amendments to the First Congress that convened under the authority of the Constitution. The first national Congress met in New York City in the sultry summer of 1789. Debate in the Senate was desultory. Some argued that the whole matter should be postponed for at least one year, while others denigrated the importance of the subject. Richard Henry Lee raised objections to Mason's proposed preamble, which he said allowed "a careless reader … to suppose that the amendments desired by the states had been graciously granted.... But when the thing done is compared with that desired, nothing can be more unlike."[28]

The Senate divided Madison's remaining measures into twelve proposed amendments, which, after a few more changes in conference with the House, were jointly approved on September 25, 1789, and submitted to the states for ratification. In Prince Edward County, Patrick Henry threw the pamphlet containing the twelve amendments on his office table and told his law clerks that "Virginia had been outwitted."[29]

The rise to national prominence of Mason protégés Jefferson and Monroe mollified Mason, but he was never fully reconciled to the Constitution. A second Constitutional Convention was never called, and Mason continued to be concerned about the broad jurisdiction of the federal courts, the power of Congress to regulate elections, the ability of a simple majority of Congress to adopt navigation laws, and the lack of an executive council.

Thomas Jefferson, who had monitored the debate from France, shared many of Mason's reservations, but he subtly encouraged Mason to accept the Constitution. Mason showed signs of a softening attitude. During the debate over Gouverneur Morris's nomination to be United States Minister to France, Monroe asked Mason for his opinion on the Senate's power to "advise and consent." Could the Senate, Monroe asked, make its own selection if it rejected the president's nominee? It could not, Mason wrote, although the "Constitution ... wisely & Properly directs" that ambassadors had to be approved by the Senate. Earlier Mason had condemned the Senate's role in the confirmation process.[30]

By this time, 1791, Washington was president of the United States. And there was still another satisfaction for Mason before the year ended. The looked-for letter came at last. The "Bill of Rights" had been pushed through its slow stages of ratification by the states—Virginia, the first state to consider the amendments, was actually the last to accept them—and, on December 15, 1791, when the last state gave its approval, the first ten amendments became a permanent part of the Constitution of the United States. In his final year of life, Mason received some vindication. The adoption of his amendments pleased him greatly: "I have received much Satisfaction from the Amendments to the federal Constitution, which have lately passed from the House of Representatives."[31]

The Bill of Rights became the bedrock of Americans' rights and liberties. But the men who made it happen did not call it that, or even see it that way. Nobody seems to have referred to either the twelve amendments proposed by Congress or the ten that were ratified by the end of 1791 as a "bill of rights." Washington's letter transmitting the amendments to the states for their consideration referred only to "the amendments proposed to be added to the Constitution of the United States." And on March 1, 1792, Secretary of State Thomas Jefferson sent state governors official notice merely of "the ratifications by three fourths of the Legislatures."

Madison, who referred to some of the amendments he had proposed as "what may be called a bill of rights," did not use that term for the amendments Congress sent out for enactment. He referred to them as a "plan of amendments." As one author has commented, "The proposed amendments did not, in fact, look like a bill or declaration of rights as Americans of the late eighteenth century knew them. Thanks to Roger Sherman, they were at least grouped together—but at the end of the Constitution, like the afterthought they were, not at its beginning, as with most state declarations of rights. Moreover, they did not open, like the Virginia declaration of rights and other state documents modeled on it, with a declaration that all men had 'certain inherent rights' or any of the other general principles Americans had come to expect in bills or declarations of rights."[32]

In fact, according to legal historian Akhil Reed Amar, before the enactment of the Fourteenth Amendment to the Constitution in 1868, "the Supreme Court never—not once—referred to the 1792 decalogue as 'the' or 'a' bill of rights." As late as 1880, one Supreme Court justice declared that the federal Constitution, "unlike most modern ones, does not contain any formal declaration or bill of rights." As one constitutional historian has concluded, "Eventually ... the country got a federal Bill of Rights.... It emerged from a series of Supreme Court cases, beginning in the 1920s, that used the Fourteenth Amendment to make the first ten amendments powerful protectors of the people's right to 'equal protection of the laws' and not to be deprived of 'life, liberty, or property without due process of law' by the states as well as the federal government. The document itself—or rather Congress's official copy of the twelve amendments it proposed in September 1789—made its first major public appearance on the 1947 Freedom Train, and a few years later, in 1952, the Bill of Rights went on display in the National Archives along with the Declaration of Independence and the Constitution."[33] Until the courts "incorporated" the Bill of Rights, applying them to the states under the Fourteenth Amendment, those rights protected Americans only against the power of the federal government. States were exempt and could, if the several legislatures wished, pass laws establishing a church, limiting the press, outlawing seditious speech, or restricting the right of assemblage.

The First Amendment is, arguably, the most famous and debated amendment in the Bill of Rights. Madison deftly combined Mason's five fundamental civil liberties into this amendment. There are several important components to the First Amendment, not the least of which is the first five words, "Congress shall make no law ..." This established a pattern for the next nine amendments.

Mason went further, protecting a free press, which he thought had been essential in the years leading up to the American War for Independence. Mason argued that it kept governments honest or at the very least exposed political transgressions. Perhaps this is why both Jefferson and Madison, in the Virginia and Kentucky Resolutions, fervently opposed the Sedition Law of 1798 as a violation of the First Amendment.[34] One of Mason's greatest concerns, both as a Revolutionary and drafter of the Bill of Rights, was that the press should be free and independent. Mason pointed out that nothing in the Constitution as originally written forbade the government from restricting the press. He offered a hypothetical example: "Suppose oppressions should arise under this government, and a writer should dare to stand forth, and expose to the community at large the abuses of those powers; could not Congress, under the idea of providing for the general welfare, and under their own construction, say that this was destroying the general peace, encouraging sedition, and poisoning the minds of the people ... could they not, in order to provide against this, lay a dangerous restriction on the press?"[35]

Mason's original version of the Second Amendment, guaranteeing the right to bear arms, defined the militia as "all men, able to bear arms." The Maryland Ratifying Convention had wanted the militia to be subject to martial law only "in time of war, invasion, or rebellion." Mason said in the Virginia Ratifying Convention that the militia "consist now of the whole people, except a few public officers." That is, the militia was everyone, "composed of the body of people trained in arms," not the modern "National Guard." Every man had to be armed for the "defense of themselves and their own state, or the United States," in the words of the Pennsylvania Ratifying Convention—so as to render a standing army unnecessary. When the amendment was up for debate in the House, no one questioned that intent. In fact, Elbridge Gerry made his understanding of the amendment quite clear. "What, sir, is the use of a militia? It is to prevent the establishment of a standing army, the bane of liberty ... Whenever Governments mean to invade the rights and liberties of the people, they always attempt to destroy the militia, in order to raise an army...."[36] Both the North Carolina and Virginia Ratifying Conventions had proposed that "the people have a right to keep and bear arms; that a well-regulated militia, composed of the body of the people trained in arms, is the proper, natural, and safe defense of a free state; that standing armies, in time of peace, are dangerous to liberty, and therefore ought to be avoided."[37] The Third Amendment forbids the government to impose soldiers on the households of citizens in peacetime.

The Fourth through Eighth Amendments were designed by Mason to protect the lives, liberty, and property of the people. All these Amendments restrict the judicial power of the United States government and were intended to quiet one of the main criticisms of the Constitution, namely that the Constitution did not define trial by jury or protect the rights of the accused. Mason had hammered on this issue during the ratification debates. State constitutions typically outlined these essential liberties in their respective declarations of rights. But because the Supreme Court was to have jurisdiction "both as to Law and Fact," and because Congress could establish inferior tribunals that could destroy the state court systems, Mason argued that the federal judiciary would trample the rights of the people. The Supreme Court had too much power and would not only render the state courts superfluous but also, Mason claimed "will destroy the state governments."[38] He had proposed limiting the jurisdiction of federal courts to matters of international law, admiralty jurisdiction, suits involving the United States, or suits involving two or more states,

including competing land grants from different states. He also wanted
to limit federal appellate jurisdiction to questions of law and leave
most cases arising before ratification with the state courts. One
scholar has observed what was "most striking about Mason's jurisprudence was his willingness to let state judges decide ordinary matters of federal law."[39]

And, finally, the Ninth and Tenth Amendments are designed to
protect rights that are not enumerated in the first eight Amendments:
"The enumeration in the Constitution, of certain rights, shall not be
construed to deny or disparage others retained by the people," and
"The powers not delegated to the United States by the Constitution,
nor prohibited by it to the States, are reserved to the States respectively, or to the people."

But the amendments that make up the Bill of Rights still did not
entirely satisfy Mason—he wanted more: "With two or three further
Amendments—Such as confining the federal Judiciary to Admiralty
& Maritime Jurisdiction, and to Subjects merely federal ... fixing the
Mode of Elections either in the Constitution itself (which I think
wou'd be preferable) or securing the Regulation of them to the respec-
tive States—Requiring more than a bare Majority to make Navigation
& Commercial Laws, and appointing a constitutional amenable
Council to the President, & lodging with them most of the Executive
Powers now vested in the Senate—I cou'd cheerfully put my Hand &
Heart to the new Government."

And Mason was not alone. Mason told Jefferson that he still
"apprehended great Danger to the Rights & Liberty of our Country."
Jefferson replied that he too wished "to see some amendments, further
than those which have been proposed" to fix the new government
"more surely on a republican basis," and he hoped they would be
"obtained before the want of them will do any harm." Richard Henry
Lee said that "it is essential in every free country, that common

people should have a part and share of influence, in the judicial as well as in the legislative department."[40]

Ultimately, both sides were victorious. The Constitution was ratified by the states and became the law of the land. And Mason's beloved rights, the ones he had been fighting for since the original Declaration of Rights he wrote for Virginia at the beginning of the Revolution—freedom of religion, freedom of speech, the right of trial by jury, and freedom of the press—were guaranteed by the first ten Amendments.

As one writer has pointed out, the anti-federalists' insistence on a Declaration of Rights has been vindicated by history: "Even after the adoption of the Bill of Rights, the federal government has continually violated fundamental liberties.... How much more would the Congress have tread on free speech rights were they not explicitly protected in the Constitution?"[41]

The Constitution the Founders gave us, as amended, proved more successful than its Framers could have imagined. George Mason's rhetorical question—"Was there ever an instance of a general national government extending over so extensive a country, abounding in such a variety of climates, &c., where the people retained their liberty?"[42]—has been answered with a resounding Yes by the subsequent history of America. The Bill of Rights "has guided the United States for over two centuries," one historian has noted, "as its boundaries expanded from the Mississippi to the Pacific and its influence spread over the world. The Constitution's success came less from a perfection in its design than from the sacrifices of men like [Mason.] The Constitution's critics did not get all the amendments to the Constitution they wanted, or even those they thought most important. Without their determined opposition, however, the first ten amendments would not have become a part of the Constitution ... Their example might well be their greatest gift to posterity."[43]

Over time, the Bill of Rights has proven to be as significant as the Constitution itself. It is the ultimate protection for the rights of a vast diversity of humanity who in the centuries that followed its adoption would call themselves American. As historian Gordon Wood has written, "It is what makes us a single people. It's the only thing that makes us a single people, really, because we're not a nation in any traditional sense of the term. We're the first nation in modern times to make ideology the basis of our existence."[44]

CHAPTER FIFTEEN

The Shade of Retirement

—

Death is sweeping his scythe all around us, cutting down our old friends and brandishing it over us.
—JOHN ADAMS (1816)

Mason's reluctant political career was essentially over. In the years after the Virginia Ratifying Convention, Mason remained somewhat active in local affairs but never again in national politics. He kept in contact with old colleagues, including Madison, Jefferson, and Monroe, noting that "I have been for some time in retirement and shall not probably return again to public life. Yet my anxiety for my country in these times of danger makes me sometimes dabble a little in politics and keep up a correspondence with some men upon the public stage. You know I am not apt to form opinions lightly and without due examination."[1] His son John would recall that his father "kept up constantly during his retirement, an active correspondence with many of the prominent of that day."[2]

Locally, Robert Carter had asked Mason to serve as a mediator in one of Carter's own legal squabbles. Mason tried to resist: "I am grown old & infirm, and find Business grow[s] fatigueing and irksome to me." In reality, Mason continued to do a good bit of his own

311

legal work, and his letters suggest he eventually agreed to help Carter. He also still supervised a sprawling estate—which, with enterprise, frugality, and political connections, he had made even larger. Mason settled his debts with his British creditors, although he grumbled about having to pay interest that had accrued during the American Revolution.[3] In fact, by the time of his death, Mason had paid off all his debts, and his holdings included fifteen thousand acres along the Potomac, sixty thousand acres in Kentucky, $50,000 worth of private property, $30,000 in accounts receivable, and three hundred slaves.[4]

Health problems continued to plague Mason in the final years of his life. Recurring episodes of illness left Mason saying he would "quit all public Business" had he not promised "some of my Constituents, that I would serve them another year?" The gout had struck Mason again shortly after he left the Ratifying Convention in Richmond and, he told Richard Henry Lee, "reduced me lower than I have been these twenty years." Mason soon recovered, but he remained "in a very indifferent State of Health," to which, he believed, "Vexation has not a little contributed." Health complaints appear repeatedly in Mason's letters. He wrote to Beverly Randolph in March 1790, "I have been confined by a severe fit of the Gout, ever since the Second Week in January." And to Robert Carter in September 1791, "I am at present very unwell, from a late fit of Gout in my Stomach." Despite his complaints, Mason did not consider himself disabled. Recovering from yet another episode of gout, he told his son John that his health was "tolerable" for his age. As late as January 1792, the last year of his life, Mason told John that, apart from gout, "in every other Respect, thank God, I am in good Health."[5] In fact, the aches and pains that made walking through his garden difficult somehow disappeared once he was on horseback.

In the shade of retirement at Gunston Hall, Mason looked back over the years, through the haze of war and political strife. He had done his duty. "The circumstances of our country at my entrance into life," he remarked to a visitor, "were such that every honest man felt himself compelled to take a part, and to act up to the best of his abilities." He could have done no other. In these waning years, he enjoyed the comfort of his family and his farm. It would be misleading to portray Mason's last years as an unhappy period of decline. Defeated in the greatest political battle of his career, estranged from many old allies, and tormented by frequent fits of gout, Mason had reasons to be bitter. Yet he remained active and content with Sarah at Gunston Hall, spending most of his time on the family matters that had always been his first love. Mason rarely traveled, but he remained "hospitable, cheerful, and fond of conversation."[6]

By the late spring of 1789, the family at Gunston Hall had been "reduced," in Mason's words, "from a very large to a small one." Besides Mason's wife Sarah, only his second son, William, and his youngest daughter, Elizabeth, remained at home, and Elizabeth would marry William Thornton before the end of the year.[7] Mason's son Thomson and his wife Sarah had lived at Gunston Hall until 1787, when Mason helped them build their own estate, Hollin Hall. Ann, at thirty-four the oldest daughter, had just married Rinaldo Johnson of Maryland.

Mason may have been closest to his son John, and their correspondence forms the single most important source of information about Mason's final years. John had accompanied his father to Philadelphia in 1787 but returned to Alexandria before the Convention adjourned and formed a partnership with James and Joseph Fenwick of Maryland, hoping to market American tobacco in France after the expiration of an exclusive contract between Robert Morris and the French Farmers. John left for Bordeaux, France, where Joseph Fenwick had arrived in the previous year. John Mason impressed the older man: "He is industrious attentive frugal &

reasonable ... he has courage to form resolutions & spirit to adhere to them." Mason began sending his son advice even before John left for France, writing one letter during the Ratifying Convention: "Confide as little as possible in the Merchants of the Place; at least never so far, as to give them the Power of hurting you; for they will look on your Success with a jealous & an evil Eye." He explained his financial philosophy: "Live in a frugal Style, without parade or Ostentation, avoid all unnecessary Expence...."[8]

In a letter telling John that he had declined the Virginia Assembly's appointment to the U.S. Senate, Mason commented on the French Revolution: "I heartily wish the French nation success in establishing their new government upon the principles of liberty and the sacred rights of human nature, but I dread the consequences of their affairs remaining so long in an unsettled state ... besides the risk of the most respectable part of the people (which is always found in the middle walks of life) being disgusted and worn down with so long a scene of doubt and uncertainty, not to say anarchy."[9]

Mason had resigned as justice of the peace for Fairfax County after twenty years of service. At times, Sarah became alarmed at the depression of spirit that accompanied Mason's gout, and his disaffection with politics. She was grateful for his correspondence with Jefferson, who returned from Paris in 1789 to take his place in Washington's Cabinet. He and Mason had carried on a lively correspondence. Jefferson was glad to avail himself of Mason's judgment, and Mason was eager to keep in touch with events. As we have seen, Mason sensed that Washington's warm regard for him had waned. It appeared to him that Madison was also disappointed in the stand he had taken at both Conventions.

A farmer to the end, Mason assessed his crops and harvest in a letter to John. Too much rain would make the tobacco crop "unusually bad this Year." The wheat had "suffered some Damage, & our

Hay a great deal." Omens for the corn "looked pretty good."[10] Mason had an opportunity to buy Marlborough, the Potomac plantation built by his uncle John Mercer, but he declined. Throughout his life, he refused to overextend himself financially. "There is no estate in Virginia which I should prefer to it," he told John Francis Mercer, but he had "Made it a Rule thro' Life, never, on any consideration whatever, to embarrass, or subject myself to Difficulties."[11] He won a partial judgment against William Lee for Lee's alleged mishandling of a tobacco shipment at the beginning of the war. It was one of several lawsuits spawned by Mason's extensive agricultural operations and land speculations. He often complained about "all my ill luck with lawyers."

In his final years of life, unable to sleep soundly alongside his wife Sarah on account of his gout, Mason would read well into the night, and be out of bed and reading by candlelight at six in the morning. When his eyes grew weary, Sarah would read to him. Mason spent hours alone, reading, writing, or just gazing out the window at his beautiful river. On the table beside his reading chair could be found a poem or a novel by Henry Fielding. Unlike Jefferson, who seldom ever marked a book, and then only in light pencil, Mason scribbled comments in the margins of his.

Much was left to Mason that he loved; there was still a great deal of life to the man, and he was extremely grateful for his close family and his books. Mason loved the company of his children and grandchildren. It seemed that Gunston Hall was always full in his final years. He was rarely without aches and pains, but he could still ride horseback at nearly seventy. Mason sometimes covered three miles, and he never tired of his plantation. He loved every garden and field, loved its order and productiveness. Mason's last Christmas, in 1791, brought all of Mason's children home. Gunston Hall was full of children and grandchildren; there were fires in all the once-cold hearths and holly and mistletoe in a great bunch tied to the pineapple of welcome in the hall arch. John and Tom came down from Alexandria together. Tom was living in Alexandria, and John was now on Analostan Island (since renamed Theodore Roosevelt Island) between Georgetown and the site of the future city of Washington, where Pierre L'Enfant was planning the new capital. Sally's oldest child had blossomed into a belle in her own right, carrying on the tradition of her mother and grandmother. She decorated the lapel of Mason's black silk coat with a bunch of bright red holly berries. The dining table was so long that the smallest children were seated at a smaller table near the window. When it was over, the various family coaches bore away the parents and children. They left the master of Gunston Hall happy and tired with a deep sense of gratitude for the blessings of his life.

Before the site of the new nation's permanent capital had been decided, Jefferson had visited Gunston Hall, perhaps at Washington's request, to hear Mason's views on the subject. An agreement to build a capital in the South had been part of the compromise made to pass Alexander Hamilton's funding and debt-assumption plan, but an exact location remained to be decided. Jefferson detected in Mason "a shyness" on the subject "not usual in him," which the secretary of state attributed to Mason's ownership of land near Georgetown. Mason said enough to indicate his preference for a Georgetown site over Alexandria, a rival candidate.

Jefferson, Madison, and Monroe continued to visit Gunston Hall whenever possible. In March of 1792, Mason's health problems turned severe. As he wrote to Jefferson on the twenty-ninth of that month, "This Letter was intended to have been forwarded the Day on which it is dated; but I was suddenly seized with a repeated Attack of the Gout (after having been confined for near two months before) which rendered me unable to sit up, or attend to any thing, for several

Days."[12] Yet Mason still looked forward to Jefferson's visits, and the feeling was warmly mutual. Jefferson wrote, "I have some hope of visiting Virginia in the fall, in which case I shall still flatter myself with the pleasure of seeing you. In the mean time I am with unchanged esteem & respect my dear Sir Your most obedient friend & servt, Th: Jefferson."[13] Mason replied, "Dear Sir Until I heard of your passing thro' Colchester, a few days ago, I had flattered myself with having the pleasure of seeing you at Gunston, of hearing that You enjoyed good Health, and of personally congratulating You upon Your Return to Your native Country."[14] As biographer Helen Hill Miller notes, "Thomas Jefferson, so soon to become the leader of a triumphant Republican (or Democratic) party, which was to carry out in government, as far as possible, the states' rights views of George Mason, turned with the affection and reverence of a disciple to the retired sage of Gunston Hall."[15]

Mason's health complaints seemed to multiply in the summer and early fall of 1792. The gout returned, accompanied by pneumonia and influenza. In August he described "Fevers" that left him "very weak & low" to John. In September Mason reviewed his will, which would provide generously for his family. He continued to suffer various ailments, including bouts of diarrhea and a chronic disorder of the urinary tract. He depended on his wife and doctor for relief with small doses of laudanum. That same month he complained of "an exceeding troublesome Cough." These were all signs of stomach cancer, unrecognized in the eighteenth century. Meanwhile his wife Sarah was confined to bed with a broken leg. Concerned with the health and welfare of the plantation, Mason had forty-nine slaves and several of his grandchildren inoculated for smallpox. The inoculations generally went well, but Betsy, William, and many of the household slaves were incapacitated by other ailments. "I hardly remember so sickly a season," he wrote John. Mason managed somehow to produce his last state paper, a petition to the general assembly to encourage "the Manufacture and Sale of Flour." According to historian Jeff Broadwater, "Mason proposed a series of reforms intended to make inspections less burdensome on wheat producers. Progressive farmers in the Northern Neck had long seen wheat as an alternative to tobacco, but by the early 1790s Mason, Washington, and others were becoming concerned that Virginia wheat was no longer competitive, in part because of a 1787 inspection law. The assembly made only a few limited changes, but the petition was vintage Mason."[16]

In the late months of 1792, Mason declined rapidly. He suffered severe pains in his legs and back. In chilly weather his gout and rheumatism were so debilitating that he could not walk without a cane. His teeth were almost all gone, and his hearing was failing. Three future presidents visited and corresponded with Mason in his final days. James Madison, on his occasional visits to Gunston Hall, found that Mason's "conversations were always a feast to me." James Monroe also kept up active correspondence toward the end of Mason's life. He planned a visit with Mason on his way north to take his seat in Congress as a United States senator in the fall of 1792, but he was too late. And on Sunday afternoon, October 1, 1792, Thomas Jefferson was one of the last visitors that Mason, fighting through his pain, received at Gunston Hall.

Jefferson saw Mason in the library. The older man seemed to be "recovering from a dreadful attack of the cholic," as Jefferson would write later. Jefferson noted that Mason's eyesight was failing and his hair perfectly white, but he was struck by the perseverance of Mason's spirit. The two friends sat in Mason's office, with a sweeping view upon the riverfront of Gunston Hall. As Mason talked, his voice raspy, Jefferson recorded his words with paper and a quill pen that Mason's servant James had brought him. As Mason told anecdotes of the federal Constitutional Convention in Philadelphia, Jefferson wrote them down. Both men were aware of children's voices in the garden. Two of Mason's granddaughters played under the now tall box bushes that bordered the vista. Beyond, the Potomac glistened silver in the October haze. A drone of bees added its music to the children's soft voices.

Mason said again that he "could have set his hand and heart" to the Constitution before the infamous deal between New England and "the 2 Southernmost States" to continue the slave trade and permit a simple majority to adopt navigation laws. He recalled the deep divisions within the New York delegation: Delegates Yates and Lansing, he told Jefferson, "never voted in one single instance" with Hamilton. According to author Jeff Broadwater, "Mason recalled exposing Gouverneur Morris's effort early one morning near the end of the convention to slip past a half-empty chamber an amendment depriving the states of the power to call a convention."[17]

Mason and Jefferson also talked about the problem of financial debt left from the Revolutionary War. But seeing Mason's weakened physical condition, Jefferson felt compelled to close the conversation sooner than Mason would have liked. Mason, Jefferson would tell Madison, "was perfectly communicative, but I could not in discretion let him talk as much as he was disposed."[18] He wrote down every halting, painful word Mason struggled to utter as his life ebbed away.

Although the dying Mason was no longer to be feared, the living Jefferson was to be reckoned with. He, along with Madison, was establishing the rudiments of the "Republican" Party. Jefferson had thrown his political weight behind Mason's proposed amendments to the Constitution, both by letters from France and by direct persuasion on his protégé, James Madison. And in creating a new party that was a discernible and organized alternative to the federalists, Jefferson was essentially Mason's torchbearer.

On October 6, 1792, Mason was confined to bed with an inflamed throat and severe abdominal pain. He nudged Sarah awake; she grew alarmed by his labored breathing and called for their servant James. By the time another slave kindled a fire in the early morning, Mason was breathing with difficulty and scarcely able to speak, he was in such excruciating pain. James propped his master up in a chair by the fire and sent another servant to Alexandria for Dr. Craik, the Scottish physician who had served George Washington. Meanwhile, to soothe his throat and stomach, Mason drank a syrupy blend of molasses and butter—but vomited when he tried to swallow it.

When Dr. Craik arrived, he was alarmed at Mason's grave condition. The doctor bled his patient and probably also evacuated Mason's bowels with an enema. He was dosed with quinine and Madeira by his wife and physician. Climbing into bed bedside him, Sarah kept turning Mason over to try to relieve his stomach pain. Several times Mason leaned back, holding his wife's hand. Mason's perseverance as he faced death was remarkable. He never complained, though he was dying in a particularly gruesome fashion, gasping for air "with an exceedingly Troublesome Cough." He retained control of his faculties and was resigned to his fate. The sun was brilliant at high noon, its golden light flooding Mason's beloved garden and river.[19]

On October 16, 1792, James Monroe wrote to Jefferson from Fredericksburg, Virginia. In his letter, Monroe shared his news, including plans to travel to Philadelphia—and his thoughts on Mason: "You have before this I presume heard of the death of Colo. Geo. Mason [which] was abt. the 8th of this mo[n]th of the gout in the stomach. His patriotic virtues thro[ugh] the revolution will ever be remembered by the citizens of this county, and his death at the present moment will be sensibly felt by the republican interest."[20]

A letter from Jefferson to Madison describes a stomach illness or stomach cancer as the cause of Mason's death. In the letter, written from Georgetown on October 1, 1792, Jefferson told Madison about his last visit with Mason: "I called at Gunston hall, [Gunston Hall] the proprietor [George Mason] just recovering from a dreadful attack of the cholic [colic]."[21] Washington paid a modest tribute to the memory of Mason in a letter he wrote to James Mercer from Philadelphia on November 1, 1792, the last line of which reads, "And I will also unite my regret to yours for the death of our old friend, and acquaintance Colo. Mason."[22]

Mason had died on a peaceful Sunday afternoon at Gunston Hall, October 7, 1792. The sixty-six-year-old was the oldest of his Virginia Revolutionary colleagues. There is no mystery about the date George Mason died, the place of his death, or the location of his burial. But not much is known beyond these basic facts.[23] George Mason's descendant and first biographer Kate Mason Rowland searched for information regarding his death and published what she was able to learn in her 1892 book *The Life of George Mason, 1725–1792*. Referencing a "Gunston Bible" as her source, she supplied the following information: "George Mason died at 'Gunston Hall' in the sixty-seventh year of his age, on the afternoon of Sunday, the 7th of October, 1792, and was buried by the side of his wife in the family graveyard on the estate." His body was placed as close to the side of Ann, the wife of his youth and mother of his children, as her tomb would permit. He wanted it that way. Her tomb thus became his own. For nineteen years his heart had been there anyway. On the following day, the five sons and four daughters gathered in the library of Gunston Hall for the reading of his solemn will. It had been written in 1773, just after the death of Ann and before the Revolution had begun. Mason's last will and testament began, "I, George Mason, of 'Gunston Hall,' in the parish of Truro and county of Fairfax, being of perfect and sound mind and memory and in good health, but mindful of the uncertainty of human life and the imprudence of man's leaving his affairs to be settled upon a deathbed, do make and appoint this my last Will and Testament. My soul, I resign into the hands of my Almighty Creator, whose tender mercies are over all His works, who hateth nothing that He hath made and to the Justice and Wisdom of whose dispensation I willing and cheerfully submit, humbly hoping from His unbounded mercy and benevolence, through the merits of my blessed Savior, a remission of my sins."[24]

But it is another paragraph of Mason's will that distills the essence of the man. It would behoove all Americans, who are in some sense the sons of this neglected Founding Father, to heed his words: "I recommend it to my sons from my own experience in life, to prefer the happiness of independence and a private station to the troubles and vexation of publick business, but if either their own inclinations or the necessity of the times should engage them in public affairs, I charge them on a father's blessing never to let the motives of private interest or ambition induce them to betray, nor the terrors of poverty and disgrace, or the fear of danger or of death, deter them from asserting the liberty of their country and endeavoring to transmit to their posterity those sacred rights to which themselves were born."[25]

EPILOGUE

"The Stage of Human Life"

There is nothing so rare as a truly great man.
He never thinks himself one. They do not leave dia-
ries, memoirs, autobiographies or carefully worded
inscriptions for their tombs. Like Samson, they baffle
the world and pass on seeming to say:
"Behold, I have not told it my father nor my mother,
and shall I tell it thee?"

—R. CARTER PITTMAN,
George Mason of Gunston Hall (1954)

I t is hard to explain why George Mason is not a cultural icon like his Virginia colleagues Washington, Jefferson, and Madison. His prolific writings throughout the Revolutionary years should secure Mason's recognition as the chief draftsmen for the patriotic cause. The values that he embodied throughout his life remain vital and resilient two and half centuries after the Declaration of Independence. And the rhetorical power of Mason's anti-government writings should never be underestimated as a major influence on modern-day political discourse.[1] George Mason's declarations on our natural freedoms kept government on the defensive in the eighteenth century, and they still do today. Mason's work—particularly the Bill of Rights—is not just an essential ingredient in the American political tradition, but the essence of it. Mason's contemporaries seemed to recognize the potent talents that had distilled Americans' rights into a form that would triumph in the Revolution and be vindicated in the American Experiment. Edmund Randolph, Virginia's governor, observed that Mason ranked "behind none of the sons of Virginia in knowledge of her history and interest. At a glance he saw to the bottom of every proposition which affected her."[2]

George Mason died as he lived—one of the most selfless men of his times. He was, indeed, "one of the most remarkable men ... of all countries and all times," as nineteenth-century writer John Esten Cooke described him long ago. By the time of his death, Mason had poured his last ounce of passion into the creation of his country. Never a perfect man, he had human frailties. Irritable and acerbic yet incorruptible, Mason has always inspired more respect than affection. Ambitious in his younger years, he remained a shrewd businessman. But over the years this man of deep emotions and strong convictions evolved into a statesman with extraordinary literary skills, who mapped out America's government for future generations. Whatever political disputes swirled around him, he focused on restraining government. He never allowed personal attacks to distract him from that goal. He always followed his inner compass, whose true north was "liberty."

The real significance of George Mason's role in the founding of the United States can be seen in the documents he drafted and the public stands he took—all in defense of American's rights, lives, and liberty. Mason drafted the Constitution of Virginia, which shattered the old myth of divine right and proved that men could handle their own affairs. Mason understood more than most that necessary powers must be given to a government—but he also knew that the price of increased government power was decreased liberty. Mason's political works were the creation of a genius that was democratic at heart. His Fairfax Resolves in 1774 had helped stir the Revolution, and his Virginia Declaration of Rights was the precursor to the Declaration of Independence and the Bill of Rights. Yet Mason could write of his devoted family, "[A]t my time of life, my only satisfaction and pleasure is in my children, and all my views are centered in their welfare and happiness."[3]

Jefferson called Mason's death "a great loss." Monroe believed Mason's "patriotic virtues thro' the revolution will ever be remembered by the citizens of this country."[4] Yet it seems that Mason's eloquence and talents to the cause of freedom have been largely unappreciated. Apart from a few brief obituaries, Mason's death attracted little immediate attention. Patrick Henry's death would garner much more attention; the *Virginia Gazette* placed black borders around Henry's death notice, proclaiming, "Mourn, Virginia, mourn! Your Henry is gone! Ye friends to liberty, drop a tear." No such tributes were written for Mason.

But as the historical record demonstrates, George Mason should have a place in the highest ranks of the Founders, not on account of the prestige of high office or the glamour of the battlefield, but because he is the father of our liberties. The contributions that Mason made to the preservation of Americans' freedoms and the structure of our republican government are irreplaceable.[5]

What is George Mason's legacy? One scholar has concluded that the life of George Mason was, in many respects "comparable to the life of Voltaire. Both men led their generations in formulating the political philosophy of the revolutionary state that was to come. Both had geometric gardens, Voltaire at Fernie, Mason at Gunston Hall. They shared the same shrewd understanding of humankind, shot through with the same twinges of sardonic humor which were probably not unrelated to their common enemy, the gout, but the means of their effectiveness differed."[6]

Perhaps George Mason's most influential achievement was his framing of the Virginia Declaration of Rights, a document espousing human rights for all individuals, and the precursor to both the

Declaration of Independence and the Bill of Rights. Historians of religious liberty rightly credit the major contributions of Jefferson and Madison, but Mason's writings on religious freedom are neglected, or overlooked altogether. This is an indefensible omission. Few men were more engaged than Mason in the struggle to establish the free exercise of religion, starting with his authorship of Article XVI of the Virginia Declaration of Rights. Mason eloquently and succinctly formulated the principles that would govern the debate on religious freedom in Virginia and the new United States.

Scholars disagree about how much respective weight to assign to political theory and personal leadership for the success of the American Revolution. But they all are able to acknowledge Mason's remarkable contributions to the historical record: he was one of the first political philosophers of the American Revolution, and the most influential. And his personal leadership of the anti-federalist cause gave us our Bill of Rights. Historian Forrest McDonald credits Mason with "prestige not drastically beneath Washington's and talent that far outweighed Madison's."[7] Scholar Josephine Pacheco has observed that "it is an injustice to the memory of one of our truly great men to dismiss him by saying, 'Oh, Mason didn't sign the Constitution.' In fact, except for Madison, probably no one contributed more to the actual document than did Mason. He rightly deserves to be considered one of the fathers of our national government."[8]

But to George Mason, judging by the jottings of his own quill pen, the most important considerations were the natural rights of mankind, and their defense in the Constitution and laws of his country. The road to Mason's achievements began in his uncle's library as a boy, where he studied history, legal documents, and political philosophy. He distilled it all into a deep understanding of government power and citizens' rights that would provide the intellectual fuel for the American Revolution. Mason synthesized two hundred years of history to create guarantees to ensure that the new national government would never overwhelm the states or tyrannize the people. The state constitutions that came out of the Revolution were in large part modeled on Mason's Virginia Constitution and reflected his commitment to liberty.

We admire George Washington's indomitable will and impeccable judgment, Patrick Henry's stirring rhetoric, and James Madison's intellectual depth and brilliance. In the opinion of historian Lorri Glover, George Mason combined all these qualities and more.[9] The firm, unbending quality of Mason's character can be traced back to his great-grandfather, George Mason I, the captain who rode with his king against Cromwell's army at Worcester. The Masons were imbued with a perseverance that made their presence permanent. They were home and family builders, firmly rooted where they had settled. And George Mason threw the entire power of his sterling character and intellectual endowments behind his country's cause.

A state university bears his name, his portrait hangs in the Capitol building in Washington, and statues of George Mason stand in Washington, D.C., and on the statehouse grounds in Richmond. On February 22, 1858, during the administration of Virginia Governor Wise, an equestrian statue of Washington was dedicated in the presence of a vast gathering of citizens. Next to Washington, the orator named two others: "Of Henry, Washington and Mason, none speak but with reverence, admiration and love—all were first in different characters. Here it will stand for all time commemorating a very great man whom we number among 'The dead but sceptered sovereigns who still rule Our spirit from their urns.'"[10]

Yet, despite his great contributions, Mason has never been admitted to the inner temple of American Founders with Washington, Franklin, Jefferson, Adams, Hamilton, and Madison. Mason has been called "an almost forgotten man in the pantheon of revolutionary heroes."[11] Perhaps it is because he never became president of the United States, as some of the other Founders did. But neither did Benjamin Franklin or Alexander Hamilton, and their places in the first rank of the Founders are solid. Franklin and Hamilton, though, were essentially public men, while Mason was at heart a private one.

When Mason had helped secure his political goals, he withdrew from public service. He might have aspired to higher elective office, like the other patriots with whom he made the Revolution and framed the Constitution. But the knowledge that his work was done seemed sufficient, without the trappings of power.[12] As Pauline Maier has explained, "His work on Virginia's constitution and declaration of rights earn him a fame that he, unlike other members of his generation, did not crave. He once described himself as a man who seldom meddled in public affairs, 'content with the blessings of a public station' without regard for 'the smiles and frowns of the great.'"[13] His heart was always at home, in Gunston Hall.

And he succeeded in achieving his private goals. Visitors to the Old Dominion in the nineteenth century were stunned at the poorly maintained roads and dilapidated plantation houses. Martha Jefferson Randolph, Jefferson's beloved daughter, lamented that "Virginia is no longer a home for the family of Thomas Jefferson." Dolley Madison was financially ruined at the end of her life. James Monroe only kept his estate, Oak Hill, solvent by selling land and slaves. Edmund Randolph and Henry "Light-Horse Harry" Lee could never pay off their debts. In fact, Lee was jailed for his debts in 1809.[14] The Mason family, in contrast, did not suffer such ignominies—in large part because of George Mason's loving influence and financial prudence.

Did George Mason achieve his public goals, as well? The Philadelphia Convention drafted the Constitution with no Bill of Rights. Despite Mason's vociferous objections, it was submitted to the states—and ratified. His anti-federalists were defeated. And Mason is most often remembered for refusing to sign the Constitution, which today Americans of every political stripe love and treasure. And yet, as the editor of the official papers of George Washington has said, Mason was "perhaps the greatest constitutionalist America has produced. He should be honored wherever civil and religious liberty is valued."[15] Mason deserves an equal place among the Founders.

There were two distinct creative moments in the American founding: the winning of independence and the invention of the United States. Mason was the central figure in both. No other founder can match his credentials. Mason speaks to us now because he spoke so powerfully in his time. His writings and public actions were inspired by the epic issues of the Revolution: individual rights and governmental power. He was not a politician nor a public man, but a father, husband, planter, and reluctant patriot. His unique stature is owed to his authorship of the founding documents of both the American Revolution and the American nation. Mason's genius was to answer the political challenges of his own moment decisively: Americans must declare and win their independence from Britain to secure their rights. The American confederation of states must be replaced by a national government—but a government so limited as to preserve the people's rights in perpetuity.[16]

Mason would have heartily agreed with his friend and protégé Thomas Jefferson when the man from Monticello wrote, of the turbulent times they both lived through, "And I have observed this march of civilization advancing from the sea coast, passing over us like a cloud of light, increasing our knowledge and improving our condition…and where this progress will stop no one can say." Yet Mason, unlike Jefferson, Washington, Hamilton, or Adams, never lost his equilibrium. Some of his contemporaries grasped this. "George Mason," as James Madison, his quondam political enemy, would say, "possessed the greatest talents for debate of any man I have ever seen or heard speak."[17] And the defeats that Mason suffered in the great debates of his public career were, in the end, only temporary setbacks. Ultimately his principles—and his Bill of Rights—won the day.

George Mason lived one of the most consequential lives of all time. From two and a half centuries in the past, his lasting principles shield mankind from the lash of tyrants. One scholar has truly said, "Those who carry the torch of freedom are soon forgotten—perhaps to be rediscovered centuries later."[18]

A GEORGE MASON CHRONOLOGY

DECEMBER 11, 1725 George Mason of Gunston Hall is born at the Mason family plantation in Fairfax County, Virginia.

1735 Mason's father dies in a boating accident.

1746 Mason comes of age and assumes responsibility for extensive land holdings he inherited in Virginia and Maryland.

1748 He unsuccessfully seeks election from Fairfax County to the Virginia House of Burgesses.

1749 Mason is elected a vestryman of Truro Parish. He becomes a partner in the Ohio Company, an organization that invested in land located in the Ohio River Valley.

APRIL 4, 1775 George Mason marries Ann Eilbeck from a plantation in Charles County, Maryland. At first, they live in a house on Mason's property in Dogue's Neck, Virginia.

1751 Mason is appointed treasurer of the reorganized Ohio Company, in which capacity he will serve until his death.

1754 The Seven Years' War (French and Indian War) begins when George Washington faces French forces at the forks of the Ohio River.

1758 Mason is appointed to represent Fairfax County in the Virginia House of Burgesses, in which he will serve until 1761.

1759 Construction of Gunston Hall, Mason's plantation house on the Potomac River, is completed.

FEBRUARY 10, 1763 The Peace of Paris ends the French and Indian War.

OCTOBER 7, 1763 The Royal Proclamation of 1763 forbids land claims and settlement west of the Appalachian Mountains.

1765–1766 Mason is active in the protest of the Stamp Act. He writes a letter opposing British actions to the *London Public Ledger* and signs it, "A Virginia Planter."

1769 George Mason helps to write nonimportation agreements as a resistance measure against British Parliamentary taxation. Under these agreements, colonial citizens vow to boycott British goods until their complaints are answered.

MARCH 9, 1773 Ann Eilbeck Mason dies.

JULY 1774 George Mason serves on the Fairfax County Committee of Safety and oversees the formation of an independent militia company for Virginia.

JULY 18, 1774 Mason, with assistance from George Washington and others, writes the Fairfax Resolves, stating actions to be taken against British aggression.

MAY 1775 Mason is chosen as a Fairfax County delegate to the Virginia Convention.

APRIL 19, 1775 Fighting between the colonies and Great Britain begins in Lexington and Concord, Massachusetts, initiating the War for Independence.

1776 Mason serves in the Virginia Convention in Williamsburg. He prepares drafts of the first Declaration of Rights and state Constitution in the colonies. Both are adopted after committee alterations—the Virginia Declaration of Rights on June 12 and the Virginia Constitution on June 29.

JULY 4, 1776 The Declaration of Independence, written by Thomas Jefferson on the model of Mason's Virginia Declaration of Rights, is formally announced to the world.

1777 Mason continues to represent Fairfax County in Virginia's House of Delegates (the new government created by Virginia's Constitution), and assumes major responsibility for legislation needed to continue the war.

1780 George Mason marries Sarah Brent of Stafford County, Virginia.

1781 Mason withdraws from the legislature on account of ill health.

FEBRUARY 27, 1781 Maryland becomes the last state to ratify the Articles of Confederation.

MARCH 1, 1781 The Articles take full effect.

FALL 1781 Mason helps to supply troops moving toward Yorktown for the final battle of the Revolutionary War.

OCTOBER 19, 1781 British General Cornwallis surrenders to General George Washington, ending hostilities.

1782 George Mason returns to private life.

1784 Mason is appointed to serve on a Virginia-Maryland commission to settle navigation questions on the Potomac River.

1786 He is appointed to represent Virginia as a delegate to a Federal Convention to meet in Philadelphia in May 1787 for the purpose of revising the Articles of Confederation.

MAY–OCTOBER 1787 Mason serves at the Federal Convention in Philadelphia and makes major contributions to the framing of the Constitution. He refuses to sign the Constitution and writes a list of *Objections to This Constitution of Government* explaining why.

JUNE 3–27, 1788 Mason attends the Virginia Ratifying Convention as a delegate from Stafford County. He opposes ratification and calls for a second Federal Convention.

JULY–AUGUST 1788 Mason retires from active politics and spends time assisting his sons with business ventures.

1789 The French Revolution and drafting of the Declaration of the Rights of Man, which draws heavily on Mason's Virginia Declaration of Rights.

MARCH 25, 1790 Mason is appointed to fill a vacancy in the U.S. Senate, but declines to serve.

DECEMBER 15, 1791 The first ten Amendments to the United States Constitution—the Bill of Rights, which is based largely on George Mason's Virginia Declaration of Rights—is ratified.

1792 Mason corresponds with U.S. senator James Monroe on national politics.

AUGUST–SEPTEMBER 1792 In spite of increasing poor health, Mason welcomes Thomas Jefferson to Gunston Hall and recounts events of the Federal Convention.

OCTOBER 7, 1792 George Mason dies on a peaceful Sunday afternoon at Gunston Hall.

George Mason's Drafts for the Virginia Declaration of Rights and the Virginia Constitution (1776)

T he Virginia Convention met in Williamsburg on May 6, 1776, and by May 15 had passed a resolution calling for the Virginia delegates at the Continental Congress to move for independence. At the same time, they formed a committee for drafting a bill of rights and a constitution for Virginia. George Mason took the lead on this project, and his notes below are considered the first draft of the Virginia Declaration of Rights. To this draft eight additional propositions were added by the committee before it was read to the Convention on May 27, 1776. After debate, and several amendments, the Declaration of Rights was passed unanimously on June 11, 1776.

THE VIRGINIA DECLARATION OF RIGHTS
[FIRST DRAFT, CA. MAY 20–26, 1776]

A Declaration of Rights, made by the Representatives of the good People of Virginia, assembled in full Convention; and recommended to Posterity as the Basis and Foundation of Government.

That all Men are born equally free and independant, and have certain inherent natural Rights, of which they can not by any Compact, deprive or divest their Posterity; among which are the Enjoyment of Life and Liberty, with the Means of acquiring and possessing Property, and pursueing and obtaining Happiness and Safety.

That Power is, by God and Nature, vested in, and consequently derived from the People; that Magistrates are their Trustees and Servants, and at all times amenable to them.

That Government is, or ought to be, instituted for the common Benefit and Security of the People, Nation, or Community. Of all the various Modes and Forms of Government, that is best, which is capable of producing the greatest Degree of Happiness and Safety, and is most effectually secured against the Danger of mal-administration. And that whenever any Government shall be found inadequate, or contrary to these Purposes, a Majority of the Community had an indubitable, inalianable and indefeasible Right to reform, alter or abolish it, in such Manner as shall be judged most conducive to the Public Weal.

That no Man, or Set of Men are entitled to exclusive or seperate Emoluments or Privileges from the Community, but in Consideration of public Services; which not being descendible, or hereditary, the Idea of a Man born a Magistrate, a Legislator, or a Judge is unnatural and absurd.

That the legislative and executive Powers of the State shoud be seperate and distinct from the judicative; and that the Members of the two first may be restraind from Oppression, by feeling and participating the Burthens they may lay upon the People; they should, at fixed

Periods be reduced to a private Station, and returned, by frequent, certain and regular Elections, into that Body from which they were taken.

That no part of a Man's Property can be taken from him, or applied to public uses, without the Consent of himself, or his legal Representatives; nor are the People bound by any Laws, but such as they have in like Manner assented to for their common Good.

That in all capital or criminal Prosecutions, a Man hath a right to demand the Cause and Nature of his Accusation, to be confronted with the Accusers or Witnesses, to call for Evidence in his favour, and to a speedy Tryal by a Jury of his Vicinage; without whose unanimous Consent, he can not be found guilty; nor can he be compelled to give Evidence against himself. And that no Man, except in times of actual Invasion or Insurrection, can be imprisoned upon Suspicion of Crimes against the State, unsupported by Legal Evidence.

That no free Government, or the Blessings of Liberty can be preserved to any People, but by a firm adherence to Justice, Moderation, Temperance, Frugality, and Virtue and by frequent Recurrence to fundamental Principles.

That as Religion, or the Duty which we owe to our divine and omnipotent Creator, and the Manner of discharging it, can be governed only by Reason and Conviction, not by Force or Violence; and therefore that all Men should enjoy the fullest Toleration in the Exercise of Religion, according to the Dictates of Conscience, unpunished and unrestrained by the Magistrate, unless, under Colour of Religion, any Man disturb the Peace, the Happiness, or Safety of Society, or of Individuals. And that it is the mutual Duty of all, to practice Christian Forbearance, Love and Charity towards Each other.

That in all controversies respecting Property, and in Suits between Man and Man, the ancient Tryal by Jury is preferable to any other, and ought to be held sacred.

That the freedom of the press, being the great bulwark of Liberty, can never be restrained but in a despotic government. That laws having a restrospect to crimes, & punishing offences committed before the existence of such laws, are generally danger- ous, and ought to be avoided.

N. B. It is proposed to make some alteration in this last article when reported to the house. Perhaps somewhat like the following That all laws having a retrospect to crimes, & punishing offences committed before the existence of such laws are dangerous, and ought to be avoided, except in cases of great, & evident necessity, when safety of the state absolutely requires them. This is thought to state with more precision the doctrine respecting ex post facto laws & to signify to posterity that it is considered not so much as a law of right, as the great law of necessity, which by the well known maxim is— allowed to supersede all human institutions.

Another is agreed to in committee condemning the use of general warrants; & one other to prevent the suspension of laws, or the execution of them.

The above clauses, with some small alterations, & the addition of one, or two more, have already been agreed to in the Committee appointed to prepare a declarition of rights; when this business is finished in the house, the committee will proceed to the ordinance of government.

T. L. Lee

The entire document is in George Mason's handwriting, except for the end portion beginning "That the freedom of the press," which is in Thomas Ludwell Lee's hand. The original document is in the Mason Papers at the Library of Congress.

GEORGE MASON'S DRAFT CONSTITUTION FOR VIRGINIA [JUNE 1776]

A Bill for new-modelling the form of Government and for establishing the Fundamental principles thereof in future.

Whereas George Guelf king of Great Britain and Ireland and Elector of Hanover, heretofore entrusted with the exercise of the kingly office in this government hath endeavored to pervert the same into a detestable and insupportable tyranny; by putting his negative on laws the most wholesome & necessary for ye public good;

by denying to his governors permission to pass laws of immediate and pressing importance, unless suspended in their operations for his assent, and, when so suspended, neglecting to attend to them for many years;

by refusing to pass certain other laws, unless the person to be benefited by them would relinquish the inestimable right of representation in the legislature

by dissolving legislative assemblies repeatedly and continually for opposing with manly firmness his invasions on the rights of the people;

when dissolved, by refusing to call others for a long space of time, thereby leaving the political system without any legislative head;

by endeavoring to prevent the population of our country, & for that purpose obstructing the laws for the naturalization of foreigners & raising the condition lacking appropriations of lands;

by keeping among us, in times of peace, standing armies and ships of war;

lacking to render the military independent of & superior to the civil power;

by combining with others to subject us to a foreign jurisdiction, giving his assent to their pretended acts of legislation.

for quartering large bodies of troops among us;

for cutting off our trade with all parts of the world;

for imposing taxes on us without our consent;

for depriving us of the benefits of trial by jury;

for transporting us beyond seas to be tried for pretended offences; and

for suspending our own legislatures & declaring themselves invested with power to legislate for us in all cases whatsoever;

by plundering our seas, ravaging our coasts, burning our towns and destroying the lives of our people;

by inciting insurrections of our fellow subjects with the allurements of forfeiture & confiscation;

by prompting our negroes to rise in arms among us; those very negroes whom *he hath from time to time* by an inhuman use of his negative he hath refused permission to exclude by law;

by endeavoring to bring on the inhabitants of our frontiers the merciless Indian savages, whose known rule of warfare is an undistinguished destruction of all ages, sexes, & conditions of existence;

by transporting at this time a large army of foreign mercenaries to complete the works of death, desolation & tyranny already begun with circumstances of cruelty & perfidy so unworthy the head of a civilized nation;

by answering our repeated petitions for redress with a repetition of injuries;

and finally by abandoning the helm of government and declaring us out of his allegiance & protection;

by which several acts of misrule the said George Guelf has forfeited the kingly office and has rendered it necessary for the preservation of the people that he should be immediately deposed from the same, and divested of all its privileges, powers, & prerogatives:

And forasmuch as the public liberty may be more certainly secured by abolishing an office which all experience hath shewn to be inveterately inimical thereto *or which* and it will thereupon become further necessary to re-establish such ancient principles as are friendly to the rights of the people and to declare certain others which may co-operate with and fortify the same in future.

Be it therefore enacted by the authority of the people that the said, George Guelf be, and he hereby is deposed from the kingly office within this government and absolutely divested of all it's rights, powers, and prerogatives: and that he and his descendants and all persons acting by or through him, and all other persons whatsoever shall be and forever remain incapable of the same: and that the said office shall henceforth cease and never more either in name or substance be re-established within this colony.

And be it further enacted by the authority aforesaid that the following fundamental laws and principles of government shall henceforth be established.

The Legislative, Executive and Judiciary offices shall be kept forever separate; no person exercising the one shall be capable of appointment to the others, or to either of them.

LEGISLATIVE.

Legislation shall be exercised by two separate houses, to wit a house of Representatives, and a house of Senators, which shall be called the General Assembly of Virginia.

Ho. of Representatives

The sd house of Representatives shall be composed of persons chosen by the people annually on the [1st day of October] and shall meet in General assembly on the [1st day of November] following and so from time to time on their own adjournments, or at any time when summoned by the Administrator and shall continue sitting so long as they shall think the publick service requires.

Vacancies in the said house by death or disqualification shall be filled by the electors under a warrant from the Speaker of the said house.

Electors

All male persons of full age and sane mind having a freehold estate in [one fourth of an acre] of land in any town, or in [25] acres of land in the country, and all elected persons resident in the colony who shall have paid scot and lot to government the last [two years] shall have right to give their vote in the election of their respective representatives. And every person so qualified to elect shall be capable of being elected, provided he shall have given no bribe either directly or indirectly to any elector, and shall take an oath of fidelity to the state and of duty in his office, before he enters on the exercise thereof. During his continuance in the said office he shall hold no public pension nor post of profit, either himself, or by another for his use.

The number of Representatives for each county or borough shall be so proportioned to the numbers of it's qualified electors that the whole number of representatives shall not exceed [300] nor be less than [125.] for the present there shall be one representative for every [ ] qualified electors in each county or borough: but whenever this or any future proportion shall be likely to exceed or fall short of the limits beforementioned, it shall be again adjusted by the house of representatives.

The house of Representatives when met shall be free to act according to their own judgment and conscience.

Senate

The Senate shall consist of not less than [15] nor more than [50] members who shall be appointed by the house of Representatives. One third of them shall be removed out of office by lot at the end of the first [three] years and their places be supplied by a new appointment; one other third shall be removed by lot in like manner at the end of the second [three] years and their places be supplied by a new appointment; after which one third shall be removed annually at the end of every [three] years according to seniority. When once removed, they shall be forever incapable of being re-appointed to that house. Their qualifications shall be an oath of fidelity to the state, and of duty in their office, the being [31] years of age at the least, and the having given no bribe directly or indirectly to obtain their appointment. While in the senatorial office they shall be incapable of holding any public pension or post of profit either themselves, or by others for their use.

The judges of the General court and of the High court of Chancery shall have session and deliberative voice, but not suffrage in the house of Senators.

The Senate and the house of representatives shall each of them have power to originate and amend bills; save only that bills for levying money *bills* shall be originated and amended by the representatives only: the assent of both houses shall be requisite to pass a law.

The General assembly shall have no power to pass any law inflicting death for any crime, excepting murder, & *such* those offences in the military service for which they shall think punishment by death absolutely necessary: and all capital punishments in other cases are hereby abolished. Nor shall they have power to prescribe torture in any case whatever: nor shall there be power anywhere to pardon crimes or to remit fines or punishments: nor shall any law for levying money be in force longer than [ten years] from the time of its commencement.

[Two thirds] of the members of either house shall be a Quorum to proceed to business.

EXECUTIVE.

The executive powers shall be exercised in manner following.

Administrator

One person to be called the [Administrator] shall be annually appointed by the house of Representatives on the second day of their first session, who after having acted [one] year shall be incapable of being again appointed to that office until he shall have been out of the same [three] years.

Deputy Admr.

Under him shall be appointed by the same house and at the same time, a Deputy-Administrator to assist his principal in the discharge of his office, and to succeed, in case of his death before the year shall have expired, to the whole powers thereof during the residue of the year.

The administrator shall possess the power formerly held by the king: save only that, he shall be bound by acts of legislature tho' not expressly named;

he shall have no negative on the bills of the Legislature;

he shall be liable to action, tho' not to personal restraint for private duties or wrongs;

he shall not possess the prerogatives;

of dissolving, proroguing or adjourning either house of Assembly;

of declaring war or concluding peace;

of issuing letters of marque or reprisal;

of raising or introducing armed forces, building armed vessels, forts or strongholds;

of coining monies or regulating their values;

of regulating weights and measures;

of erecting courts, offices, boroughs, corporations, fairs, markets, ports, beacons, lighthouses, seamarks.

of laying embargoes, or prohibiting the exportation of any commodity for a longer space than [40] days.

of retaining or recalling a member of the state but by legal process pro delicto vel contractu.

of making denizens.

of pardoning crimes, or remitting fines or punishments.

of creating dignities or granting rights of precedence.

but these powers shall be exercised by the legislature alone, and excepting also those powers which by these fundamentals are given to others, or abolished.

Privy Council

A Privy council shall be annually appointed by the house of representatives whose duties it shall be to give advice to the Administrator when called on by him. With them the Deputy Administrator shall have session and suffrage.

Delegates

Delegates to represent this colony in the American Congress shall be appointed when necessary by the house of Representatives. After serving [one] year in that office they shall not be capable of being re-appointed to the same during an interval of [one] year.

Treasurer

A Treasurer shall be appointed by the house of Representatives who shall issue no money but by authority of both houses.

Attorney Genrl.

An Attorney general shall be appointed by the house of Representatives

High Sheriffs, &c.

High Sheriffs and Coroners of counties shall be annually elected by those qualified to vote for representatives: and no person who shall have served as high sheriff [one] year shall be capable of being re-elected to the said office in the same county till he shall have been out of office [five] years.

Other Officers

All other Officers civil and military shall be appointed by the Administrator; but such appointment shall be subject to the negative of the Privy council, saving however to the Legislature a power of transferring to any other persons the appointment of such officers or any of them.

JUDICIARY.

The Judiciary powers shall be exercised

First, by County courts and other inferior jurisdictions:

Secondly, by a General court & a High court of Chancery:

Thirdly, by a Court of Appeals.

County Courts, &c.

The judges of the county courts and other inferior jurisdictions shall be appointed by the Administrator, subject to the negative of the privy council. They shall not be fewer than [five] in number. Their jurisdictions shall be defined from time to time by the legislature: and they shall be removable for misbehavior by the court of Appeals.

Genl. Court and High Ct. of Chancery

The Judges of the General court and of the High court of Chancery shall be appointed by the Administrator and Privy council. If kept united they shall be [5] in number, if separate, there shall be [5] for the General court & [3] for the High court of Chancery. The appointment shall be made from the faculty of the law, and of such persons of that faculty as shall have actually exercised the same at the bar of some court or courts of record within this colony for [seven] years. They shall hold their commissions during good behavior, for breach of which they shall be removable by the court of Appeals. Their jurisdiction shall be defined from time to time by the Legislature.

Court of Appeals

The Court of Appeals shall consist of not less than [7] nor more than [11] members, to be appointed by the house of Representatives: they shall hold their offices during good behavior, for breach of which they shall be removable by an act of the legislature only. Their jurisdiction shall be to determine finally all causes removed before them from the General Court or High Court of Chancery, or of the county courts or other inferior jurisdictions for misbehavior: [to try impeachments against high offenders lodged before them by the house of representatives for such crimes as shall hereafter be precisely defined by the Legislature, and for the punishment of which, the said legislature shall have previously prescribed certain and determinate pains.] In this court the judges of the General court and High court of Chancery shall have session and deliberative voice, but no suffrage.

Juries

All facts in causes whether of Chancery, Common, Ecclesiastical, or Marine law, shall be tried by a jury upon evidence given viva voce, in open court: but where witnesses are out of the colony or unable to attend through sickness or other invincible necessity, their deposition may be submitted to the credit of the jury.

Fines, &c.

All Fines or Amercements shall be assessed, & Terms of imprisonment for Contempts & Misdemeanors shall be fixed by the verdict of a Jury.

Process

All Process Original & Judicial shall run in the name of the court from which it issues.

Quorum

Two thirds of the members of the General court, High court of Chancery, or Court of Appeals shall be a Quorum to proceed to business.

RIGHTS, PRIVATE AND PUBLIC.

Lands

Unappropriated or Forfeited lands shall be appropriated by the Administrator with the consent of the Privy council.

Every person of full age neither owning nor having owned [50] acres of land, shall be entitled to an appropriation of [50] acres or to so much as shall make up what he owns or has owned [50] acres in full and absolute dominion. And no other person shall be capable of taking an appropriation.

Lands heretofore holden of the crown in fee simple, and those hereafter to be appropriated shall be holden in full and absolute dominion, of no superior whatever.

No lands shall be appropriated until purchased of the Indian native proprietors; nor shall any purchases be made of them but on behalf of the public, by authority of acts of the General assembly to be passed for every purchase specially.

The territories contained within the charters erecting the colonies of Maryland, Pennsylvania, North and South Carolina, are hereby ceeded, released, & forever confirmed to the people of those colonies respectively, with all the rights of property, jurisdiction and government and all other rights whatsoever which might at any time heretofore have been claimed by this colony. The Western and Northern extent of this country shall in all other respects stand as fixed by the charter of until by act of the Legislature one or more territories shall be laid off Westward of the Alleghaney mountains for new colonies, which colonies shall be established on the same fundamental laws contained in this instrument, and shall be free and independent of this colony and of all the world.

Descents shall go according to the laws Gavelkind, save only that females shall have equal rights with males.

Slaves

No person hereafter coming into this county shall be held within the same in slavery under any pretext whatever.

Naturalization

All persons who by their own oath or affirmation, or by other testimony shall give satisfactory proof to any court of record in this colony that they propose to reside in the same [7] years at the least and who shall subscribe the fundamental laws, shall be considered as residents and entitled to all the rights of persons natural born.

Religion

All persons shall have full and free liberty of religious opinion; nor shall any be compelled to frequent or maintain any religious institution.

Arms

No freeman shall be debarred the use of arms [within his own lands].

Standing Armies

There shall be no standing army but in time of actual war.

Free Press

Printing presses shall be free, except so far as by commission of private injury cause may be given of private action.

Forfeitures

All Forfeitures heretofore going to the king, shall go the state; save only such as the legislature may hereafter abolish.

Wrecks

The royal claim to Wrecks, waifs, strays, treasure-trove, royal mines, royal fish, royal birds, are declared to have been usurpations on common right.

Salaries

No Salaries or Perquisites shall be given to any officer but by some future act of the legislature. No salaries shall be given to the Administrator, members of the legislative houses, judges of the court of Appeals, judges of the County courts, or other inferior jurisdictions, Privy counsellors, or Delegates to the American Congress: but the reasonable expences of the Administrator, members of the house of representatives, judges of the court of Appeals, Privy counsellors, & Delegates for subsistence while acting in the duties of their office, may be borne by the public, if the legislature shall so direct.

Qualifications

No person shall be capable of acting in any office Civil, Military [or Ecclesiastical] *The Qualifications of all not otherwise directed, shall be an oath of fidelity to state and the having given no bribe to obtain their office* who shall have given any bribe to obtain such office, or who shall not previously take an oath of fidelity to the state.

None of these fundamental laws and principles of government shall be repealed or altered, but by the personal consent of the people on summons to meet in their respective counties on one and the same day by an act of Legislature to be passed for every special occasion: and if in such county meetings the people of two thirds of the counties shall give their suffrage for any particular alteration or repeal referred to them by the said act, the same shall be accordingly repealed or altered, and such repeal or alteration shall take it's place among these fundamentals and stand on the same footing with them, in lieu of the article repealed or altered.

The laws heretofore in force in this colony shall remain in force, except so far as they are altered by the foregoing fundamental laws, or so far as they may be hereafter altered by acts of the Legislature.

George Mason's Objections to the Federal Constitution (1787)

Objections to This Constitution of Government
There is no Declaration of Rights, and the laws of the general government being paramount to the laws and constitution of the several States, the Declarations of Rights in the separate States are no security. Nor are the people secured even in the enjoyment of the benefit of the common law.

In the House of Representatives there is not the substance but the shadow only of representation; which can never produce proper information in the legislature, or inspire confidence in the people; the laws will therefore be generally made by men little concerned in, and unacquainted with their effects and consequences.

The Senate have the power of altering all money bills, and of originating appropriations of money, and the salaries of the officers of their own appointment, in conjunction with the president of the United States, although they are not the representatives of the people or amenable to them.

These with their other great powers, viz.: their power in the appointment of ambassadors and all public officers, in making treaties, and in trying all impeachments, their influence upon and connection with the supreme Executive from these causes, their duration of office and their being a constantly existing body, almost continually sitting, joined with their being one complete branch of the legislature, will destroy any balance in the government, and enable them to accomplish what usurpations they please upon the rights and liberties of the people.

The Judiciary of the United States is so constructed and extended, as to absorb and destroy the judiciaries of the several States; thereby rendering law as tedious, intricate and expensive, and justice as unattainable, by a great part of the community, as in England, and enabling the rich to oppress and ruin the poor.

The President of the United States has no Constitutional Council, a thing unknown in any safe and regular government. He will therefore be unsupported by proper information and advice, and will generally be directed by minions and favorites; or he will become a tool to the Senate—or a Council of State will grow out of the principal officers of the great departments; the worst and most dangerous of all ingredients for such a Council in a free country; From this fatal defect has arisen the improper power of the Senate in the appointment of public officers, and the alarming dependence and connection between that branch of the legislature and the supreme Executive.

Hence also spuring that unnecessary officer the Vice- President, who for want of other employment is made president of the Senate, thereby dangerously blending the executive and legislative powers, besides always giving to some one of the States an unnecessary and unjust pre-eminence over the others.

The President of the United States has the unrestrained power of granting pardons for treason, which may be sometimes exercised to screen from punishment those whom he had secretly instigated to commit the crime, and thereby prevent a discovery of his own guilt.

By declaring all treaties supreme laws of the land, the Executive and the Senate have, in many cases, an exclusive power of legislation; which might have been avoided by proper distinctions with respect to treaties, and requiring the assent of the House of Representatives, where it could be done with safety.

By requiring only a majority to make all commercial and navigation laws, the five Southern States, whose produce and circumstances are totally different from that of the eight Northern and Eastern States, may be ruined, for such rigid and premature regulations may be made as will enable the merchants of the Northern and Eastern States not only to demand an exhorbitant freight, but to monopolize the purchase of the commodities at their own price, for many years, to the great injury of the landed interest, and impoverishment of the people; and the danger is the greater as the gain on one side will be in proportion to the loss on the other. Whereas requiring two-thirds of the members present in both Houses would have produced mutual moderation, promoted the general interest, and removed an insuperable objection to the adoption of this government.

Under their own construction of the general clause, at the end of the enumerated powers, the Congress may grant monopolies in trade and commerce, constitute new crimes, inflict unusual and severe punishments, and extend their powers as far as they shall think proper; so that the State legislatures have no security for the powers now presumed to remain to them, or the people for their rights.

There is no declaration of any kind, for preserving the liberty of the press, or the trial by jury in civil causes; nor against the danger of standing armies in time of peace.

The State legislatures are restrained from laying export duties on their own produce.

Both the general legislature and the State legislature are expressly prohibited making ex post facto laws; though there never was nor can be a legislature but must and will make such laws, when necessity and the public safety require them; which will hereafter be a breach of all the constitutions in the Union, and afford precedents for other innovations.

This government will set out a moderate aristocracy: it is at present impossible to foresee whether it will, in its operation, produce a monarchy, or a corrupt, tyrannical aristocracy; it will most probably vibrate some years between the two, and then terminate in the one or the other.

The general legislature is restrained from prohibiting the further importation of slaves for twenty odd years; though such importations render the United States weaker, more vulnerable, and less capable of defence.

(The George Mason Manuscript Collection)

Acknowledgments

I wish to thank the following people who contributed significantly to improving the manuscript: first and foremost, my agent, John Rudolph, who championed the book and did not give up on me, and my excellent editor at Regnery, Elizabeth Kantor, who greatly improved the book and made it much better. And of my readers, who invaluably read and critiqued the book, my special thanks goes to Art Downey, a colleague of my father's from the White House, and a good friend. I am also indebted to the library, resources, and personnel at Gunston Hall, especially Director Scott Stroh and Samantha Dorsey.

Finally, and most importantly, I want to thank both my children, Tori and Will, for encouraging me to keep writing books. You have filled my life with love and laughter, and keep me young at heart.

Notes

Preface

1. Joseph Ellis, *A Legacy of Myth and Contradiction, Thomas Jefferson, American's Enduring Revolutionary*, Foreword, 8; *Time*, 2015: "These have become the most important 55 words in American history, the essence of the American creed." (Declaration of Independence).

2. Robert A. Rutland, *George Mason: Reluctant Statesman* (Baton Rouge: LSU Press, 1980), Kindle edition, 80.

3. Helen Hill Miller, *George Mason: Gentleman Revolutionary* (Chapel Hill: University of North Carolina Press, 1975); Helen Hill Miller, *George Mason of Gunston Hall* (Virginia: The Board of Regents of Gunston Hall, 1958); see also Helen Hill Miller, *George Mason, Constitutionalist* (Simon Publications, 1938).

4. For character sketches of the Founders, see Gordon S. Wood, *Revolutionary Characters: What Made the Founders Different* (New York: Penguin, 2006); Douglass Adair, "Fame and the Founding Fathers," in *Fame and the Founding Fathers: Essays by Douglass Adair*, ed. Trevor Colbourn (Indianapolis, IN: Liberty Fund, 1998); Joanne B. Freeman, *Affairs of Honor: National Politics in the New Republic* (New Haven: Yale University Press, 2001); and John Kaminski, *The Great Virginia*

Triumvirate: George Washington, Thomas Jefferson, and James Madison in the Eyes of Their Contemporaries (Charlottesville: University of Virginia Press, 2010). For Jefferson, see Francis D. Cogliano, *Thomas Jefferson: Reputation and Legacy* (Charlottesville: University of Virginia Press, 2006). For Washington, see Richard Brookhiser, *Founding Father: Rediscovering George Washingto*n (New York: Free Press, 1996), 131–36; and *Paul K. Longmore, The Invention of George Washington* (Berkeley: University of California Press, 1988).

5.   Joseph Ellis, "American Sphinx: The Contradictions of Thomas Jefferson," *Civilization: The Magazine of the Library of Congress*, Nov–Dec 1994, 1606-1827 1 Digital Collections 1 Library of Congress: "Thomas Jefferson [is] so integral part of the public domain, [that] he has daring power outside the academic world as well. The admiration for Jefferson [is] as much a psychological as a political phenomenon. He could walk past the slave quarters on Mulberry Row at Monticello without qualms or guilt while daydreaming about the rights of man with utter sincerity. He could purchase the finest and most expensive art and furniture for his many residences, all the while idealizing the pastoral virtues of the sturdy farmer. He could fall in love with beautiful women in fits of rhapsodic passion but never allow the deepest secrets of his soul to be shared with any living creature. He was, like us, layered and conflicted but, as we wish to be, always in control, the perfect model for his beloved ideal of 'self-government.'"

6.   Joseph Ellis, *The Quartet* (New York: Vintage, 2016), 36.

7.   Jon Meacham, *Jefferson, The Art of Power*, I book edition, 654; see also Kevin J. Hayes, *The Mind of a Patriot: Patrick Henry and the World of Ideas* (Charlottesville: University of Virginia Press, 2008); Jeff Broadwater, *George Mason, Forgotten Founder* (Chapel Hill: University of North Carolina Press, 2006); Richard Brookhiser, *James Madison* (New York: Basic Books, 2011); and Ron Chernow, *Washington, a Life* (New York: Penguin, 2010).

8.   Historian David O. Stewart, author of *The Summer of 1787 (1363)*, concludes that "The resemblances between the two documents are too close not to conclude that Jefferson began with Mason's Declaration before him and revised it for his purposes."; Joseph Ellis, *American Sphinx*: "The *Pennsylvania Gazette* published Mason's words the same day they were adopted in Williamsburg. Since Jefferson's version of the same thought was

drafted sometime that following week, and since we know that he regarded the unfolding events in Virginia as more significant than what was occurring in Philadelphia and that he was being kept abreast by courier, it also strains credulity to deny the influence of Mason's language on his own."; Mason's Declaration of Rights was distinctive and different from previous, or later, manifestos in one significant sense. For it was not just a rejection of British authority but also an assertion of the need to create state governments to replace discredited British rule; Maier, *American Scripture, 722*: Jefferson's words, "that all men are created equal; that they are endowed by their Creator with certain unalienable rights; that among these are life, liberty, and the pursuit of happiness"—were originally adapted from a draft of the Virginia Declaration of Rights written by George Mason and amended by a committee of the Virginia convention. In fact, the words of the Mason draft made their way into several other revolutionary state bills of rights, and seem to have had a far greater impact than either the Declaration of Independence or the Declaration of Rights that the Virginia convention finally adopted, both of which were themselves descended from the Mason draft. What might seem to be minor differences of wording are critical in tracing its lineage. Where the Declaration of Independence said men were "created equal," the Mason/committee draft asserted that all men are born equally free and independent, and have certain inherent natural rights, of which they cannot, by any compact, deprive or divert their posterity; among which are the enjoyment of life and liberty, with the means of acquiring and possessing property, and pursuing and obtaining happiness and safety; see Maier, *American Scripture*: "As this book makes plain, I dissent from any suggestion that Jefferson was alone responsible for the Declaration of Independence, or that the document most worth studying and admiring is his draft, or that the full story of the Declaration can be told apart from that of the Independence it declared and the process that led to it.... ."; Jefferson's Declaration "was based upon the first three provisions of the Mason/committee draft of Virginia's Declaration of Rights. Jefferson began with Mason's statement "that all men are born equally free and independant," which he rewrote to say they were "created equal & independent," then (on his "original rough draft") cut out the "& independent." Mason said that all men had "certain inherent natural rights, of which they cannot, by any compact, deprive or divest their posterity,"

which Jefferson compressed marvelously into a statement that men derived
from their equal creation "rights inherent & inalienable," then moved the
noun to the end of the phrase so it read "inherent & inalienable rights."
Among those rights, Mason said, were "the enjoyment of life and liberty,
with the means of acquiring and possessing property, and pursuing and
obtaining happiness and safety," which Jefferson again shortened first to
"the preservation of life, & liberty, & the pursuit of happiness," and then
simply to "life, liberty, & the pursuit of happiness; Maier, *American
Scripture*: "Selby, *Revolution in Virginia*, 103, says that Pennsylvania,
Massachusetts, and four of the other five states that adopted bills of rights in
the next decade drew on the Mason/committee draft (Delaware, Maryland,
Vermont, and New Hampshire), and that North Carolina seems to have
been more influenced by the final version as adopted by the Virginia
convention—which, of course, was itself based on the Mason draft. On the
use specifically of Mason's language on equality and natural rights, see Boyd
I: 413; Dumbauld, *The Declaration of Independence*, 54 (and see also 77);
D.W. Brogan quoted in Philip F. Detweiler, "The Changing Reputation of
the Declaration of Independence: The First Fifty Years," WMQ, 3d Ser.,
IXX (1962), 557. 65. Boyd I: 213, and Decent Respect, 91. 66. JCC II: 129,
and Boyd I: 199. 67. Committee of Secret Correspondence to Silas Deane,
Philadelphia, July 8 and August 7, 1776, in LDC IV: 405, 635–36."

9.   Maier, *American Scripture*: "On the development and influence of the
Virginia Declaration, see John Selby, *The Revolution in Virginia*, 1775-1783
(Williamsburg, 1988), 101–4, 106–10. The committee draft, it seems, was
far more widely circulated and more influential than that finally adopted by
the Virginia Convention, which, Selby says, was virtually lost for some forty
years[…] The committee version of the Virginia Declaration of Rights had
been published earlier—it appeared, for example, in the Pennsylvania
Evening Post on June 6, and later in the Pennsylvania Ledger—but the
Gazette republication seems especially important since it coincided with the
appointment and early meetings of the drafting committee. The kinship of
the Declaration of Independence with Mason's Virginia Declaration was
noted in John C. Fitzpatrick, *The Spirit of the Revolution* (Boston and New
York, 1924), 2-3, 5-6, and more recently in Lucas, "Justifying America," 87,
which, however, claims that it is impossible to know how much Jefferson was
influenced by the Mason document. Boyd, in his *Declaration of*

Independence, 21–22, insisted that Jefferson was "a recognized master, not an imaginative imitator," and dismissed Jefferson's debt to the Mason/committee draft as "not yet proved" and something that will "in all probability remain a matter of opinion." However, a careful comparison of the various drafts of the Declaration, which Becker sorted out, with the Mason/committee draft makes it clear that Jefferson began with that draft and gradually altered it. Such a comparison will be made later. It is, however, impossible to know whether the idea of using the Mason/committee draft came out of the Committee of Five or, as Fitzpatrick assumed, "the clarion note of liberty in [the draft Virginia Declaration's] first three sections found sympathetic echo" in Jefferson's "brain; he seized upon them and, with the artist's perfect judgment, commenced the Declaration with the trumpet blast of their bold principles" (6). See also Robert A. Rutland, ed., *The Papers of George Mason*, 1725-92 (Chapel Hill, 1970), I, 275–91, for drafts of the document and a brief discussion of its evolution and influence. 60. Congressional vote of 11 June in JCC V: 428-29; Hancock to Certain States, Philadelphia, July 6, 1776, in LDC IV: 396. 61. From *the Pennsylvania Gazette*, June 12, 1776. 62. Compare the draft Virginia Declaration in the Pennsylvania Gazette for June 12, 1776, with the Declaration as finally adopted in William W. Hening, ed., *Laws of Virginia, IX* (Richmond, 1821), 109–112, and the English Declaration in Schwoerer, Declaration of Right."

10. Foreword to Robert A. Rutland's book *George Mason: Reluctant Statesman*, https://www.law.gmu.edu/about/mason_man.
11. Kate Mason Rowland, *The Life of George Mason*, 1725–1792 (New York: G. Putnam's Sons, 1892), ix.
12. Pauline Maier, *Ratification* (New York: Simon and Schuster, 2011), 298; *Mason Papers*, 3:963; *Notes of Debates in The Federal Convention of 1787 Reported by James Madison*. Ed. Adrienne Koch (Athens, OH: Ohio University Press, 1966), 493. Bill O'Reilly, *Killing England*, (New York: Henry Holt and Co., 2017), 1408: "The thirty-seven words for the Presidential Oath of Office, which have been used to swear in every American president since Washington, are written into the U.S. Constitution. They were penned in 1787 by delegates to the Constitutional Convention."

13. Henry Mayer, *A Son of Thunder* (New York: Grove Press, 2007), 1798: At the Virginia ratifying convention in 1788, "No listener could ever forget how Henry drew shivers by reminding jurors that 'blood is concerned' in their decision. Nor could people forget how Henry spiked the testimony of a woman who had witnessed something through a keyhole. 'Which eye did you peep with?' he asked. When the laughter had subsided, he turned from the flustered witness to the court, flung out his arms and said, 'Great God, deliver us from eavesdroppers!' When a Scotch merchant named John Hook sued one of Henry's neighbors for the value of two steers impressed during the war, Henry spoke feelingly of the wartime sacrifices patriots had made and described the joyous celebration that followed the British surrender at Yorktown. What notes of discord disturbed the general joy? Henry asked, and he convulsed the courtroom with the answer, 'They are the notes of John Hook, hoarsely bawling through the American camp, "beef! beef! beef!"'"

14. Ellis, *The Quartet*: "My interpretation here tends to deviate from the mainstream because his most distinguished biographers see him primarily as a political philosopher. I see him as a political strategist, whose ideas were developed in specific contexts, usually in response to arguments he sought to counter and, in this case, political developments that he had not anticipated. His greatest gift was intellectual agility, not consistency."

15. Ellis, *The Quartet*, 38.

16. R. Carter Pittman, *George Mason of Gunston Hall*, 15 Ala. Law. 196 1954, 196–208.

17. Josephine F. Pacheco, *George Mason and The Constitution* 59 N.Y. St. B.J. 10 1987.

18. Ibid., 11.

19. For political portraits of James Madison, see Lance Banning, *The Sacred Fire of Liberty: James Madison and the Founding Federal Republic* (Ithaca, NY: Cornell University Press, 1995); and Drew R. McCoy, *The Last of the Fathers: James Madison and the Republican Legacy* (Cambridge, UK: Cambridge University Press, 1989); Maier, *Ratification*, 155–211.

20. Jeff Broadwater, *Forgotten Founder*, 307; Branchi, "*Memoirs of the Life and Voyages of Doctor Philip Mazzei, Part I*" 169–70; Rakove, *Madison*, 13–14.

21. Hayes, *The Mind of a Patriot: Patrick Henry and the World of Ideas* (Charlottesville: University of Virginia Press, 2008); Jeff Broadwater, *George*

Mason, Forgotten Founder (Chapel Hill: University of North Carolina Press, 2006); Richard Brookhiser, *James Madison* (New York: Basic Books, 2011); and Ron Chernow, *Washington, a Life* (New York: Penguin, 2010).

22. Glover, *Founders as Fathers*, Introduction; see also Jeff Broadwater, *George Mason, Forgotten Founder* (Chapel Hill: University of North Carolina Press, 2006).

23. Glover, *Founders as Fathers*, 1067.

24. See Ellis, *Revolutionary Summer*, 15: "John Adams emerged as the leader of the radical faction in the Continental Congress [in 1776]. He did not look the part. By the time he turned forty-one in 1776, he was already losing his teeth and what remained of his hair. At five foot six he was shorter than most males of his time, with a torso that his enemies compared to a cannonball."

25. Mason's Declaration of Rights was distinctive and different from previous, or later, manifestos in one significant sense. For it was not just a rejection of British authority but also an assertion of the need to create state governments to replace discredited British rule." Ellis, *Revolutionary Summer: The Birth of American Independence*, 23.

26. R. Carter Pittman, *George Mason of Gunston hall*, 15 Ala. Law. 196 1954, 196–208; R. Carter Pittman, "Introduction," in Marian Buckley Cox, *Glimpse of Glory: George Mason of Gunston Hall* (Richmond, 1954), xvii (first quotation); R. Carter Pittman, "George Mason and the Rights of Men," *Florida Law Journal* 25 (1951): 252 (second quotation).

Prologue

1. *Founding Fathers: America's Great Leaders and the Fight for Freedom*, Special Edition, *National Geographic,* Introduction (2016), 4.

2. The riverfront was the main entryway in the eighteenth century, with most travelers and guests coming to Gunston Hall from the Potomac River. After arriving at the wharf at Gunston, guests would enter the garden through a side gate into the Boxwood Allee.

3. Kate Mason Rowland, *The Life of George Mason, 1725–1792* (New York: G.P. Putnam's Sons, 1892), 86–87.

4. Lorri Glover, *Founders as Fathers, The Private Lives and Politics of the American Revolution (New Haven and London,* Yale University Press, 2014), 276.

5. Ibid., 306.

6. My understanding and interpretation of Washington is based on a number of sources, most notably a reading of the official Washington Papers and the character sketch in Joseph Ellis's biography, *His Excellency: George Washington* (New York, 2004). The scholarship on Washington is voluminous, but four other books strike me as crucial to an understanding of him: Ron Chernow, *Washington: A Life* (New York: Penguin Press, 2011); Marcus Cunliffe, *George Washington: Man and Monument* (Boston, 1958); Peter Henriques, *Realistic Visionary: A Portrait of George Washington* (Charlottesville, VA, 2006); and Don Higgenbotham, ed., *George Washington Reconsidered* (Charlottesville, VA, 2001).

7. Glover, *Founders as Fathers*, 138.

8. Ibid., 88; George Mason to George Washington, 9 April 1768, Gunston Hall Library and Archives; Miller, *George Mason*, 74–75, 84; Broadwater, *Forgotten Founder*, I book Edition, 57–58.

9. David O. Stewart, *The Summer of 1787* (New York: Simon & Schuster, 2007), 42.

10. Bill O'Reilly and Martin Dugard, *Killing England: The Brutal Struggle for American Independence* (New York: Henry Holt and Co., 2017), 1303: Washington was stricken with smallpox as a nineteen-year-old. "He endured three weeks of suffering before the illness passed, but in the process, he became an ardent believer in smallpox inoculation, a highly controversial practice at the time. It involved placing a small amount of pus from an infected victim into an incision on the body of a healthy person. This would result in a mild form of smallpox, one that could sometimes be fatal, but when successful, it gave the individual a lifetime of immunity from the disease. Thus, in 1776, as Martha Washington came to stay with her husband in Massachusetts, the general vigorously urged her to get inoculated. Despite great misgivings, she did, with no ill effects."

11. *National Geographic*, Abigail Adams, 66.

12. "Dr. James Thatcher of the Continental Army," *Parade Magazine*, January 22, 2017, 14.

13. Kevin J. Hayes, *The Mind of a Patriot: Patrick Henry and the World of Ideas* (Charlottesville: University of Virginia Press, 2008); Jeff Broadwater, *George Mason, Forgotten Founder* (Chapel Hill: University of North Carolina Press, 2006); Richard Brookhiser, *James Madison* (New York: Basic Books, 2011); and Chernow, *Washington*.

14. O'Reilly and Dugard, *Killing England*, 1297.

15. Henriques, *Realistic Visionary*; and Don Higginbotham, ed., *George Washington Reconsidered* (Charlottesville, VA: University of Virginia Press, 2001); see also the Papers of George Washington: www.gwpapers.virginia. edu.

16. R. Walton Moore, "George Mason, The Statesman," *William and Mary Quarterly*, Vol. 13, No. 1 (Jan., 1933), 10–17; Published by: Omohundro Institute of Early American History and Culture, http://www.jstor.org/ stable/1922831, Accessed: 13-05-2017 18:16 UTC.

17. See Richard Brookhiser, *James Madison* (New York: Basic Books, 2011); Thomas Fleming, *The Intimate Lives of the Founding Fathers* (New York: Smithsonian/HarperCollins, 2009); and Harlow Giles Unger, *The Unexpected George Washington: His Private Life* (Hoboken, NJ: John Wiley and Sons, 2006).

18. Ron Chernow, *Washington*, 41; *PWP*, 10:333.; See Hayes, *The Mind of a Patriot*; Broadwater, *Forgotten Founder*.

19. Ellis, *The Quartet*, 66; see also Pauline Maier, *Ratification: The People Debate the Constitution, 1787–1788* (New York: Simon and Schuster, 2010), chs. 9–10; and Kaminski et al., *Documentary History of the Ratification*, vols. 8–10. 4. For sovereignty and constitutionalism, see Gordon S. Wood, *The Creation of the American Republic, 1776–1787* (Chapel Hill: University of North Carolina Press, 1969); Lance Banning, *Conceived in Liberty: The Struggle to Define the New Republic*, 1789– 1793 (Lanham, MD: Rowman and Littlefield, 2004); Jack Rakove, *Original Meanings: Politics and Ideas in the Making of the Constitution* (New York: Viking, 1996); and Bernard Bailyn, *Ideological Origins of the American Revolution* (Cambridge, MA: Harvard University Press, 1967). For anti-federalists, see Saul Cornell, *The Other Founders: Anti-Federalism and the Dissenting Tradition in America, 1788–1828* (Chapel Hill: University of North Carolina Press, 1999). 5. The wide-ranging and extensive work on early national politics includes Lance Banning, *The Jeffersonian Persuasion:*

Evolution of a Party Ideology (Ithaca, NY: Cornell University Press, 1978); Stanley Elkins and Eric McKitrick, *The Age of Federalism* (New York: oxford University Press, 1993); Joanne B. Freeman, *Affairs of Honor: National Politics in the New Republic* (New Haven: Yale University Press, 2001).

20. Ellis, *The Quartet*, Appendix A, 1081.

21. Joseph Ellis, "American Sphinx: The Contradictions of Thomas Jefferson," *Civilization: The Magazine of the Library of Congress*, Nov–Dec 1994, 1606-1827 1 Digital Collections 1 Library of Congress, 1034: "Like Henry, Hamilton was a youthful prodigy of impoverished origins—John Adams later called him 'a bastard brat of a Scotch pedlar'—whose visible craving for greatness violated the understated code of the true Virginia aristocrat. To make matters worse, Hamilton as an opponent was equally formidable on his feet and in print. Jefferson recalled his clashes with Hamilton in cabinet meetings as a form of martyrdom and warned Madison to draft all newspaper attacks."

22. *The Making of the Constitution*, PBS television, 1998; Ron Chernow, *Alexander Hamilton* (London: Penguin Books, 2005), 68: "Charming and impetuous, romantic and witty, dashing and headstrong, Hamilton offers the biographer an irresistible psychological study. For all his superlative mental gifts, he was afflicted with a touchy ego that made him querulous and fatally combative.... He has also emerged as the uncontested visionary in anticipating the shape and powers of the federal government. At a time when Jefferson and Madison celebrated legislative power as the purest expression of the popular will, Hamilton argued for a dynamic executive branch and an independent judiciary, along with a professional military, a central bank, and an advanced financial system. Today, we are indisputably the heirs to Hamilton's America."

23. Chernow, *Washington*, 1895; WWR, 4:605.; Maier, *Ratification*, 141.

24. Chernow, *Washington*, 1903; PWCF, 4:332; Hayes, *The Mind of a Patriot: Patrick Henry and the World of Ideas* (Charlottesville: University of Virginia Press, 2008); Jeff Broadwater, *George Mason, Forgotten Founder* (Chapel Hill: University of North Carolina Press, 2006); Richard Brookhiser, *James Madison* (New York: Basic Books, 2011); and Ron Chernow, *Washington, a Life* (New York: Penguin, 2010).

25. Chernow, *Washington*, 1904; *WWR*, 631.; Chernow, *Washington, A life,* I
book edition, 1728; See also, Hayes, *The Mind of a Patriot: Patrick Henry
and the World of Ideas* (Charlottesville: University of Virginia Press, 2008);
Jeff Broadwater, *George Mason, Forgotten Founder* (Chapel Hill:
University of North Carolina Press, 2006); Richard Brookhiser, *James
Madison* (New York: Basic Books, 2011); and Ron Chernow, *Washington*.

26. Randolph to Washington, Richmond, January 4, 178[7], and Madison to
Washington, Richmond, December 24, 1786, in *PGWCS IV*: 500–01, 474–
75; and Washington to Henry Knox, Mount Vernon, February 3, 1787,
PGWCS V; Pauline Maier *Ratification, I book edition*, 68.

27. For Mason's suspicion of federal authority, see Broadwater, *Forgotten
Founter*, ch. 1; Helen Hill Miller, *George Mason, Gentleman
Revolutionary* (Chapel Hill: University of North Carolina Press, 1975); and
Jack Rakove, *Revolutionaries: A New History of the Invention of America*
(Boston: Houghton Mifflin Harcourt, 2010), 166–167. This discussion of
the Mason family comes principally from Pamela C. Copeland and Richard
K. MacMaster, *The Five George Masons: Patriots and Planters of Virginia
and Maryland* (Charlottesville: University Press of Virginia, 1975), 1–88.
For women's property rights, see *Marylynn Salmon, Women and the Law
of Property in Early America* (Chapel Hill: University of North Carolina
Press, 1986). 8; Miller, *George Mason*, 26; Copeland and MacMaster, *Five
George Masons*, 56, 73. 9. Quoted in Copeland and MacMaster, *Five
George Masons*, 77–78. 10. Miller, *George Mason*, 44. See also Rakove,
Revolutionaries, 157–169; Broadwater, *George Mason*, ch. 1; Peter
Wallenstein, *"Flawed Keepers of the Flame: The Interpreters of George
Mason,"* *VMHB* 102 (1994): 229–60. 11; see alsoTerry K. Dunn, ed., *The
Recollections of John Mason: George Mason's Son Remembers His Father
and Life at Gunston Hall* (Marshall, VA: EPM Publications, 2004).

Chapter One: Origins

1. Lorri Glover, *Founders as Fathers, The Private Lives and Politics of the
American Revolution* (New Haven and London, Yale University Press,
2014), 27.

2. Jeff Broadwater, *George Mason, Forgotten Founder* (Chapel Hill:
University of North Carolina Press, 2006), 1258, fn 1: "Mason's

nineteenth-century biographer, Kate Mason Rowland, listed George Mason along with George Washington, Thomas Jefferson, and other revolutionary-era patriots as descendants of Cavaliers. Rowland, Mason, 1:1. For most of them, the truth was less romantic. Jefferson's English roots, for example, are wholly obscure. See Malone, Jefferson, 1:4–8. Washington, by contrast, could trace his lineage to some prominent Royalists, but the first Washington in the colonies had been 'a merchant adventurer,' not an aristocrat. Randall, George Washington, 10. For an introduction to the historiographical debate, see Fischer and Kelly, Bound Away, 35–43, 311 (n. 44). The best history of the Mason family is Copeland and MacMaster, Five George Masons ... "

3.   Ron Chernow, *Washington: A Life* (New York: The Penguin Press, 2011), 75. Foundational works on Virginia in this era include Edmund S. Morgan, *American Slavery, American Freedom: The Ordeal of Colonial Virginia* (New York: W. W. Norton, 1975); Rhys Isaac, *The Transformation of Virginia, 1740–1790* (Chapel Hill: University of North Carolina Press, 1982); T. H. Breen, *Tobacco Culture: The Mentality of the Great Tidewater Planters on the Eve of Revolution* (Princeton, NJ: Princeton University Press, 1985); and Charles Sydnor, *Gentlemen Freeholders: Political Practices in Washington's Virginia* (Chapel Hill: University of North Carolina Press, 1952). More recent explorations include Emory G. Evans, A "Topping People": The Rise and Decline of Virginia's Old Political Elite, 1680–1790 (Charlottesville: University of Virginia Press, 2009); and Brent Tarter, *The Grandees of Government: The Origins and Persistence of Undemocratic Politics in Virginia* (Charlottesville: University of Virginia Press, 2013). For limits of elite control, see Woody Holton, *Forced Founders: Indians, Debtors, Slaves, and the Making of the American Revolution in Virginia* (Chapel Hill: University of North Carolina Press, 1999); and Michael A. McDonnell, *The Politics of War: Race, Class, and Conflict in Revolutionary Virginia* (Chapel Hill: University of North Carolina Press, 2007).

4.   Mason properties included: Accokeek, the first plantation of the Mason Family; Analostan (now Theodore Roosevelt Island), home to our George Mason's son John Mason; Chopawamscic, the childhood home of our George Mason; Hollin Hall, home to our George's brother Thomson; Lexington, home to Mason's son George V; Mattawoman, the childhood home of Ann Eilbeck Mason, our George's wife; Marlborough, home to his uncle, John Mercer; and two other Mason family plantations, Stump Creek

and Woodbridge. The Mason family eventually owned upwards of seventy-five thousand acres. R. Walton Moore George Mason, *The Statesman*; The William and Mary Quarterly, Vol. 13, No. 1 (Jan., 1933), pp. 10-17, Published by: Omohundro Institute of Early American History and Culture, http://www.jstor.org/stable/1922831, accessed: May 13, 2017.

5.   Terry K. Dunn, ed., *The Recollections of John Mason: George Mason's Son Remembers His Father and Life at Gunston Hall* (Marshall, VA.: EPM Publications, 2004), 40.

6.   Henry C. Riely, "George Mason," *The Virginia Magazine of History and Biography*, Vol. 42, No. 1 (Jan. 1934), 1–17, published by Virginia Historical Society, http://www.jstor.org/stable/4244557 accessed December 28, 2015.

7.   "Headright" refers to the practice, begun by the Virginia Company, of awarding fifty acres to anyone who paid for the transportation of an immigrant to the colony. Because headrights were sometimes traded and because patents were not always sought in a timely manner, it is impossible to determine whether George Mason I personally brought eighteen settlers to Virginia and, if so, when. See Morgan, *American Slavery*, 94, 171–73, 219, 405–6.

8.   Glover, *Founders as Fathers*, 128.

9.   "Among the first known uses of the word revolution to describe political change was the Glorious Revolution in 1689, which saw England's King James II removed from the throne." Bill O'Reilly and Martin Dugard, *Killing England: The Brutal Struggle for American Independence* (New York: Henry Holt and Co., 2017), 118.

10. See O'Reilly, *Killing England*, 1339: "Formed in 1619, this body was the first elected legislature in America. Originally known as the House of Burgesses, it was dubbed the House of Delegates in 1776. Its last act as the 'House of Burgesses' was to vote in favor of independence."

11. Gordon S. Wood, *Revolutionary Characters* (New York: Penguin Press, 2006), 560.

12. Kate Mason Rowland, *The Life of George Mason* (New York: Russell &: Russell, Inc., 1964); Broadwater, *Forgotten Founder*.

13. Rowland, *The Life of George Mason*, 34.

14. Ibid., 38.

15. Ibid.

16. Broadwater, *Forgotten Founder*, 63.
17. There was a George Mason V and a George Mason VI, but no George Mason VII. George Mason VI's second-born son was named George Thomson Mason. As George Mason VI had married his cousin, Elizabeth Thomson Mason, daughter of his uncle Thomson Mason, this name honored both sides of the family—which actually was the same family, anyway. Second Lieutenant George Thomson Mason of the U.S. Second Dragoons was killed in action near Brownsville, TX, in 1846, in a skirmish known as the Thornton Affair, which is considered the first battle of the Mexican War. Lieutenant George Thomson Mason died childless.
18. Chernow, *Washington*, 50.
19. Ibid., 51.
20. Broadwater, *Forgotten Founder*, 46.
21. Jon Meacham, *Thomas Jefferson, The Art of Power* (New York: Random House, 2012), 259.
22. Rowland, *The Life of George Mason*, 46.
23. Ibid., 51–52.
24. Ibid.
25. Chernow, *Washington*, 65.
26. George Mason to unknown, 2 October 1778, PGM, 1:433.
27. Chernow, *Washington*, 70.
28. Ibid.: "A university education would have spared him [Washington] a gnawing sense of intellectual inadequacy. We know that he regretted his lack of Latin, Greek, and French—the major intellectual adornments of his day—since he lectured wards in later years on their importance."
29. Ibid., 71.

Chapter Two: Ann Eilbeck Mason

1. Kate Mason Rowland, *The Life and Correspondence of George Mason, 1725–1792* (New York: Russell & Russell, 1964; reprint of 1892 volume), vol. I.; Terry K. Dunn, ed., *The Recollections of John Mason: George Mason's Son Remembers His Father and Life at Gunston Hall* (Marshall, VA: EPM Publications, 2004).
2. "The latter had become especially important to Virginians," historian Thomas Fleming noted. "It, too, was an offshoot of the growing fondness

for emotion in poetry and novels. A woman, especially, felt inferior if she was deficient in such sensibilities." Thomas Fleming, *The Intimate Lives of the Founding Fathers* (New York: Harper Collins, 2009), 1146.

3. Pamela C. Copeland and Richard K. MacMaster, *The Five George Masons, Patriots and Planters of Virginia and Maryland* (Lorton, VA: The Board of Regents of Gunston Hall, 1989), xxxvii.

4. Lorri Glover, *Founders as Fathers, The Private Lives and Politics of the American Revolution* (New Haven and London, Yale University Press, 2014), 639.

5. Rowland, *The Life and Correspondence of George Mason.*

6. Glover, *Founders as Fathers*, 69; Jan Ellen Lewis, "Motherhood and the Construction of the Male Citizen in the United States, 1750–1850," in *Constructions of the Self*, ed. George Levine (New Brunswick, NJ: Rutgers University Press, 1992), 143–63.

7. Jeff Broadwater, *George Mason, Forgotten Founder* (Chapel Hill: . University of North Carolina Press, 2006), 53; Rowland, *Life and Correspondence of George Mason*, 1:55–58; Mason Family Bible Entries, 4 April 1750–11 April 1780, *PGM*, 1:480–83.

8. Rowland, *The Life and Correspondence of George Mason*; Dunn, *Recollections.*

9. Dunn, *Recollections*, 68, fn 16.; Rowland, *Life and Correspondence of George Mason*, 56.

10. Rowland, *Life and Correspondence of George Mason*; Dunn, *Recollections of John Mason.*

11. Ibid.
12. Ibid.
13. Ibid.
14. Ibid.

15. For women's roles, see Catherine Allgor, *Parlor Politics: In Which the Ladies of Washington Help Build a City and a Government* (Charlottesville: University Press of Virginia, 2000); *Cynthia A. Kierner, Beyond the Household: Women's Place in the Early South, 1700–1835* (Ithaca, NY: Cornell University Press, 1998); Linda Kerber, *Women of the Republic: Intellect and Ideology in Revolutionary America* (Chapel Hill: University of North Carolina Press, 1980); and Lewis, "Motherhood and the Construction of the Male Citizen"143–63.

16. Cokie Roberts, *Founding Mothers* (New York: Harper Collins, 2005), 69.

17. Roberts, *Founding Mothers*, 77.

18. Marie Kimball, "Thomas Jefferson's Cook Book," *William and Mary Quarterly*, Second Series, 19 (2/April, 1939), 238–39, published by Omohundro Institute of Early American History and Culture, http://www.jstor.org/stable/1922859, accessed January 14, 2012.

19. Roberts, *Founding Mothers*, 159.

20. Ibid., 71.

21. Ibid., 73; Kimball, "Thomas Jefferson's Cook Book," 238–39

22. Philip Mazzei, *My Life and Wanderings* (American Institute of Italian Studies, 1980), 209; fn. 57, 405.

23. Ibid.

24. Ibid.

25. Rowland, *Life and Correspondence of George Mason*; Dunn, *Recollections of John Mason*.

26. Jon Meacham, *Thomas Jefferson, The Art of Power* (New York: Random House, 2012), 434.

27. Ibid., 432; see also Hyland, *Martha Jefferson An Intimate Life with Thomas Jefferson*, Kindle edition, 99.

28. See in general Hyland, *Martha Jefferson An Intimate Life with Thomas Jefferson*, Ch. 8 and Ch. 14.

29. Dunn, *Recollections*, 47–49.

30. Ibid.

31. Broadwater, *Forgotten Founder*, 304; Mason Family Bible entries, 4 April 1750-11 April 1780, *PGM*, 480–83; "Last Will and Testament" 20 March 1773, PGM, 147–60; Dunn, *Recollections*, 65.

32. Dunn, *Recollections*, 47–49.

33. Ibid.

34. Ibid.

Chapter Three: Gunston Hall

1. By the early years of the nineteenth century, tobacco, the "money" crop of the colonial period, was no longer profitable in Northern Virginia. Wheat and other grains were grown, cattle were raised, and extensive fisheries operated at Gunston, but the plantation was not profitable and was several

times offered for sale by the Mason family. After the last Mason owner sold the estate, it was later acquired by Col. Edward Daniels, a Northern officer who had admired it during the Civil War. Daniels, an amateur astronomer, added the tower to the roof in the 1870s. Gunston passed subsequently to the Specht and Kester families, and in December 1912, Paul Kester, author and playwright, sold it to its last private owner, Louis Hertle of Chicago. Mr. and Mrs. Hertle made many improvements to Gunston Hall and deeded the estate in 1932 to the Commonwealth of Virginia to be managed and supervised by a board of regions from the National Society of the Colonial Dames of America (http://www.gunstonhall.org/). Gunston Hall was among the nation's first properties to be declared a national historic landmark, the country's highest status of historic resource designation.

2. Robert A. Rutland, *George Mason, Reluctant Statesman* (Baton Rouge: Louisiana State University Press, 1961).

3. Joseph Ellis, *American Sphinx: The Character of Thomas Jefferson* (New York: Knopf, 1997), 297.

4. Jeff Broadwater, *George Mason, Forgotten Founder* (Chapel Hill: University of North Carolina Press, 2006), 85.

5. Ibid., 11.

6. Kate Mason Rowland, *The Life of George Mason, 1725–1792* (New York: Russell & Russell, 1964; reprint of 1892 volume), 58

7. Daniel L. Dreisbach, "George Mason's Pursuit of Religious Liberty in Revolutionary Virginia," *The Virginia Magazine of History and Biography*, Vol. 108, No. 1 (2000), 25–44, Published by: Virginia Historical Society, http://www.jstor.org/stable/4249815.

8. Dreisbach, "Pursuit of Religious Liberty," 25–44.

9. GM to Richard Henry Lee, April 12, 1779, *PGM*, 2:498, 590–92; Broadwater, *Forgotten Founder*, 618; *Journal of the House of Delegates of the Commonwealth of Virginia, 1777–80*, November 1, 1777, 9. At the same time, the House began its day with a prayer, employed a chaplain— Reverend James Madison, cousin of the future president—and even ordered Reverend Madison to prepare a Thanksgiving Day sermon. Ibid., November 4, 1777, 12, 71.

10. Dreisbach, "Pursuit of Religious Liberty," 40.

11. Philip Slaughter and Edward Louis Goodwin, *The History of Truro Parish in Virginia (1907)* (Whitefish, MT: Kessinger Publishing, LLC, 2010), 143–50.
12. Robert Rutland, "George Mason and the Origins of the First Amendment," 87–100.
13. Broadwater, *Forgotten Founder*: "Catholics who refused to attend Anglican services, were disenfranchised. In 1762 the right to vote of Mason's Catholic neighbor George Brent was challenged, but Brent was allowed to vote apparently because, whatever his personal beliefs, he was not a "recusant convict." Kennedy, JHB, 1761–1765, 126–30; See generally Hening, *Statutes*, 3:172, 238; 4:133–34, 477; Syndor, *American Revolutionaries*, 35–37; Dinnerstein and Palsson, *Jews in the South*, 5; Kolp, *Gentlemen and Freeholders*, 43–49."
14. Dreisbach, "Pursuit of Religious Liberty," 5.
15. Scott Muir Stroh III, "Envisioning the Future at Gunston Hall," *Gunston Grapevine*, Summer 2016, http://www.gunstonhall.org/docs/Summer-2016-Grapevine.pdf.
16. Stroh, "Envisioning the Future."
17. Jack McLaughlin, *Jefferson and Monticello* (New York: Henry Holt, 1988),1620.
18. Ibid., 251.
19. Broadwater, *Forgotten Founder*, 72.
20. Brent Tarter, "'A Raft Which Will Never Sink': Virginians and the Defense of Republicanism," *The Virginia Magazine of History and Biography*, Vol. 99, No. 3, (July 1991), 279–304, http://www.jstor.org/stable/4249228 Accessed: 26-12-2015 06:16 UTC.
21. Rowland, *The Life of George Mason*, Vol. 1, 106.
22. Ibid., 106–7.
23. Terry K. Dunn, ed., *The Recollections of John Mason: George Mason's Son Remembers His Father and Life at Gunston Hall* (Marshall, VA: EPM Publications, 2004), 73–78.
24. Ibid., 71.
25. See Dunn, *Recollections*.
26. As a widow, Mason's mother did not want her two younger children, Thomson and Mary, to feel slighted in their inheritance. She saved enough money to make a land deal known as the "Wild Lands" purchase.

Eventually, Ann bought ten thousand acres in Loudoun County that extended north from Leesburg. She divided the land between her daughter Mary and Thomson. In 1760, Thomson added to his property in Loudoun County by purchasing the "Raspberry Plain" acreage from Aeneas Campbell.

27. Fiske Kimball, "Gunston Hall," *Journal of the Society of Architectural Historians*, Vol. 13, No. 2 (May 1954), 38, http://www.jstor.org/stable/987683.

28. George Mason's statement of endorsement for William Buckland, dated November 8, 1759. Original owned by Daniel R. Randall, Annapolis, Maryland. Photostat copy in the Library of Congress, http://www.gunstonhall.org/newsletter/Grapevine-Fall-2012.pdf.

29. When Buckland designed the garden porch at Gunston Hall, he apparently adopted plate XXXI of *Gothic architecture*, one of fifteen architectural pattern books listed in his estate inventory. One of the pattern books in Buckland's library was *Chippendale's designs*. The reversed scallops on the canopy of the Chinese sofa may have inspired the cornice designs in the Chinese room at Gunston Hall, the earliest known use of Chinese motifs in colonial architecture. Buckland's estate inventory list many books, including one noted as *Swans British treasury*, likely Abraham Swan's *The British Architect*. This British design guide converts each in architecture to fit eighteenth-century taste. Many of the images likely served as prototypes for the elaborate woodwork throughout Gunston Hall.

30. McLaughlin, *Jefferson and Monticello*, 1699.

31. Robert Rutland, ed., Letter to Alexander Henderson, July 18, 1763, *George Mason Papers*, Vol. 1, 56.

32. Broadwater, *Forgotten Founder*, 77; see B. Brown, *The Library of George Mason*.

33. Broadwater, *Forgotten Founder*, 68; Edmund Randolph, *History of Virginia*, ed. Arthur Shaffer (Charlottesville: University Press of Virginia, 1970), 202; Helen H. Miller, *George Mason: Gentleman Revolutionary* (Chapel Hill: University of North Carolina Press, 1975), 21–22.

34. Broadwater, *Forgotten Founder*, 68.

35. Lorri Glover, *Founders as Fathers, The Private Lives and Politics of the American Revolution (New Haven and London,* Yale University Press, 2014), 34.

36. Dunn, *Recollections*, 65.

37. Excavations at Gunston Hall unearthed liquor bottle seals affixed to wine and spirit bottles belonging to George and Ann Mason.

38. Rims of salt-glazed stoneware have been found at excavation sites at Gunston Hall and suggest the Masons owned one or more dinner or dessert sets of salt-glazed stoneware. Many teawares were imported from China; others were made in England based on Chinese designs.

39. See Bill O'Reilly and Martin Dugard, *Killing England: The Brutal Struggle for American Independence* (New York: Henry Holt and Co., 2017), 1325–26: "The modern practice of bathing or showering by submersion was not widely practiced in America until the nineteenth century. For this reason, the room for conducting daily ablutions was known as a privy instead of a bathroom. In the absence of flush toilets, an individual either used a chamber pot or an outdoor privy. For the latter, it was necessary to dig a trench deep into the ground outside a building for use as a toilet, line the hole with bricks, then fit a wooden seat over the opening. 'Bathing' in 1776 consisted of cleaning the face and hands with a cloth wetted in a small washbasin in one's bedchamber. Once the act of cleansing by submersion in water eventually became a common practice, there was great debate over whether cold or hot water was better for the body. Cold-water bathing was considered a form of personal strength, while the use of warm water was seen as a sign of indulgence."

40. Dunn, *Recollections*, 53.

41. Rowland, *The Life of George Mason*, 104.

42. Philologist Walter William Skeat in *A Concise Etymological Dictionary of the English Language* (1895) wrote that "hogshead" is a corruption of the original Old Dutch oxhooft meaning oxhead. "No doubt the cask was at first named from the device or brand of an 'ox-head' upon it," he wrote.

43. Dunn, *Recollections*, 72.

44. Glover, *Founders as Fathers*, 1032.

45. Kate Mason Rowland, cited in Robert Rutland, *The Papers of George Mason* (Chapel Hill: University of North Carolina Press, 1970).

46. Dunn, *Recollections*, 51.

47. Ibid., 51–53; Broadwater, *Forgotten Founder*, 76.

48. Dunn, *Recollections*, 51–53.

49. Ibid.

50. Ibid.
51. Ron Chernow, *Washington: A Life* (New York: Penguin Press, 2011), 775.
52. Dunn, *Recollections,* 43–46.
53. Ibid.
54. Broadwater, *Forgotten Founder,* 79.
55. O'Reilly, *Killing England,* 1245.
56. Rowland, *The Life of George Mason,* 82.
57. Broadwater, *Forgotten Founder,* 80, 82.
58. Ibid., 82.
59. "Mason Sightings," *Gunston Grapevine,* Spring 2015, http://www.gunstonhall.org/docs/Spring-2015-Grapevine.pdf.

Chapter Four: The Two Georges

1. Peter R. Henriques, "An Uneven Friendship: The Relationship between George Washington and George Mason." *Virginia Magazine of History and Biography,* Vol. 97 (April 1989), http://www.jstor.org/stable/4249070, 185.
2. Ibid., 186.
3. Ibid., 185–204.
4. Ibid., 185.
5. Ron Chernow, *Washington: A Life* (New York: Penguin Press, 2011), 415; Jefferson, *Writings,* 1319.
6. Gerard W. Gawalt, *George Mason and George Washington: The Power of Principe* (Scotts Valley, CA: CreateSpace Independent Publishing Platform, 2012), 4.
7. Ibid.
8. Ibid.
9. Chernow, *Washington,* 413, (John Rhodehamel, ed. *George Washington Writings.* New York, 1997), 483. Letter to Bushrod Washington, January 15, 1783.
10. Chernow, *Washington,* 722.
11. Ibid., 1614–15.
12. Ibid., 1613; *PWCF,* 3:90, Letter to Fairfax, June 30, 1785.
13. *PWCF,* 6:111, Letter to Alexander Spotswood, February 13, 1788; Chernow, *Washington,* 1612.
14. Chernow, *Washington,* 1614; *Diaries,* A, XVIII.

15. Kate Mason Rowland, *The Life of George Mason, 1725–1792* (New York: Russell & Russell, 1964; reprint of 1892 volume), 122.
16. Gawalt, *George Mason and George Washington*, 15.
17. Henriques, "An Uneven Friendship," 360.
18. Gawalt, *George Mason And George Washington*, 12.
19. Ibid., 12–13.
20. Henriques, "An Uneven Friendship," 360.
21. Ibid.
22. Ibid.
23. Ibid.
24. Joseph Ellis, *His Excellency: George Washington* (New York: Random House, 2004), 232.
25. Ibid., 239.
26. Henriques, "An Uneven Friendship," 360.
27. Ibid.
28. Ibid.
29. "George Washington to George Mason," March 27, 1779, in John C. Fitzpatrick, ed., *The Writings of George Washington*, 39 vols. (Washington, DC: U.S. Government Printing Office, 1931–1944), 299.
30. Ibid.
31. Ibid., 488.
32. Ellis, *His Excellency*, 526.
33. Ibid., 525–26.
34. Ibid., 526.
35. Douglas Southall Freeman et al., *George Washington: A Biography*, 7 vols. (New York: Charles Scribner's Sons, 1948–1957), 89.
36. Ellis, *His Excellency*, 783.
37. Gawalt, *George Mason And George Washington*, 2.
38. Ibid., 12–13.
39. Ibid., 14–15.
40. John E. Ferling, "'The Strictest Rectitude': The Character of General Washington," *Virginia Cavalcade*, Vol. 38, No. 2, Autumn 1988, 90.
41. Henriques, "An Uneven Friendship," 185–204.
42. Ibid.
43. Ibid.
44. Ibid.

45. Ibid.
46. "George Mason and the Constitution," *Gunston Hall: Home of George Mason*, http://gunstonhall.org/georgemason/essays/constitution.html, accessed February 12, 2019; Robert A. Rutland, ed., *The Papers of George Mason* (Chapel Hill, NC: University of North Carolina Press, 1970), 3:1142.
47. Mason to John Mason, July 5, 1792, Rutland, *Papers of George Mason*; David O. Stewart, *The Summer of 1787* (New York: Simon & Schuster, 2007), 2139; See also Dunn, *Recollections*.
48. "From George Washington to J. Foy Chase, 22 December 1783," Founders Online, accessed February 12, 2019, https://founders.archives.gov/documents/Washington/99-01-02-12220.
49. Henriques, "An Uneven Friendship," 185–204.
50. Ibid.
51. Ibid.
52. Ibid.
53. Ibid.
54. "Redemptioners" were European immigrants who gained passage to the American colonies by selling themselves into indentured servitude. They arrived after long, often arduous voyages with no guarantee that anyone would pay their way and no prospect of returning to the Old World. The German redemptioner in this case had sailed to Baltimore where his indenture was purchased by Col. William Fitzhugh, who in turn, sold it to George Mason. Col. Fitzhugh had told Mason that the coachman was "an exceeding good driver, & careful of horses, but lazy, & quarelsom among the servants."
55. Frank N. Barker, "Would You Hire This Man?," *Gunston Grapevine*, Summer 2016, http://www.gunstonhall.org/docs/Summer-2016-Grapevine.pdf.
56. Ibid.
57. Chernow, *Washington*, 2448, 4209; Moncure Daniel Conway, ed., *The Writings of Thomas Paine*, 4 vols. (New York: G. P. Putnam, 1896; reprint: New York: AMS Press, 1967), 705.
58. Chernow *Washington*, 2448, 4209; Conway, *The Writings of Thomas Paine*, 705.
59. Rhodehamel, *Washington*, 39.

60. Ellis, *His Excellency*, 18.

61. Gawalt, *George Mason And George Washington*, 1.

Chapter Five: The Ohio Company

1. The Ohio Valley consisted of the modern-day state states of Ohio, parts of Pennsylvania, West Virginia, and Indiana.

2. Fred Anderson, *George Washington Remembers: Reflections on the French and Indian War* (Lanham, MD: Rowman & Littlefield Publishers, 2004), 71; Ron Chernow, *Washington: A Life* (New York: Penguin Press, 2011), 112.

3. Jeff Broadwater, *George Mason, Forgotten Founder* (Chapel Hill: University of North Carolina Press, 2006), 222.

4. Ibid., 207.

5. Ibid., 235.

6. See in general Broadwater, *Forgotten Founder*, Chapter One, "A Retreat of Heroes."

7. Broadwater, *Forgotten Founder*, 141.

8. Ibid., 144.

9. Ibid., 128.

10. GM to Robert Dinwiddie, September 9th 1761, PGM, 1:46:-47; Broadwater, *Forgotten Founder*, 129.

11. Broadwater, *Forgotten Founder*, 132.

12. Ibid., 133.

13. Ibid., 155.

14. Ibid., 133.

15. See Broadwater, *Forgotten Founder*, Chapter One, and p. 225.

16. Joseph J. Ellis, *Revolutionary Summer: The Birth of American Independence*, (New York: Vintage, 2013), 7.

17. "Extracts from the Virginia Charters, with Some Remarks on Them Made in the Year 1773," http://www.virginia1774.org/ExtractsFromVirginiaCharter.html; Kenneth P. Bailey, "George Mason, Westerner," *The William and Mary Quarterly*, Vol. 23, No. 4, October 1943, http://www.jstor.org/stable/1923192, 412–13.

18. Brent Tarter, "George Mason and the Conservation of Liberty," *The Virginia Magazine of History and Biography*, Vol. 99, No. 3, July 1991, http://www.jstor.org/stable/4249228, 279–304.

19. Helen Hill Miller, *George Mason, Constitutionalist* (Cambridge: Harvard University Press, 1938), 82.

20. Broadwater, *Forgotten Founder*, 144.

21. Ibid., 150.

22. Ibid., 156.

23. Ibid., 177.

24. Ibid., 183.

Chapter Six: Revolutionary

1. See "Virginia Nonimportation Resolutions, 17 May 1769," Founders Online website, accessed February 13, 2019, https://founders.archives.gov/documents/Jefferson/01-01-02-0019; Jeff Broadwater, *George Mason, Forgotten Founder* (Chapel Hill: University of North Carolina Press, 2006), 2078: "The essay Mason told Washington he was writing to popularize nonimportation may have appeared in the Virginia papers as two letters from 'Atticus' in May 1769. Certainly the points made in the second letter—for example, that the abolition of the slave and tobacco trades would encourage domestic industry and the immigration of English workers—could have come from Gunston Hall. Otherwise little more than tradition identifies Mason as Atticus. Conceivably, Atticus could have been two people: Mason, who wrote the second letter, and another writer, perhaps the unknown copyist who helped Mason with the nonimportation agreement, who drafted the first. But the theory is largely conjecture. See ibid., 106–9. Ragsdale believes Mason was Atticus. Ragsdale, A Planters' Republic, 77."

2. The Resolves provided a concise summary of American constitutional concerns on such issues as taxation, representation, judicial power, and military matters; a proposal for the creation of a nonimportation effort to be levied against British goods; a call for a general congress of the colonies to convene for the purpose of preserving the Americans' rights as Englishmen; and a condemnation of the practice of importing slaves as an "unnatural trade"; Broadwater, *Forgotten Founder*, 2095: "Although Mason has almost universally been regarded as the author of the Fairfax Resolves, Sweig, 'A

New Found Washington Letter,' 283–91, argues that they were primarily a committee effort. To be sure, other writers may have influenced the resolves; Richard Henry Lee had prepared his own draft before Dunmore dissolved the House of Burgesses, and undoubtedly Mason conferred with Lee when both men were in Williamsburg. Richard Henry Lee to Samuel Adams, 23 June 1774, in Force, American Archives, 4:445–46. But all the evidence points toward Mason as the principal, if not the sole, author of the Fairfax Resolves. The oldest known copy is in his handwriting, and he presented the resolves to the Fairfax freeholders. More significantly, drafting the resolves was the kind of task that often fell to Mason, and they echoed his voice, as when they declare the colonists were 'Descendants not of the Conquered, but of the Conquerors.... '"

3. Va. Declaration of Rights, Section 3, https://www.archives.gov/founding-docs/virginia-declaration-of-rights.

4. Broadwater, *Forgotten Founder*, 375.

5. *Diaries* A, 110; Ron Chernow, *Washington: A Life* (New York: Penguin Press, 2011), 427; The modern-day Christiana Campbell's tavern in restored colonial Williamsburg.

6. "Thomas Jefferson (1743–1826)," Special Collections Research Center Wiki website, accessed February 13, 2019, https://scdbwiki.swem.wm.edu/wiki/index.php?title=Thomas_Jefferson_(1743-1826); Jefferson's Autobiography, 1821.

7. Chernow, *Washington*, 427.

8. GM to Cockburn, May 26, 1774, *PGM* 1:191; Lorri Glover, *Founders as Fathers, The Private Lives and Politics of the American Revolution (New Haven and London,* Yale University Press, 2014), 266; see also Terry K. Dunn, ed., *The Recollections of John Mason: George Mason's Son Remembers His Father and Life at Gunston Hall* (Marshall, VA: EPM Publications, 2004).

9. Born in 1632, John Locke entered a world in flux. The Age of Enlightenment was upending the centuries-old trust in faith, replacing it with science and rationality. Locke spent fifteen years at Oxford before finally settling on medicine. He eventually went to London as the physician for Lord Cooper, Chancellor of the Exchequer. There Locke began helping Cooper with governmental affairs. An outspoken opponent of absolute monarchy, Cooper was imprisoned twice. When he fled to Holland in 1682, Locke followed.

Locke published his great four-volume opus, *An Essay Concerning Human Understanding*, in 1689. He also wrote the influential *Two Treatises of Government*, refuting the divine right of kings. His ideas echo through American ideals of freedom and morality; Broadwater, *Forgotten Founder*, 2071: " … Locke's mutual commitment to the right of armed resistance to an arbitrary government, a highly salient point, to say the least, to the American revolutionaries. On Locke's contribution to modern notions of individual rights and equality, see Breen, 'Ideology and Nationalism,' 34–39."

10. R. Walton Moore, "George Mason, The Statesman," *The William and Mary Quarterly*, Vol. 13, No. 1, January 1933, accessed May 13, 2017, http://www.jstor.org/stable/1922831.

11. Broadwater, *Forgotten Founder*, 77, 212.

12. On January 9, 1776, Thomas Paine published his pamphlet *Common Sense* setting forth his arguments in favor of American independence. Although little used today, pamphlets were an important medium for the spread of ideas in the sixteenth through nineteenth centuries. Originally published anonymously, *Common Sense* advocated independence for the American colonies from Britain and is considered one of the most influential pamphlets in American history. Credited with uniting average citizens and political leaders behind the idea of independence, it played a remarkable role in transforming a colonial squabble into the American Revolution. At the time Paine wrote *Common Sense*, most colonists considered themselves to be aggrieved Britons. Paine fundamentally changed the tenor of colonists' argument with the Crown when he wrote the following: "Europe, and not England, is the parent country of America. This new world hath been the asylum for the persecuted lovers of civil and religious liberty from every part of Europe. Hither they have fled, not from the tender embraces of the mother, but from the cruelty of the monster; and it is so far true of England, that the same tyranny which drove the first emigrants from home, pursues their descendants still…. "; Thomas Paine, *Common Sense*, (Philadelphia: Independence Hall Association, 1999–2019), http://www.ushistory.org/paine/commonsense/.

13. Broadwater, *Forgotten Founder*, 480, 481, 486.

14. Chester James Antieau, *Natural Rights and The Founding Fathers—The Virginians*, 17 Wash. & Lee L. Rev. 43-79 (1960), http://scholarlycommons.

law.wlu.edu/wlulr/vol17/iss1/4; The American Catholic website, accessed
February 13, 2019, https://the-american-catholic.com/tag/saint-robert-
bellarmine/.

15. Antieau, *Natural Rights and The Founding Fathers*; The American Catholic
website, accessed February 13, 2019, https://the-american-catholic.com/tag/
saint-robert-bellarmine/.

16. *PWC*, 10: 119-25, "Fairfax County Resolves, July 19, 1774; Chernow,
Washington, 2755.

17. For the full text of the Fairfax Resolves see Philip P. Kurland and Ralph
Lerner, ed., *The Founders Constitution*, Vol.1: Major Themes (Indianapolis:
Liberty Fund, 1986), 633–34.

18. Antieau, *Natural Rights and The Founding Fathers*.

19. Jon Meacham, *Thomas Jefferson, The Art of Power* (New York: Random
House, 2012), 472; Isaac Samuel Harrell, *Loyalism in Virginia: Chapters in
the Economic History of the Revolution* (Durham, NC: Duke University
Press, 1926).

20. Joseph J. Ellis, *Revolutionary Summer: The Birth of American
Independence* (New York: Vintage, 2013), 23.

21. Gordon S. Wood, *Revolutionary Characters* (New York: Penguin Press,
2006), 296.

22. R. Carter Pittman, *George Mason of Gunston Hall, Father of the American
Bill of Rights* 15 Ala. Law. 196 1954, 203.

23. According to historian Alfred Young in his 1999 book *The Shoemaker and
the Tea Party*, the term "Boston Tea Party" was not seen in print until 1834
in the first biography of George Robert Twelves Hewes, *A Retrospect of the
Tea Party*, by James Hawkes. Hewes, a struggling cobbler, was reputed to be
one of the final remaining participants of the destruction of the tea in Boston
Harbor. Contemporary references to the affair included "Boston harbor a
teapot tonight," "The Destruction of the Tea," "the Boston Affair," and even
British Admiral Montagu's the "Indian Caper."

24. *PTJ, I:106*; Meacham, *Thomas Jefferson*, 474–75.

25. *PTJ, I:106*; Meacham, *Thomas Jefferson*, 475.

26. Broadwater, *Forgotten Founder*, 219; GM to Committee of Merchants in
London, June 6, 1766, PGM 1:65-66.

27. Glover, *Founders as Fathers*, 308; George Mason, Remarks on Annual
Elections for the Fairfax Independent Company, April 1775, PGM, 1:231;

Thomas Paine, *Common Sense*, in Philip S. Foner, ed., *The Complete Writings of Thomas Paine* (New York: Citadel Press, 1945), 1:30–31.

28. Christopher Hitchens, *Thomas Paine's Rights of Man* (New York: Grove Press, 2008), 28.

29. Center for the Study of the American Constitution website, http://csac.history.wisc.edu/4.%20virginia.pdf.

30. Ellis, *American Sphinx*, 215: "On June 20, 1775, Thomas Jefferson arrived in Philadelphia in an ornate carriage, called a phaeton, along with four horses and three slaves. The roughly three-hundred-mile trip from Williamsburg had taken him ten days, in part because the roads were poor and poorly marked—twice he had been forced to hire guides to recover the route—and in part because he had dawdled in Fredricksburg and Annapolis to purchase extra equipment for his entourage. As the newest and youngest member of Virginia's delegation to the Continental Congress, he obviously intended to uphold the stylish standard of the Virginia gentry … "

31. Glover, *Founders as Fathers*, 267, 285; Helen H. Miller, *George Mason: Gentleman Revolutionary* (Chapel Hill: University of North Carolina Press, 1975), 108–9.

32. GM to William Ramsay, July 11, 1775; *PGM* 1:239; Glover, *Founders as Fathers*, 268.

33. GM to Martin Cockburn, August 22, 1775, *PGM* 1: 250; Glover, *Founders as Fathers*, 270.

34. Edmund Randolph, *History of Virginia*, ed. Arthur Shaffer (Charlottesville: University Press of Virginia, 1970), 255; Broadwater, *Forgotten Founder*, 388.

35. Edmund Pendleton to Thomas Jefferson, 24 May 1776, in Mays, Pendleton Papers, 1:180–81; Broadwater, *Forgotten Founder*.

36. Bill O'Reilly and Martin Dugard, *Killing England: The Brutal Struggle for American Independence* (New York: Henry Holt and Co., 2017), 1325:

37. Glover, *Founders as Fathers*, 272.

38. O'Reilly, *Killing England*, 1380: "Grog is a mixture of rum and water, named after its inventor, British vice admiral Edward Vernon, who was fond of wearing a suit made of grogram (a coarse fabric woven from silk, mohair, or wool) and went by the nickname 'Old Grog.' The standard ration was a half pint of rum mixed with a quart of water per day."

39. O'Reilly, *Killing England*, 1398.

40. He would miss the May 1777 session while he recovered from a smallpox
    vaccination. And he was habitually late for the start of the assemblies; the
    pull of his cloistered family played an even larger part in his absences than
    his health. George Mason to George Wythe, 14 June 1777; PGM, 1:345–46.
    Smallpox ravaged America during the war. PGM, 2:663 M, 1:345–46;
    PGM, 2:663; Miller, *Gentleman Revolutionary*, 173.

41. Broadwater, *Forgotten Founder*, 1823: In the Virginia debates on the Federal
    Constitution held in Richmond in 1788, "Mason and Henry tried to work
    together. No evidence exists that Mason resented Henry's preeminence as an
    orator, and Grigsby describes them as 'walking arm in arm' from the Swan
    to the New Academy, but Henry was more opportunistic in his arguments
    and more extreme in his objectives. His rhetoric was much more strident
    than it had been in Philadelphia, and unfounded rumors circulated that
    Mason and Henry might resort to force to prevent the convention from
    ratifying the Constitution. Mason was often described as the 'first man in
    every assembly in which he sat,' but he took a secondary role to Patrick
    Henry in the Richmond debates. 'The powers of Henry,' in a large assembly,
    one contemporary observed, 'are incalculable.' Another put the matter less
    charitably: 'In such as Assembly he must to be sure be better adapted to
    carry his point & lead the ignorant people astray than any other person upon
    earth.'"

42. Jefferson to William Wirt, 4 August 1805, in Stan V. Henkels, "Jefferson's
    Recollections of Patrick Henry," *Pennsylvania Magazine of History and
    Biography*, Vol. 24, No. 4, 1910, 395; Glover, *Founders as Fathers*, 1028.

43. Jefferson to William Wirt, 4 August 1805, in Henkels, *Jefferson's
    Recollections of Patrick Henry*, 395; Glover, *Founders as Fathers*, 1028;
    Ellis, *American Sphinx*: "All of Jefferson's surviving observations on Henry
    date from a later time, when their friendship had turned sour (Jefferson
    claimed that Henry was 'avaritious & rotten hearted' and always spoke
    'without logic, without arrangement … '). Compared with Henry, Jefferson
    epitomized the diametrically different sensibility of the refined and
    disciplined scholar. As far as we know, he never rose to deliver a single
    speech in the Continental Congress. John Adams recalled, with a mingled
    sense of admiration and astonishment, that 'during the whole Time I sat with
    him in Congress, I never heard him utter three sentences together.' No one,
    however, including the ever-skeptical Adams, ever doubted his radical

credentials. His clear denunciation of British authority in Summary View put him on record as an opponent of moderation. But he was utterly useless in situations that demanded the projection of a public presence. He was almost as inadequate in behind-the-scenes arm twisting and cajoling, which were the specialty of John's cousin Sam Adams. He was simply too shy and withdrawn to interact easily."

44. GM To Cockburn, May 26, 1774, PGM 1:190; GM to Richard Henry Lee, 18 may 1776, PGM 1: 271; Glover, *Founders as Fathers*, 282.

45. Glover, *Founders as Fathers*, 282; GM to Cockburn, May 26, 1774, PGM 1:190; GM to Richard Henry Lee, 18 may 1776, PGM 1: 271.

46. GM To Cockburn, May 26, 1774, PGM 1:190; GM to Richard Henry Lee, 18 may 1776, PGM 1: 271; Glover, *Founders as Fathers*, 282.

47. Cecelia M. Kenyon, "Constitutionalism in Revolutionary America," Vol. 20, *Constitutionalism*, 1979, accessed September 20, 2017, http://www.jstor.org/stable/24219128; although the conscience did not say much about slavery, only that: "No person hereafter coming into this county shall be held within the same in slavery under any pretext whatever."

48. Josephine F. Pacheco, ed., *Antifederalism: The Legacy of George Mason* (Fairfax, VA: George Mason University Press, 1992), 20.

49. Ellis, *Sphinx*, 251: "[Jefferson's] selection to serve on the Virginia delegation in Philadelphia was a fortunate accident. Jefferson was not elected to the original delegation in 1774; he was not considered a sufficiently prominent figure to be included with the likes of George Washington, Patrick Henry, Edmund Pendleton and Peyton Randolph. In 1775, however, he was chosen as a potential substitute for Randolph—Jefferson was regarded as Randolph's political godson—in anticipation of Randolph's decision to abandon his post at Philadelphia in order to assume leadership of what was regarded as the more important business back in Virginia. It would be fair to say that Jefferson made the list of acknowledged political leaders in the Old Dominion, but just barely, and largely because of his ties by blood and patronage with the Randolph circle. If his arrival in Philadelphia in June 1775 marked his entry into national affairs, he entered by the side door."

50. Pittman, *15 Ala. Law.* 196 1954, 198.

51. Thomas Jefferson, *Autobiography*; Henry S. Randall, *The Life of Thomas Jefferson*, 3 vols. (New York, 1858), 198.

52. Mason, Va. Declaration of Rights; http://www.gunstonhall.org/.

53. Ibid.
54. Antieau, *Natural Rights and The Founding Fathers.*
55. Jefferson to Thomas Nelson, May 16, 1776; Boyd, I: 292; Ellis, *American Sphinx*, 244.
56. Ellis, *American Sphinx*, 292, 295: "His obvious preoccupation with the ongoing events at the Virginia convention, which was drafting the Virginia constitution at just this time, is also crucial to remember. Throughout late May and early June couriers moved back and forth between Williamsburg and Philadelphia, carrying Jefferson's drafts for a new constitution to the convention and reports on the debate there to the Continental Congress. On June 12 the Virginians unanimously adopted a preamble drafted by George Mason that contained these words: 'All men are created equally free and independent and have certain inherent and natural rights ... among which are the enjoyment of life and liberty, with the means of acquiring and possessing property, and pursuing and obtaining happiness and safety.' *The Pennsylvania Gazette* published Mason's words the same day they were adopted in Williamsburg."
57. Pauline Maier, *American Scripture: Making the Declaration of Independence* (New York: Vintage, 1998), 48.
58. Ellis, *American Sphinx*, 292–95.
59. Ibid., 254: "All in all, Jefferson's prescriptions for the new Virginian republic were an impressive blend of traditional forms and selective reforms. They establish the historically correct, if unorthodox, context for answering the proverbial question: What was Jefferson thinking about on the eve of his authorship of the Declaration of Independence? The answer is indisputable. He was not thinking, as some historians have claimed, about John Locke's theory of natural rights or Scottish commonsense philosophy. He was thinking about Virginia's new constitution. An aspect of his thinking proved directly relevant for the task he was about to assume. In his preamble to the first and third drafts of the Virginia constitution, he composed a bill of indictment against George III. One could see glimmerings of these charges against the British monarch in *Summary View*, then even more explicit accusations in Causes and Necessities."; Maier, *American Scripture*, 478: "[Jefferson] applied the same gift in drafting the Declaration of Independence, which was as much in keeping with the values of his time as it facilitated the completion of his task under the constraints he faced in June

1776.16 In the end, the draft Declaration of Independence submitted to Congress by the Committee of Five was so much the work of Thomas Jefferson that it can justly be called 'Jefferson's draft.' But within the committee and, above all, later, when Congress let loose its collective editorial talent on Jefferson's prose, other men made more substantial and constructive contributions to the Declaration of Independence than pleased Jefferson at the time, and far more than he remembered in the 1820s. Jefferson's Draft: The Charges Against the King Whatever written directions or 'minutes' the Committee of Five gave Jefferson have long since disappeared."

60. David O. Stewart, *The Summer of 1787* (New York: Simon & Schuster, 2007), 1364.

61. David McCullough, *John Adams* (New York: Simon & Shuster, 2004), 1071.

62. Maier, *American Scripture*, 477; see also Ellis, *American Sphinx*.

63. Maier, *American Scripture*, 1179: "On the development and influence of the Virginia Declaration, see John Selby, *The Revolution in Virginia, 1775–1783* (Williamsburg, 1988), 101–4, 106–10. The committee draft, it seems, was far more widely circulated and more influential than that finally adopted by the Virginia Convention, which, Selby says, was virtually lost for some forty years[...] The committee version of the Virginia Declaration of Rights had been published earlier—it appeared, for example, in the Pennsylvania Evening Post on June 6, and later in the Pennsylvania Ledger—but the Gazette republication seems especially important since it coincided with the appointment and early meetings of the drafting committee. The kinship with Mason's Declaration was noted in John C. Fitzpatrick, *The Spirit of the Revolution* (Boston and New York, 1924), 2–3, 5–6, and more recently in Lucas, "Justifying America," 87, which, however, claims that it is impossible to know how much Jefferson was influenced by the Mason document. Boyd, in his *Declaration of Independence*, 21-22, insisted that Jefferson was "a recognized master, not an imaginative imitator," and dismissed Jefferson's debt to the Mason/committee draft as "not yet proved" and something that will "in all probability remain a matter of opinion." However, a careful comparison of the various drafts of the Declaration, which Becker sorted out out, with the Mason/committee draft makes it clear that Jefferson began with that draft

and gradually altered it. Such a comparison will be made later. It is, however, impossible to know whether the idea of using the Mason/committee draft came out of the Committee of Five or, as Fitzpatrick assumed, "the clarion note of liberty in [the draft Virginia Declaration's] first three sections found sympathetic echo" in Jefferson's "brain; he seized upon them and, with the artist's perfect judgment, commenced the Declaration with the trumpet blast of their bold principles" (6). See also Robert A. Rutland, ed., *The Papers of George Mason*, 1725-92 (Chapel Hill, 1970), I, 275-91, for drafts of the document and a brief discussion of its evolution and influence. 60. Congressional vote of 11 June in JCC V: 428-29; Hancock to Certain States, Philadelphia, July 6, 1776, in LDC IV: 396. 61. From *the Pennsylvania Gazette*, June 12, 1776. 62. Compare the draft Virginia Declaration in the Pennsylvania Gazette for June 12, 1776, with the Declaration as finally adopted in William W. Hening, ed., *Laws of Virginia, IX* (Richmond, 1821), 109-112, and the English Declaration in Schwoerer, Declaration of Right."

64. Maier, *American Scripture*, 595.
65. Ibid., 476: "Jefferson managed to find two [influences]. One was the draft preamble for the Virginia constitution that he had just finished and which was itself based upon the English Declaration of Rights; the other, a preliminary version of the Virginia Declaration of Rights, had been drafted for the convention sitting in Williamsburg by George Mason, an older man whom Jefferson knew and respected. By modern lights, Jefferson's use of texts by other authors might be considered to detract from his achievement. In the eighteenth century, however, educated people regarded with disdain the striving for novelty. Achievement lay instead in the creative adaptation of preexisting models to different circumstances, and the highest praise of all went to imitations whose excellence exceeded that of the examples that inspired them. Young men were taught to copy and often to memorize compelling passages from their readings for future use since you could never tell when, say, a citation from Cicero might come in handy. Jefferson had not only a good memory but, as his biographer Dumas Malone observed, 'a rare gift of adaptation.'"
66. Maier, *American Scripture*, 566.
67. Jon Meacham, "Free to be Happy," *Time* 2015 special issue, 24.
68. Ellis, *American Sphinx*, 316: "By the time Jefferson arrived in Philadelphia Adams himself had begun to emerge as one of the most effective public

speakers in the Congress, a man whose own throbbing ego had lashed itself to the cause of independence, and whose combination of legal learning and sheer oratorical energy had overwhelmed more moderate delegates in a powerful style that seemed part bulldog and part volcano. Meanwhile the elevated status of the Virginia delegation derived primarily from its reputation for oratorical brilliance. Edmund Pendleton was the silver-haired and silver-tongued master of the elegant style. Jefferson later described him as the 'ablest man in debate I have ever met with.' Pendleton's specialty was the cool and low-key peroration that hypnotized the audience, while his arguments waged a silent guerrilla war against its better judgment. Richard Henry Lee was more inflammable and ostentatious. If Pendleton's technique suggested a peaceful occupation, Lee was a proponent of the all-out invasion. Opponents winced whenever he rose to speak, knowing as they did that their arguments were about to be carried off to oblivion in a whirlwind of words."

69. See O'Reilly, *Killing England*, 2211: "Congress appointed a committee of five men to craft the Declaration of Independence: Jefferson, Franklin, Adams, Robert Sherman of Connecticut, and Robert Livingston from New York. Jefferson was chosen to do the actual writing because of previous documents he had written on the subject of independence. He then ran the document past the rest of the committee for a critique. Franklin's insight was highly regarded, but there were some who thought the author, printer, and political theorist might have tried to insert too much humor into the document if he had been the writer."

70. Glover, *Founders as Fathers*, 284. See also, Miller, *Gentleman Revolutionary*, 153-155; Broadwater, *Forgotten Founder*, 77-82.

71. R. Carter Pittman, *The Declaration of Independence: Its Antecedents and Authors;* C:\Users\whyland\Documents\IT\IT\FINAL BOOK\RESEARCH ARTICLES\POLITICAL\The Declaration of Independence_ Its Antecedents and Authors.html.

72. Glover, *Founders as Fathers*, 284. See also Miller, *Gentleman Revolutionary*, 153–55; Broadwater, *Forgotten Founder*, 77–82.

73. The Works of John Adams, Vol. 4, 220.

74. Broadwater, *Forgotten Founder*, 461.

75. Ibid., 392.

76. The three authoritative studies of the chronology and different drafts of the
Declaration are: Julian Boyd, *The Declaration of Independence: The
Evolution of the Text* (Princeton, 1945), John H. Hazelton, *The Declaration
of Independence* (New York, 1906) and Pauline Maier's *Sacred Scriptures:
Making the Declaration of Independence* (New York, 1997). For a
convenient summary of the many myths about the signing ceremony, see
Charles Warren, *"Fourth of July Myths,"* WMQ, II (1945), 242–48; Maier,
American Scripture: "Selby, Revolution in Virginia, 103, says that
Pennsylvania, Massachusetts, and four of the other five states that adopted
bills of rights in the next decade drew on the Mason/committee draft
(Delaware, Maryland, Vermont, and New Hampshire), and that North
Carolina seems to have been more influenced by the final version as adopted
by the Virginia convention—which, of course, was itself based on the Mason
draft. On the use specifically of Mason's language on equality and natural
rights, see Chapter IV, below. 64. Boyd I: 413; Dumbauld, The Declaration
of Independence, 54 (and see also 77); D.W. Brogan quoted in Philip F.
Detweiler, "The Changing Reputation of the Declaration of Independence:
The First Fifty Years," WMQ, 3d Ser., IXX (1962), 557; 65 Boyd I: 213, and
Decent Respect, 91. 66. JCC II: 129, and Boyd I: 199. 67. Committee of
Secret Correspondence to Silas Deane, Philadelphia, July 8 and August 7,
1776, in LDC IV: 405, 635–36."

Chapter Seven: The Virginia Constitution

1. Bill O'Reilly and Martin Dugard, *Killing England: The Brutal Struggle for
American Independence* (New York: Henry Holt and Co., 2017), 1315:
"The thirteen colonies were broken up into three distinctions: royal colonies
(New York, New Hampshire, New Jersey, Virginia, North Carolina, South
Carolina, Georgia), proprietary colonies (Maryland, Pennsylvania,
Delaware), and charter colonies (Massachusetts, Connecticut, and Rhode
Island; Massachusetts would later become a royal colony). Royal colonies
were administered by officials chosen by the king; charter colonies were self-
governed, with rights and privileges granted to them through a written
contract with the king; proprietary colonies were lands deeded to an
individual by the king, with full governing rights."

2. Lorri Glover, *Founders as Fathers, The Private Lives and Politics of the American Revolution (New Haven and London,* Yale University Press, 2014), 475.

3. Joseph J. Ellis, *Revolutionary Summer: The Birth of American Independence* (New York: Vintage, 2013), ix–x, 1.

4. Ellis, *Revolutionary Summer,* 99.

5. Thomson Gale, "Niccolo Machiavelli," Encyclopedia.com, International Encyclopedia of the Social Sciences, 2008, accessed February 13, 2019, https://www.encyclopedia.com/people/social-sciences-and-law/political-science-biographies/niccolo-machiavelli.

6. Ralph Ketcham, *James Madison, A Biography* (Charlottesville and London: University Press of Virginia, 1994), 71.

7. Cecelia M. Kenyon, "Constitutionalism in Revolutionary America," Vol. 20, *Constitutionalism,* 1979, accessed September 20, 2017, http://www.jstor.org/stable/24219128; Texts of the three constitutions are reprinted in Francis Newton Thorpe, compiler, *The Federal and State Constitution, Colonial Charters, and Other Organic Laws of the State, Territories, and Colonies Now or Heretofore Forming the United States of America,* 7 vols. (United States Congress, Constitutionalism in Revolutionary America 121 1909). The Massachusetts constitution in vol. 3, 1888–923; the Pennsylvania constitution in vol. 5, 3081–92; the Virginia constitution in vol. 7, 3812–19; For a concise account of the several plans available for consideration by the Virginia Convention, see the editorial note in Julian P. Boyd, ed., *The Papers of Thomas Jefferson* (Princeton: Princeton University Press, 1950), vol. I, 329–37. The three drafts of Jefferson's plan, plus other notes and documents, including the constitution as adopted by the convention, are printed on pp. 337–86; For a full account of George Mason's role and copies of Mason's drafts and the Declaration of Rights and Constitution as adopted, see Robert A. Rutland, ed., *The Papers of George Mason 1725-1792,* 3 vols. (Chapel Hill, NC: University of North Carolina Press, 1970), vol. I, 274–91, 295–310;

8. Joseph Ellis, *American Sphinx: The Character of Thomas Jefferson* (New York: Knopf, 1997), 252.

9. Brent Tarter, "George Mason and the Conservation of Liberty," *Virginia Magazine of History and Biography,* Vol. 99, No. 3, "A Raft Which Will Never Sink": Virginians and the Defense of Republicanism (Jul., 1991),

accessed December 26, 2015, http://www.jstor.org/stable/4249228, 279–304.

10. Jeff Broadwater, *George Mason, Forgotten Founder* (Chapel Hill: University of North Carolina Press, 2006): "Schreeven et al., *Revolutionary Virginia*, 7:594–98, 603–6 (nn. 18–40). Not only did the Cary committee fail to keep a record of its deliberations, but neither Mason's original draft nor the committee's final report has survived. Critical to recreating the evolution of the Virginia Constitution is William Fleming's letter to Jefferson of 22 June 1776, which contained an annotated copy of the printed constitution of 19–20 June, from which Mason's original can be reconstructed. Fortunately, a supplemental report from the committee to the convention, dated 24 June 1776, also survived. Julian Boyd collected and attempted to reconcile the surviving drafts in Boyd et al., *Papers of Thomas Jefferson*, 1:337–77. Boyd did the ground-breaking work; Van Schreeven et al., *Revolutionary Virginia*, sets out the transition from one draft to the next in minute detail but in an accessible fashion. Except for language that can be traced to Jefferson's draft, it is virtually impossible to know who originated a particular amendment."

11. Mason's Plan for the Virginia Constitution of 1776, PGM, 1:299–302; Boyd et al., Papers of Thomas Jefferson, 1:366–69. 50; Broadwater, *Forgotten Founder*, 451; *PGM* 1:299-302.

12. See Robert A. Rutland, *George Mason, Reluctant Statesman* (Baton Rouge: Louisiana State University Press, 1961).

13. Letter from John Adams to Richard Henry Lee, 15 November 1775; https://founders.archives.gov/documents/Adams/06-03-02-0163.

14. Helen H. Miller, *George Mason: Gentleman Revolutionary* (Chapel Hill: University of North Carolina Press, 1975), 142–43.

15. Kenyon, "Constitutionalism in Revolutionary America."

16. It is ironic that, eighty-five years after Richard Henry Lee made the case for independence, another Lee from the same bloodline, General Robert E. Lee, waged a war that divided the nation in two.

17. Virginia Constitution, http://www.gunstonhall.org/.

18. Broadwater, *Forgotten Founder*, 480.

19. Harlow G. Unger, *Lion of Liberty: Patrick Henry and the Call to a New Nation,* (Cambridge, MA: Da Capo Press, 2011), 115.

20. St. George Tucker, *Blackstone's Commentaries with Notes of Reference to the Constitution and Laws of the Federal Government of the United States*

and of the Commonwealth of Virginia, 5 vols. (Philadelphia: William Young Birch & Abraham Small, 1803; reprint, New York: Augustus M. Keller, 1969), 1:83–91.

21. Miller, *Gentleman Revolutionary*, 145–48.

22. Wythe to Thomas Jefferson, 27 July 1776, https://lawlibrary.wm.edu/wythepedia/index.php/Wythe_to_Thomas_Jefferson,_27_July_1776.

23. James C. Ballagh, ed., *The Letters of Richard Henry Lee*, 2 vols. (New York: Macmillan, 1911), 2:492–94.

24. A. E. Dick Howard, "For the Common Benefit": Constitutional History in Virginia as a Casebook for the Modern Constitution-Maker, Virginia Law Review, Vol. 54, No. 5, Symposium: State Constitutional Revision (Jun., 1968), 816–902, Virginia Law Review, accessed September 20, 2017, http://www.jstor.org/stable/1071893.

25. Ballagh, *The Letters of Richard Henry Lee*, 2:492–94.

26. James Madison, *Prefatory note. The debates in 1776 on the Declaration of Rights*, 581.

27. Broadwater, *Forgotten Founder*, 504.

28. *PGM* 1:304–9; Broadwater, *Forgotten Founder*, 468.

29. GM to Mr. Brent, October 2, 1778, *PGM*, 2:433-39; Broadwater, *Forgotten Founder*, 478.

30. Broadwater, *Forgotten Founder*, 471.

31. The Seal of Virginia is officially described in the Code of Virginia (1950), §1-500, https://en.wikipedia.org/wiki/Flag_and_seal_of_Virginia.

Chapter Eight: War and Death

1. Terry K. Dunn, ed., *The Recollections of John Mason: George Mason's Son Remembers His Father and Life at Gunston Hall* (Marshall, VA: EPM Publications, 2004), 36.

2. Ibid., 36.

3. Ibid., 44.

4. GM to unknown 6 December 1770, PGM 1:129; Lorri Glover, *Founders as Fathers, The Private Lives and Politics of the American Revolution (New Haven and London,* Yale University Press, 2014), 174.

5. Glover, *Founders as Fathers*, 175.

6. Ibid., 1104. *Alexandra Gazette,* March 21, 1849, Gunston Hall Library and Archives.
7. "Children of George Mason of Gunston Hall," Gunston Hall website, accessed February 14, 2019, http://www.gunstonhall.org/georgemason/mason_family/sarah_eilbeck_mason.html; Papers of George Mason, II: 810.
8. See "James Craik," George Washington's Mount Vernon website, accessed February 14, 2019, http://www.mountvernon.org/digital-encyclopedia/article/james-craik/: "After the Revolutionary war's conclusion, Craik opened a medical practice in Alexandria, Virginia, and visited Mount Vernon frequently, serving as Washington's personal physician. In 1798, with Washington briefly called from his retirement to command the army in preparation for a possible war with France, Craik was named his chief medical officer. With war averted, Craik continued his medical practice in Alexandria. On December 13, 1799, Craik was summoned to Mount Vernon to attend to a gravely ill Washington. Serving with two other doctors, Craik repeatedly attempted to cure what ailed the sickly former president. Washington passed away the next day, despite the best efforts of his long time friend and physician. Craik lived the rest of his life in Alexandria where he passed away in 1814 and was buried in the cemetery of the Old Presbyterian Meeting House."
9. Glover, *Founders as Fathers,* 154; *Mason Family Bible,* in Kate Mason Rowland, *The Life of George Mason, 1725–1792* (New York: Russell & Russell, 1964; reprint of 1892 volume), Vol. 1, 162–63.
10. Dunn, *The Recollections of John Mason,* 48.
11. Ibid.
12. Ibid.
13. March 9, 1773, was the date of Ann's death.
14. Dunn, *The Recollections of John Mason,* 49.
15. Broadwater; *Forgotten Founder,* 305; GM to Brent, 2 October, 1778, PGM, 1: 433–39.
16. British Lord Sandwich, in a speech in the House of Lords.
17. Ron Chernow, *Washington: A Life* (New York: Penguin Press, 2011), 775–76; James R. Gaines, *For Liberty and Glory: Washington, Lafayette, and Their Revolutions* (New York: W. W. Norton & Company, 2008), 44.
18. Bill O'Reilly and Martin Dugard, *Killing England: The Brutal Struggle for American Independence* (New York: Henry Holt and Co., 2017), 1301: The

name comes from the number of knotted cord tentacles attached to the whip handle.

19. O'Reilly, *Killing England*, 1330: The British troops, who despised the Americans, also feared their fate should they be taken captive by the colonists. "Many English believe the Americans to be cannibals. A rumor circulates throughout the British ranks that Americans are fond of slitting open a man's body to stuff it with dry wood, then setting the wood afire as a form of torture."

20. Chernow, *Washington*, 776; Gary Wills, *Cincinnatus: George Washington and the Enlightenment* (New York: Doubleday, 1984), 187.

21. Joseph J. Ellis, *Revolutionary Summer: The Birth of American Independence* (New York: Vintage, 2013), 3.

22. Ellis, *Revolutionary Summer*, 30; There is some debate as to Washington's actual height: "in instructions to his tailor, he described himself as six feet tall. Fellow officers in the French and Indian War described him as six foot two. Measurements of his corpse for his coffin list him at six foot three and a half. Adams had been the one to nominate him as American military commander in June 1775, later explaining that he was the obvious choice, in part because he was a Virginian and Virginia's support for the still-undeclared war was critical, and in part because he was a full head taller than anyone else in the room."

23. Ellis, *Revolutionary Summer*, 30–31.

24. John H. Rhodehamel, *George Washington: The Wonder of the Age* (New Haven and London: Yale Universality Press, 2017), 31; GW to Catharine Sawbridge Macaulay Graham, Jan. 9, 1790, FO/NA, http://founders. archives.gov/documents/Washington/05-02-02-030-0003); Dorothy Twohig, ed., *The Papers of George Washington, Presidential Series, vol. 4, 8 Sept. 1789–15 Jan. 1790*, (Charlottesville: University Press of Virginia, 1993), 551–54.

25. Broadwater, *Forgotten Founder*, 393; GM to Washington, 2 April 1776, PGM 1:266–69.

26. Chernow, *Washington*, 581–82; Paul K. Longmore, *The Invention of George Washington* (Berkeley: University of California Press, 1988),149.

27. Broadwater, *Forgotten Founder*, 390.

28. Glover, *Founders as Fathers*, 362; Mason to Henry Lee, 13 December 1780, PGM 2: 679-680.

29. Rowland, *The Life of George Mason*, 370.

30. Dunn, *Recollections*.

31. J. S. Skinner, ed., "Shooting Extraordinary," *American Turf Register and Sporting Magazine*, Vol. 1, 1830. 400. No. 8. Google EBook. Web: And more than one descendant became known as a keen sportsman, especially George Mason VI, Mason's grandson. As the story is told, the "extraordinary shooting" by Mason's grandson took place on the grounds of Colonel Smith near Alexandria, D.C. Witnesses told the magazine of Mason's expertise in marksmanship: "[Mason] killed forty-nine partridges without missing a single shot. The same gentleman killed two bucks, running, at one shot, with a rifle loaded with a single ball. He once shot at eight partridges, flying, and killed them all. I saw him strike a playing card six times running with a pistol, at the distance of thirty yards ... I have frequently seen him take a pistol in each hand, distance ten yards, and in the act of advancing rapidly, strike a lath with each. He can throw into the air two apples at once, and strike each with a double barrel gun, before they fall. I once saw him put a bandage over his eyes so that he could not possibly see, and turn loose ten partridges, one at a time and kill three at the ten shots."

32. Dunn, *Recollections*, 43

33. Ibid., 10.

34. Glover, *Founders as Fathers*; George Mason to unknown, 2 October 1778, PGM, 1:435; Patrick Henry, "Rough Resolution in favor of Independence," May 1776, PHC, 1:395 (second quotation); William Jameson, Charlotte County clerk, to Paul Carrington and Thomas Read, 23 April 1776, PHC, 1:374 (last quotation).

35. Glover, *Founders as Fathers*, 349; GW to George Mason, 22 October 1780, PGM 2:678; For a sample of Washington's steady stream of complaints about lack of support for the Continental Army, see the following: GW to Board of War, 11 November 1778, WW 13:244–46; GW to Benjamin Harrison, 18–30 December 1778, WW 13:463–68; GW to Committee of Conference, 13 January 1779, WW 14:3–12.

36. Ellis, *Revolutionary Summer*, 208, 224, footnote 22: Interesting to note is that Ellis solicited the opinions of four distinguished historians of the American Revolution in response to this question: "Would the demise of the Continental Army and the capture of George Washington in 1776 have changed the outcome of the American Revolution? Edmund Morgan,

Gordon Wood, and David Hackett Fischer all said no, though all agreed that the way the war played out would have been different. Ed Lengel, editor of the Washington Papers, disagreed on the grounds that Washington was indispensable and irreplaceable."

37. Glover, *Founders as Fathers*, 349; GW to George Mason, 22 October 1780, PGM 2:678.

38. John E. Selby, *Revolution in Virginia 1775–1783* (Charlottesville: University of Virginia Press, 2007), 213.

39. GM to Thomas Jefferson, 6 October 1780, PGM, 2:675–77.

40. Michael Kranish, *Flight from Monticello: Thomas Jefferson at War* (New York, 2010), 274; Mary Beacock Fryer and Christopher Dracott, *John Graves Simcoes, 1752–1806: A Biography* (Toronto: Dundurn Press, 1998), 75. See O'Reilly, *Killing England*, 1372: "Despite the fact that rape and other atrocities were hanging offenses, such acts occurred among the British soldiers. An example is the British headquarters notation of March 14, 1778, stating that a Cpl. John Fisher was sentenced to be hanged by the neck until dead for 'a rape on the body of Maria Nicolls, a woman child of nine years of age.' In the case of Maria Nicolls, whose father was a sergeant in the British Army, she refused to share her story until exacting a promise from her own mother 'that if she would not beat her, she would tell.'"

41. George Mason, "George Mason to George Mason Jr.," June 3, 1781, last updated January 22, 2013, http://www.consource.org/document/george-mason-to-george-mason-jr-1781-6-3-2/.

42. Ibid.

43. Chernow, *Washington*, 2601; Letter to Alexander Hamilton February 25, 1799, PWRT, 3:398.

44. Mason, "George Mason to George Mason Jr."

45. See O'Reilly, *Killing England*, 1361: "Arnold was also known to give his horse a bit of rum before a fight. Many American soldiers drank before battle, leading the British soldiers to denounce them as drunkards."

46. Glover, *Founders as Fathers*, 396; Mason, "Mason to George Mason Jr." On the issue of destroying estates, "Forty-three-year-old Lund Washington went on board the [British warship] *Savage* carrying a small amount of poultry as a gift to the ship's captain, pleading that Mount Vernon be spared. Later, Lund sent large amounts of livestock to the ship as a gift. George Washington, seeing this as aiding and abetting the enemy, was

furious when Lafayette informed him what had happened—yet Lund Washington's actions saved the Mount Vernon estate from being destroyed." See O'Reilly, *Killing England*, 1361.

47. George Mason, "George Mason to Pearson Chapman," May 31, 1781, last updated January 22, 2013, http://www.consource.org/document/george-mason-to-pearson-chapman-1781-5-31/.

48. *National Geographic, Founding Fathers*, Special Publication 2016, 76; O'Reilly, *Killing England*, 2127: "Banastre Tarleton, a man no less notorious than Benedict Arnold, returned to England a hero. The noted British artists Thomas Gainsborough and Joshua Reynolds both painted his portrait, and the one by Reynolds still hangs in London's National Gallery. Tarleton was elected to Parliament in 1790, where he staunchly defended the slave trade while still remaining a member of the British military, being promoted to major general in 1794. He maintained a fifteen-year affair with Mary Robinson, the former lover of King George IV, before finally marrying an illegitimate daughter of the Fourth Duke of Ancaster in 1798. Banastre Tarleton died in 1833 at the age of seventy-nine and is buried in Lancaster Cemetery in Lancashire, England."

49. Thomas Fleming, *The Intimate Lives of the Founding Fathers* (New York: Harper Collins, 2009), 968.

50. Broadwater, *Forgotten Founder*, 662; Mason, "George Mason to Pearson Chapman."

51. Glover, *Founders as Fathers*, 396; Mason to George Mason Jr. 3 June 1781, PGM 2:690.

52. A lengthy exploration of the war lies beyond the scope of this project. See Edward Countryman, *The American Revolution*, rev. ed. (New York: Hill and Wang, 2003); John Ferling, *Almost a Miracle: The American Victory in the War of Independence* (New York: Oxford University Press, 2007); Robert Middlekauff, *The Glorious Cause: The American Revolution, 1763–1789*, 2nd rev. ed. (New York: Oxford University Press, 2005); and Charles Royster, *A Revolutionary People at War: The Continental Army and American Character, 1775–1783* (Chapel Hill: University of North Carolina Press, 1979). For class and racial tensions in Virginia, see Michael A. McDonnell, *The Politics of War: Race, Class, and Conflict in Revolutionary Virginia* (Chapel Hill: University of North Carolina Press, 2007); and Alan

Taylor, *The Internal Enemy: Slavery and War in Virginia*, 1772–1832 (New York: W. W. Norton, 2013).

53. James Madison, "From James Madison to Philip Mazzei, 7 July 1781," Founders Online website, https://founders.archives.gov/documents/Madison/01-03-02-0091.

54. On the circumstances that made victory at Yorktown possible, see Richard M. Ketchum, *Victory at Yorktown: The Campaign That Won the Revolution* (New York: Henry Holt & Co., 2004), 1–28.

55. Chernow, *Washington*, 1482; WWR 513 "General Orders" April 18, 183.

Chapter Nine: A New Constitution for a New Country

1. Jeff Broadwater, *George Mason, Forgotten Founder* (Chapel Hill: University of North Carolina Press, 2006), 551; GM TO Mr. Brent, 2 October 1778, PGM, 1:433–39; GM to James Mercer, 5 February, 1780; PGM, 2: 61718; Pamela C. Copeland and Richard K. MacMaster, *The Five George Masons, Patriots and Planters of Virginia and Maryland* (Lorton, VA: The Board of Regents of Gunston Hall, 1989), 208–9.

2. Marian Buckley Cox, *Glimpse of Glory: George Mason of Gunston Hall* (Richmond: Garrett & Massie, 1954).

3. Denise McHugh, "Family of George Mason (IV) of Gunston Hall: A Close Look at George Mason's Second Wife: Sarah Brent Mason," Gunston Hall website, accessed February 15, 2019, http://www.gunstonhall.org/georgemason/mason_family/sarah_brent.html; Cox, *Glimpse of Glory*.

4. McHugh, "Family of George Mason (IV) of Gunston Hall."

5. Cox, *Glimpse of Glory*.

6. McHugh, "Family of George Mason (IV) of Gunston Hall."

7. Cox, *Glimpse of Glory*, 185.

8. Gordon S. Wood, *Revolutionary Characters: What Made the Founders Different* (New York: Penguin Press, 2006), 214–15: "There was something direct and earthy about Paine. He wore no masks over his fiery black eyes. His appearance was careless and slovenly, with a large nose reddened from too much drink. His dress was drab and coarse, his wig worn and tattered. One observer noted in 1792, 'He is the very picture of a journeyman tailor who has been drunk and playing at nine pins for the first three days of the

week, and is returning to his work on Thursday.' Paine was never quite able to shed his lowly corset maker origins and the effects of all those years living in poverty and obscurity near the bottom of English society. No wonder people said that 'he is better in print than in the flesh.' Paine never really assimilated to gentry status the way Franklin did. To be sure, he moved in aristocratic and gentlemanly circles, especially after his fame had been established in 1776. His writings became an entrée into liberal gentry society and enabled him to mingle with Washington, Jefferson, and Lafayette."

9. "I think every age has some major issue that people understand as an agenda for that generation, a major problem that is to be resolved. In the 18th century, clearly it was the problem of government. How could you design a government, a new government, a government that didn't have kings, didn't have hereditary rule, that could function, that could be stable?" Pauline Maier, *Ratification: The People Debate the Constitution, 1787–88* (New York: Simon & Schuster, 2010), 137. Maier's work is the authoritative scholarly study of the ratification process. The documents for each state ratifying convention are published in DHRC, a massive editorial project nearing completion; PBS television special.

10. "Creating the United States," Library of Congress website, accessed February 15, 2019, https://www.loc.gov/exhibits/creating-the-united-states/road-to-the-constitution.html.

11. "George Mason and the Constitution," Gunston Hall website, accessed February 15, 2019, http://www.gunstonhall.org/georgemason/essays/constitution.html; Robert A. Rutland, *The Papers of George Mason* (Chapel Hill: University Press of North Carolina, 1970), 3:903–4.

12. "George Mason and the Constitution," https://founders.archives.gov/documents/Washington/99-01-02-10768; George Washington, "From George Washington to Benjamin Harrison, Sr.," March 4, 1783, http://founders.archives.gov/documents/Washington/99-01-02-10768

13. James Madison, "To Thomas Jefferson from James Madison," December 10, 1783, https://founders.archives.gov/documents/Jefferson/01-06-02-0301.

14. James Madison, *Letters and Other Writings of James Madison: 1769–1793*, Vol. 1, (Philadelphia: J. B. Lippincott & Company, 1865), 238.

15. "George Mason and the Constitution"; Rutland, *The Papers of George Mason*, 2:799–800.

16. Numerous historians have written detailed analysis and commentary of the important Annapolis conference; see "Annapolis Convention," George Washington's Mount Vernon website, accessed February 15, 2019, http://www.mountvernon.org/digital-encyclopedia/article/annapolis-convention/: "Held September 11-14, 1786, the Annapolis Convention was a meeting incipiently aimed at constructing uniform parameters to regulate trade between states during a time of political turbulence and economic strain. While chartered as a purely commercial convening, and attended by only a handful of delegates from five states, the Annapolis Convention served as a decisive stepping-stone to the Constitutional Convention, effectively laying the catalytic groundwork for our nation's constitutional formation. The Convention's attendees, 'dictated by an anxiety for the welfare of the United States,' came to the collective realization that trade was altogether unseverable from the widespread 'embarrassments' characterizing the then-present state of affairs, and that to discuss commerce without first addressing the inadequacies of America's broader political framework was thoroughly unavoidable. Articulating these sentiments in a report issued to all states and Congress, the Annapolis delegates recommended a convention be held in Philadelphia the following year; the Constitutional Convention was subsequently held from May to September, 1787."

17. Randolph to Madison, 12 June 1786; DLC: *Madison Papers*; "To Thomas Jefferson from James Madison."

18. Rutland, *The Papers of George Mason, II*, 858; James Madison, "From James Madison to Thomas Jefferson," May 12, 1786, https://founders.archives.gov/documents/Madison/01-09-02-0007.

19. Broadwater, *Forgotten Founder*, 748.; Letter of Madison to Jefferson, April 23, 1787.

20. Lorri Glover, *Founders as Fathers, The Private Lives and Politics of the American Revolution (New Haven and London,* Yale University Press, 2014), 62.; GM TO Washington, 2 April 1776, PGM 1:267; see also Broadwater, *Forgotten Founder,* chapter one.

21. Broadwater, *Forgotten Founder,* 1289: "After arriving in Philadelphia with his son John, and at least two slaves, Mason complained to George Jr. that they had found 'travelling very expensive, from eight to nine Dollars Per Day.' Mason's per diem was six dollars. Fortunately their room cost only twenty-five shillings a day, in Pennsylvania currency, 'so that I hope I shall

be able to defray my Expenses with my public Allowance; & more than that I do not wish.'"

22. Broadwater, *Forgotten Founder*, 1286.
23. Pauline Maier, *Ratification: The People Debate the Constitution* (New York: Simon and Schuster, 2010), 83; DHRC, I: 192–204, 197.
24. Maier, *Ratification*, 2776, footnote 24; Broadwater, *Forgotten Founder*, 74–75, 107. Mason to GW, April 2 1776, and to Cockburn, April 18, 1784, PGM I: 267, II: 799–800.
25. Philip B. Kurland and Ralph Lerner, ed., "Convention: Virginia General Assembly," The Founders' Constitution website, December 1, 1786, http://press-pubs.uchicago.edu/founders/documents/v1ch6s3.html; Farrand 3:559–61.
26. Ron Chernow, *Washington: A Life* (New York: Penguin Press, 2011), 1737; PWCF 4:474–75; Letter from Madison, December 24, 1786.
27. Chernow, *Washington*, 1506.
28. Ibid., 1741; PWCF 5:96. Letter form Henry Knox, March 19, 1787.
29. Chernow, Washington, 1743; Wood, *Revolutionary Characters*, 45.
30. Henry Mayer, *A Son of Thunder: Patrick Henry and the American Republic* (New York: Grove Press, 1991), 1433-34.
31. Mayer, *A Son of Thunder*, 1434; Patrick Henry reply, 13 February 1787, WWH, 2:311; Grigsby, Virginia Convention of 1788, 1:32 n. 36.
32. Max Farrand, ed., *The Records of the Federal Convention of 1787*, Vols. I–III (New Haven: Yale University Press, 1966; originally 1911), 559–61; Broadwater, *Forgotten Founder*, 1283.
33. Josephine Pacheco, "George Mason and The Constitution," *New York State Bar Journal* October 1987, 10–12.
34. Mason to George Mason Jr., June 1, 1787, *PGM*, 3:890-94.; Broadwater, *Forgotten Founder*, 774.
35. Pacheco, "George Mason and The Constitution," 10–12.
36. Mason to George Mason Jr., June 1, 1787, *PGM*, 3:890-94.; Broadwater, *Forgotten Founder*, 774.
37. Broadwater, *Forgotten Founder*, 1272.
38. Mayer, *A Son of Thunder*, 35.
39. George Mason, "Letter to George Mason Jr.," TeachingAmericanHistory.org, May 20, 1787, http://teachingamericanhistory.org/library/document/

george-mason-to-george-mason-jr-2/; PGM 3:879-92; Farrand, *The Records of the Federal Convention of 1787*, 3:58–59.

40. Gerry would later serve as vice president of the United States, and died of a heart attack while riding in his carriage to the Senate.

41. Broadwater, *Forgotten Founder*, 806; PGM 3:879–92; Farrand, *The Records of the Federal Convention of 1787*, 3:58–59.

42. Joe Wolverton, II, J. D., "1787 Constitutional Convention: Why the Secrecy Rule?," The New American website, May 28, 2014, https://www. thenewamerican.com/culture/history/item/18356-1787-constitutional-convention-why-the-secrecy-rule; PGM 3:879-92; Farrand, *The Records of the Federal Convention of 1787*, 3:58–59.

Chapter Ten: The Philadelphia Convention

1. Thomas Fleming, *The Great Divide* (New York: Da Capo Press, 2015), 36.; TJ to WS Smith, September 28, 1787, PTJ Digital.

2. Jeff Broadwater, *George Mason, Forgotten Founder* (Chapel Hill: University of North Carolina Press, 2006), 1281:"Of the Virginia delegates, Randolph, Madison, and Mason—especially Madison and Mason— dominated the floor debates. When the two of them were in agreement, they formed a formidable alliance; when they disagreed, which they often did, the exchange could be electric."

3. David O. Stewart, *The Summer of 1787* (New York: Simon & Schuster, 2007), 260; Max Farrand, ed., *The Records of the Federal Convention of 1787*, Vol. III (New Haven: Yale University Press, 1966; originally 1911), 550 (unpublished "Preface to Debates in the Convention of 1787.")

4. *National Geographic, Founding Fathers Special Edition*, 102; Stewart, *The Summer of 1787*, 260; Farrand, *Recordds*, 550 (unpublished "Preface to Debates in the Convention of 1787.")

5. Fleming, *The Great Divide*, 4; Stewart, *The Summer of 1787*, 46.

6. Ron Chernow, *Washington: A Life* (New York: Penguin Press, 2011), 1721; Herbert Baxter Adams, *The Life and Writings of Jared Sparks: Comprising Selections from His Journals and Correspondance*, Vol 1 (Whitefish, MT: Kessinger Publishing, LLC, 2007) 567.

7. Broadwater, *Forgotten Founder*, 1310.

8.   Ibid., 467; Jefferson to A.B. Woodward, April 3, 1825, in Andrew Lipscomb, ed., *The Writings of Thomas Jefferson*, Vol. 16 (Washington, DC: Thomas Jefferson Memorial Association, 1904–1905), 166–67; Kate Mason Rowland, *The Life of George Mason, 1725–1792* (New York: Russell & Russell, 1964; reprint of 1892 volume), 248–49; Edmund Randolph, *History of Virginia*, ed. Arthur Shaffer (Charlottesville: University Press of Virginia, 1970), 192.

9.   George Mason, "Letter to George Mason Jr." June 1, 1787, see PGM 3:892–893, http://teachingamericanhistory.org/library/document/george-mason-to-george-mason-jr/.

10.   Lorri Glover, *Founders as Fathers, The Private Lives and Politics of the American Revolution (New Haven and London,* Yale University Press, 2014), 862; GM to GM Jr. June 1 1787, PGM 3:892–893; "ourselves and our Posterity"; John P. Kaminski, Gaspare J. Saladino, Richard Leffler, Charles H. Schoenleber, and Margaret A. Hogan, ed., *The Documentary History of the Ratification of the Constitution Digital Edition*, (Charlottesville: University of Virginia Press, 2009), http://rotunda.upress.virginia.edu/founders/RNCN-02-08-02-0001-0118 [accessed 08 Jun 2017] Original source: Commentaries on the Constitution, Volume XIII: Commentaries on the Constitution, No. 1.

11.   PWR 8:61. Letter to Robert Morris, January 13, 1777; Chernow, *Washington*, 1032.

12.   Glover, *Founders as Fathers*, 1115; Pauline Maier, *Ratification: The People Debate the Constitution* (New York: Simon and Schuster, 2010), 94; Robert F. Dalzell Jr. and Lee Baldwin Dalzell, *George Washington's Mount Vernon: At Home in Revolutionary America* (Oxford: Oxford University Press, 1998), 103–112, quotations at 109 and 111.

13.   See Ron Chernow, *Alexander Hamilton* (London: Penguin Books, 2005), 2024: " … The eighty-one-year-old Benjamin Franklin, the ancient Philadelphian, with his mostly bald head, lank strands of side hair, and double chin, was bedeviled by gout and excruciating kidney stones. He often discoursed to Hamilton and other delegates under the canopy of a mulberry tree in his courtyard, sometimes with his fond grandson Benjamin Franklin Bache looking on. Legend has it that when the enfeebled Franklin first came to the convention, he was borne aloft on a sedan chair, toted by four convicts conscripted from the Walnut Street jail. Nevertheless, with exemplary

dedication, he showed up for every session of the four-month convention … "

14. Chernow, *Washington*: "In the absence of Martha's company, Washington continued to gravitate toward alluring female society. When he dined at a club composed of the city's leading gentlemen, he noted that they invited female family members on alternate Saturdays. Not surprisingly, Washington chose that day to attend, specifying, 'This was the ladies day.' Several times he called upon Elizabeth Powel and dusted off a musty streak of gallantry. As he wrote to her on July 23, "Gen[era]l Washington presents his respectful compliments to Mrs. Powel and will do himself the honor of calling upon her at or before 5 o'clock (in his carriage) in hopes of the pleasure of conducting her to Lansdown this evening."

15. GM to George Mason Jr., May 20, 1787, PGM, 3: 879-92; Broadwater, *Forgotten Founder*, 460.

16. GM to George Mason Jr., May 20, 1787, PGM, 3: 879-92; Broadwater, *Forgotten Founder*, 460.

17. Stewart, *The Summer of 1787*, 1153

18. Two of the delegates would later die under mysterious circumstances, presumed murdered. In 1806, George Wythe of Virginia was fed poison by a grandnephew and heir. John Lansing of New York disappeared in 1829 after checking into a hotel room. Delegate Elbridge Gerry's most lasting impact on American politics came in 1812 when, as governor of Massachusetts, he signed a law creating such distorted voting districts that they were compared to a salamander, or a "gerrymander."

19. Chernow, *Washington*, 1976.

20. Letter from Thomas Jefferson to John Adams, August 30, 1787. Text from the Digital Edition of the Adams Papers; "Constitution of the United States—A History," National Archives website, accessed February 15, 2019, https://www.archives.gov/founding-docs/more-perfect-union; Gordon Lloyd, "The Constitutional Convention: Selected Correspondence from the Convention," TeachingAmericanHistory.org, accessed February, 15, 2019, http://teachingamericanhistory.org/convention/correspondence/.

21. Primary research on the debates draws upon Madison's notes in Debates and on five secondary accounts by distinguished historians: Max Farrand, *The Framing of the Constitution of the United States* (New Haven, CT, 1913); Catherine Drinker Bowen, *Miracle at Philadelphia* (Boston, 1966);

Jack N. Rakove, *Original Meanings: Politics and Ideas in the Making of the Constitution* (New York, 1996); Carol Berkin, *A Brilliant Solution: Inventing the American Constitution* (New York, 2003); and finally Richard Beeman, *Plain, Honest Men: The Making of the American Constitution* (New York, 2009); Wood, *Revolutionary Characters*, 574: "When in 1776 the revolutionaries met in their conventions to discuss the forms of their new state constitutions, they felt no need either to report what they said or to extract vows of secrecy to prevent leaks of what they said to the people out of doors. As a result, we know very little of what went on during those momentous closed meetings in the months surrounding the Declaration of Independence. Apparently the leaders believed that nearly everyone who counted and ought to hear what was said was within the legislative or convention halls. A decade later, however, by 1787, the situation had become very different. In many of the states, particularly Pennsylvania and Massachusetts, legislative debates had begun to be reported by a growing number of newspapers (which now included dailies), and political leaders had developed a keen, even fearful awareness of a larger political society existing outside the legislative chambers. Politics no longer seemed an exclusively gentlemanly business, and consequently gentlemen in public discussions increasingly found themselves forced to concede to the popular and egalitarian ideology of the Revolution … "

22. For a succinct summary of Mason's and other founders' growing concern about "majoritarian excess," see Robert Middlekauff, *The Glorious Cause: The American Revolution, 1763–1789* (Oxford: Oxford University Press, 2007), 651–54. For the popular view of Mason as a champion of states' rights, see Rowland, *The Life of George Mason*, 2:139–79. See also Catherine Drinker Bowen, *Miracle at Philadelphia: The Story of the Constitutional Convention May to September 1787* (New York: Back Bay Books, 1986), 105, for the argument Mason believed "a strong central government lay counter to the republican ideas for which the Revolution had been fought." Irving Brant belabored the point but was close to the truth when he wrote "there was no dominating defensive force for State Rights in the Convention." Irving Brant, *James Madison*, Vol. 3 (Indianapolis: Bobbs-Merrill, 1941), 128. Luther Martin, who left the convention before the signing ceremony, may have been the one prominent Anti-Federalist with a coherent philosophy of states' rights. Saul Cornell, *The Other Founders:*

Anti-Federalism and the Dissenting Tradition in America, 1788–1828
(Chapel Hill: University of North Carolina Press, 1999), 61–62.

23. George Mason to Beverley Randolph (June 30, 1787) Philadelphia June
30th 1787, http://www.consource.org/document/george-mason-to-beverley-
randolph-1787-6-30/, http://teachingamericanhistory.org/library/document/
george-mason-to-beverley-randolph/.

24. See Brent Tarter, "George Mason and the Conservation of Liberty,"
Virginia Magazine of History and Biography, Vol. 99, No. 3, "A Raft
Which Will Never Sink": Virginians and the Defense of Republicanism (July
1991), 279–304.

25. Martin S. Sheffer, "Presidential Power and Limited Government,"
Presidential Studies Quarterly, Vol. 21, No. 3, Ordered Liberty (Summer
1991), 471-488, accessed September 20, 2017, http://www.jstor.org/
stable/27550767. For a specific analysis of the philosophies themselves,
particularly the consolidated nationalism of Alexander Hamilton and
Gouverneur Morris, the democratic nationalism of James Wilson, and the
republican nationalism of James Madison, see Conyers Read, ed., *The
Constitution Reconsidered* (New York: Macmillan, 1938); William W.
Crosskey, *Politics and the Constitution in the History of the United States*,
2 vols. (Chicago: University of Chicago Press, 1953); Paul Eidelberg, *The
Philosophy of the American Constitution* (New York: Free Press, 1968).

26. Chernow, *Washington*, 1966–1967; Gordon S. Wood, *Empire of Liberty: A
History of the Early Republic, 1789–1815* (Oxford: Oxford University
Press, 2009), 73; Quote of Pierce Butler, Founding Father, Conservapedia,
accessed February 15, 2019, https://www.conservapedia.com/Pierce_
Butler_(Founding_Father)#Quotes.

27. See James Thomas Flexner, *George Washington*, Vol. 3 (Boston: Little,
Brown and Company, 1965), 133–34; see also Miller, *Gentleman
Revolutionary*, 245.

28. Wood, *Revolutionary Characters*, 120; TJ letter to David Humphrey,
March 18, 1789, in *Papers of Thomas Jefferson*, 14: 679.

29. Wood, *Revolutionary Characters*, 122–23; Louise B. Dunbar, *A Study of
"Monarchical" Tendencies in the United States from 1776 to 1801*, in
Illinois Studies in the Social Sciences, 10(1922), 99–100.

30. Wood, *Revolutionary Characters*, 122–23; Louise B. Dunbar, *A Study of
"Monarchical" Tendencies*, 99–100. And Washington was not beyond

severe criticism when he became president. This vilification of the first president climaxed with an open letter to him in July 1796 written by none other than the great pamphleteer of the Revolution, Thomas Paine accused him of vanity and Stuart-like pride; he was a man whose integrity was questionable, whose politics were duplicitous, and whose character was "chameleon-colored." See Wood, *Revolutionary Characters*.

31. During the Revolutionary War, Washington himself had required his soldiers and officers to call him "Excellency." The term often preceded another one of his titles, thus "His Excellency General George Washington," signifying that Washington was separate from the other generals in the Continental Army. According to one historian, "It was a source of deep frustration to Washington that he was looked down upon by the British military leadership. Using this title was yet another way to show that he was their equal. Despite this, General Howe, in particular, refused to acknowledge Washington as anything other than a contemptuous rebel.": Brent Tarter, "George Mason and the Conservation of Liberty," *The Virginia Magazine of History and Biography*, Vol. 99, No. 3, "A Raft Which Will Never Sink": Virginians and the Defense of Republicanism (Jul., 1991), 279–304 Published by: Virginia Historical Society Stable URL: http://www.jstor.org/stable/4249228.

32. Martin S. Sheffer, "Presidential Power and Limited Government," *Presidential Studies Quarterly,* Vol. 21, No. 3, Ordered Liberty (Summer, 1991), 471–88; Published by: Wiley on behalf of the Center for the Study of the Presidency and Congress Stable URL: http://www.jstor.org/stable/27550767, Accessed: 20-09-2017 18:01.

33. Ibid.

34. ibid.

35. Chernow, *Washington*, 1966–67.

36. Sheffer, "Presidential Power and Limited Government."

37. DAFC, V: 128, 131, 192. William Patterson's "New Jersey Plan" would have instituted a plural "federal executive." Like the Virginia Plan, New Jersey's alternative purported to enlarge and correct the Articles of Confederation. Some elements were common to both. The New Jersey Plan gave Congress the power to regulate trade, though it would still have to make requisitions on the states for funds; those requisitions would be based on the number of free citizens plus three-fifths of all others. Congress would elect an executive

for a single term and could remove him upon application by a majority of state governors. And a national judiciary would apply the law of the United States, which would be supreme.

38. Brion McClanahan, *The Founding Fathers' Guide to the Constitution* (Washington, DC: Regnery History, 2012), 1313.; Farrand, *The Records of the Federal Convention of 1787*, Vol., 4, 17–18.

39. McClanahan, *Founding Fathers*, 1313.; DAFC IV, 17-18.

40. Article 2, Section 1, Clause 1: Records of the Federal Convention, http://press-pubs.uchicago.edu/founders/documents/a2_1_1s4.html.

41. Maier, *Ratification*, 326–27.

42. Ibid.; PGM III: 991–93 and note 993–94; Farrand, *The Records of the Federal Convention of 1787*, Vol. 2, 637–40.

43. For a succinct summary of Mason's and other founders' growing concern about "majoritarian excess," see Middlekauff, *The Glorious Cause*, 651–54. For the popular view of Mason as a champion of states' rights, see Rowland, *The Life of George Mason*, 2:139–79. See also Bowen, *Miracle at Philadelphia*, 105, for the argument Mason believed "a strong central government lay counter to the republican ideas for which the Revolution had been fought." Irving Brant belabored the point but was close to the truth when he wrote "there was no dominating defensive force for State Rights in the Convention." Brant, *James Madison*, Vol. 3, 128. Luther Martin, who left the convention before the signing ceremony, may have been the one prominent Anti-Federalist with a coherent philosophy of states' rights. Cornell, *The Other Founders*, 61–62.

44. "George Mason's Objections to the Constitution," Gunston Hall website, accessed February 15, 2019, http://www.gunstonhall.org/library/archives/manuscripts/objections.html. Mason was perhaps clairvoyant as the modern-day president utilizes both a foreign and domestic council: the National Security Council and the Council of Economic advisors.

45. McClanahan, *Founding Fathers*, 1364; Farrand, Documentary History XVI 33–35.

46. The Debates in the Federal Convention of 1787: Which Framed the Constitution ... Vol. 3, p. 491, Document 4 Records of the Federal Convention Article 2, Section 1, Clause 1, http://press-pubs.uchicago.edu/founders/print_documents/a2_1_1s4.html.

47. Ibid.

48. McClanahan, *Founding Fathers*, 1407; DAFC, III:483–84.

49. Documentary History XIV: 185.

50. McClanahan, *Founding Fathers*, 2543; Documentary History, XIV:11

51. Letter from Thomas Jefferson to John Adams, 13 November 1787, https://founders.archives.gov/documents/Jefferson/01-12-02-0342.

52. Ibid.; Stewart, *The Summer of 1787*, 1026.

53. Wood, *Revolutionary Characters*, 135.

54. Cameron Kistler, "The Anti-Federalists and Presidential War Power," *Yale Law Journal*, Vol. 121, No. 2 (November 2011), 459–68; Published by: The Yale Law Journal Company, Inc., http://www.jstor.org/stable/23079337, Accessed: 20-09-2017 17:59 UTC; The Virginia Convention (June 5, 1788), in John P. Kaminski, Gaspare J. Saladino, Richard Leffler, Charles H. Schoenleber, and Margaret A. Hogan, ed., *The Documentary History of the Ratification of the Constitution Digital Edition*, (Charlottesville: University of Virginia Press, 2009), http://rotunda.upress.virginia.edu/founders/RNCN-02-08-02-0001-0118. [hereinafter Documentary History] The Virginia Convention (June 9,1788), in 9 Documentary History, supra note 8, at 1050, 1069.

55. Michael D. Ramsey, *Text and History in the War Powers Debate: A Reply to Professor Yoo*, 69 U. Chi. L. Rev. 1685, 1712 n.95 (2002); See Ramsey, supra note 7, at 1712.; See generally Jack N. Rakove, *Original Meanings: Politics and Ideas in the Making of the Constitution* (New York: Vintage Books ed. 1997), 151–52 (noting the Anti-Federalist faith in the traditional axioms of constitutional design.

56. McClanahan, *Founding Fathers*, 1295; Farrand, *The Records of the Federal Convention of 1787*, Vol. 1, 71.

57. McClanahan, *Founding Fathers*, 883.

58. The Convention ultimately turned the task of recasting all the initiatives of Presidential and Congressional power approved so far over to a "Committee of Detail" composed of Randolph, Wilson, Ellsworth, John Rutledge, and Nathaniel Gorham of Massachusetts. And the sweltering weather continued to make the delegates anxious to end their business. "At each inhaling of air," wrote one visitor to Philadelphia, "one worries about the next one. The slightest movement is painful." Many of the delegates from nearby states took the opportunity to return home while others fled to the countryside. Washington, in his usual taciturn style, recorded in his journal, "In company

with Mr. Govr. Morris and in his Phaeton with my horses, went up to one Jane Moore's (in whose house we lodged) in the vicinity of Valley Forge to get Trout." When they reconvened on August 6th, the delegates were eager to move the executive power business toward a conclusion.

59. Documentary history XVI: 479.

60. McClanahan, *Founding Fathers*, 1544.; Elliot, ed., *The Debates in the Several States Conventions on the Adoption of the federal Convention as recommended by the general convention at Philadelphia in 1787*, DAFC, III, 496.

61. McClanahan, *Founding Fathers*, 1544.

62. Ibid., 1568.

63. McClanahan, The Founding Fathers Guide to the Constitution, Kindle edition p. 1830; Documentary History XVI: 387-90.

64. McClanahan, *Founding Fathers*, 1439; Farrand, *The Records of the Federal Convention of 1787*, Vol. 2, 66.

65. McClanahan, *Founding Fathers*, 1439; Farrand, *The Records of the Federal Convention of 1787*, Vol 1, 65.

66. McClanahan, *Founding Fathers*, 1474; DAFC, III: 500.

67. He also feared the president would be too apt to select nominees from the small group of lawyers the president would know in the nation's capital. Mason put little faith in Senate confirmation as a barrier to bad presidential appointments. "The false complaisance which usually prevails in such cases will prevent a disagreement to the first nominations." Broadwater, *Forgotten Founder*, 2602; Farrand, Documentary History I: 86; II: 41–42, 82–83.

68. Alpheus T. Mason and Richard H. Leach, *In Quest of Freedom* (2nd ed., Englewood Cliffs: Prentice-Hall, 1973), 88.

69. Ibid.

70. Volume 3, Page 491, Document 4 Records of the Federal Convention Article 2, Section 1, Clause 1, http://press-pubs.uchicago.edu/founders/print_documents/a2_1_1s4.html.

71. Broadwater, *Forgotten Founder*, 894; Farrand, *The Records of the Federal Convention of 1787*, Vol. 1, 68–69; Vol. 2, 31, 118–119.

72. Broadwater, *Forgotten Founder*, 99; Farrand, *The Records of the Federal Convention of 1787*, Vol. 2, 497–502, 524–25

73. McClanahan, *Founding Fathers*, 1798; Farrand, *The Records of the Federal Convention of 1787*, Vol. *The Records of the Federal Convention of 1787*, Vol. 1, 80.

74. Broadwater, *Forgotten Founder*, 939; Farrand *The Records of the Federal Convention of 1787*, Vol. 2, 497–502.

75. Jack N. Rakove, "Philadelphia Story," *Wilson Quarterly* (1976-), Vol. 11, No. 2 (Spring, 1987), 105–21 Published by: Wilson Quarterly, Stable URL: http://www.jstor.org/stable/40257842, accessed: 12-12-2016 22:35 UTC.

76. Broadwater, *Forgotten Founder*, 816; Farrand, *The Records of the Federal Convention of 1787*, Vol. 3, 94.

77. Joseph Ellis, *American Sphinx: The Character of Thomas Jefferson* (New York: Knopf, 1997), 1521.

Chapter Eleven: Objections

1. R. Walton Moore "George Mason, The Statesman," *William and Mary Quarterly*, Vol. 13, No. 1 (January 1933), http://www.jstor.org/stable/1922831 Accessed: 13-05-2017 18:16 UTC, 10–17; Representative Beck of Pennsylvania, based on Mr. Beck's lectures at Oxford

2. Jeff Broadwater, *George Mason, Forgotten Founder* (Chapel Hill: University of North Carolina Press, 2006), 841; Max Farrand, ed., *The Records of the Federal Convention of 1787*, Vol. 1 (New Haven: Yale University Press, 1966; originally 1911), 48–50. See also C. Smith, *Wilson*, 221–25.

3. The evolution of Mason's objections to the Constitution can be traced in the following documents, all in PGM, vol. 3: "Notes on the Committee of Detail Report," 934–48; "Notes on Proposed Changes to Committee of Style Report," ca. 13 September 1787, 983–85; "Objections on the Committee of Style Report," ca. 16 September 1787, 991–94; GM to Thomas Jefferson, 26 May 1788, 1044–46; Memorandum of Thomas Jefferson, 30 September

4. Broadwater, *Forgotten Founder*, 868; GM to Beverly Randolph, 30 June 1787, PGM 3:918–19.

5. Farrand, *The Records of the Federal Convention of 1787*, Vol. 3; https://www.usconstitution.net/constframe.html; http://memory.loc.gov/cgi-bin/query/r?ammem/hlaw:@field(DOCID+@lit(fr003134)).

6. Ibid.

7.   For a succinct summary of the Framers' growing concern about "majoritarian excess," see Robert Middlekauff, *The Glorious Cause: The American Revolution, 1763–1789* (Oxford: Oxford University Press, 2007), 651–54. For the popular view of Mason as a champion of states' rights, see Kate Mason Rowland, *The Life of George Mason, 1725–1792* (New York: Russell & Russell, 1964; reprint of 1892 volume), 2:139–79.

8.   Maier, *Ratification*, 333.

9.   "Richard Henry Lee, Rhetoric and Rebellion," Lee Family Digital Archive, accessed February 15, 2019, http://leefamilyarchive.org/reference/theses/rhl-taylor/02.html.

10. So solemn was Washington in tone and temperament that there was a story, whether literal or apocryphal, told about Alexander Hamilton and Robert Morris. Hamilton and Morris had discussed how Washington's body language signaled to keep a respectful distance. Hamilton urged, then wagered Morris that he would not dare greet Washington with a friendly pat on the back. Taking up the challenge, Morris found Washington standing alone by the fireplace in a drawing room and gently slapped him on the shoulder: "My dear general, how happy I am to see you look so well." Washington fixed Morris with a frigid stare and stony silence. Morris melted into the shadows, with Hamilton smiling in the background. Ron Chernow, *Washington: A Life* (New York: Penguin Press, 2011), 1768; Edmund S. Morgan, *The Genius of George Washington* (New York: Norton, 1980), 5.

11. "Richard Henry Lee, Rhetoric and Rebellion."

12. Chernow, *Washington*, 1722; Chernow, *Alexander Hamilton*, 223.

13. Broadwater, *Forgotten Founder*, 1008; Farrand, *The Records of the Federal Convention of 1787*, Vol. 2, 581, 587–88.

14. "Amendments to the Constitution," June 8, 1789, https://founders.archives.gov/documents/Madison/01-12-02-0126; James Madison, "Speech on Amendments to the Constitution," TeachingAmericanHistory.org, June 8, 1789, http://teachingamericanhistory.org/library/document/speech-on-amendments-to-the-constitution/.

15. David O. Stewart, *The Summer of 1787* (New York: Simon & Schuster, 2007), 1079; ED (Elliot's Debates), VOL. III, 446 (June 16, 1788), http://memory.loc.gov/ammem/amlaw/lwed.html.

16. Thomas Fleming, *The Great Divide* (New York: Da Capo Press, 2015), 37; Jefferson to Madison, Dec 20 1787; PTJ Digital; Ellis, *The Quartet*, 959; JM TO TJ, 18 November 1788, 15 March 1789, RL (Republic of Letters : The Correspondence of letters between Thomas Jefferson and James Madison 1776-1826, 3 vols. New York, 1995) 1:567, 587.

17. Broadwater, *Forgotten Founder*, 987; Farrand, *The Records of the Federal Convention of 1787*, Vol. 2, 478–79. Memorandum for Maryland Delegates, 31 August 1787, PGM, 3: 974–75.

18. Broadwater, *Forgotten Founder*, 1009; Farrand, *The Records of the Federal Convention of 1787*, Vol. 2, 581, 585–88.

19. Carol Berkin, *The Bill of Rights: The Fight to Secure America's Liberties* (New York: Simon & Schuster, 2016).

20. Stewart, *The Summer of 1787*, 839–40; Hutson, 199–200 (*Washington Diary*).

21. Broadwater, *Forgotten Founder*, 1013; Farrand, *The Records of the Federal Convention of 1787*, Vol. 2, 565–80; Madison to Jefferson, 24 October 1787, Farrand, *The Records of the Federal Convention of 1787*, Vol. 3, 135–36; Ralph Ketcham, *James Madison, A Biography* (Charlottesville and London: University Press of Virginia, 1994), 222.

22. William Findley spoke for many others in 1796 when he said that the people who had raised objections to the Constitution during the ratification struggle were "called Anti-federalists, as a name of reproach," and then added, "I do, and always did, treat the appellation with contempt."

23. Morris's death, in 1816, was gruesome even by the standards of the time. Suffering a painful blockage of the urinary tract, he tried to open it himself with a piece of whalebone from his wife's undergarments. He was found dead of the attempt.

24. Stewart, *The Summer of 1787*, 1134; Farrand, *The Records of the Federal Convention of 1787*, Vol. 2, 645, 641–43.

25. Ibid.

26. Farrand, *The Records of the Federal Convention of 1787*, 582.

27. Ibid.

28. Mason Papers, 3:903-4; Max Farrand, ed., *The Records of the Federal Convention of 1787*, 4 vols. (New Haven: Yale University Press, 1937), 4:75–76. Rutland thinks Mason may not have written these words, but he wrote

about the same thing to Arthur Lee on May 21. Mason Papers, 3:882; Pacheco, *New York State Bar Journal*, 12.

29. Chernow, *Washington*; Fahim, "George Washington Letter Found in Scrapbook," *New York Times*, April 27, 2007, 31; Maxey, Portrait of Elizabeth Willing Powel, 30, 32

30. Fleming, *The Great Divide*, 33; GW to Lafayette, June 18, 1788, PGW digital.

31. Chernow, *Washington*, 1794; Robert A. Goldwin, *From Parchment to Power: How James Madison Used the Bill of Rights to Save the Constitution*, (Aei Press, 1997), 59.

32. Chernow, *Washington*, 1814; PWP 4:1 Letter to James Craik, September 8, 1789.a

Chapter Twelve: A Slow Poison

1. The scholarship on slavery in this era is extensive. Foundational works include Ira Berlin, *Many Thousands Gone: The First Two Centuries of Slavery in North America* (Cambridge, MA: Harvard University Press, 1998); Ira Berlin and Ronald Hoffman, eds., *Slavery and Freedom in the Age of the American Revolution* (Urbana: University of Illinois Press, 1986); Kathleen M. Brown, *Good Wives, Nasty Wenches, and Anxious Patriarchs: Gender, Race, and Power in Colonial Virginia* (Chapel Hill: University of North Carolina Press, 1996); Allan Kulikoff, *Tobacco and Slaves: The Development of Southern Cultures in the Chesapeake, 1680–1800* (Chapel Hill: University of North Carolina Press, 1986); and Edmund S. Morgan, *American Slavery, American Freedom: The Ordeal of Colonial Virginia* (New York: W. W. Norton, 1975); Bill O'Reilly and Martin Dugard, *Killing England: The Brutal Struggle for American Independence* (New York: Henry Holt and Co., 2017), 1322: "Slavery was legal and condoned in all thirteen colonies, but by 1776 only Georgia and South Carolina still allowed the importation of slaves. Many members of Congress, including Thomas Jefferson, not just owned slaves but also sold them as a form of commerce. However, the issue of slavery was making many Americans uncomfortable. One of them was Jefferson. He blamed King George for bringing slavery to America. His original language in the Declaration concerning freedom caused considerable debate in Congress, particularly from Georgia and

South Carolina. It was later modified to avoid the slavery issue. The congressional delegates deleted the following paragraph: He [George III] has waged cruel war against human nature itself, violating its most sacred rights of life and liberty in the persons of a distant people who never offended him, captivating & carrying them into slavery in another hemisphere or to incur miserable death in their transportation thither. This piratical warfare, the opprobrium of infidel powers, is the warfare of the Christian King of Great Britain. Determined to keep open a market where Men should be bought & sold, he has prostituted his negative for suppressing every legislative attempt to prohibit or restrain this execrable commerce among us, and to purchase that liberty of which he has deprived them, by murdering the people on whom he has obtruded them: thus paying off former crimes committed against the Liberties of one people, with crimes which he urges them to commit against the lives of another. Although those words disappeared from the Declaration of Independence, Jefferson kept them in his private library"; "This is a cancer that we must get rid of," wrote Charles Thomson from Philadelphia. "It is a blot on our character that must be wiped out. If it cannot be done by religion, reason and philosophy, confident I am that it will one day be by blood." Charles Thomson to Jefferson, November 2, 1785, ibid., IX, 9–10. 50.

2.   David O. Stewart, *The Summer of 1787* (New York: Simon & Schuster, 2007), 924: "The brutality of the passage from Africa, and the high mortality rate among the enslaved, were widely reviled. While the Convention sat, a Philadelphia magazine carried an emotional depiction of the journey: The rolling sea hurries the heaving hearts: the sighing souls escape! ... The groans of a hundred men, the sighs of a hundred women, the cries of a hundred youths are one! ... Silence prevails, and the dead bodies are thrown to the watchful sharks, whose ravenous jaws are glutted with the flesh of men! The markets in the west are full of slaves. The fathers of oppression are there: their flinty hearts regard them as beasts of burden."

3.   Max Farrand, ed., *The Records of the Federal Convention of 1787*, Vol. 2 (New Haven: Yale University Press, 1966; originally 1911), 199, 319, 349, 451, 370; Pauline Maier, *Ratification: The People Debate the Constitution* (New York: Simon and Schuster, 2010), 300.

4.   DHRC X: 1338–39, 1341; Maier, *Ratification, 1647.*

5. Maier, *Ratification*, 1609; John Tyler, another delegate to the Virginia ratifying convention in 1788, particularly condemned the "wicked clause" allowing the slave trade to continue until 1808.

6. See Berlin, *Many Thousands Gone*; Berlin, *Slavery and Freedom in the Age of the American Revolution*; Brown, *Good Wives, Nasty Wenches, and Anxious Patriarchs*; Kulikoff, *Tobacco and Slaves*; and Morgan, *American Slavery, American Freedom*.

7. Theodore Roosevelt and John T. Morse Jr. (contributor), *American Statesmen: The Constructive Period. Gouvernor Morris*, Vol. 8 (Leopold Classic Library, 2016), 138; Farrand, *The Records of the Federal Convention of 1787*, Vol. 3, 271, 282; Stewart, *The Summer of 1787*, 928: "Not that the slave trade lacked for defenders. General Pinckney would speak for many in 1788 when he declared his commitment to it: [W]hile there remained one acre of swamp-land uncleared of South Carolina, I would raise my voice against restricting the importation of negroes. I am as thoroughly convinced as that gentleman is, that the nature of our climate, and the flat, swampy situation of our country, obliges us to cultivate our lands with negroes, and that without them South Carolina would soon be a desert waste. In the same remarks, General Pinckney stressed that many Convention delegates opposed the slave trade, which he attributed to 'the religious and political prejudices of the Eastern and Middle States,' while Virginia 'was warmly opposed to our importing more slaves.'"

8. "George Mason's Slaves," Gunston Hall website, accessed February 17, 2019, http://www.gunstonhall.org/georgemason/slavery/slaves.html.

9. Jeff Broadwater, *George Mason, Forgotten Founder* (Chapel Hill: University of North Carolina Press, 2006), 66; Terry K. Dunn, ed., *The Recollections of John Mason: George Mason's Son Remembers His Father and Life at Gunston Hall* (Marshall, VA: EPM Publications, 2004), 60–61, 78–80.

10. Kate Mason Rowland, *The Life of George Mason, 1725–1792* (New York: Russell & Russell, 1964; reprint of 1892 volume), 103.

11. Lorri Glover, *Founders as Fathers, The Private Lives and Politics of the American Revolution* (New Haven and London, Yale University Press, 2014), 792; see in general Dunn, *Recollections*.

12. See in general Dunn, *Recollections*; Glover, *Founders as Fathers*, 632.

13. Glover, *Founders as Fathers*, 633; see also Dunn, *Recollections*.

14. On the role of slavery in the convention, see Paul Finkelman, *Slavery and the Founders: Race and Liberty in the Age of Jefferson* (London: Routledge, 1996), 1–30.

15. Glover, *Founders as Fathers*, 792; see also, Dunn, *Recollections.*

16. "George Mason's Slaves," Gunston Hall website.

17. See foundational works including Berlin, *Many Thousands Gone*; Berlin, *Slavery and Freedom in the Age of the American Revolution*; "George Mason's Slaves," Gunston Hall website.

18. "George Mason's Slaves," Gunston Hall website.

19. Similar to Jefferson's Monticello, where the slaves basically had their own place of abode at Mulberry Row; "George Mason's Slaves," Gunston Hall website.

20. "George Mason's Slaves," Gunston Hall website.

21. Ron Chernow, *Washington: A Life* (New York: Penguin Press, 2011), 399.

22. Glover, *Founders as Fathers*, 801–2; Paul Jennings, *A Colored Man's Reminiscences of Madison*, (Ithica, NY: Cornell University Library, 1865), 11–15. For slavery in Jefferson's white house, see Lucia C. Stanton, *"Those who Labor for My Happiness,": Slavery at Jefferson's Monticello* (Charlottesville: University of Virginia Press, 2012), ch. 3; Chernow, *Washington*, 374, 1784; "Whatever his own nascent abolitionist views, George Washington wasn't about to make an open stand at the [constitutional] convention and joined other delegates in daydreaming that slavery would fade away at some nebulous future date. Isolated critics branded Washington a hypocrite for clinging to his slaves after a revolution fought in the name of freedom. At the Massachusetts convention that ratified the Constitution, one speaker deplored his status as a slaveholder. "Oh, Washington, what a name he has had! How he has immortalized himself!" he exclaimed, then remarked that Washington "holds those in slavery who have as good a right to be free as he has. He is still for self and, in my opinion, his character has sunk 50 percent." A Massachusetts newspaper, echoing this charge, regretted that Washington had "wielded the sword in defense of American liberty yet at the same time, was, and is to this day, living upon the labors of several hundreds of miserable Africans as freeborn as himself."; Broadwater, *Forgotten Founder*: "When private manumissions produced a notable increase in the number of free blacks in Virginia, the legislature responded by increasing restrictions on them until, by 1806, it

required all newly freed blacks to leave the state within twelve months."
Winthrop D. Jordan, *White over Black: American Attitudes toward the
Negro, 1550–1812* (Chapel Hill: Omohundro Institute and University of
North Carolina Press, 2012), 348. Hostility toward free blacks was hardly
unique to Virginia. At the same time that Massachusetts, in 1788, banned
the slave trade, it also banned voluntary immigration from Africa. Ibid.,
410–11.

23. Jean B. Lee, *Experiencing Mount Vernon: Eyewitness Accounts, 1784–
1865* (Charlottesville: University of Virginia Press, 2006), 69; Chernow,
Washington, 382, 2110: "Still, Washington remained a tough master.
Slavery depended on exerting a sizable degree of terror to cow slaves into
submission. Before the war Washington had shipped two difficult slaves to
the West Indies, where life expectancy was short in the tropical climate. In
March 1793, when [Washington's overseer] Whitting told Washington
about a refractory slave named Ben, Washington replied that, if he persisted
in his misbehavior, Whitting should warn Ben that "I will ship him off as I
did Waggoner Jack for the West Indies, where he will have no opportunity
to play such pranks." While Washington ordinarily did not allow slaves to
be whipped, he sometimes condoned it if all else failed. Such was the case in
January 1793 with a slave named Charlotte, whom Martha had found
"indolent" and "idle." "Your treatment of Charlotte was very proper,"
Washington advised Whitting, "and if she, or any other of the servants, will
not do their duty by fair means or are impertinent, correction (as the only
alternative) must be administered."

24. PWP, 12:524. Letter to Anthony Whitting, May 5, 1793; Chernow,
Washington, 382.

25. Lee, *Experiencing Mount Vernon*, 69; Chernow, *Washington*, 382, 2110.

26. Chernow, *Washington*, 374, 1784.

27. *Diaries*, 5:260. Washington's Diary entries for January 3 and 4, 1788;
Chernow, *Washington*, 1656.

28. Madison to Jefferson, July 30, 1793, in James Morton Smith, *The Republic
of Letters: The Correspondence between Thomas Jefferson and James
Madison* (New York: W. W. Norton & Company, 1995), 2:798.; Glover,
Founders as Fathers, 843.

29. PWC, 9:70. Letter to Daniel Jenifer Adams, July 20, 1772; Chernow,
Washington, 372

30. Henry Wiencek, *An imperfect God: George Washington, His Slaves and the Creation of America* (New York: Farrar, Straus and Giroux, 2003), 45; Chernow, *Washington*, 372.

31. "George Mason's Slaves," Gunston Hall website.

32. *PWP*, 12: 634. Letter to Anthony Whitting, May 26, 1793; Chernow, *Washington*, 389.

33. "George Mason's Slaves," Gunston Hall website.

34. Ibid.

35. Ibid.

36. Ibid.

37. Ibid.

38. Ibid.

39. "Scheme for Repleving Goods" *PGM*, 1:161; Robert A. Rutland, *George Mason and the War for Independence* (Williamsburg, VA: Virginia Independence Bicentennial Commission), 1976, 13; Broadwater, *Forgotten Founder*, 190.

40. *WWR*, 594, Letter to Robert Morris, April 12, 1786; Chernow, *Washington*, 1636.

41. William Peden, ed., *Notes on the State of Virginia* (Chapel Hill: University of North Carolina, 1955), 138, 163; Joseph Ellis, *American Sphinx: The Character of Thomas Jefferson* (New York: Knopf, 1997), 444, 1573:"More has been written on Jefferson and slavery than any other subject in the Jefferson corpus. And here there is nothing like a scholarly consensus. The best defense of Jefferson's record is Douglas L. Wilson, 'Thomas Jefferson and the Character Issue,' *Atlantic Monthly*, CCLXX (1992), 61–78. The most sustained scholarly attack of Jefferson's record is Paul Finkelman, 'Jefferson and Slavery: "Treason Against the Hopes of the World,"' Onuf, ed., *Jeffersonian Legacies*, 181–221. The standard survey of the subject is Miller, *The Wolf by the Ears*. The deepest probe into the psychological issues at stake is Jordan, *White over Black*, 429–81. The best look at the Virginia context is McColley, *Slavery and Jeffersonian Virginia*. The most extensive effort to understand his latter-day procrastinations is Freehling, *The Road to Disunion*, 122–57. And this merely scratches the proverbial surface."

42. Patrick Henry, 18 January 1773, *PHC*, 1:152–153; "This is a cancer that we must get rid of," wrote Charles Thomson from Philadelphia to Thomas Jefferson. "It is a blot on our character that must be wiped out. If it cannot

be done by religion, reason and philosophy, confident I am that it will one day be by blood." Charles Thomson to Jefferson, November 2, 1785, ibid., IX, 9–10. 50; Glover, *Founders as Fathers*, 250; George Mason essay, 23 December 1765, PGM, 1:61; Patrick Henry, 18 January 1773, *PHC*, 1:152–1530

43. Robert Meade, *Patrick Henry*, 2 volumes (Philadelphia and New York, 1957–1969) 1:299–300; *WWH (William Wirt Henry, Patrick Henry, Correspondence and Speeches*, 3 volumes (New York, 1891), 1:152–53; Henry Mayer, *A Son of Thunder: Patrick Henry and the American Republic* (New York: Grove Press, 1991), 651.

44. PGM, 1:277, 287–89; Glover, *Founders as Fathers*, 603.

45. Dunn, *Recollections*, 12–13; Broadwater, *Forgotten Founder*, 957; Farrand, *The Records of the Federal Convention of 1787*, 2:369–71; PGM, 3:965-66; The George Mason essay, 23 December 1765, PGM, 1:61; Patrick Henry, 18 January 1773, PHC, 1:152–153; On the role of slavery in the convention, see Paul Finkelman, *Slavery and the Founders: Race and Liberty in the Age of Jefferson* (London, 1996), 1–30; *Founding Brothers: The Revolutionary Generation* (New York, 2000), 81–119.

46. Pittman, *The Alabama Lawyer: Official Organ State Bar of Alabama*, Volume 15; The Documentary History of the Ratification of the Constitution: Ratification of the Constitution by the States, Maryland (2).

47. Stewart, *The Summer of 1787*, 498–502; The Virginia Plan was a set of fifteen proposals that the governor of Virginia Edmund Randolph presented to the delegates of the Constitutional Convention in Philadelphia, on May 29, 1787. These resolutions essentially outlined a new form of government. The Virginia delegates proposed a strong national government that could make and enforce laws and collect taxes. The plan would establish a federal system of government under which the people would be governed by both the state and national governments. Another feature of this proposal was a bicameral legislature, in which representation would be proportional to a state's population. Larger states favored this element of the plan; see "The Virginia Plan, May 29, 1787," Educations @ Library of Virginia website, accessed February 18, 2019, http://edu.lva.virginia.gov/online_classroom/shaping_the_constitution/doc/virginia_plan.

48. George Mason to, 22 August 1787, PGM, 3:966; Peden, *Notes on the State of Virginia*, 163; Glover, *Founders as Fathers*, 768; "George Mason's

Slaves," Gunston Hall website; see Ellis, *American Sphinx*: "More has been
written on Jefferson and slavery than any other subject in the Jefferson
corpus. And here there is nothing like a scholarly consensus. The best
defense of Jefferson's record is Douglas L. Wilson, 'Thomas Jefferson and
the Character Issue,' Atlantic Monthly, CCLXX (1992), 61–78. The most
sustained scholarly attack of Jefferson's record is Paul Finkelman, 'Jefferson
and Slavery: "Treason Against the Hopes of the World,"' Onuf, ed.,
Jeffersonian Legacies, 181–221. The standard survey of the subject is Miller,
The Wolf by the Ears. The deepest probe into the psychological issues at
stake is Jordan, *White over Black*, 429–81. The best look at the Virginia
context is McColley, Slavery and Jeffersonian Virginia. The most extensive
effort to understand his latter-day procrastinations is Freehling, *The Road to
Disunion*, 122."; Joseph Ellis, "American Sphinx: The Contradictions of
Thomas Jefferson," *Civilization: The Magazine of the Library of Congress*,
November–December 1994 : "*White over Black*, a magisterial reappraisal of
race relations in early America that featured a section on Jefferson. Jordan's
book, which won the major prizes, offered a subtle and psychologically
sophisticated assessment of Jefferson's attitudes toward slavery and blacks,
suggesting that he was emblematic of white American society in the way his
deep-seated racist values were hidden within folds of his personality. White
over Black was hardly a heavy-handed indictment of Jefferson. Jordan's
major point was that racism had infiltrated the American soul very early in
our history and that Jefferson simply provided the most resonant example of
the virulence of racist values and the commingling of racial and sexual
drives."

49. "George Mason's Slaves," Gunston Hall website.
50. Ibid. Yet one scholar remained skeptical of Mason's professed opposition to
    slavery. "Mason sought the curtailment of the trade not as a preliminary step
    toward emancipation but as a measure essential to the security of slavery. He
    sought to strengthen, not weaken [the institution]."
51. Mason, *Virginia Ratification Debates*, 11 June 1788, DHRC, 9:1161;
    Glover, *Founders as Fathers*, 756;
52. WWR 1002–3. Letter to Lawrence Lewis, August 4, 1797; Chernow,
    Washington, 2544.
53. PTJRS, VII, 652; Jon Meacham, *Thomas Jefferson, The Art of Power* (New
    York: Random House, 2012), 2637.

54. Meacham, *Jefferson*, 2629; Miller, *Wolf by the Ears: Thomas Jefferson and Slavery* (Charlottesville: University of Virginia Press, 1991).

55. https://founders.archives.gov/documents/Madison/99-02-02-0521; James Madison, September 1825.

56. "Scheme for Replevying Goods," PGM 1:61; Rutland, *George Mason and the War for Independence*, 13; Broadwater, *Forgotten Founder*, 13, 179–80.

57. "Scheme for Replevying Goods," PGM 1:61; Rutland, *George Mason and the War for Independence*, 13; Broadwater, *Forgotten*, 13, 190.

58. Robert A. Rutland, "Framing and Identifying the First Ten Amendments," in Leonard W. Levy and Dennis J. Mahoney, eds., *The Framing and Ratification of the Constitution* (London: MacMillan Publishing Co., 1987), 305; Margaret Stimmann Branson, "George Mason: The Reluctant Founder," Center for Civic Education website, accessed February 18, 2019, http://www.civiced.org/resources/curriculum/mason#note28.

59. "George Mason's Slaves," Gunston Hall website.

60. Helen Hill Miller, *George Mason, Constitutionalist* (Cambridge: Harvard University Press, 1938), 180–213.

61. "George Mason's Slaves," Gunston Hall website.

62. "George Mason's Objections to the Constitution," Gunston Hall website, accessed February 18, 2019, http://www.gunstonhall.org/library/archives/manuscripts/objections.html.

63. Helen H. Miller, *George Mason: Gentleman Revolutionary* (Chapel Hill: University of North Carolina Press, 1975), 254.

64. "George Mason's Objections to the Constitution," Gunston Hall.

65. Peter Wallenstein, "Flawed Keepers of the Flame: The Interpreters of George Mason," *Virginia Magazine of History and Biography*, 102: 2 (1994), 229–260, JSTOR, www.jstor.org/stable/4249431.

66. Ellis, *American Sphinx*, 741: "For one brief moment, in 1789, [Jefferson] seemed to entertain a bold, if somewhat bizarre, scheme whereby emancipated slaves would be 'intermingled' with imported German peasants on fifty-acre farms where both groups could learn proper work habits. But even this short-lived proposal served only to expose the inherent intractability of the postemancipation world as Jefferson tried to imagine it. His fundamental conviction, one that he never questioned, was that white and black Americans could not live together in harmony. He had already

explained why in Notes: 'Deep rooted prejudices entertained by the whites; ten thousand recollections, by the blacks, of the injuries they have sustained; new provocations … '"; Ibid., 1326: "He was no longer convinced that the end of slavery was near. Certainly he would never live to see it: 'I leave it, therefore, to time.' Silence had become his official policy."

67. History.com Editors, "Missouri Compromise," History, October 29, 2009, last updated September 11, 2018, http://www.history.com/topics/missouri-compromise: "In the years leading up to the Missouri Compromise of 1820, tensions began to rise between pro-slavery and anti-slavery factions within the U.S. Congress and across the country. They reached a boiling point after Missouri's 1819 request for admission to the Union as a slave state, which threatened to upset the delicate balance between slave states and free states. To keep the peace, Congress orchestrated a two-part compromise, granting Missouri's request but also admitting Maine as a free state."

68. *A Dissertation on Slavery: With a Proposal for the Gradual Abolition of It, In the State of Virginia (1796)*; James Rutledge Roesch, State's Rights Vol. 2: St. George Tucker's Views on the Constitution, Jul 17, 2014, https://www. abbevilleinstitute.org/review/states-rights-vol-2-st-george-tuckers-views-on-the-constitution/; "St. George Tucker was born in 1752 in Bermuda. At the age of 19, Tucker left Bermuda for Virginia, where he studied law at the College of William & Mary under George Wythe (mentor to Thomas Jefferson, John Marshall, Henry Clay, and other Southern luminaries). When colonial courts closed in protest against taxation without representation, Tucker smuggled arms from the West Indies to Virginia and South Carolina. During the American Revolution, Tucker enlisted as a major in the Virginia militia, and fought with honor at Guilford's Court House and Yorktown. By the war's end, he had advanced to lieutenant colonel. In 1786, Tucker was a delegate to the Annapolis Convention—the prelude to the Philadelphia Convention. Tucker then took up a professorship at his alma mater, and later served as a state and federal judge. His classes, which he insisted on teaching from his Williamsburg home in order to have full access to his library, soon became famous. Although his courses were based on Blackstone's voluminous legal commentaries, Tucker believed that his students required formal education in the American (as well as Virginian) innovations of British law. To teach his students the principles of American constitutional law, Tucker annotated Blackstone with commentaries of his

own. At first, he simply read his annotations to his classes, but in 1803, after encouragement from his friends, Tucker published his commentaries. At the time, Tucker's commentaries—the first systematic analysis of American constitutionalism—were widely accepted as authoritative, and were even cited by the Supreme Court in many significant rulings."

69. Chad Vanderford, "A Dissertation on Slavery: With a Proposal for the Gradual Abolition of It, In the State of Virginia (1796)," *Encyclopedia Virginia, Virginia Foundation for the Humanities,* https://www. encyclopediavirginia.org/A_Dissertation_on_Slavery_With_a_Proposal_ for_the_Gradual_Abolition_of_It_In_the_State_of_Virginia_1796#start_ entry.

70. Ibid.

71. Ibid.

72. Ibid.

73. Ibid.

74. Ibid.

75. Ibid.

76. Ibid.

77. Stephen E. Ambrose, "Founding Fathers and Slaveholders," *Smithsonian Magazine,* November 2202, https://www.smithsonianmag.com/history/ founding-fathers-and-slaveholders-72262393/#5ZsZeCA7OJqatYWF.99

78. Broadwater, *Forgotten Founder,* 755, 1098; Rowland, *Mason,* 2:161–62. "Rowland's denial of Mason's abolitionist tendencies commences a lyrical defense of "the old slave-holding aristocracy of the South." Mason is reborn as an abolitionist in Bowen, *Miracle at Philadelphia,* 95; and W. Miller, *Business of May Next,* 118."

79. Broadwater, *Forgotten Founder,* 757.

80. Ibid.

81. Ambrose, "Founding Fathers and Slaveholders."

82. Ibid.

83. Glover, *Founders as Fathers,* 602.

84. Mason, Ratification Debates, June 11, 1788 in *DHRC,* 9:1161; Glover, *Founders as Fathers,* 603.

85. Glover, *Founders as Fathers,* 604.

86. Chernow, *Washington,* 1622: "Lafayette's abolitionism may have been influenced by his wartime association with James Armistead, a slave who

served under him in Virginia and operated as a valuable spy, infiltrating the British lines under the guise of being an escaped slave. When Washington received Lafayette's letter, the war was winding down and he was dwelling on his impaired finances. His economic well-being depended on slavery, so that whatever his theoretical sympathy with Lafayette's idea, he could not have been thrilled by the timing. Not wanting to disillusion his worshipful protégé, he replied the way a fond father might write to an ardent but impractical son: "The scheme, my dear Marq[ui]s, which you propose as a precedent to encourage the emancipation of the black people of this country … is a striking evidence of the benevolence of your heart."

87. Chernow, *Washington*, 1621.
88. *WWR*, 1110. Letter from Lafayette to Washington, February 5, 1783; Chernow, *Washington*, 1621.
89. Lafayette To Washington, February 5, 1783, in *Lafayette in the Age of the American Revolution*, 5 Vols., 5:90–93; Glover, *Founders as Fathers*, 616.
90. Chernow, *Washington*, 1627.
91. Glover, *Founders as Fathers*, 617.
92. Ibid.
93. Madison to James Madison Sr, September 8, 1783, *PJM (Congressional)*, 7: 304; Glover, *Founders as Fathers*, 620.
94. Patrick Henry to January 18, 1773, *PHC*, 1:153; Glover, *Founders as Fathers*, 626; Patrick Henry to January 18, 1773, *PHC*, 1:153.
95. Glover, *Founders as Fathers*, 626.
96. That was the same reason that Dolley Madison gave when contending with her decidedly undeferential "maid," Sukey. An exasperated Dolley conceded that it was "terribly inconvenient to do without her." Dolley Madison to Anna Cuttts, c. July 23 1818 in *The Selected Letters of Dolley Payne Madison*, 231; Glover, *Founders as Fathers*, 627.
97. Glover, *Founders as Fathers*, 807–8.
98. Madison, June 6, 1787, in Eliot, *Debates in the Several State Conventions*, 5:162; Glover, *Founders as Fathers*, 627–28.
99. Glover, *Founders as Fathers*, 860.
100. Madison, June 6, 1787, in Eliot, *Debates in the Several State Conventions*, 5: 162; Glover, *Founders as Fathers*, 627–28.
101. "George Mason's Slaves," Gunston Hall website.

102. Peter Wallenstein, "Flawed Keepers of the Flame," *The Virginia Magazine of History and Biography*, vol. 102, no. 2, April 1994; "George Mason's Slaves," Gunston Hall website.

103. Wallenstein, "Flawed Keepers of the Flame."

104. "George Mason's Slaves," Gunston Hall website.

105. See, for example, Stewart, *The Summer of 1787*, 204: "Slavery was the original sin in which the nation was conceived."

106. Ellis, *Revolutionary Summer*, 24.

107. Ibid.; AP 3:411.

108. Wood, *Revolutionary Characters*, 42.

109. Ellis, *American Sphinx*, 1462.

110. Stewart, *The Summer of 1787*, 1244.

111. Richard Jerome, "Seven Pillars of Freedom," *Time Special Edition: Founding Fathers*, 7.

Chapter Thirteen: The Virginia Ratifying Convention

1. "Mason Family Genealogy," George Mason's Gunston Hall, accessed February 18, 2019, http://www.gunstonhall.org/index.php/george-mason/mason-family.

2. Robert A. Rutland and Charles F. Hobson, eds., *The Papers of George Mason* (Chapel Hill: University Press of North Carolina, 1970), 10:226–27.

3. "From George Washington to George Mason," Founders Online, October 7, 1787, https://founders.archives.gov/documents/Washington/04-05-02-0330; "To George Washington to George Mason," Founders Online, October 7, 1787, https://founders.archives.gov/documents/Washington/04-05-02-0331.

4. "From George Washington to George Mason," Founders Online, October 7, 1787, https://founders.archives.gov/documents/Washington/04-05-02-0330; "To George Washington to George Mason," Founders Online, October 7, 1787, https://founders.archives.gov/documents/Washington/04-05-02-0331.

5. Pauline Maier, *Ratification: The People Debate the Constitution* (New York: Simon and Schuster, 2010), 274; Donald Jackson and Dorothy Twohig, eds., *The Diaries of George Washington*, 4 vols. (Charlottesville: University Press of Virginia, 1976–1978), 186–87.

6. Ron Chernow, *Alexander Hamilton* (London: Penguin Books, 2005), 2136.

7. Ibid., 1072.

8. Letter from John Dawson to James Madison, September 25, 1787.

9. Gordon S. Wood, *Revolutionary Characters: What Made the Founders Different* (New York: Penguin Press, 2006), 587: "The Federalist writers and speakers … responded as eighteenth-century gentlemen would: with the traditional elitist weapons of satire and invective, saturating the political climate with vituperation and venom the likes of which have never been equaled in our national history. But such verbal abuse and ridicule—against democracy, demagoguery, vulgarity—were rhetorical devices designed for a different culture from that which America was creating. Such calumny and invective as the Federalists expressed were supposed to be calculated and deliberately exaggerated, not a genuine expression of the satirists' inner emotions, and were justifiable because they were the result of the righteous indignation that any gentleman would feel in similar circumstances."

10. DHRC, John P. Kaminski, Gaspare J. Saladino, Richard Leffler, Charles H. Schoenleber, and Margaret A. Hogan, ed., *The Documentary History of the Ratification of the Constitution Digital Edition* (Charlottesville: University of Virginia Press, 2009). Canonic URL: http://rotunda.upress.virginia.edu/ founders/RNCN-03-13-02-0177-0002 [accessed 08 Jun 2017] Original source: Commentaries on the Constitution, Volume XIII: Commentaries on the Constitution, No. 1.

11. Ibid.; Hughes, a lawyer, was in Alexandria to attend the Fairfax County court. He had just visited Gates at the latter's plantation.

12. Ibid.

13. *New York Morning Post*, 1 November; New Haven Gazette, 8 November; state Gazette of South Carolina, 24 December; State Gazette of North Carolina, 7 February. During a debate in the Constitutional Convention on 31 August, Mason declared "that he would sooner chop off his right hand than put it to the Constitution as it now stands" (Farrand, II, 479). He repeated the statement in a debate in the House of Delegates on 25 October. (See "The General Assembly Calls a State Convention," 25–31 October, above.)

14. Kaminski, DHRC; *New York Morning Post*, 1 November; New Haven Gazette, 8 November; state Gazette of South Carolina, 24 December; State Gazette of North Carolina, 7 February. During a debate in the Constitutional Convention on 31 August, Mason declared "that he would

sooner chop off his right hand than put it to the Constitution as it now stands" (Farrand, II, 479). He repeated the statement in a debate in the House of Delegates on 25 October. (See "The General Assembly Calls a State Convention," 25–31 October, above.)

15. R. Carter Pittman, *George Mason of Gunston Hall, Father of the American Bill of Rights* 15 Ala. Law. 196 1954.

16. "To George Mason from George Washington," Founders Online, October 7, 1787, https://founders.archives.gov/documents/ Washington/04-05-02-0331; Mason's enclosure, his Objections to the Constitution of Government Formed by the Convention (DLC:GW), is included in CD-ROM:GW and is printed in Rutland, *The Papers of George Mason*, 3:991–94. For the text of Mason's statement and its publication beginning in November, see George Mason: Objections to the Constitution, in Kaminski and Saladino, Documentary History of the Ratification of the Constitution, 8:41–46. GW made an abstract of Mason's statement, c.7 Oct. 1787, on the cover. For the reaction of GW and James Madison to Mason's criticism of the Constitution, see GW to Madison, 10 Oct., and Madison to GW, 18 October. It was through the agency of GW's secretary Tobias Lear that Mason's "Objections to the Constitution" first appeared in print on 22 Nov. in the Virginia Journal, and Alexandria Advertiser. Lear wrote John Langdon on 3 Dec. that George Mason had given his objections "in manuscript to persons in all parts of the country where he supposed they would make an impression, but avoided publishing them.—I waited for a long time in expectation that they would appear in the publick papers, but finding they did not, I conveyed a copy of them to the printer of the Virginia Journal who published them, this has had a good effect as the futility of them strikes every unprejudiced person who reads them.—I have answered some of them & am now answering the rest, but as it is under an assumed signature, it is not known, even to the General, by whom it is done" (Kaminski, DHRC, 8:196–98). Lear's attack on Mason's "Objections" under the name of "Brutus appeared in the Virginia Journal, and Alexandria Advertiser; Mason's "Objections" were printed in newspapers throughout the country.

17. Nelson, a planter, was governor in 1781. He represented York County in the House of Burgesses, 1701–1776, the revolutionary conventions, 1774–1776, and in the House of Delegates, 1777–1781, 1782–1784, and 1786–1788. He

was a delegate to Congress, 1775–1777, 1779, and a signer of the
Declaration of Independence. Nelson apparently did not answer Washington
until July 17, 1788 (not found), three weeks after Virginia had ratified the
Constitution. Harrison (1726–179)—-a planter, and governor from 1781 to
1784—represented Charles City County in the House of Burgesses, 1748–
1776, the revolutionary conventions, 1774–1775, and the House of
Delegates, 1776–1781, 1787–1791 lie was a delegate from Surry, 1785–1786,
and Speaker of the House, 1778–1781, 1785–1786. Harrison was a delegate
to Congress, 1774–1777, and a signer of the Declaration of Independence.
He represented Charles City County in the state Convention, where he voted
against ratification of the Constitution. He replied to Washington on
October 4(below). Henry was governor from 1776 to 1779 and again from
1784 to 1786.

18. George Washington to Patrick Henry, Benjamin Harrison, and Thomas
Nelson, Jr., Mount Vernon, 24 September; Kaminski, DHRC.

19. Jon Meacham, *Thomas Jefferson, The Art of Power* (New York: Random
House, 2012), 1216; PTJ XII, 332, 350–51.

20. Meacham, *Jefferson*, 1216–18; PTJ XII, 332, 350–51.

21. Meacham, *Jefferson*, 1216–18; PTJ XII, 332, 350–51.

22. Lorri Glover, *Founders as Fathers, The Private Lives and Politics of the
American Revolution (New Haven and London,* Yale University Press,
2014), 901.

23. GW to Charles Carter, 7 December 1787, *PWCS 5*: 492; Joseph J. Ellis, *The
Quartet: Orchestrating the Second American Revolution, 1783–1789* (New
York: Alfred A. Knopf, 2015), 780.

24. Ron Chernow, *Washington: A Life* (New York: Penguin Press, 2011), 547,
2434.

25. Peter R. Henriques, "An Uneven Friendship: The Relationship between
George Washington and George Mason." *Virginia Magazine of History and
Biography*, Vol. 97 (April 1989), http://www.jstor.org/stable/4249070, 185–
204; George Washington to Samuel Thaws, 8 Jan. I 788, in ibid. XXIX, 360.

26. Chernow, *Washington*, 547, 1998. fn 26, *PWP*, 4:1, Letter from Washington
to James Clark, September 8, 1789.

27. Carol Berkin, *The Bill of Rights: The Fight to Secure America's Liberties*
(New York: Simon & Schuster, 2016), 28; Jeff Broadwater, *George Mason,
Forgotten Founder* (Chapel Hill: University of North Carolina Press, 2006),

1119; *Philadelphia Independent Gazetteer*, 4 April 1788; Lear to Langdon 3 April 1788, Rutland, *Ordeal of the Constitution*, 196.

28. Henriques, "An Uneven Friendship."

29. From George Washington to James Madison, 10 October 1787 https:// founders.archives.gov/GEWN-04-05-02-0334.

30. Letter from GM to John Mason, March 13, 1789, PGM 3:1142; Glover, *Founders as Fathers*, 921.

31. Henriques, "An Uneven Friendship."

32. George Mason, Virginia Ratification Debates, 11 June 1788, in Kaminski, DHRC, 9:1161. See also Debates in the Federal Convention, 22 August 1787, in James Madison, August 31, 1787, in *The Debates in the Several State Conventions, on the Adoption of the Federal Constitution*, ed. Jonathan Elliot, 5 vols. (Philadelphia: J. B. Lippincott, 1901)d, 5:457–61; Virginia Ratification debates, 17 June 1788, in Kaminski et al., DHRC, 10:1338–44; and George Mason to Thomas.

33. Boyd, *Politics of Opposition*, 102–10; Oliver Perry Chitwood, *Richard Henry Lee, Statesman of the Revolution* (Morgantown: West Virginia University Library, 1967), 180–82; J. Kent McGaughy, *Richard Henry Lee of Virginia: A Portrait of an American Revolutionary* (Lanham, MD: Rowman & Littlefield Publishers, Inc., 2003), 197–98. Henry has traditionally been seen as the public face of Virginia anti-federalism, with Mason and Lee providing the intellectual leadership. See Robert Rutland, *The Ordeal of the Constitution* (Norman, OK: University of Oklahoma, 1965), 222–23. Lee's influence rested in large part on his assumed authorship of the anonymous "Letters from the Federal Farmer," but contemporary scholarship has questioned that assumption, see Joseph Kent McGaughy, "The Authorship of *The Letters from the Federal Farmer*, Revisited," *New York History*, Vol. 70, No. 2, April 1989, 153–70.

34. GM to Martin Cockburn, 26 May, 1774, PGM, 1:190; Glover *Founders as Fathers*, 45; George Mason, Virginia Ratification Debates, 11 June 1788, in Kaminski, DHRC, 9:1161. See also *Debates in the Federal Convention*, 22 August 1787, in Elliot, *The Debates in the Several State Conventions*, 5:457–61; Virginia Ratification debates, 17 June 1788, in Kaminski, DHRC, 10:1338–1344; and George Mason to Thomas; Patrick Henry, Virginia Ratification Debates, 4 June 1788, in Kaminski, DHRC, 9:930–31. See also Pauline Maier, *Ratification*.

35. Glover, *Founders as Fathers*, 872; Hugh Blair Grigsby, *The History of the Federal Convention of 1788*, Vol. 1, ed. R. A. Brock (Richmond: Virginia Historical Society, 1890), 42.

36. Glover, *Founders as Fathers*, 873--74; For Virginia's ratification debates, see also Maier, *Ratification*, chapters 9–10.

37. Glover, *Founders as Fathers*, 892; George Mason, Virginia Ratification Debates, 11 June 1788, in Kaminski, DHRC, 9:1161. See also Debates in the Federal Convention, 22 August 1787, in Elliot, *The Debates in the Several State Conventions*, 5:457–461; Virginia Ratification debates, 17 June 1788, in Kaminski, DHRC, 10:1338–44; and George Mason to Thomas.

38. For Virginia's ratification debates, see also Maier, *Ratification*, chapters 9–10.

39. Ibid.

40. Ibid.

41. Ibid.

42. Ibid.

43. Ibid.

44. Ibid., 368–69; Letter from Lee to Elbridge Gerry September 29, 1787; For Virginia's ratification debates, see also Pauline Maier, *Ratification*, chapters 9–10.

45. Broadwater, *Forgotten Founder*, 1819.

46. Henry Mayer, *A Son of Thunder: Patrick Henry and the American Republic* (New York: Grove Press, 1991), 919.

47. Ibid., 920.

48. Ellis, *The Quartet*, 868.

49. Making of the constitution, PBS (1997).

50. http://csac.history.wisc.edu/ag_randolph.pdf.

51. Ibid.

52. "Letter from Thomas Jefferson to James Madison," Founders Online, August 11, 1793, https://founders.archives.gov/documents/Jefferson/01-26-02-0599.

53. Madison predicted that Henry would do anything in his power to throw sand into the gears of the new federal government, arguing that Virginia's representative "will commit suicide on his own authority." One of Henry's first acts was to block Madison's election to the Senate. For Virginia's ratification debates, see also Maier, *Ratification*, chapters 9–10.

54. Thomas Rogers Hunter, "The First Gerrymander? Patrick Henry, James Madison, James Monroe, and Virginia's 1788 Congressional Districting," *Early American Studies: An Interdisciplinary Journal*, Vol. 9, No. 3, Fall 2011, https://muse.jhu.edu/article/448116, 781–820.
55. Maier, *Ratification*, 1513–17; Robert D. Meade, *Patrick Henry: Practical Revolutionary* (Philadelphia, 1969), 360.
56. For Virginia's ratification debates, see also Maier, *Ratification*, chapters 9–10.
57. Maier, *Ratification*, 1513–17; Meade, *Practical Revolutionary*, 360.
58. Maier, *Ratification*, 1489; DHRC IX 937–40.
59. Broadwater, *Forgotten Founder*, 1818.
60. Making of the constitution, PBS (1997).
61. Ibid.
62. For Virginia's ratification debates, see also Maier, *Ratification*, chapters 9–10.
63. See appendix for the full list of Mason's Objections.
64. Thomas Fleming, *The Great Divide* (New York: Da Capo Press, 2015), 43.
65. "From James Madison to George Washington," Founders Online, June 4, 1788, https://founders.archives.gov/documents/Madison/01-11-02-0060; see also Fleming, *The Great Divide*.
66. Maier, *Ratification*, 1599–1600; DHRC X 1269–72 and also Henry at 1274-78.
67. Maier, *Ratification*, 1622; DHRC X 1365-95.
68. Maier, *Ratification*; DHRC X: 1258–99. 79. See, for example, the interventions at ibid., 1290 (Nicholas) and 1294–95 (Madison). 80. Ibid., 1259–69. 81. Ibid., 1269–72, and also Henry at 1274–78. 82. Ibid., 1272–74, and also 1269. 83. Ibid., 1278–83, 1304, 1306–07, 1312. 84. Ibid., 1292, 1320–21, 1317–19. 85. Ibid., 1338–39, 1341.
69. "George Mason Speech," TeachingAmericanHistory.org, June 4, 1788, http://teachingamericanhistory.org/library/document/george-mason-speech/.
70. "Elliot's Debates: Volume 3," in Gordon Lloyd, "Ratification of the Constitution," TeachingAmericanHistory.org, June 23, 1788, http://teachingamericanhistory.org/ratification/elliot/vol3/june23/.
71. John Marshall, "On the Federal Constitution," Bartleby.com, June 10, 1788, http://www.bartleby.com/268/8/21.html.
72. Ibid.

73. "Elliot's Debates: Volume 3," in Gordon Lloyd, "Ratification of the Constitution," TeachingAmericanHistory.org, June 6, 1788, http://teachingamericanhistory.org/ratification/elliot/vol3/june6/

74. "Elliot's Debates: Volume 3," In Convention, Richmond, Tuesday, June 17, 1788.

75. "Elliot's Debates: Volume 3," In Convention, Richmond, Wednesday, June 11, 1788, http://teachingamericanhistory.org/ratification/elliot/vol3/june11/. James Madison to Margaret B. Smith, September 1830, JM Writings, 9:405. For the Mason-Jefferson-Madison connection, see James Morton Smith, *The Republic of Letters: The Correspondence between Thomas Jefferson and James Madison* (New York: W. W. Norton & Company, 1995); Lance Banning, *Jefferson and Madison: Three Conversations from the Founding* (Madison, WI: Madison House, 1995); and Andrew Burstein and Nancy Isenberg, *Madison and Jefferson* (New York: Random House, 2010). See also Joseph J. Ellis, *Founding Brothers: The Revolutionary Generation* (New York: Knopf, 2000); Peter R. Henriques, "An Uneven Friendship: The Relationship Between George Washington and George Mason," VMHB 97 (1989): 185–204; John P. Kaminski, *The Great Virginia Triumvirate: George Washington, Thomas Jefferson, and James Madison in the Eyes of Their Contemporaries* (Charlottesville: University of Virginia Press, 2010).

76. Broadwater, *Forgotten Founder*, 1138–39; Quoted in David John Mays, *Letters and Papers of Edmund Pendleton, 1734–1803* (Charlottesville: University Press of Virginia, 1963), 2:233, See also DHRC, 9:933.

77. Glover, *Founders as Fathers*, 898–99; Fleming, *The Great Divide*, 43–44; Maier, *Ratification*, 267.

78. Glover, *Founders as Fathers*, 863–64.

79. Maier, *Ratification*, 1760; Nelson at DHRC X: 1701, and also 1560–62 for accounts of the meeting and Mason's address, including one that claims Henry spoke against continued resistance to the Constitution; Broadwater, *Forgotten Founder*, 236–37.

80. Fleming, *The Great Divide,* 44-45.

81. Maier, *Ratification*, 1804.

Chapter Fourteen: The True Father of the Bill of Rights

1. Don P. Halsey, "Virginia's Part in Framing the National Constitution," *Virginia Law Register*, Vol. 11, No. 11 (March 1926), 641–54, http://www.jstor.org/stable/1108518, 650.

2. Joseph J. Ellis, *The Quartet: Orchestrating the Second American Revolution, 1783–1789* (New York: Alfred A. Knopf, 2015), 831–32.

3. "To George Washington from Lund Washington," Founders Online, April 28, 1790, https://founders.archives.gov/documents/Washington/05-05-02-0230.

4. Pauline Maier, *Ratification: The People Debate the Constitution* (New York: Simon and Schuster, 2010), 1790–91.

5. Chris Derose, *Founding Rivals: Madison vs. Monroe, the Bill of Rights, and the Election That Saved a Nation* (Washington, DC: Regnery History, 2011), 205.

6. Ibid., 212, 224–25, 228–30.

7. "From James Madison to George Eve," Founders Online, January 2, 1789, https://founders.archives.gov/documents/Madison/01-11-02-0297.

8. JM to Thomas Mann Randolph, 13 January 1789, MP 11:416; Ellis, *The Quartet*, 947.

9. *The Founders' Constitution*, Volume 5, Amendment X, Document 6, August 18, 1789, http://press-pubs.uchicago.edu/founders/documents/amendXs6.html.

10. History.com Editors, "Freedom of the Press," History, December 7, 2017, last updated August 21, 2018, https://www.history.com/topics/united-states-constitution/freedom-of-the-press.

11. Henry Mayer, *A Son of Thunder: Patrick Henry and the American Republic* (New York: Grove Press, 1991).

12. Jonathan Elliot, ed., *The Debates in the Several State Conventions on the Adoption of the Federal Constitution as Recommended by the General Convention at Philadelphia in 1787*, Vol. 2, (New York: Burt Franklin Reprints, 1974); Mayer, *A Son of Thunder*.

13. Proposed Amendment, *PGM*, 3:1057–58; Jeff Broadwater, *George Mason, Forgotten Founder* (Chapel Hill: University of North Carolina Press, 2006), 1105.

14. Mayer, *A Son of Thunder*, 1491: "That 'great adversary,' pensive in defeat, stood quietly as Pendleton made a brief appeal for patience and urged the delegates 'to breathe peace and hope to the people.' After declaring the convention adjourned sine die, Pendleton hobbled from the chair and took a seat on a front bench, where he tearfully bade goodbye to the delegates crowded around him. Henry clasped Pendleton's hand, then called for his horse and went home."

15. Broadwater, *Forgotten Founder*, 957.

16. Brion McClanahan, *The Founding Fathers' Guide to the Constitution* (Washington, DC: Regnery History, 2012), 2390.

17. JM to Thomas Mann Randolph, 13 January 1789, MP 11:416; Ellis, *The Quartet*, 947.

18. Ellis, *The Quartet*, 945; RL 1:548–49.

19. Maier, *Ratification*, 1830.

20. Madison to Jefferson, October 17, 1788, quoted in Maier, *Ratification*, 1832.

21. Letter to John Mason on July 31, 1789; Broadwater, *Forgotten Founder*, 3456; Gordon Lloyd, "Did Madison Flip-Flop?: 'Circumstances Are Now Changed,'" TeachingAmericanHistory.org, accessed February 18, 2019, http://teachingamericanhistory.org/bor/themes/flip-flop/.

22. Maier, *Ratification*, 1462.

23. Ibid., 1472.

24. Papers of James Madison, Madison's speech of June 8, 1789 in *PJM* XII: 203; Maier, *Ratification*, 1848.

25. Maier, *Ratification*, 1852.

26. *PJM XII*:201–02; Maier, *Ratification*, 1852.

27. Mayer, *Son of Thunder*, 1331.

28. Ibid., 1335.

29. Ibid., 1341.

30. "To Thomas Jefferson from George Mason," Founders Online, March 16, 1790, http://founders.archives.gov/documents/Jefferson/01-16-02-0135.

31. "George Mason to Samuel Griffin," ConSource, September 8, 1789, http://consource.org/document/george-mason-to-samuel-griffin-1789-9-8-2/. Broadwater, *Forgotten Founder*, 1190; GM to John Mason, 31 July 1789, PGM 3:1162–68.

32. Maier, Pauline, *Ratification*, 1891.

33. Ibid., 463–64, 466–67.

34. McClanahan, *The Founding Fathers' Guide to the Constitution*, 2552.

35. Mayer, *Son of Thunder*, 1454.

36. McClanahan, *The Founding Fathers' Guide to the Constitution*, 2643.

37. Elliot, *The Debates in the Several State Conventions* (DAFC, III:659; IV: 244); McClanahan, *The Founding Fathers' Guide to the Constitution*, 2625.

38. Broadwater, *Forgotten Founder*, 938–39.

39. Ibid., 939,

40. McClanahan, *The Founding Fathers' Guide to the Constitution*.

41. Chris Derose, *Founding Rivals: Madison vs. Monroe, the Bill of Rights, and the Election that Saved a Nation* (Washington, DC: Regnery History, 2013, 185.

42. McClanahan, *The Founding Fathers' Guide to the Constitution*.

43. Maier, *Ratification*.

44. Wood, Gordon PBS television special, "Liberty" (1991).

Chapter Fifteen: The Shade of Retirement

1. George Mason letter January 8, 1783; "George Mason and the Constitution," Gunstons Hall website, accessed February 19, 2019, http:// www.gunstonhall.org/georgemason/essays/constitution.html

2. Jeff Broadwater, *George Mason, Forgotten Founder* (Chapel Hill: University of North Carolina Press, 2006), 1181.

3. Ibid., 1209.

4. Ibid., 1947.

5. GM TO William Aylett 8 June 1777, PGM 1:343–45, GM to Thomas Jefferson, 3 April 1779 PGM, 2:494–97; Broadwater, *Forgotten Founder*, 547–48; GM TO William Aylett 8 June 1777, PGM 1:343–45, GM to Thomas Jefferson, 3 April 1779 PGM, 2:494–97.

6. Broadwater, *Forgotten Founder*, 1181.

7. Ibid., 1949.

8. GM to John Mason, 12 June 1788, PGM 3: 1072–73; Broadwater, *Forgotten Founder*, 1217.

9. Marian Buckley Cox, *Glimpse of Glory: George Mason of Gunston Hall* (Richmond: Garrett & Massie, 1954), 211.

10. GM to John Mason, 2 September 1789, PGM 3:1128–30; Broadwater, *Forgotten Founder*, 1208; GM to John Mason, 2 September 1789, PGM 3:1128–30.

11. Broadwater, *Forgotten Founder*, 1209.

12. "To Thomas Jefferson from George Mason," Founders Online, March 16, 1790, http://founders.archives.gov/documents/Jefferson/01-16-02-0135.

13. "From Thomas Jefferson to George Mason," Founders Online, June 13, 1790, http://founders.archives.gov/documents/Jefferson/01-16-02-0295.

14. "To Thomas Jefferson from George Mason," Founders Online, March 16, 1790, http://founders.archives.gov/documents/Jefferson/01-16-02-0135.

15. See Helen Hill Miller, *George Mason, Constitutionalist* (Cambridge: Harvard University Press, 1938), Chapter XIV; "To Thomas Jefferson from George Mason," Founders Online, March 16, 1790, http://founders. archives.gov/documents/Jefferson/01-16-02-0135; Broadwater, *Forgotten Founder*, 1236–37; Notes on a Conversation with George Mason 30 September 1792, in Boyd et al PTL 24:428–29.

16. Broadwater, *Forgotten Founder*, 1234.

17. Ibid., 1236–37; Notes on a Conversation with George Mason, 30 September 1792, in Boyd et al PTL 24:428–29.

18. Broadwater, *Forgotten Founder*, 1238–39.

19. Pamela C. Copeland and Richard K. MacMaster, *The Five George Masons, Patriots and Planters of Virginia and Maryland* (Lorton, VA: The Board of Regents of Gunston Hall, 1989), 245.

20. "Monroe, James. Letter to Thomas Jefferson, 16 Oct. 1792. Manuscript. *The Thomas Jefferson Papers.* American Memory. Lib. Of Congress. 20 Mar. 2013 http://memory.loc.gov/cgi-bin/query/r? ammem/mtj:@ field(DOCID+@lit(jm010070))," quoted in Claudia J. Wendling, "George Mason: His Illness, Death, and Funeral," *Gunston Grapevine*, Spring 2013, http://www.gunstonhall.org/newsletter/spring2013grapevine.pdf.

21. "Jefferson, Thomas. Letter to James Madison, 1 Oct. 1792. *The Works of Thomas Jefferson.* Ed. Paul L. Ford. Reprint ed. Vol. 7. G.P. Putnam's Sons, 1904. Print. Google Book Search. Web. 20 Mar. 2013," quoted in Wendling, "George Mason: His Illness, Death, and Funeral."

22. See Kate Mason Rowland, *The Life of George Mason, 1725–1792*, Vol. 2 (New York: Russell & Russell, 1964; reprint of 1892 volume), 365; Mason, George. Letter to John Mason, 20 Aug. 1792, College of William & Mary,

Williamsburg, Va. Transcription: Robert A. Rutland and Charles F. Hobson, eds., *The Papers of George Mason*, Vol. 3 (Chapel Hill: University Press of North Carolina, 1970), 1271–73. "George Mason to John Mason," ConSource, August 20, 1792, http://www.consource.org/document/george-mason-to-john-mason-1792-8-20/20130122083252/; "Monroe, James. Letter to Thomas Jefferson, 16 Oct. 1792. Manuscript. *The Thomas Jefferson Papers*. American Memory. Lib. Of Congress. 20 Mar. 2013 http://memory.loc.gov/cgi-bin/query/r? ammem/mtj:@field(DOCID+@ lit(jm010070))," quoted in Wendling, "George Mason: His Illness, Death, and Funeral;" "Jefferson, Thomas. Letter to James Madison, 1 Oct. 1792. *The Works of Thomas Jefferson*. Ed. Paul L. Ford. Reprint ed. Vol. 7. G.P. Putnam's Sons, 1904. Print. Google Book Search. Web. 20 Mar. 2013," quoted in Wendling, "George Mason: His Illness, Death, and Funeral."

23. Wendling, "George Mason: His Illness, Death, and Funeral."
24. Mason Last Will & Testament, 20 March 1773, PGM 1:147; Wendling, "George Mason: His Illness, Death, and Funeral."
25. Ibid.

Epilogue: "The Stage of Human Life"

1. Perhaps the most effective articulator of Mason's ideology in recent political history was Ronald Reagan, whose belief in less government, individual freedoms, and American destiny sprung out of Mason's lexicon.
2. Randolph, quoted in Warren M. Billings, "Virginians and the Origins of the Bill of Rights," in Patrick T. Conley and John P. Kaminski, eds., *The Bill of Rights and the States: The Colonial and Revolutionary Origins of American Liberties* (Madison, WI: Madison House, 1992), 337.
3. David O. Stewart, *The Summer of 1787* (New York: Simon & Schuster, 2007), 1214.
4. Monroe to Jefferson, 16 October 1792, PTJ, 24:489–91; Jefferson to James Madison, 17 October 1792, PTJ 24:493–94; Jeff Broadwater, *George Mason, Forgotten Founder* (Chapel Hill: University of North Carolina Press, 2006), 1238–39; Monroe to Jefferson, 16 October 1792, PTJ, 24:489-91; Jefferson to James Madison, 17 October 1792, PTJ 24: 493–94.

5. Henry C. Riely, "George Mason," *Virginia Magazine of History and Biography*, Vol. 42, No. 1, January 1934, http://www.jstor.org/ stable/4244557, 1–17.

6. Riely, "George Mason."

7. Forrest McDonald, *E Pluribus Unum: The Formation of the American Republic, 1776–1790*, 2nd ed. (Indianapolis: Liberty Press, 1979), 265.

8. Josephine Pacheco, *George Mason and the Constitution*, 59 N.Y. St. B.J. 61 1987, 11.

9. Lorri Glover, *Founders as Fathers, The Private Lives and Politics of the American Revolution* (New Haven and London, Yale University Press, 2014), 1065.

10. Walton Moore, "George Mason, The Statesman," *William and Mary Quarterly*, Vol. 13, No. 1, January 1933, http://www.jstor.org/ stable/1922831, 10–17.

11. Broadwater, *Forgotten Founder*, 1188; Margaret Stimmann Branson, "George Mason, Reluctant Founder," Center for Civic Education, accessed February 19, 2019, http://www.civiced.org/resources/curriculum/mason.

12. See in general Glover, *Founders as Fathers*.

13. Pauline Maier, *Ratification: The People Debate the Constitution* (New York: Simon and Schuster, 2010), 280; Mason to the Committee of Merchants in London, June 6, 1766, PGM I:71; Moore, "George Mason, The Statesman."

14. Glover, *Founders as Fathers*, 1009–11; Herbert E. Sloan, *Principle and Interest: Thomas Jefferson and the Problem of Debt* (New York: Oxford University Press, 1995) 26–27.

15. Moore, "George Mason, The Statesman."

16. Jon Meacham, *Thomas Jefferson, The Art of Power* (New York: Random House, 2012), 2763.

17. John P. Kennedy, *Memoirs of the Life of William Wirt*, Vol 1 (Philadelphia: Lea and Blanchard, 1849), 352; R. Carter Pittman, *George Mason of Gunston Hall, Father of the American Bill of Rights* 15 Ala. Law. 196, 1954.

18. Pittman, *George Mason of Gunston Hall*.

Selected
Bibliography

A uthor Catherine Drinker Bowen once said that biographers should "not…startle with new material but…persuade with old." I can lay no claim to a wealth of unexplored material on Mason's life: no secret diary or family scandal. I have worked from the available primary sources to describe both the man and his times with as much detail as possible. The following bibliography represents my attempt to cite the primary and secondary sources that most influenced my research on George Mason's life and times. Almost of all these collection of papers are digitalized by the Library of Congress or the most prestigious college libraries in the country, and can be accessed online.

WORKS CITED BY ABBREVIATIONS

Adams Diary: Diary of John Adams, made available by the Massachusetts Historical Society at http://www.masshist.org/ digitaladams/aea!diary/.

ED: Debates of the state ratifying conventions, gathered in *Elliot's Debates*, made available by the Library of Congress at http:// memory.loc.gov/ammem/amlaw/lwed.html.

DGW: Donald Jackson and Dorothy Twohig, eds. *The Diaries of George Washington*, 4 vols. Charlottesville: University Press of Virginia, 1976–1978.

DHRC:. John P. Kaminski, Gaspare J. Saladino, Richard Leffler, Charles H. Schoenleber and Margaret A. Hogan, eds. *The Documentary History of the Ratification of the Constitution Digital Edition* Charlottesville: University of Virginia Press, 2009. Canonic URL: http://rotunda.upress.virginia.edu/founders/ RNCN-02-08-02-0001-0118.

Diaries, GW: Donald Jackson and Dorothy Twohig, eds. *The Diaries of George Washington*, 6 vols. Charlottesville, 1976–1979.

Diaries: A. Dorothy Twohig, ed. *George Washington's Diaries: An Abridgment.* Charlottesville, 1999. MTV Library of the Mount Vernon Ladies' Association, Mount Vernon, VA.

DNCB: William S. Powell, ed., Dictionary of North Carolina Biography, 6 vols. Chapel Hill, NC, and London, 1979–1996.

Farrand: Max Farrand, ed., The Records of the Federal Convention of 1787, rev. ed. in 4 vols., (New Haven, Connecticut, and London: 1966). Vol. IV, Supplement to James H. Hutson, ed., Max Farrand's The Records of the Federal Convention of 1787. New Haven, Connecticut, and London, 1987.

FLDA: *Family Letters Digital Archive*, Thomas Jefferson Foundation, Inc., accessed 2012 http://www.monticello.org/familyletters.

FOUNDERS ONLINE: Founders Online, National Archives (http:// founders.archives.gov/documents/Washington/05-10-02-0211-0001).

PGW: Robert F. Haggard and Mark A. Mastromarino, eds. *The Papers of George Washington, Presidential Series.* Charlottesville: University Press of Virginia, 2002.

FP: William B. Willcox et al., eds. *The Papers of Benjamin Franklin,* 28 vols. to date. New Haven, 1959.

JCC: Washington C. Ford, ed. *Journals of the Continental Congress, 1776–1789,* 34 vols. Washington, DC: U.S. Government Printing Office, 1931–44. Journals of the Continental Congress, made available by the Library of Congress at http://memory.loc.gov/ ammem/amJaw/lawhome.html.

JHB: *Journals of the House of Burgesses of Virginia.*

JM: Writings Gaillard Hunt, ed. *The Writings of James Madison,* 9 vols. New York: G. P. Putnam's Sons, 1900–1910.

JP: Julian Boyd et al., eds. *The Papers of Thomas Jefferson,* 28 vols. to date. Princeton, 1950–.

LA: *Library of America, The American Revolution: Writings from the War of Independence.* New York, 2001. Selections and notes by John Rhodehamel.

LC: Library of Congress.

LDC: Paul H. Smith et al., eds. *Letters of Delegates to Congress, 1774–1789,* 26 vols. Washington, DC, 1976–2000. Made available by the Library of Congress at http://memory.loc.gov/ammem/ amJaw/lawhome.html.

PAH: Harold C. Syrett, ed. *The Papers of Alexander Hamilton,* Vols. 3–5. New York, 1962.

PGM: Robert A. Rutland, ed., *The Papers of George Mason, 1725–1792*, 3 vols. Chapel Hill: University of North Carolina Press, 1970.

PGW-Col S: W. W. Abbot and Dorothy Twohig, eds., *The Papers of George Washington: The Colonial Series*, 10 vols. Charlottesville: University Press of Virginia, 1983–1995.

PGW-Conf S: W. W. Abbot, ed. *The Papers of George Washington: Confederation Series*, 6 vols. Charlottesville: University Press of Virginia, 1992–.

PGW-PS: Dorothy Twohig, ed. *The Papers of George Washington: The Presidential Series*, 11 vols. Charlottesville: University Press of Virginia, 1987–.

PGW (Retirement): W. W. Abbot et al., eds. *The Papers of George Washington, Retirement Series*, 4 vols. Charlottesville: University Press of Virginia, 1998–1999.

PGW (War): Philander D. Chase et al., eds. *The Papers of George Washington, Revolutionary War Series*, 20 vols. Charlottesville: University Press of Virginia/University of Virginia Press, 1985–present.

PGW-R WS: Philander D. Chase, ed. *The Papers of George Washington: The Revolutionary War Series*, 14 vols. Charlottesville: University Press of Virginia, 1985–. Preface.

PH: T. C. Hammond, ed. *The Parliamentary History of England*, 30 vols. London, 1806–1820.

PHC William: Wirt Henry, *Patrick Henry: Life, Correspondence and Speeches*, 3 vols. New York: Charles Scribner's Sons, 1891.

PJM (Congressional): William T. Hutchinson et al., eds. *The Papers of James Madison*, [Congressional Series], 17 vols. Chicago: University of Chicago.

PJM (Presidential): Robert A. Rutland et al., eds. *The Papers of James Madison, Presidential Series*, 6 vols. Charlottesville: University Press of Virginia/University of Virginia Press, 1984–present; Digital Edition (hereafter PJM Digital), ed J.C.A. Stagg. Charlottesville, 2010.

PJM (Retirement): David B. Mattern et al., eds. *The Papers of James Madison, Retirement Series*, 1 vol. Charlottesville: University of Virginia Press, 2009–present.

PJM (State): Robert J. Brugger et al., eds. *The Papers of James Madison, Secretary of State Series*, 8 vols. Charlottesville: University Press of Virginia/University of Virginia Press, 1986–present.

PTJ: Julian P. Boyd et al., eds. *The Papers of Thomas Jefferson*, 36 vols. Princeton, NJ: Princeton University Press, 1950–present.

PTJ (Retirement): J. Jefferson Looney, ed. *The Papers of Thomas Jefferson, Retirement Series*, 7 vols. Princeton, NJ: Princeton University Press, 2004–present; Digital Edition (hereafter PTJ Digital), ed. Barbara B. Oberg and J. Jefferson Looney. Charlottesville, 2008–2014.

PWR: W. W. Abbott, Dorothy Twohig, and Philander Chase, eds. *The Papers of George Washington: Revolutionary War Series*, 12 vols. to date. Charlottesville, 1985–.

VMHB: *Virginia Magazine of History and Biography.*

WMQ: *William and Mary Quarterly.*

WWF: John C. Fitzpatrick, ed. *The Writings of George Washington,* 39 vols. Washington, DC, 1931–1944.

WWR: John Rhodehamel, ed. *George Washington, Writings* New York, 1997.

MANUSCRIPT COLLECTIONS

American Philosophical Society, Philadelphia, PA

Carter-Smith Papers (transcripts)

Cheshire Collection

George Mason Manuscript Collection

George Mason Papers, Library of Congress

George Mason Family Papers, Gunston Hall, Virginia

George Mason's Slaves, Records and Notes, Gunston Hall, Virginia

George Washington Papers, Library of Congress

Gunston Hall School Records

International Center for Jefferson Studies, Monticello, Charlottesville, Va.

James Madison Papers Library of Congress

James Monroe Papers, Library of Congress, Washington, DC

John Mason Papers

Mason Family Manuscript Collection

Martin Cockburn Ledger, Library of Congress

Thomas Jefferson Papers, Library of Congress

Thomson Francis Mason Papers

Thomas Grimke Rhett Papers

Washington Family Papers, Library of Congress

BOOKS, ARTICLES, AND DISSERTATIONS

Abbot, W. W., ed. *The Papers of George Washington: Confederation Series*. 6 vols. Charlottesville: University Press of Virginia, 1992–1997.

Abbot, W. W., and Dorothy Twohig, eds. *The Papers of George Washington: The Colonial Series*. 10 vols. Charlottesville: University Press of Virginia, 1983–1995.

Adair, Douglass, ed. "James Madison's Autobiography." *William and Mary Quarterly*, 3rd ser., 2 (April 1945): 191–209.

Adams, Charles Francis, ed. *Letters of Mrs. Adams*. 2 vols. Boston, 1840.

Adams, William Howard. *The Paris Years of Thomas Jefferson*. New Haven, 1997.

Allgor, Catherine. "Margaret Bayard Smith's 1809 Journey to Monticello and

Montpelier: The Politics of Performance in the Early Republic." *Early American Studies*.

———. *Parlor Politics: In Which the Ladies of Washington Help Build a City and a Government*. Charlottesville, 2000.

———. *A Perfect Union: Dolley Madison and the Creation of the American Nation*. New York, 2006.

Allen, W. B., and Gordon Lloyd, eds. *The Essential Antifederalist*. 2nd ed. Lanham, MD: Rowman & Littlefield, 2002.

Appleby, Joyce. "Commercial Farming and 'the Agrarian Myth' in the Early Republic." *Journal of American History* 68 (1982): 833–49.

———. *Inheriting the Revolution: The First Generation of Americans.* Cambridge, MA, 2000.

Aries, Philippe. *The Hour of Our Death.* Translated by Helen Weaver. New York, 1981.

Bailey, Kenneth P. "George Mason: Westerner." *William and Mary Quarterly,* 2nd ser., 23 (October 1943): 409–17.

Bailyn, Bernard, ed. *Pamphlets of the American Revolution, 1750–1776.* Cambridge: Harvard University Press, 1965.

Bailyn, Bernard, and John B. Hench, eds. *The Press and the American Revolution.* Boston, 1981.

Ball, Charles. *Fifty Years in Chains; The Life of an American Slave.* Indianapolis, 1859.

Ballagh, James C., ed. *The Letters of Richard Henry Lee,* 2 vols. New York: Macmillan, 1911.

Banning, Lance. "The Constitutional Convention." In *The Framing and Ratification of the Constitution.* Edited by Leonard W. Levy and Dennis J. Mahoney, 112–31. New York: Macmillan, 1987.

———. "Virginia, Sectionalism and the General Good." In Ratifying the Constitution. Edited by Michael Allen Gillespie and Michael Lienesch.

Bardaglio, Peter V. *Reconstructing the Household: Families, Sex, and the Law in the Nineteenth-Century South.* Chapel Hill, 1995.

Barker, Frank N., *What's in Betsy's Pocket/What's in John's Haversack: A New Look at the Hands-on History Touch Museum at Gunston Hall.* http://www.gunstonhall.org/docs/Spring-2015-Grapevine.pdf.

Bear, James A. Jr., ed. *Jefferson at Monticello.* Charlottesville, 1967.

Bear, James A. Jr., and Lucia Stanton, eds. *Jefferson's Memorandum Books: Accounts, with Legal Records and Miscellany.* 2 vols. Princeton, 1997.

Bearss, Sara B., et al., eds. *Dictionary of Virginia Biography.* Richmond, 1988–.

Beckerdite, Luke. *Architect-Designed Furniture in Eighteenth-Century Virginia: The Work of William Buckland and William Bernard Sears. American Furniture.* Milwaukee, WI: Chipstone Foundation, 1994, 29–48. William Buckland was a joiner/carpenter hired as an indentured servant by George Mason in 1755. He supervised the interior decoration of Gunston Hall. William Bernard Sears was a carver who is responsible for much of the detailed carvings of Gunston Hall.

———. "William Buckland and William Bernard Sears: The Designer and the Carver." Journal of Early Southern Decorative Arts 8 (November 1982): 7–40.

———. *William Buckland and William Bernard Sears: The Designer and the Carver.* Journal of Early Southern Decorative Arts, 8 (November 1982), 7–40.

———. *William Buckland Reconsidered: Architectural Carving in Chesapeake Maryland, 1771-1774.* Journal of Early Southern Decorative Arts, 8 (November 1982), 43–88.

Beirne, Rosamund and John H. Scarff. *William Buckland, 1734–1774: Architect of Virginia and Maryland.* Lorton, VA: The Board of Regents of Gunston Hall and Hammond-Harwood House

Association, 1958. Provides information on Buckland's early career. Several the houses credited to Buckland in this book are no longer thought to have been by his hand.

Bell, Whitfield J., Jr. *Patriot-Improvers: Biographical Sketches of Members of the American Philosophical Society.* 2 vols. Philadelphia, 1997–1999.

Berkin, Carol. *First Generation Women in Colonial America.* New York: Hill and Wang, 1996.

———. *Revolutionary Mothers: Women in the Struggle for American Independence.* New York, 2005.

Betts, Edwin Morris, ed. *Thomas Jefferson's Farm Book.* Chapel Hill, 2002.

Betts, Edwin Morris, and James Adam Bear Jr., eds. *The Family Letters of Thomas Jefferson.* Columbia, Missouri, 1966.

Birle, Ann Lucas, and Lisa A. Francavilla, eds. *Thomas Jefferson's Granddaughter in Queen Victoria's England: The Travel Diary of Ellen Wayles Coolidge, 1838-1839.* Boston, 2011. The Boston Directory. Boston, 1828.

Bisbee, M. Lauren. *Land & Labor: Gunston Hall Plantation Life in the 18th Century.* Lorton, VA: Board of Regents, Gunston Hall, 1994.

Blackstone, William. *Commentaries on the Laws of England.* Oxford, 1765.

Blanton, Wyndham B. "Washington's Medical Knowledge and Its Sources." Annals of Medical History, 4 (1932).

Bond, Beverly W., Jr. "The Quit-Rent System in the American Colonies." American Historical Review 17 (April 1912): 496–516.

Bouldin, Powhatan. *Home Reminiscences of John Randolph of Roanoke*. Danville and Richmond, 1887.

Bowling, Kenneth R. "'A Tub to the Whale': The Founding Fathers and the Adoption of the Federal Bill of Rights." Journal of the Early Republic 8 (Fall 1988): 223–51.

Boyd, Julian, et al., eds. *The Papers of Thomas Jefferson*. 31 vols. Princeton: Princeton University Press, 1950–2003.

Brady, Patricia. *Martha Washington: An American Life*. New York, 2005.

Branchi, E. C., trans. "Memoirs of the Life and Voyages of Doctor Philip Mazzei, Part I." *William and Mary Quarterly*, 2nd ser., 9 (July 1929): 161–74.

———. "Memoirs of the Life and Voyages of Doctor Philip Mazzei, Part II." *William and Mary Quarterly*, 2nd ser., 9 (October 1929): 247–64.

Brand, Barbara Allston. *The Work of William Buckland in Maryland, 1771–1774*. Master's thesis, George Washington University, 1978.

Broadwater, Jeff, *George Mason. Forgotten Founder*. Chapel Hill: University of North Carolina Press, 2006.

Brock, R. A., ed. *The Official Records of Robert Dinwiddie*. 5 vols. Richmond: Virginia Historical Society, 1883–1884.

Brodie, Fawn M. *Thomas Jefferson: An Intimate History*. New York, 1974.

Brookhiser, Richard, *Founding Father: Rediscovering George Washington*. New York: The Free Press, 1996: 54.

Brown, Bennie, ed. *Buckland: Master Builder of the 18th Century*. Lorton, VA: Board of Regents of Gunston Hall, 1977.

———. "The Ownership of Architecture Books in Colonial Virginia." In Kenneth Hafertepe and James F. O'Gorman. *American Architects and Their Books to 1848*. Amherst: University of Massachusetts Press, 2001. 17–33. Discusses the books owned by William Buckland.

———. *Jefferson's Secrets: Death and Desire at Monticello*. New York, 2005.

Bryan, Helen. *Martha Washington. First Lady of Liberty.* New York: John Wiley & Sons, Inc., 2002.

Buckley, Thomas E. *The Great Catastrophe of My Life: Divorce in the Old Dominion*. Chapel Hill, 2002.

Burstein, Andrew. *The Inner Jefferson: Portrait of a Grieving Optimist*. Charlottesville, 1995.

———. *Jefferson's Secrets: Death and Desire at Monticello*. New York, 2005.

Butterfield, L. H., et al., eds. *Adams Family Correspondence*. Cambridge, Mass.,1963–.

Cary, Virginia Randolph. *Letters on Female Character, Addressed to a Young Lady on the Death of Her Mother.* Richmond, 1828.

Chase, Philander D., ed. *The Papers of George Washington: The Revolutionary War Series*. 14 vols. Charlottesville: University Press of Virginia, 1985–.

Chastellux, Marquis de. *Travels in North America in the Years 1780, 1781*. Vol I and II. Howard C. Rice, Jr., ed. Chapel Hill: University of North Carolina Press, 1963.

Chernow, Ron. *Washington: A Life*. New York: Penguin Press, 2011.

———. *Alexander Hamilton*. New York, 2004.

Chester, James Antieau. *Natural Rights And The Founding Fathers-The Virginians*, 17 Wash. & Lee L. Rev. 43–79 (1960). http://scholarlycommons.law.wlu.edu/wlulr/vol17/iss1/4; https://the-american-catholic.com/tag/saint-robert-bellarmine.

Clement, J. ed. *Noble Deeds of American Women; with Biographical Sketches of Some of the More Prominent*. With an introduction by Mrs. L. H. Sigourney. Buffalo, NY: Jewett, Thomas and Co., 1851.

Clinton, Catherine. *The Plantation Mistress: Woman's World in the Qui South*. New York, 1982.

Clinton, Catherine, and Michele Gillespie, eds. *The Devil's Lane: Sex and Race in the Early South*. New York, 1997.

Cockerham, Anne Z., Arlene W. Keeling, and Barbara Parker. "Seeking Refuge at Monticello: Domestic Violence in Thomas Jefferson's Family." Magazine of Albemarle County History 64 (2006): 34–42.

Cogliano, Francis D. *Thomas Jefferson: Reputation and Legacy*. Charlottesville, 2006.

Cohen, William. "Thomas Jefferson and the Problem of Slavery." Journal of American History 56 (1969): 503–26.

Conley Patrick and Kaminski John P, eds. *The Bill of Rights and the States: The Colonial and Revolutionary Origins of American Liberties*. Madison, WI: Madison House, 1992. 335–69.

Copeland, Pamela C. and Richard K. MacMaster. *The Five George Masons, Patriots and Planters of Virginia and Maryland*. Lorton, VA: The Board of Regents of Gunston Hall, 1989.

Cott, Nancy F. *No Small Courage: A History of Women in the United States*. New York: Oxford University Press, 2000.

Conway, Moncure Daniel, ed. *The Writings of Thomas Paine*. 4 vols. New York: G. P. Putnam, 1896; reprint, New York: AMS Press, 1967.

Cox, Marian Buckley. *Glimpse of Glory, George Mason of Gunston Hall*, Garrett & Massie, Richmond, 1954.

Cripe, Helen. *Thomas Jefferson and Music*. Charlottesville, 1974.

Cullen, Charles T. "Jefferson's White House Dinner Guests." White House History 17 (2006): 25–43.

Cullen, Charles T., and Herbert A. Johnson, eds. *The Papers of John Marshall*. Chapel Hill, 1974–.

Cunningham, Noble E., Jr. *The Jeffersonian Republicans in Power: Party Operations,*

1801–1809. Chapel Hill, 1963.

Davis, Richard Beale, ed. *The Abbe Correa in America, 1812–1820: The Contributions of the Diplomat and Natural Philosopher to the Foundations of our Nation*. Philadelphia, 1955.

Dabney, William M. "Jefferson's Albemarle: History of Albemarle County, Virginia, 1727–1829." Ph.D. diss., University of Virginia, 1951.

Daniels, Jonathan. *The Randolphs of Virginia*. Garden City, NY, 1972.

Davidson, Cathy N. *Revolution and the Word: The Rise of the Novel in America*. New York, 1988.

Dawidoff, Robert. *The Education of John Randolph of Roanoke*. New York, 1979.

DePauw, Linda Grant, Charlene Bangs Bickford, Helen E. Veit, and Kenneth R. Bowling, eds. *Documentary History of the First*

Federal Congress of the United States of America. Baltimore and London, 1972–.

Doyle, Nora. "'The Highest Pleasure of Which Woman's Nature Is Capable': BreastFeeding and the Sentimental Maternal Ideal in America, 1750–1860." *Journal of American History* 97 (20n): 958–73.

Dreisbach, Daniel L. "George Mason's Pursuit of Religious Liberty in Revolutionary Virginia." *Virginia Magazine of History and Biography*, Vol. 108, No. 1 (2000): 25–44, Published by: Virginia Historical Society, Stable URL: http://www.jstor.org/stable/4249815.

Duncan, Louis C. *Medical Men in the American Revolution, 1775–1783*. Carlisle Barracks, PA: Medical Field Service School, 1931.

Dunn, Terry K., ed. *The Recollections of John Mason: George Mason's Son Remembers His Father and Life at Gunston Hall*. Marshall, VA: EPM Publications, 2004.

Dunn, Susan. *Dominion of Memories: Jefferson, Madison, and the Decline of Virginia*. New York, 2007.

Egerton, Douglas R. *Gabriel's Rebellion: The Virginia Slave Conspiracies of 1801 and 1802*. Chapel Hill, 1993.

Egnal, Marc. "The Origins of the Revolution in Virginia: A Reinterpretation." *William and Mary Quarterly*, 3rd ser., 37 (July 1980): 401–28.

Ellet, Elizabeth F. Ellet, Elizabeth F. *The Women of the American Revolution*. New York: Baker & Scribner, 1849.

Elliott, Jonathan, ed. "James Madison, 31 August 1787," in *The Debates in the Several State Conventions, on the Adoption of the*

Federal Constitution. 5 vols. (Philadelphia: J. B. Lippincott, 1901), 5:502.

Ellis, Joseph. *His Excellency George Washington.* New York: Random House, 2004.

———. *After the Revolution.* New York: Norton, 1979.

———. *American Creation: Triumphs and Tragedies at the Founding of the Republic.* New York, 2007.

———. *American Sphinx: The Character of Thomas Jefferson.* New York: Knopf, 1997.

———. *Founding Brothers: The Revolutionary Generation.* New York: Alfred A. Knopf, 2001.

———. *Passionate Sage.* New York: Norton, 1993.

———. *Revolutionary Summer: The Birth of American Independence.* Vintage: Reprint edition 2014.

———. *The Quartet: Orchestrating the Second American Revolution, 1783–1789.* Kindle Edition, Alfred A. Knopf, 2015.

Ellis, Richard. "The Persistence of Antifederalism after 1789." In *Beyond Confederation: Origins of the Constitution and American National Identity.* Edited by Richard R. Beeman, Stephen Botein, and Edward C. Carter II. Chapel Hill: University of North Carolina Press, 1987. 295–314.

Evans, Emory G. "Planter Indebtedness and the Coming of the Revolution in Virginia." *William and Mary Quarterly,* 3rd ser., 19 (October 1962): 511–33.

Farrand, Max, ed., *The Records of the Federal Convention of 1787.* 3 Vols. New Haven: Yale University Press, 1911, 1937, 1966.

Finkelman, Paul. "Slavery and the Constitutional Convention: Making a Covenant with Death." In *Beyond Confederation: Origins of the Constitution and American National Identity.* Edited by Richard R. Beeman, Stephen Botein, and Edward C. Carter II, Chapel Hill: University of North Carolina Press, 1987. 188–225.

———. "Slavery at the Philadelphia Convention," *This Constitution, a Bicentennial Chronicle.* no. 18. (Spring/Summer 1988): 25.

———. "Thomas Jefferson and Antislavery: The Myth Goes On." *Virginia Magazine of History and Biography* 102 (1994): 193–228.

Fitzpatrick, John C., ed. *The Writings of George Washington.* 39 vols. Washington, DC: U.S. Government Printing Office, 1931–1944.

Fleming, Thomas, *The Great Divide.* New York: Da Capo Press, 2015.

———. *The Intimate Lives of the Founding Fathers.* New York: Harper Collins, 2009.

Force, Peter, ed. *American Archives.* 4th ser. 6 vols. Washington, DC: St. Clair and Force, 1837–1846.

Ford, Washington C., ed. *Journals of the Continental Congress, 1776–1789.* 34 vols. Washington, DC: U.S. Government Printing Office, 1904–1937.

Ford, Paul Leicester, ed. *The Writings of Thomas Jefferson.* 10 vols. New York: G. P. Putnam's Sons, 1892–1899.

Freehling, William W. "The Founding Fathers and Slavery." American Historical Review 77 (February 1972): 81–93.

——. "The Founding Fathers, Conditional Antislavery, and the Nonradicalism of the American Revolution." In *The Reintegration of American History: Slavery and the Civil War*. Edited by William W. Freehling. New York: Oxford University Press, 1994. 12–33.

Freeman, Douglas Southall et al., *George Washington. A Biography*. 7 vols., New York: Charles Scribner's Sons, 1948–1957.

Gaines, William H., Jr. *Thomas Mann Randolph: Thomas Jefferson's Son-in-Law*. Baton Rouge, LA, 1966.

Ganter, Herbert L. "The Machiavellianism of George Mason." *William and Mary Quarterly*, 2nd ser., 17 (April 1937): 239–64.

Gillespie, Michael Allen and Michael Lienesch. Lawrence: University Press of Kansas, 1989. 261–99.

Gilmer, George R. *Sketches of Some of the First Settlers of Upper Georgia, of the Cherokees, and of the Author*. New York, 1855.

Glasse, Hannah. *The Art of Cookery Made Plain and Easy*. Multiple editions after the first edition of 1747.

Glover, Lorri, *Founders as Fathers, The Private Lives and Politics of the American Revolution*. New Haven and London: Yale University Press, 2014.

Gordon-Reed, Annette. *The Hemingses of Monticello*. New York, 2008.

——. *Thomas Jefferson and Sally Hemings: An American Controversy*. Charlottesville, 1997.

Hall, James Anthony. *William Buckland's Anglo-Palladian Interior Ornamentation at Gunston Hall*. Master's thesis, University of Virginia, 1978.

Halsey, Don P. "Virginia's Part in Framing the National Constitution." *Virginia Law Register*, New Series, Vol. 11, No. 11 (March 1926): 641–54, Published by: Virginia Law Review, Stable URL: http://www.jstor.org/stable/1108518, 650.

Harper, Marilyn. *What It Ought to Have Been: Three Case Studies of Early Restoration Work in Virginia.* Master's thesis, George Washington University, 1989. Includes early restoration attempts at Gunston Hall. Gunston Hall Library & Archives December 2009.

Hayes, Kevin J. *The Road to Monticello: The Life and Mind of Thomas Jefferson.* New York, 2008.

Hemphill, John M., ed. "John Wayles Rates His Neighbors." *Virginia Magazine of History and Biography* 66 (July 1958): 302–6.

Hess, Karen ed. *Martha Washington's Booke of Cookery.* New York: Columbia University Press, 1981.

Henriques, Peter R. "An Uneven Friendship: The Relationship between George Washington and George Mason." *Virginia Magazine of History and Biography* 97 (April 1989): 185–204.

Hobson, Charles F. "The Negative on State Laws: James Madison and the Crisis of Republican Government." *William and Mary Quarterly* 36: 2 (April 1979): 215–35.

Hunt, Gaillard, ed. *The Writings of James Madison.* 9 vols. New York: G. P. Putnam's Sons, 1900–1910.

Huntington, Bill, and Culhane Kevin, *Gunston Hall, the Birth of L.S.U., W. T. Sherman and George Mason Graham.* http://www.gunstonhall.org/docs/Summer-2016-Grapevine.pdf.

Hutchinson, William T., and William M. E. Rachal, et al., eds. *The Papers of James Madison.* 17 vols. Chicago: University of Chicago

Press; Charlottesville: University Press of Virginia, 1962–1991.

Hutson, James, ed., *Supplement to Max Farrand's The Records of the Federal Convention of 1787.* New Haven: Yale University Press, 1987.

Hyneman, Charles S., and Donald S. Lutz, eds. *American Political Writing during the Founding Era, 1760–1805.* 2 vols. Indianapolis: Liberty Fund, 1983.

Inashima, Paul Y., *A Landmark Lost in Time: Finding the Tea Table.* http://www.gunstonhall.org/newsletter/Grapevine-Winter-2012.pdf.

———. The Mason Family Fisheries. http://www.gunstonhall.org/docs/Summer-2016-Grapevine.pdf.

Isaac, Rhys. "Stories and Constructions of Identity: Folk Tellings and Diary Inscriptions in Revolutionary Virginia." In *Through a Glass Darkly: Reflections on Personal identity in Early America*, edited by Ronald Hoffman, Mechal Sobel, and Fredrika J. Teute. UNC Press Books, 1997.

Joyner, Georgina Louise. *William Buckland in England and America: His Apprenticeship, English Early Georgian Influences on his Style and New Evidence at Gunston Hall.* Master's thesis, University of Notre Dame, 1985.

Kimball, Fiske. *Gunston Hall, Journal of the Society of Architectural Historians,* Vol. 13, No. 2. (May 1954): 3–8 Published by: University of California Press on behalf of the Society of Architectural Historians Stable URL: http://www.jstor.org/stable/987683.

Jackson, Donald, and Dorothy Twohig, eds. *The Diaries of George Washington.* 4 vols. Charlottesville: University Press of Virginia, 1976–1978.

Journal of the House of Delegates of the Commonwealth of Virginia. Richmond: Commonwealth of Virginia, 1776–.

Journal of the House of Delegates of the Commonwealth of Virginia, 1777–1780. Richmond: Thomas W. White, 1827.

Journal of the House of Delegates of Virginia, 1776. Williamsburg: Alexander Purdie, undated.

Journals of the House of Burgesses of Virginia, 1766–1769. Richmond: Colonial Press, 1906.

Keane, John, *Tom Paine: A Political Life,* Boston, 1995..

Kennedy, John Pendleton, ed. *Journal of the House of Burgesses of Virginia, 1761–1765.* Richmond: Colonial Press, 1907.

Kerber, Linda K. *Women of the Republic: Intellect and Ideology in Revolutionary America* (Chapel Hill: University of North Carolina Press, 1980).

Kern, Susan. "The Material World of the Jeffersons at Shadwell." *William and Mary Quarterly,* 3rd ser., 62 (2005): 213–42.

Ketcham, Ralph, ed. *The Anti-Federalist Papers and the Constitutional Convention Debates.* New York: Signet, 2003.

———. *James Madison, A Biography.* Charlottesville and London: University Press of Virginia, 1994.

Kierner, Cynthia A. *Beyond the Household: Women's Place in the Early South, 1700–1835.* Ithaca, KY, 1998.

———. *Martha Jefferson Randolph, Daughter of Monticello: Her Life and Times,* The University of North Carolina Press; Reprint edition (2014).

———. "The Dark and Dense Cloud Perpetually Lowering Over Us: Gender and the Decline of the Gentry in Postrevolutionary Virginia." *Journal of the Early Republic* 20 (2000): 185–217.

———. *Scandal at Bizarre: Rumor and Reputation in Jefferson's America*. New York, 2004.

———. *Southern Women in Revolution: Personal and Political Narratives, 1776–1800*. Columbia, SC, 1998.

Kimball, Fiske. *Gunston Hall, Journal of the Society of Architectural Historians*, Vol. 13, No. 2 (May 1954): 3-8. Published by: University of California Press on behalf of the Society of Architectural Historians Stable URL: http://www.jstor.org/stable/987683.

Kimball, Marie. *Jefferson: The Scene of Europe, 1784 to 1789*. New York, 1950.

———. *Thomas Jefferson's Cookbook*. Charlottesville, 1979.

Knox, J. H. Mason Jr. "The Medical History of George Washington, His Physicians, Friends and Advisers," *Bulletin of the Institute of the History of Medicine*, 1 (1933).

Kranish, Michael. *Flight from Monticello: Thomas Jefferson at War*. New York, 2010

Kukla, Jon. M. *Jefferson's Women*. New York, 2007.

Kurland, Philip B., and Ralph Lerner, eds. *The Founders' Constitution*. 4 vols. Chicago: University of Chicago of Chicago Press, 1987.

Labaree, Leonard W., ed. *The Papers of Benjamin Franklin*. 36 vols. New Haven: Yale University Press, 1959–2001.

Leepson, Marc. *Saving Monticello: The Levy Family's Epic Quest to Restore the House That Jefferson Built.* New York, 2001.

Levasseur, Auguste. *Lafayette in America in 1824 and 1825: Journal of a Voyage to the United States.* Translated by Alan R. Hoffman. Manchester, NH, 2006.

Lewis, Jan. *The Pursuit of Happiness: Family and Values in Jefferson's Virginia.* Cambridge, Eng., 1983.

———. "The Republican Wife: Virtue and Seduction in the Early Republic." *William and Mary Quarterly*, 3rd ser., 44 (1987): 689–721.

Lewis, Jan, and Kenneth A. Lockridge. "'Sally Has Been Sick': Pregnancy and Family Limitation among Virginia Gentry Women, 1780–1830." *Journal of Social History* 22 (1988): 5–20.

Lewis, Jan and Peter S. Onuf., eds. *Sally Hemings and Thomas Jefferson: History, Memory, and Civic Culture.* Charlottesville, 1999.

Lewis, Jan, et al. "Forum: Thomas Jefferson and Sally Hemings Redux." *William and Mary Quarterly*, 3rd ser., 57 (2000): 121–210.

Lewis, William Terrell. *Genealogy of the Lewis Family in America.* Louisville, KY, 1893.

Lockridge, Kenneth A. *On the Sources of Patriarchal Rage: The Commonplace Books of William Byrd and Thomas Jefferson and the Gendering of Power in the Eighteenth Century.* New York, 1992.

Lovell, Margaretta M. *Art in a Season of Revolution: Painters, Artists, and Patrons in Early America.* Philadelphia, 2005.

Lipscomb, Andrew, ed. *The Writings of Thomas Jefferson.* 20 vols. Washington, DC: Thomas Jefferson Memorial Association, 1904–1905.

Locke, John. *Two Treatises of Government.* Edited by Peter Laslett. Cambridge: Cambridge University Press, 1988.

Looney, J. Jefferson, et al., eds. *The Papers of Thomas Jefferson: Retirement Series.* Princeton, 2004–.

Lounsbury, Carl R. "'An Elegant and Commodious Building': William Buckland and the Design of the Prince William County Courthouse." *Journal of the Society of Architectural Historians,* Vol. 46, No. (September): 228–40. Published by: University of California Press on behalf of the Society of Architectural Historians Stable URL: http://www.jstor.org/stable/990228.

Madison, James. *Journal of the Federal Convention Vol 1 & 2.* Chicago: E. H. Scott, 1893.

Maier, Pauline. *Ratification: The People Debate the Constitution.* New York: Simon and Schuster, 2010.

———. *From Resistance to Revolution: Colonial Radicals and the Development of American Opposition to Britain, 1765–1776.* New York: Random House, 1972.

———. *American Scripture: Making the Declaration of Independence,* Vintage; 1st Vintage Books Ed edition (1998). This is the standard work on the subject.

Malone, Dumas. *Jefferson and His Time.* 6 vols. Boston, 1951–1982.

———. *Jefferson and the Ordeal of Liberty.* Boston, 1962.

———. *Jefferson the President: First Term, 1801–1805.* Boston, 1970.

———. *Jefferson the President: The Second Term, 1805–1809.* Boston, 1974.

———. *Jefferson the Virginian.* Boston, 1948.

———. *The Sage of Monticello.* Boston. 1982.

———. *Thomas Jefferson and the Rights of Man.* Boston, 1951.

Marchione, Margherita, et al., .eds. *Philip Mazzei: Selected Writings and Correspondence.* 2 vols. Prato, 1983.

Mason, Jonathan. *Extracts from a Diary kept by the Hon. Jonathan Mason of a Journey from Boston to Savannah in the Year 1804.* Cambridge, MA, 1885.

Matson, Cathy D., ed. *The Economy of Early America: Historical Perspectives and New Directions.* Philadelphia, 2006.

Mayer, Henry, *A Son of Thunder, Patrick Henry and the American Republic.* New York: Grove Press, 1991.

Mays, David John, ed. *The Letters and Papers of Edmund Pendleton, 1734–1803.* 2 vols. Charlottesville: University Press of Virginia, 1967.

Maxham, Robert M. *The Colonial Plantations of George Mason.* North Springfield, VA, 1975.

Mazzei, Philip. *My Life and Wanderings.* American Institute of Italian Studies, 1980.

McCullough, David. *John Adams.* New York: Simon & Schuster, 2004.

McHugh, Denise. *Family of George Mason (IV) of Gunston Hall: A Close Look at George Mason's Second Wife: Sarah Brent Mason.* http://www.gunstonhall.org/georgemason/mason_family/sarah_brent.html.

McIlwaine, H.R., ed. *The Journals of the House of Burgesses of Virginia, 1758–1761.* Richmond: Colonial Press, 1908.

McLaughlin, Jack. *Jefferson and Monticello.* New York: Henry Holt, 1988.

Meacham, Jon. *Thomas Jefferson, The Art of Power.* New York: Random House, 2012.

Meade, Bishop [William]. *Old Churches, Ministers and Families of Virginia.* 2 vols. Philadelphia, 1857.

Miller, John Chester, *The Wolf by the Ears: Thomas Jefferson and Slavery.* (1977; reissued by U. Of Virginia Press, 1991).

Helen Hill Miller, *George Mason, Constitutionalist.* Cambridge: Harvard University Press, 1938.

———. *George Mason. Gentleman Revolutionary.* Chapel Hill: University of North Carolina Press, 1975.

———. *George Mason of Gunston Hall.* Lorton, VA: The Board of Regents of Gunston Hall, 1985.

———. "John Mercer of Marlborough: A Portrait of an Irascible Gentleman." *Virginia Cavalcade* 27 (Autumn 1976): 74–85.

Minnick, John. "Patriot George Mason-Framer of Liberty." *SAR Magazine.* (Fall 1980), LXXV, no. 2.

Minutes of the Vestry: Truro Parish, Virginia, 1732–1785. Baltimore: Gateway Press, 1995.

Montague, Lee Ludwell, ed. "Cornelia Lee's Wedding, As Reported in a Letter from Ann Calvert Stuart to Mrs. Elizabeth Lee, October 19, 1806." *Virginia Magazine of History and Biography* 80 (1972): 453–60.

Mordecai, Samuel. *Richmond in By-Gone Days*. 1856. Richmond. 1946.

Morgan, Edmund S. *American Slavery, American Freedom: The Ordeal of Colonial Virginia*. New York: W. W. Norton, 1975.

Moore, R. Walton. "George Mason, The Statesman." *William and Mary Quarterly*, Vol. 13, No. 1 (January 1933), 10–17. Published by: Omohundro Institute of Early American History and Culture Stable URL: http://www.jstor.org/stable/1922831 Accessed: 13-05-2017 18:16 UTC.

Morgan, Edmund S. *The Birth of the Republic, 1763–89*. Chicago, 1956. This is the seminal statement of the constitutional issues at stake in the 1760s.

Morison, Samuel E., ed. *Sources and Documents Illustrating the American Revolution, 1764–1788*. New York: Oxford University Press, 1929.

Morris, Gouverneur. *A Diary of the French Revolution*. 2 vols. Edited by Beatrix Cary Davenport. Boston, 1939.

Mulkearn, Lois, comp. *George Mercer Papers Relating to the Ohio Company of Virginia*. Pittsburgh: University of Pittsburgh Press, 1954.

Neins, Allan, ed. *Diary of John Quincy Adams: American Political, Social, and Intellectual Life from Washington to Polk*. New York, 1929.

Norton, Mary Beth. *Ladies of Liberty*. New York: Harper Collins, 2009.

———. *Liberty's Daughters: The Revolutionary Experience of American Women, 1750–1800*. Ithaca, NY: Cornell University Press, 1996.

———. *Separated by Their Sex: Women in Public and Private in the Colonial Atlantic World*. Ithaca, NY, 2011.

O'Connor, Thomas H. *The Athens of America*: Boston, 1825–1845. Amherst, MA, 2006.

Onuf, Peter S., ed. *Jeffersonian Legacies*. Charlottesville: University of Virginia Press, 1993.

Pacheco, Josephine F., ed. *Antifederalism: The Legacy of George Mason*. Fairfax, VA: George Mason University Press, 1992.

———. *George Mason and The Constitution* 59 N.Y. St. B.J. 61 1987

PBS, *The Making of the Constitution: Liberty,* Host Forrest Sawyer, 1998.

Peterson, Merrill D., ed. *The Portable Jefferson*. New York: Penguin Books, 1977.

———, ed. *The Writings of Thomas Jefferson*. New York: Library of America, 1984.

———. *Visitors to Monticello*. Charlottesville, 1989.

———. *The Jefferson Image in the American*. New York: Vintage, 1970.

Pilcher, James Evelyn. *The Surgeon Generals of the Army of the United States of America: A Series of Biographical Sketches of the Senior Officers of the Military Medical Service from the American Revolution to the Philippine Pacification*. Carlisle, PA: Association of Military Surgeons, 1905.

Pittman, R. Carter, *George Mason of Gunston Hall, Father of the American Bill of Rights* 15 Ala. Law. 196 1954

Pittman, R. Carter. *The Declaration of Independence Its Antecedents and Authors*. C:\Users\whyland\Documents\IT\IT\FINAL BOOK\

RESEARCH ARTICLES\POLITICAL\The Declaration of Independence_ Its Antecedents and Authors.html.

Pocock, Robert. *Memorials of the Family of Tufton, Earls of Thanet.* Gravesend, 1800.

Radbill, Samuel X., ed. *The Autobiographical Ana of Robley Dunglison, M.D.* Philadelphia, 1963.

Rakove, Jack. *Declaring Rights: A Brief History with Documents.* Boston: Bedford Books, 1998.

———. "James Madison and the Bill of Rights," *This Constitution, a Bicentennial Chronicle.* no. 18 (Spring/Summer 1988): 4.

———. *Revolutionaries: A New History of the Invention of America.* New York: Houghton Mifflin Harcourt, 2010.

———. *James Madison and the Creation of the American Republic.* 2nd ed. New York: Longman, 2002.

———. *Original Meanings: Politics and Ideas in the Making of the Constitution.* New York: Alfred A. Knopf, 1997.

———. *The Ordeal of the Constitution: The Antifederalists and the Ratification Struggle of 1787–1788.* Norman: University of Oklahoma Press, 1961.

———. *The Beginnings of National Politics: An Interpretive History of the Continental Congress.* New York, 1979. 91–92.

———. *Revolutionaries: A New History of the Invention of America.* Boston and New York, 2010.

Randall, Henry S. *The Life of Thomas Jefferson.* 3 vols. New York, 1858.

Randall, Willard Sterne. *George Washington. A Life.* New York: Henry Holt and Co., 1997.

Randolph, Edmund. *History of Virginia.* Edited by Arthur Shaffer. Charlottesville: University Press of Virginia, 1970.

Randolph, Mary. *The Virginia House-Wife.* Edited by Karen Hess. Columbia, SC,

1984.

Randolph, Sarah N. *The Domestic Life of Thomas Jefferson.* New York, 1871.

Randolph, Thomas Jefferson, ed. *The Writings of Thomas Jefferson.* 4 vols. Charlottesville, 1829.

"Randolph and Tucker Letters." *Virginia Magazine of History and Biography* 43 (1935): 41-46.

Rawlings, Mary, ed. *Early Charlottesville: Recollections of James Alexander, 1828–1874.* Charlottesville, 1963.

Reese, George, ed. *The Official Papers of Francis Fauquier, Lieutenant Governor of Virginia, 1758–1768.* 3 vols. Charlottesville: University Press of Virginia, 1980–1982.

Rhodehamel, John H. *George Washington: Wonder of the Age.* New Haven and London: Yale Universality Press, 2017.

Rice, Howard C., ed. *Travels in North America in the Years 1780, 1781 and 1782 by the Marquis de Chastelleux.* 2 vols. Chapel Hill, 1963.

Roberts, Cokie. *Founding Mothers.* New York: Harper Collins, 2005.

Robinson, William E. *Jefferson's Granddaughter: Speech of Hon. William E. Robinson, of New York, in the House of Representatives.* Friday, March 14, 1884. Washington, DC, 1884.

Rothman, Joshua D. *Notorious in the Neighborhood: Sex and Families across the Color Line in Virginia, 1787–1861*. Chapel Hill, 2003.

Rowland, Kate Mason. *The Life and Correspondence of George Mason, 1725–1792*. New York: Russell & Russell, 1964; reprint of 1892 volume.

Royall, Anne Newpon. *Sketches of History, Life and Manners in the United States, by a Traveller*. New Haven, 1826.

Rudolph, Frederick, ed. *Essays on Education in the Early Republic*. Cambridge, MA, 1965.

Runes, Dagobert G., ed. *The Selected Writings of Benjamin Rush*. New York, 2007.

Rutland, Robert A. *The Birth of the Bill of Rights*. Boston: Northeastern University Press, 1983.

———. *George Mason and the War for Independence*. Williamsburg, VA: Virginia Independence Bicentennial Commission, 1976.

———. *George Mason, Reluctant Statesman*. Baton Rouge: Louisiana State University Press, 1961.

———. *The Papers of George Mason*. Chapel Hill: The University Press of North Carolina, 1970.

———. *"George Mason's 'Objections' and the Bill of Rights," This Constitution, a Bicentennial* Chronicle. no. 18 (Spring/Summer 1988): 11.

Scharff, Virginia. *The Women Jefferson Loved*. New York, 2010.

Schiff, Stacy. *A Great Improvisation: Franklin, France, and the Birth of America*. New York, 2005.

Schwartz, Bernard, ed. *The Bill of Rights: A Documentary*

Scribner, Robert L. and Tarter, Brent, comp. and ed. *Virginia Independence Bicentennial Commission. Revolutionary Virginia: The Road to Independence, a Documentary Record, Vol 7: Independence and the Fifth Convention, 1776.* Charlottesville: University Press of Virginia, 1983.

Selby, John E. "Henry Lee, John Adams, and the Virginia Constitution of 1776." *Virginia Magazine of History and Biography* 84, No. 4 (October 1976): 387–400.

Smith, Margaret Bayard. *The First Forty Years of Washington Society.* Edited by Galliard Hunt. New York, 1906.

———. *What Is Gentility? A Moral Tale.* Washington, DC, 1828.

———. *A Winter in Washington; or, Memoirs of the Seymour Family.* New York, 1824.

Smith, Paul H., et al, eds., *Letters of Delegates to Congress, 1774–1789*, 26 vols. Washington, DC, 1976–2000.

Stanton, Lucia. *Free Some Day: The African American Families of Monticello.* Charlottesville, 2000.

———. "The Other End of the Telescope: Jefferson through the Eyes of His Slaves." *William and Mary Quarterly*, 3rd ser., 57 (2000): 139–52.

———. "A Well-Ordered Household: Domestic Servants in Jefferson's White House." *White House History* 17 (2006): 4-23.

Stein, Susan M. *The Worlds of Thomas Jefferson at Monticello.* New York, 1993.

Stewart, David O. *The Summer of 1787.* New York: Simon & Schuster, 2007.

Sullivan, Bill. *What Winter Weather Was Really Like in 18th-Century Williamsburg.* January 11, 2017. http://makinghistorynow. com/2017/01/what-winter-weather-was-really-like-in-18th-century-williamsburg/.

Syrett, Harold C., ed. *The Papers of Alexander Hamilton.* 27 vols. New York: Columbia University Press, 1961–1987.

Tarter, Brent. "Reflections on the Church of England in Colonial Virginia." *Virginia Magazine of History and Biography* 112 (2004): 338–71.

Taylor, Robert, ed. *The Papers of John Adams.* 12 vols. Cambridge: Harvard University Press, 1977–.

Thomas, Robert E. "The Virginia Convention of 1788: A Criticism of Beard's An Economic Interpretation of the Constitution." *Journal of Southern History* 19 (February–November 1953): 63–73.

Ticknor, George. *Life, Letters, and Journals of George Ticknor.* 2 vols. Boston, 1876.

Tinkcom, Margaret Bailey, ed. "Caviar along the Potomac: Sir Augustus John Foster's 'Notes on the United States,' 1804–1812." *William and Mary Quarterly*, 3rd ser., 8 (1951): 68–107.

Townsend, Edward Booth. *Country Life in America as Lived by Ten Presidents of the United States.* New York, 1947.

Trenchard, John, and Thomas Gordon. *Cato's Letters: Essays on Liberty, 1720–1723.* 2 vols. Edited by Ronald Hamoway. Indianapolis: Liberty Fund, 1995.

Tucker, St. George. *Blackstone's Commentaries with Notes of Reference to the Constitution and Laws of the Federal Government of the United States and of the Commonwealth of*

Virginia. 5 vols. Philadelphia: William Young Birch & Abraham Small, 1803; reprint, New York: Augustus M. Keller, 1969.

Twohig, Dorothy, ed. *The Papers of George Washington: The Presidential Series*. 11 vols. Charlottesville: University Press of Virginia, 1987–.

Van Horne, John C., and Lee W. Formwalt, eds. *The Correspondence and Miscellaneous Papers of Benjamin Henry Latrobe*. 3 vols. New Haven, 1984–1988.

Varon, Elizabeth R. *We Mean to Be Counted: White Women and Politics in Antebellum Virginia*. Chapel Hill, 1998.

Vedder, Sarah E. *Reminiscences of the District of Columbia, or Washington City, Seventy-Nine years Ago, 1830–1909*. St. Louis, 1909.

Wallenstein, Peter. *Cradle of America: Four Centuries of Virginia History*. Lawrence, KS, 2007.

———. "Flawed Keepers of the Flame: The Interpreters of George Mason." *Virginia Magazine of History and Biography* 102 (April 1994): 229–60.

Ward, John William. *Andrew Jackson: Symbol for an Age*. New York, 1962.

Wayson, Billy Lee. *Martha Jefferson Randolph: The Education of a Republican Daughter and Plantation Mistress, 1702–1609*. Ph.D. diss., University of Virginia, 2008.

Webster, Noah. *A Collection of Essays and Fugitive Writings: On Moral, Historical, Political and Literary Subjects*. Boston, 1790.

Weems, Mason Locke. *The Life of Washington: A New Edition with Primary Documents and Introduction*. Edited by Peter S. Onuf. Armonk, NY: M. E. Sharpe, 1996.

Weld, Isaac Jr. *Travels through the States of North America and the Provinces of Upper and Lower Canada, during the years 1795, 1796, and 1797.* 3rd ed. 2 vols. London, 1800.

Wendling, Claudia J. "Shooting Extraordinary." *American Turf Register and Sporting Magazine.* Edited by J. S. Skinner. Vol. 1.: J.S. Skinner, 1830.

Wendling, Claudia, and Jerry Foster. *Sarah Brent Mason's Pocket Watch: 'Breguet, à Paris.* http://www.gunstonhall.org/docs/Fall-2016-Grapevine.pdf.

Wenger, Mark R. "Thomas Jefferson and the Virginia State Capitol." *Virginia Magazine of History and Biography* 101 (1993): 77–102.

Wiencek, Henry, *An Imperfect God: George Washington, His Slaves and the Creation of America.* New York: Farrar, Straus and Giroux, 2003.

Williams, Dorothy Hunt. *Historic Virginia Gardens: Preservations by the Garden Club of Virginia.* Charlottesville, VA: University Press of Virginia, 1975. One chapter includes list of plants and detailed landscape drawings for the restoration of the gardens at Gunston Hall.

Woods, Edgar. "Thomas Jefferson's Design for Remodeling the Governor's Palace." *Winterhur Portfolio* 32 (1997): 223–42. Albemarle County in Virginia. Charlottesville, 1901.

Wood, Gordon S. *The American Revolution: A History.* New York: Modern Library, 2002.

——. *Revolutionary Characters.* New York: Penguin Press, 2006.

——. "The Problem of Sovereignty," WMQ 68 (October 2011).

ONLINE SOURCES

A great deal of original material about the Constitutional Convention and the delegates has been gathered and made available online (see **FOUNDERS ONLINE**). I relied on materials assembled in the following sources:

American National Biography Online. www.anb.org/ articles/03-00500.html

Annals of Congress. http://rs6.10c.gov /ammem/ amlaw/lwac.html.

"Household Accounts Maintained by Anne Cary Randolph, 1805– 1808."

Correspondence of George Washington, James Madison, and Thomas Jefferson, made available by the Library of Congress at http:// mem01y.loc.gov/ ammem/browse/ListSome. php?category=Presidents (cited, respectively, as Washington Papers, Madison Papers, and Jefferson Papers).

Debates of the state ratifying conventions, gathered in Elliot's Debates, made available by the Library of Congress at http://memory.loc. gov/ ammem/amlaw/lwed.html (cited as **ED**).

George Mason Papers. http://www.gunstonhall.org/library/archives/ finding_aids/gm_finding_aid.html. memory.loc.gov/ ammem/ collections/Jeffferson_papers / ser7v011.html.

Gunston Hall. http://www.gunstonhall.org/; http://librarycatalog. mountvernon.org/cgi-bin/koha/opac-main.pl.

Monticello. www.monticello.org.

Monticello Explorer. www.explorer.monticello.org /text/index.php.

Mt Vernon. http://www.mountvernon.org/digital-encyclopedia/.

National Register of Historic Places. Edgehill Nomination. http:j/165.176.125.227/ registers/Counties/Albemarle/002-0026_ Edgehill_1982_Final_Nomination.pdf.

Senate Journal. http://memory.loc.gov / ammem/amlaw/ lwsj.html.

Shulman, Holly C., ed. The Dolley Madison Digital Edition. Charlottesville, 2004. http://p8o8o- rotunda. upress.virginia.ed u.mutex.gmu.edu /dmde/default.xqy.

The Thomas Jefferson Encyclopedia. http://wiki.momicello.org/ mediawik.i/index.php/Thomas_Jefferson_Encyclopedia.

Thomas Jefferson Foundation, Inc. Family Letters Digital Archive. http://retirementseries.dataformat.com.

University of Virginia Geospatial and Statistical Data Center. Historical Census Data Browser. http://mapserver.lib.virginia.edu/.

Virginia Newspapers Project. www.lva.virginia.gov/public/vnp/.

Index